THE CROSS OF CHRIST

'God forbid that I should boast of anything but the
cross of our Lord Jesus Christ' (Galatians 6:14, NEB)

Dedicated
to
Frances Whitehead
in gratitude for
30 years of outstandingly loyal
and efficient service
1956 – 1986

The royalties payable on the sales of this book have been assigned to the Evangelical Literature Trust, which exists to make available books such as this one to pastors and Christian leaders in the Third World and in Eastern Europe. Enquiries and donations should be sent to the Honorary Administrator, The Rev. John Hayden, The Church House, Stoke Park Drive, Ipswich, Suffolk IP2 9TH.

THE CROSS OF CHRIST

John R. W. Stott

*Rector Emeritus of All Souls Church, Langham Place,
and President of Christian Impact*

INTER-VARSITY PRESS

Inter-Varsity Press
38 De Montfort Street, Leicester LE1 7GP, England

First edition 1986
Reprinted 1986, 1987

Second edition (with study guide) 1989
Reprinted 1990, 1991, 1992

British Library Cataloguing in Publication Data

Stott, John R. W. (John Robert Walmsley) *1921–*
    The cross of Christ – New ed.
    1. Christian doctrine. Atonement
    I. Title
    232′.3

ISBN 0–85110–674–9

Set in Linotron Sabon
Text typeset in Great Britain by
Input Typesetting Ltd, London, SW19 8DR
Printed in England by Clays Ltd, St Ives plc

*Inter-Varsity Press, England, is the book-publishing division of
the Universities and Colleges Christian Fellowship (formerly the
Inter-Varsity Fellowship), a student movement linking Christian
Unions in universities and colleges throughout the United Kingdom
and Republic of Ireland, and a member movement of the
International Fellowship of Evangelical Students. For information
about local and national activities, write to UCCF, 38 De Montfort
Street, Leicester LE1 7GP.*

Contents

Conclusion: The pervasive influence of the cross   338

Preface

I count it an enormous privilege to have been invited by Inter-Varsity Press to write a book on that greatest and most glorious of all subjects, the cross of Christ. I have emerged from the several years of work involved spiritually enriched, with my convictions clarified and strengthened, and with a firm resolve to spend the rest of my days on earth (as I know the whole redeemed company will spend eternity in heaven) in the liberating service of Christ crucified.

It is appropriate that a book on the cross should form part of the Golden Jubilee celebrations of Inter-Varsity Press, to which (under its dedicated leaders Ronald Inchley and Frank Entwistle) the whole Christian reading public is greatly indebted. For the cross is at the centre of the evangelical faith. Indeed, as I argue in this book, it lies at the centre of the historic, biblical faith, and the fact that this is not always everywhere acknowledged is in itself a sufficient justification for preserving a distinctive evangelical testimony. Evangelical Christians believe that in and through Christ crucified God substituted himself for us and bore our sins, dying in our place the death we deserved to die, in order that we might be restored to his favour and adopted into his family. Dr J. I. Packer has rightly written that this belief 'is a distinguishing mark of the world-wide evangelical fraternity' (even though it 'often gets misunderstood and caricatured by its critics'); it 'takes us to the very heart of the Christian gospel'.[1]

The centrality of the cross has certainly been a vital factor in the history of what is now the Universities and Colleges Christian

---

[1] J. I. Packer, 'What Did the Cross Achieve?', p. 3.

Fellowship, together with the world body to which it is affiliated, namely the International Fellowship of Evangelical Students. Two events, which took place earlier in this century, were particularly important.

The first was the disaffiliation in 1910 of the Cambridge Inter-Collegiate Christian Union (founded in 1877) from the Student Christian Movement (founded in 1895). CICCU members were conscious of standing in the tradition of Bilney, Tyndale, Latimer, Ridley and Cranmer, the great names of the Cambridge Reformation. They also looked back with pride and affection to Charles Simeon, who for 54 years (1782–1836) as Vicar of Holy Trinity Church had faithfully expounded the Scriptures and, as his memorial plaque testifies, 'whether as the ground of his own hopes or as the subject of all his ministrations, determined to know nothing but Jesus Christ and him crucified'. It is not surprising, therefore, that they were becoming increasingly disenchanted with the liberal tendencies of the SCM, and specially with its weak doctrines of the Bible, the cross and even the deity of Jesus. So when Tissington Tatlow, General Secretary of the SCM, met CICCU members in March 1910, the vote to disaffiliate the Union was taken. The following year Howard Mowll (later to be Archbishop of Sydney and Primate of Australia) became President of CICCU and helped to establish it on firm evangelical foundations from which it has never been moved.[2]

After the First World War ended in 1918, many ex-servicemen went up to Cambridge as students. CICCU by now was much smaller than the SCM. Yet the SCM leaders (notably Charles Raven, the Dean of Emmanuel) made overtures to the CICCU, hoping that they would re-join and supply the missing devotional warmth and evangelistic thrust. To resolve the issue, Daniel Dick and Norman Grubb (President and Secretary of CICCU) met the SCM committee in the rooms in Trinity Great Court of their secretary, Rollo Pelly. Here is Norman Grubb's own account of the crucial issue:

> After an hour's talk, I asked Rollo point-blank, 'Does the SCM put the atoning blood of Jesus Christ central?' He hesitated, and then said, 'Well, we acknowledge it, but not necessarily central.' Dan Dick and I then said that this settled the matter for us in the CICCU. We could never join something that did not maintain the atoning blood of Jesus Christ as its centre; and we parted

[2] See *Archbishop Mowll* by Marcus L. Loane, especially pp. 43–61. See also *Whatever Happened to the Jesus Lane Lot?* by O. R. Barclay, especially pp. 65–70.

company.[3]

This decision not only confirmed the pre-war vote to disaffiliate, but 'was also the real foundation of the I.V.F., for it was only a few months later that the realization dawned on us that if a C.I.C.C.U. was a necessity in Cambridge, a union of the same kind was also a necessity in every University of the world'.[4] The first Inter-Varsity Conference was held in London in December 1919.

During this period Norman Grubb quoted 1 Corinthians 15:3–4 as a key text in their thinking: 'For I delivered to you as of first importance what I also received, that Christ died for our sins in accordance with the scriptures, that he was buried, that he was raised on the third day in accordance with the scriptures' (RSV). It would be hard to square with this the SCM's 1919 Aim and Basis, which included the following statement about the cross: 'it is only as we see on Calvary the price of suffering paid day by day by God himself for all human sin, that we can enter into the experience of true penitence and forgiveness, which sets us free to embark upon a wholly new way of life. . . . This is the meaning of the Atonement.'[5] But we have respectfully to respond that the meaning of the atonement is not to be found in *our* penitence evoked by the sight of Calvary, but rather in what *God* did when in Christ on the cross he took our place and bore our sin.

This distinction between an 'objective' and 'subjective' understanding of the atonement needs to be made clear in every generation. According to Dr Douglas Johnson, the first General Secretary of the IVF, this discovery was the turning-point in the ministry of Dr Martyn Lloyd-Jones, who occupied an unrivalled position of evangelical leadership in the decades following the Second World War. He confided in several friends that 'a fundamental change took place in his outlook and preaching in the year 1929'. He had, of course, emphasized from the beginning of his ministry the indispensable necessity of the new birth. But, after preaching one night in Bridgend, South Wales, the minister challenged him that 'the cross and the work of Christ' appeared to have little place in his preaching. He went 'at once to his favourite secondhand bookshop and asked the proprietor for the two standard books on the Atonement. The bookseller . . . produced R. W. Dale's *The Atonement* (1875) and James Denney's *The Death of Christ* (1903). On his return home he gave himself to study, declining both lunch and tea, and causing his wife such anxiety that she

[3] Norman P. Grubb, *Once Caught, No Escape*, p. 56.
[4] F. Donald Coggan (ed.), *Christ and the Colleges*, p. 17.
[5] Tissington Tatlow, *Story of the SCM*, p. 630.

telephoned her brother to see whether a doctor should be called. But when he later emerged, he claimed to have found 'the real heart of the gospel and the key to the inner meaning of the Christian faith'. So the content of his preaching changed, and with this its impact. As he himself put it, the basic question was not Anselm's 'why did God become man?' but 'why did Christ die?'.[6]

Because of the vital importance of the atonement, and of an understanding of it which reclaims from misrepresentation the great biblical concepts of 'substitution', 'satisfaction' and 'propitiation', two things have greatly surprised me. The first is how unpopular the doctrine remains. Some theologians evince a strange reluctance to subscribe to it, even when its biblical basis becomes clear to them. I think, for example, of that noted Methodist New Testament scholar, Vincent Taylor. His careful and comprehensive scholarship is exemplified in his three books on the cross – *Jesus and His Sacrifice* (1937), *The Atonement in New Testament Teaching* (1940) and *Forgiveness and Reconciliation* (1946). He employs many adjectives to describe the death of Christ, such as 'vicarious', 'redemptive', 'reconciling', 'expiatory', 'sacrificial' and especially 'representative'. But he cannot bring himself to call it 'substitutionary'. After a close examination of primitive Christian preaching and belief, of Paul, Hebrews and John, he writes of the work of Christ: 'In none of the passages we have examined is it described as that of a substitute. . . . Nowhere have we found any support for such views.'[7] No, Christ's work was 'a ministry accomplished on our behalf, but not in our stead' (p. 270). Yet even as Vincent Taylor made these astonishing statements, he was clearly uneasy in making them. Their vehemence leaves us unprepared for the concessions which he later feels obliged to make. 'Perhaps the most striking feature of New Testament teaching concerning the representative work of Christ', he writes, 'is the fact that it comes so near, without actually crossing, the bounds of substitutionary doctrine. Paulinism, in particular, is within a hair's breadth of substitution' (p. 288). He even confesses of New Testament theologians that 'too often we are content to deny substitution without replacing it' (p. 289), and that it is a notion 'we have perhaps been more anxious to reject than to assess' (p. 301). What, however, I shall try to show in this book, is that the biblical doctrine of atonement is substitutionary from beginning to end. What Vincent Taylor shrank from was not the doctrine

[6] I am grateful to Dr Douglas Johnson for supplying me with this information, which supplements the account given by Iain H. Murray in *David Martyn Lloyd-Jones*, pp. 190–191.

[7] Vincent Taylor, *Atonement*, p. 258.

itself, but the crudities of thought and expression of which the advocates of substitution have not infrequently been guilty.

My second surprise, in view of the centrality of the cross of Christ, is that no book on this topic has been written by an evangelical author for thoughtful readers (until two or three years ago) for nearly half a century. True, there have been several small paperbacks, and there have been some scholarly works. I would like to pay special tribute to the outstanding labours in this field of Dr Leon Morris of Melbourne, Australia. His *Apostolic Preaching of the Cross* (1955) has put all of us in his debt, and I am glad that he has brought its contents within reach of lay people in *The Atonement* (1983). He has made himself master of the extensive literature of the ages on this theme, and his *The Cross in the New Testament* (1965) remains probably the most comprehensive survey available. From it I quote with warm endorsement his statement that 'the cross dominates the New Testament' (p. 365).

Until the recent publication, however, of Ronald Wallace's *The Atoning Death of Christ* (1981) and Michael Green's *The Empty Cross of Jesus* (1984), I do not know of an evangelical book for the readership I have in mind since H. E. Guillebaud's *Why the Cross?* (1937), which was one of the very first books published by IVF. It was a courageous work, meeting the critics of a substitutionary atonement head on, and asking the three questions: (1) 'is it Christian?' (*i.e.* compatible with the teaching of Jesus and his apostles); (2) 'is it immoral?' (*i.e.* compatible or incompatible with justice); and (3) 'is it incredible?' (*i.e.* compatible or incompatible with such problems as time and the transfer of guilt).

My concern is to range more widely, for this is not a book on the atonement only, but on the cross. After the three introductory chapters which form Part One, I come in Part Two to what I have called 'the heart of the cross', in which I argue for a truly biblical understanding of the notions of 'satisfaction' and 'substitution'. In Part Three, I move on to the three great achievements of the cross, namely saving sinners, revealing God and conquering evil. But Part Four grapples with areas which are often omitted from books on the cross, namely what it means for the Christian community to 'live under the cross'. I try to show that the cross transforms everything. It gives us a new, worshipping relationship to God, a new and balanced understanding of ourselves, a new incentive to give ourselves in mission, a new love for our enemies, and a new courage to face the perplexities of suffering.

In developing my theme, I have had in mind the triangle of Scripture, tradition and the modern world. My first anxiety has been to be true to the Word of God, allowing it to say what it has to say and not asking it to say what I might want it to say. There is no alternative to careful exegesis of the text. Secondly, I have endeavoured to share some of the fruits of my reading. In seeking to understand the cross, one cannot ignore the great works of the past. To be disrespectful of tradition and of historical theology is to be disrespectful of the Holy Spirit who has been actively enlightening the church in every century. Then, thirdly, I have tried to understand Scripture, not only in its own light and in the light of tradition, but also in relation to the contemporary world. I have asked what the cross of Christ says to us at the end of the twentieth century.

In daring to write (and read) a book about the cross, there is of course a great danger of presumption. This is partly because what actually happened when 'God was reconciling the world to himself in Christ' is a mystery whose depths we shall spend eternity plumbing; and partly because it would be most unseemly to feign a cool detachment as we contemplate Christ's cross. For willy-nilly we are involved. Our sins put him there. So, far from offering us flattery, the cross undermines our self-righteousness. We can stand before it only with a bowed head and a broken spirit. And there we remain until the Lord Jesus speaks to our hearts his word of pardon and acceptance, and we, gripped by his love and brimful of thanksgiving, go out into the world to live our lives in his service.

I am grateful to Roger Beckwith and David Turner for reading portions of the manuscript and for their helpful comments. I thank my four most recent study assistants – Mark Labberton, Steve Ingraham, Bob Wismer and Steve Andrews. Steve Andrews has been characteristically meticulous in reading the MS, compiling the bibliography and indices, checking references and correcting the proofs.

But I reserve until last my heartfelt thanks to Frances Whitehead who in 1986 completes thirty years as my secretary. This book is the umpteenth she has typed. I cannot speak too highly of her efficiency, helpfulness, loyalty, and undiminished enthusiasm for the work of the Lord. With much gratitude I dedicate this book to her.

Christmas 1985   JOHN STOTT

Abbreviations

The English text of biblical quotations is that of the New International Version, unless stated to the contrary.

AG *A Greek-English Lexicon of the New Testament and Other Early Christian Literature* by William F. Arndt and F. Wilbur Gingrich (University of Chicago Press and Cambridge University Press, 1957).

AV The Authorized (King James') Version of the Bible, 1611.

JB The Jerusalem Bible (Darton, Longman and Todd, 1966).

LXX The Old Testament in Greek according to the Septuagint, 3rd century BC.

NEB The New English Bible (NT 1961, 2nd edition 1970; OT 1970).

NIV The New International Version of the Bible (NT 1973; OT 1979).

RSV The Revised Standard Version of the Bible (NT 1946, 2nd edition 1971; OT 1952).

Part One

Approaching the cross

1

The centrality of the cross

Do you know the painting by Holman Hunt, the leader of the Pre-Raphaelite Brotherhood, entitled 'The Shadow of Death'? It depicts the inside of the carpenter's shop in Nazareth. Stripped to the waist, Jesus stands by a wooden trestle on which he has put down his saw. He lifts his eyes towards heaven, and the look on his face is one of either pain or ecstasy or both. He also stretches, raising both arms above his head. As he does so, the evening sunlight streaming through the open door casts a dark shadow in the form of a cross on the wall behind him, where his tool-rack looks like a horizontal bar on which his hands have been crucified. The tools themselves remind us of the fateful hammer and nails.

In the left foreground a woman kneels among the wood chippings, her hands resting on the chest in which the rich gifts of the Magi are kept. We cannot see her face because she has averted it. But we know that she is Mary. She looks startled (or so it seems) at her son's cross-like shadow on the wall.

The Pre-Raphaelites have a reputation for sentimentality. Yet they were serious and sincere artists, and Holman Hunt himself was determined, as he put it, to 'do battle with the frivolous art of the day', its superficial treatment of trite themes. So he spent 1870–73 in the Holy Land, and painted 'The Shadow of Death' in Jerusalem, as he sat on the roof of his house.[1] Though the idea is historically fictitious, it is also theologically true. From Jesus' youth, indeed even from his birth, the cross cast its shadow ahead of him. His death was central to his mission. Moreover, the church

[1] See *Pre-Raphaelite Paintings* from the Manchester City Art Gallery, where 'The Shadow of Death' hangs, by Julian Treuherz.

has always recognized this.

Imagine a stranger visiting St Paul's Cathedral in London. Having been brought up in a non-Christian culture, he knows next to nothing about Christianity. Yet he is more than a tourist; he is personally interested and keen to learn.

Walking along Fleet Street, he is impressed by the grandeur of the building's proportions, and marvels that Sir Christopher Wren could have conceived such an edifice after the Great Fire of London in 1666. As his eyes attempt to take it in, he cannot help noticing the huge golden cross which dominates the dome.

He enters the cathedral and stands at its central point, under the dome. Trying to grasp the size and shape of the building, he becomes aware that its ground plan, consisting of nave and transepts, is cruciform. He walks round and observes that each side chapel contains what looks to him like a table, on which, prominently displayed, there stands a cross. He goes downstairs into the crypt to see the tombs of famous men such as Sir Christopher Wren himself, Lord Nelson and the Duke of Wellington: a cross is engraved or embossed on each.

Returning upstairs, he decides to remain for the service which is about to begin. The man beside him is wearing a little cross on his lapel, while the lady on his other side has one on her necklace. His eye now rests on the colourful, stained-glass east window. Though he cannot make out the details from where he is sitting, he cannot fail to notice that it contains a cross.

Suddenly, the congregation stands up. The choir and clergy enter, preceded by somebody carrying a processional cross. They are singing a hymn. The visitor looks down at the service paper to read its opening words:

> We sing the praise of him who died,
>   Of him who died upon the cross;
> The sinner's hope let men deride,
>   For this we count the world but loss.

From what follows he comes to realize that he is witnessing a Holy Communion service, and that this focuses upon the death of Jesus. For when the people around him go forward to the communion rail to receive bread and wine, the minister speaks to them of the body and blood of Christ. The service ends with another hymn:

> When I survey the wondrous cross
>   On which the Prince of glory died,

My richest gain I count but loss,
   And pour contempt on all my pride.

Forbid it, Lord, that I should boast
   Save in the cross of Christ my God;
All the vain things that charm me most,
   I sacrifice them to his blood.

Although the congregation now disperses, a family stays behind.
They have brought their child to be baptized. Joining them at the
font, the visitor sees the minister first pour water over the child
and then trace a cross on its forehead, saying 'I sign you with the
cross, to show that you must not be ashamed to confess the faith
of Christ crucified . . .'.

The stranger leaves the cathedral impressed, but puzzled. The
repeated insistence by word and symbol on the centrality of the
cross has been striking. Yet questions have arisen in his mind.
Some of the language used has seemed exaggerated. Do Christians
really for the sake of the cross 'count the world but loss', and
'boast' in it alone, and 'sacrifice' everything for it? Can the Christian faith be accurately summed up as 'the faith of Christ crucified'?
What are the grounds, he asks himself, for this concentration on
the cross of Christ?

The sign and symbol of the cross

Every religion and ideology has its visual symbol, which illustrates
a significant feature of its history or beliefs. The lotus flower, for
example, although it was used by the ancient Chinese, Egyptians
and Indians, is now particularly associated with Buddhism. Because
of its wheel shape it is thought to depict either the cycle of birth
and death or the emergence of beauty and harmony out of the
muddy waters of chaos. Sometimes the Buddha is portrayed as
enthroned in a fully open lotus flower.

Ancient Judaism avoided visual signs and symbols, for fear of
infringing the second commandment which prohibits the manu-
facture of images. But modern Judaism now employs the so-called
Shield or Star of David, a hexagram formed by combining two
equilateral triangles. It speaks of God's covenant with David that
his throne would be established for ever and that the Messiah
would be descended from him. Islam, the other monotheistic faith
which arose in the Middle East, is symbolized by a crescent, at
least in West Asia. Originally depicting a phase of the moon, it
was already the symbol of sovereignty in Byzantium before the

19

Muslim conquest.

The secular ideologies of this century also have their universally recognizable signs. The Marxist hammer and sickle, adopted in 1917 by the Soviet government from a nineteenth-century Belgian painting, represent industry and agriculture; and they are crossed to signify the union of workers and peasants, of factory and field. The swastika, on the other hand, has been traced back some 6,000 years. The arms of its cross are bent clockwise to symbolize either the movement of the sun across the sky, or the cycle of the four seasons, or the process of creativity and prosperity ('svasti' being a Sanskrit word for 'well-being'). At the beginning of this century, however, it was taken up by some German groups as a symbol of the Aryan race. Then Hitler took it over, and it became the sinister sign of Nazi racial bigotry.

Christianity, then, is no exception in having a visual symbol. The cross was not its earliest, however. Because of the wild accusations which were levelled against Christians, and the persecution to which they were exposed, they 'had to be very circumspect and to avoid flaunting their religion. Thus the cross, now the universal symbol of Christianity, was at first avoided, not only for its direct association with Christ, but for its shameful association with the execution of a common criminal also'.[2] So on the walls and ceilings of the catacombs (underground burial-places outside Rome, where the persecuted Christians probably hid), the earliest Christian motifs seem to have been either non-committal paintings of a peacock (supposed to symbolize immortality), a dove, the athlete's victory palm or, in particular, a fish. Only the initiated would know, and nobody else could guess, that *ichthys* ('fish') was an acronym for *Iesus Christos Theou Huios Sotēr* ('Jesus Christ, Son of God, Saviour'). But it did not remain the Christian sign, doubtless because the association between Jesus and a fish was purely acronymic (a fortuitous arrangement of letters) and had no visual significance.

Somewhat later, probably during the second century, the persecuted Christians seem to have preferred to paint biblical themes like Noah's ark, Abraham killing the ram instead of Isaac, Daniel in the lions' den, his three friends in the fiery furnace, Jonah being disgorged by the fish, some baptisms, a shepherd carrying a lamb, the healing of the paralytic and the raising of Lazarus. All these were symbolic of Christ's redemption, while not being in themselves incriminating, since only the instructed would have

[2] Michael Gough, *Origins of Christian Art*, p. 18. See also J. H. Miller, 'Cross' and 'Crucifix'; *Christian World*, ed. Geoffrey Barraclough; and *Cross and Crucifix* by Cyril E. Pocknee.

been able to interpret their meaning. In addition, the Chi-Rho monogram (the first two letters of the Greek word *Christos*) was a popular cryptogram, often in the form of a cross, and sometimes with a lamb standing before it, or with a dove.

A universally acceptable Christian emblem would obviously need to speak of Jesus Christ, but there was a wide range of possibilities. Christians might have chosen the crib or manger in which the baby Jesus was laid, or the carpenter's bench at which he worked as a young man in Nazareth, dignifying manual labour, or the boat from which he taught the crowds in Galilee, or the apron he wore when washing the apostles' feet, which would have spoken of his spirit of humble service. Then there was the stone which, having been rolled from the mouth of Joseph's tomb, would have proclaimed his resurrection. Other possibilities were the throne, symbol of divine sovereignty, which John in his vision of heaven saw that Jesus was sharing, or the dove, symbol of the Holy Spirit sent from heaven on the Day of Pentecost. Any of these seven symbols would have been suitable as a pointer to some aspect of the ministry of the Lord. But instead the chosen symbol came to be a simple cross. Its two bars were already a cosmic symbol from remote antiquity of the axis between heaven and earth. But its choice by Christians had a more specific explanation. They wished to commemorate as central to their understanding of Jesus neither his birth nor his youth, neither his teaching nor his service, neither his resurrection nor his reign, nor his gift of the Spirit, but his death, his crucifixion. The crucifix (that is, a cross to which a figure of Christ is attached) does not appear to have been used before the sixth century.

It seems certain that, at least from the second century onwards, Christians not only drew, painted and engraved the cross as a pictorial symbol of their faith, but also made the sign of the cross on themselves or others. One of the first witnesses to this practice was Tertullian, the North African lawyer-theologian who flourished about AD 200. He wrote:

At every forward step and movement, at every going in and out, when we put on our clothes and shoes, when we bathe, when we sit at table, when we light the lamps, on couch, on seat, in all the ordinary actions of daily life, we trace upon the forehead the sign [the cross].[3]

Hippolytus, the scholar-presbyter of Rome, is a particularly

[3] Tertullian, *De Corona*, Ch. III, p. 94.

interesting witness, because he is known to have been 'an avowed reactionary who in his own generation stood for the past rather than the future'. His famous treatise *The Apostolic Tradition* (*c.* AD 215) 'claims explicitly to be recording only the forms and models of rites *already* traditional and customs *already* long-established, and to be written in deliberate protest against innovations'.[4] When he describes certain 'church observances', therefore, we may be sure that they were already being practised a generation or more previously. He mentions that the sign of the cross was used by the bishop when anointing the candidate's forehead at Confirmation, and he recommends it in private prayer: 'imitate him (Christ) always, by signing thy forehead sincerely: for this is the sign of his passion.' It is also, he adds, a protection against evil: 'When tempted, always reverently seal thy forehead with the sign of the cross. For this sign of the passion is displayed and made manifest against the devil if thou makest it in faith, not in order that thou mayest be seen of men, but by thy knowledge putting it forth as a shield.'[5]

There is no need for us to dismiss this habit as superstitious. In origin at least, the sign of the cross was intended to identify and indeed sanctify each act as belonging to Christ.

In the middle of the third century, when another North African, Cyprian, was Bishop of Carthage, a terrible persecution was unleashed by the Emperor Decius (AD 250–251) during which thousands of Christians died rather than offer sacrifice to his name. Anxious to strengthen the morale of his people, and to encourage them to accept martyrdom rather than compromise their Christian faith, Cyprian reminded them of the ceremony of the cross: 'let us take also for protection of our head the helmet of salvation . . . that our brow may be fortified, so as to keep safe the sign of God.'[6] As for the faithful who endured prison and risked death, Cyprian praised them in these terms: 'your brows, hallowed by God's seal . . . reserved themselves for the crown which the Lord would give.'[7]

Richard Hooker, the sixteenth-century Anglican theologian and Master of the Temple in London, applauded the fact that the early church Fathers, in spite of heathen scorn at the sufferings of Christ, 'chose rather the sign of the cross (*sc.* in baptism) than any other outward mark, whereby the world might most easily discern always what they were'.[8] He was aware of the forthright objections of the

[4] Gregory Dix (ed.), *Apostolic Tradition of St Hippolytus*, p. xi.
[5] *Ibid.*, pp. 68–69. [6] Cyprian, *Ad Thibaritanos* IX.
[7] Cyprian, *De Lapsis* 2.
[8] Richard Hooker, *Ecclesiastical Polity*, Book V, Ch. lxv.20, 'Of the Cross in Baptism'.

Puritans. 'Crossing and such like pieces of Popery,' they were
saying, 'which the church of God in the Apostles' time never knew',
ought not to be used, for human inventions ought not to be added
to divine institutions, and there was always the danger of superstitious misuse. As King Hezekiah destroyed the brazen serpent, so
crossing should be abandoned. But Hooker stood his ground. In
'matters indifferent', which were not incompatible with Scripture,
Christians were free. Besides, the sign of the cross had a positive
usefulness: it is 'for us an admonition . . . to glory in the service
of Jesus Christ, and not to hang down our heads as men ashamed
thereof, although it procure us reproach and obloquy at the hands
of this wretched world'.[9]

It was Constantine, the first emperor to profess to be a Christian,
who gave added impetus to the use of the cross symbol. For
(according to Eusebius), on the eve of the Battle of Milvian Bridge
which brought him supremacy in the West (AD 312–313), he saw
a cross of light in the sky, along with the words *in hoc signo vinces*
('conquer by this sign'). He immediately adopted it as his emblem,
and had it emblazoned on the standards of his army.

Whatever we may think of Constantine and of the development
of post-Constantinian 'Christendom', at least the church has faithfully preserved the cross as its central symbol. In some ecclesiastical
traditions the candidate for baptism is still marked with this sign,
and the relatives of a Christian who after death is buried rather
than cremated are likely to have a cross erected over his grave.
Thus from Christian birth to Christian death, as we might put it,
the church seeks to identify and protect us with a cross.

The Christians' choice of a cross as the symbol of their faith is
the more surprising when we remember the horror with which
crucifixion was regarded in the ancient world. We can understand
why Paul's 'message of the cross' was to many of his listeners
'foolishness', even 'madness' (1 Cor. 1:18, 23). How could any
sane person worship as a god a dead man who had been justly
condemned as a criminal and subjected to the most humiliating
form of execution? This combination of death, crime and shame
put him beyond the pale of respect, let alone of worship.[10]

Crucifixion seems to have been invented by 'barbarians' on the
edge of the known world, and taken over from them by both
Greeks and Romans. It is probably the most cruel method of
execution ever practised, for it deliberately delayed death until

[9] *Ibid.*, Book V, Ch. lxv.6.
[10] See especially pp. 1–10 of *Crucifixion* by Martin Hengel, whose original title was *Mors turpissima crucis*, 'the utterly vile death of the cross',
an expression first used by Origen.

maximum torture had been inflicted. The victim could suffer for days before dying. When the Romans adopted it, they reserved it for criminals convicted of murder, rebellion or armed robbery, provided that they were also slaves, foreigners or other non-persons. The Jews were therefore outraged when the Roman general Varus crucified 2,000 of their compatriots in 4 BC, and when during the siege of Jerusalem the general Titus crucified so many fugitives from the city that neither 'space . . . for the crosses, nor crosses for the bodies' could be found.[11]

Roman citizens were exempt from crucifixion, except in extreme cases of treason. Cicero in one of his speeches condemned it as *crudelissimum taeterrimumque supplicium*, 'a most cruel and disgusting punishment'.[12] A little later he declared: 'To bind a Roman citizen is a crime, to flog him is an abomination, to kill him is almost an act of murder: to crucify him is – What? There is no fitting word that can possibly describe so horrible a deed.'[13] Cicero was even more explicit in his successful defence in 63 BC of the elderly senator Gaius Rabirius who had been charged with murder: 'the very word "cross" should be far removed not only from the person of a Roman citizen, but from his thoughts, his eyes and his ears. For it is not only the actual occurrence of these things (sc. the procedures of crucifixion) or the endurance of them, but liability to them, the expectation, indeed the mere mention of them, that is unworthy of a Roman citizen and a free man.'[14]

If the Romans regarded crucifixion with horror, so did the Jews, though for a different reason. They made no distinction between a 'tree' and a 'cross', and so between a hanging and a crucifixion. They therefore automatically applied to crucified criminals the terrible statement of the law that 'anyone who is hung on a tree is under God's curse' (Dt. 21:23). They could not bring themselves to believe that God's Messiah would die under his curse, strung up on a tree. As Trypho the Jew put it to Justin the Christian apologist, who engaged him in dialogue: 'I am exceedingly incredulous on this point.'[15]

So then, whether their background was Roman or Jewish or both, the early enemies of Christianity lost no opportunity to ridicule the claim that God's anointed and man's Saviour ended his life on a cross. The idea was crazy. This is well illustrated by

[11] See the accounts given by Josephus in *Antiquities* xvii.10.10 and *Jewish War* V.xi.1.
[12] Cicero, *Against Verres* II.v.64, para. 165.
[13] *Ibid.*, II.v.66, para. 170.
[14] Cicero, *In Defence of Rabirius* V.16, p. 467.
[15] Justin Martyr, *Dialogue with Trypho a Jew*, Ch. lxxxix.

a graffito from the second century, discovered on the Palatine Hill in Rome, on the wall of a house considered by some scholars to have been used as a school for imperial pages. It is the first surviving picture of the crucifixion, and is a caricature. A crude drawing depicts, stretched on a cross, a man with the head of a donkey. To the left stands another man, with one arm raised in worship. Unevenly scribbled underneath are the words ALEXAMENOS CEBETE (*sc. sebete*) THEON, 'Alexamenos worships God'. The cartoon is now in the Kircherian Museum in Rome. Whatever the origin of the accusation of donkey-worship (which was attributed to both Jews and Christians), it was the concept of worshipping a crucified man which was being held up to derision.

One detects the same note of scorn in Lucian of Samosata, the second-century pagan satirist. In *The Passing of Peregrinus* (a fictitious Christian convert whom he portrays as a charlatan) he lampoons Christians as 'worshipping that crucified sophist himself and living under his laws' (p. 15).

The perspective of Jesus

The fact that a cross became the Christian symbol, and that Christians stubbornly refused, in spite of the ridicule, to discard it in favour of something less offensive, can have only one explanation. It means that the centrality of the cross originated in the mind of Jesus himself. It was out of loyalty to him that his followers clung so doggedly to this sign. What evidence is there, then, that the cross stood at the centre of Jesus' own perspective?

Our only glimpse into the developing mind of the boy Jesus has been given us in the story of how at the age of 12 he was taken to Jerusalem at Passover and then left behind by mistake. When his parents found him in the temple, 'sitting among the teachers, listening to them and asking them questions', they scolded him. They had been anxiously searching for him, they said. 'Why were you searching for me?' he responded with innocent astonishment. 'Didn't you know I had to be in my Father's house?' (Lk. 2:41–50). Luke tells the story with a tantalizing economy of detail. We must therefore be careful not to read into it more than the narrative itself warrants. This much we may affirm, however, that already at the age of 12 Jesus was both speaking of God as 'my Father' and also feeling an inward compulsion to occupy himself with his Father's affairs. He knew he had a mission. His Father had sent him into the world for a purpose. This mission he must perform; this purpose he must fulfil. What these were emerges gradually in the narrative of the Gospels.

The evangelists hint that Jesus' baptism and temptation were both occasions on which he committed himself to go God's way rather than the devil's, the way of suffering and death rather than of popularity and acclaim. Yet Mark (who is followed in this by Matthew and Luke) pinpoints a later event when Jesus began to teach this clearly. It was the watershed in his public ministry. Having withdrawn with his apostles to the northern district round Caesarea Philippi in the foothills of Mount Hermon, he put to them the direct question who they thought he was. When Peter blurted out that he was God's Messiah, immediately Jesus 'warned them not to tell anyone about him' (Mk. 8:29–30). This injunction was consistent with his previous instructions about keeping the so-called 'Messianic secret'. Yet now something new took place: Jesus

> then began to teach them that the Son of Man must suffer many things and be rejected by the elders, chief priests and teachers of the law, and that he must be killed and after three days rise again. He spoke plainly about this (Mk. 8:31–32).

'Plainly' translates *parrēsia*, meaning 'with freedom of speech' or 'openly'. There was to be no secret about this. The fact of his Messiahship had been secret, because its character had been misunderstood. The popular Messianic expectation was of a revolutionary political leader. John tells us that at the peak of Jesus' Galilean popularity, after feeding the five thousand, the crowds had 'intended to come and make him king by force' (Jn. 6:15). Now that the apostles had clearly recognized and confessed his identity, however, he could explain the nature of his Messiahship and do so openly. Peter rebuked him, horrified by the fate he had predicted for himself. But Jesus rebuked Peter in strong language. The same apostle who in confessing Jesus' divine Messiahship had received a revelation from the Father (Mt. 16:17), had been deceived by the devil to deny the necessity of the cross. 'Out of my sight, Satan!' Jesus said, with a vehemence which must have astonished his hearers. 'You do not have in mind the things of God, but the things of men.'[16]

This incident is usually referred to as the first 'prediction of the passion'. There had been passing allusions before (*e.g.* Mk. 2:19–20); but this was quite unambiguous. The second was made a little later, as Jesus was passing through Galilee incognito. He said to the Twelve:

---

[16] Mk. 8:31ff.; *cf.* Mt. 16:21ff.; Lk. 9:22ff.

'The Son of Man is going to be betrayed into the hands of men. They will kill him, and after three days he will rise' (Mk. 9:31).

Mark says that the disciples did not understand what he meant, and were afraid to ask him. Matthew adds that they were 'filled with grief' (Mk. 9:30–32; *cf.* Mt. 17:22–23). This was probably the time when, according to Luke, Jesus 'resolutely set out for Jerusalem' (9:51). He was determined to fulfil what had been written of him.

Jesus made his third 'prediction of the passion' when they were heading for the Holy City. Mark introduces it with a graphic description of the awe which the Lord's resolution inspired in them:

> They were on their way up to Jerusalem, with Jesus leading the way, and the disciples were astonished, while those who followed were afraid. Again he took the Twelve aside and told them what was going to happen to him. 'We are going up to Jerusalem,' he said, 'and the Son of Man will be betrayed to the chief priests and teachers of the law. They will condemn him to death and will hand him over to the Gentiles, who will mock him and spit on him, flog him and kill him. Three days later he will rise.'

Luke adds his comment that 'everything that is written by the prophets about the Son of Man will be fulfilled'.[17]

This threefold repetition of the passion prediction adds a note of solemnity to Mark's narrative. It is in this way that he deliberately prepares his readers, as Jesus deliberately prepared the Twelve, for the terrible events which were to take place. Putting the three predictions together, the most impressive emphasis is neither that Jesus would be betrayed, rejected and condemned by his own people and their leaders, nor that they would hand him over to the Gentiles who would first mock and then kill him, nor that after three days he would rise from death. It is not even that each time Jesus designates himself 'Son of Man' (the heavenly figure whom Daniel saw in his vision, coming in the clouds of heaven, being given authority, glory and sovereign power, and receiving the worship of the nations) and yet paradoxically states that as Son of Man he will suffer and die, thus with daring originality combining the two Old Testament Messianic figures, the Suffering Servant of Isaiah 53 and the reigning Son of Man of Daniel 7. More impressive still is the determination he both expressed and exemplified. He

[17] Mk. 10:32–34; *cf.* Mt. 20:17–19; Lk. 18:31–34.

must suffer and be rejected and die, he said. Everything written of him in Scripture *must* be fulfilled. So he set his face towards Jerusalem, and went ahead of the Twelve in the road. Peter's negative comment he instantly recognized as Satanic and therefore instantly repudiated.

Although these three predictions form an obvious trio because of their similar structure and wording, the Gospels record at least eight more occasions on which Jesus alluded to his death. Coming down from the mountain where he had been transfigured, he warned that he would suffer at the hands of his enemies just as John the Baptist had done,[18] and in response to the outrageously selfish request of James and John for the best seats in the kingdom, he said that he himself had come to serve, not to be served, and 'to give his life as a ransom for many'.[19] The remaining six allusions were all made during the last week of his life, as the crisis drew near. He saw his death as the culmination of centuries of Jewish rejection of God's message, and foretold that God's judgment would bring Jewish national privilege to an end.[20] Then on the Tuesday, mentioning the Passover, he said he was going to be 'handed over to be crucified'; in the Bethany home he described the pouring of perfume over his head as preparing him for burial; in the upper room he insisted that the Son of Man would go just as it was written about him, and gave them bread and wine as emblems of his body and blood, thus foreshadowing his death and requesting its commemoration. Finally, in the Garden of Gethsemane he refused to be defended by men or angels, since 'how then would the Scriptures be fulfilled that say it must happen in this way?'.[21] Thus the Synoptic evangelists bear a common witness to the fact that Jesus both clearly foresaw and repeatedly foretold his coming death.

John omits these precise predictions. Yet he bears witness to the same phenomenon by his seven references to Jesus' 'hour' (usually *hōra* but once *kairos*, 'time'). It was the hour of his destiny, when he would leave the world and return to the Father. Moreover, his hour was in the Father's control, so that at first it was 'not yet', though in the end he could confidently say 'the hour has come'.

[18] Mt. 17:9–13; Mk. 9:9–13; *cf.* Lk. 9:44.
[19] Mk. 10:35–45; Mt. 20:20–28.
[20] Mk. 12:1–12; *cf.* Mt. 21:33–46; Lk. 20:9–19.
[21] For the Passover saying see Mt. 26:2; for the 'burial' references Mk. 14:3–9 and *cf.* Mt. 26:6–13; for the woe on Judas Mk. 14:10 ff. and *cf.* Mt. 26:14 ff. and Lk. 22:22; for the institution of the supper Mk. 14:22–25 and *cf.* Mt. 26:26–29, Lk. 22:14–20 and 1 Cor. 11:23–26; and for the arrest Mt. 26:47–56 and *cf.* Mk. 14:43–50, Lk. 22:47–53 and Jn. 18:1–11.

When Jesus said to his mother at the Cana wedding after the wine had run out, and to his brothers when they wanted him to go to Jerusalem and advertise himself publicly, 'My time has not yet come', the surface meaning was plain. But John intended his readers to detect the deeper meaning, even though Jesus' mother and brothers did not.[22] John continues to share this secret with his readers, and uses it to explain why Jesus' apparently blasphemous statements did not lead to his arrest. 'They tried to seize him,' he comments, 'but no-one laid a hand on him, because his time had not yet come.'[23] Only when Jesus reaches Jerusalem for the last time does John make the reference explicit. When some Greeks asked to see him, he first said, 'The hour has come for the Son of Man to be glorified' and then, after speaking plainly of his death, he went on: 'Now my heart is troubled, and what shall I say? "Father, save me from this hour"? No, it was for this very reason I came to this hour. Father, glorify your name!'[24] Then twice in the upper room he made final references to the time having come for him to leave the world and to be glorified.[25]

However uncertain we may feel about the earlier allusions to his 'hour' or 'time', we can be in no doubt about the last three. For Jesus specifically called his 'hour' the time of his 'glorification', which (as we shall see later) began with his death, and added that he could not ask to be delivered from it because this was the reason he had come into the world. Indeed, the paradox John records can hardly have been accidental, that the hour for which he had come into the world was the hour in which he left it. Mark makes matters yet more explicit by identifying his 'hour' with his 'cup'.[26]

From this evidence supplied by the Gospel writers, what are we justified in saying about Jesus' perspective on his own death? Beyond question he knew that it was going to happen – not in the sense that all of us know we will have to die one day, but in the sense that he would meet a violent, premature, yet purposive death. More than that, he gives three intertwining reasons for its inevitability.

First, he knew he would die because of the hostility of the Jewish national leaders. It appears that this was aroused quite early during the public ministry. His attitude to the law in general, and to the sabbath in particular, incensed them. When he insisted on healing a man with a shrivelled hand in a synagogue on a sabbath day, Mark tells us that 'the Pharisees went out and began to plot with

[22] Jn. 2:4; 7:8.
[23] Jn. 7:25 ff. especially v.30, and 8:12 ff. especially v.20.
[24] Jn. 12:20–28.   [25] Jn. 13:1; 17:1.
[26] Jn. 12:27; 13:1; Mk. 14:35, 41. *Cf.* Mt. 26:18.

the Herodians how they might kill Jesus' (3:6). Jesus must have been aware of this. He was also very familiar with the Old Testament record of the persecution of the faithful prophets.[27] Although he knew himself to be more than a prophet, he also knew he was not less, and that therefore he could expect similar treatment. He was a threat to the leaders' position and prejudices. According to Luke, after his reading and exposition of Isaiah 61 in the Nazareth synagogue, in which he seemed to be teaching a divine preference for the Gentiles, 'all the people in the synagogue were furious . . . . They got up, drove him out of the town, and took him to the brow of the hill on which the town was built, in order to throw him down the cliff'. Luke adds that 'he walked right through the crowd and went on his way' (4:16–30). But it was a narrow escape. Jesus knew that sooner or later they would get him.

Secondly, he knew he would die because that is what stood written of the Messiah in the Scriptures. 'The Son of Man will go just as it is written about him' (Mk. 14:21). Indeed, when referring to the Old Testament prophetic witness, he tended to couple the death and resurrection, the sufferings and glory, of the Messiah. For the Scriptures taught both. And the Lord was still insisting on this after he had risen. He said to the disciples on the road to Emmaus: ' "Did not the Christ have to suffer these things and then enter his glory?" And beginning with Moses and all the Prophets, he explained to them what was said in all the Scriptures concerning himself' (Lk. 24:25–27; *cf.* verses 44–47).

One would dearly love to have been present at this exposition of 'Christ in all the Scriptures'. For the actual number of his recognizable quotations from the Old Testament, in relation to the cross and resurrection, is not large. He predicted the falling away of the apostles by quoting from Zechariah that when the shepherd was struck the sheep would be scattered.[28] He concluded his Parable of the Tenants with a telling reference to the stone which, though rejected by the builders, subsequently became the building's capstone or cornerstone.[29] And while hanging on the cross, three of his so-called 'seven words' were direct quotations from Scripture: 'My God, my God, why have you forsaken me?' being Psalm 22:1, 'I thirst' coming from Psalm 69:21, and 'Father, into your hands I commit my spirit' from Psalm 31:5. These three psalms all describe the deep anguish of an innocent victim, who is suffering

[27] Joachim Jeremias develops this argument in *Central Message*. See especially p. 41.
[28] Zc. 13:7; Mt. 26:31; Mk. 14:27.
[29] Ps. 118:22; Mt. 21:42; Mk. 12:10–11; Lk. 20:17. *Cf.* Acts 4:11; 1 Pet. 2:7.

both physically and mentally at the hands of his enemies, but who at the same time maintains his trust in his God. Although of course they were written to express the distress of the psalmist himself, yet Jesus had evidently come to see himself and his own sufferings as their ultimate fulfilment.

It is, however, from Isaiah 53 that Jesus seems to have derived the clearest forecast not only of his sufferings, but also of his subsequent glory. For there the servant of Yahweh is first presented as 'despised and rejected by men, a man of sorrows, and familiar with suffering' (v.3), on whom the Lord laid our sins, so that 'he was pierced for our transgressions' and 'crushed for our iniquities' (vv.5–6), and then, at the end of both chapters 52 and 53, is 'raised and lifted up and highly exalted' (52:13) and receives 'a portion among the great' (53:12), as a result of which he will 'sprinkle many nations' (52:15) and 'justify many' (53:11). The only straight quotation which is recorded from Jesus' lips is from verse 12, 'he was numbered with the transgressors'. 'I tell you that this must be fulfilled in me,' he said (Lk. 22:37). Nevertheless, when he declared that he 'must suffer many things' and had 'not come to be served, but to serve, and to give his life as a ransom for many' (Mk. 8:31; 10:45), although these are not direct quotations from Isaiah 53, yet their combination of suffering, service and death for the salvation of others points straight in that direction. Moreover Paul, Peter, Matthew, Luke and John – the major contributors to the New Testament – together allude to at least eight of the chapter's twelve verses. What was the origin of their confident, detailed application of Isaiah 53 to Jesus? They must have derived it from his own lips. It was from this chapter more than from any other that he learnt that the vocation of the Messiah was to suffer and die for human sin, and so be glorified.

The opposition of the hierarchy and the predictions of Scripture, however, do not in themselves explain the inevitability of Jesus' death. The third and most important reason why he knew he would die was because of his own deliberate choice. He was determined to fulfil what was written of the Messiah, however painful it would be. This was neither fatalism nor a martyr complex. It was quite simply that he believed Old Testament Scripture to be his Father's revelation and that he was totally resolved to do his Father's will and finish his Father's work. Besides, his suffering and death would not be purposeless. He had come 'to seek and to save what was lost' (Lk. 19:10). It was for the salvation of sinners that he would die, giving his life as a ransom to set them free (Mk. 10:45). So he set his face steadfastly to go to Jerusalem. Nothing would deter or deflect him. Hence the reiterated 'must' when he spoke of his death. The Son of Man *must* suffer many things and be rejected. Everything that was written about him *must* be fulfilled. He refused to appeal for angels to rescue him, because then the Scriptures would not be fulfilled which said that it *must* happen in this way. Was it not *necessary* for the Christ to suffer before entering his glory?[30] He felt under constraint, even under compulsion: 'I have a baptism to undergo, and how distressed I am (RSV 'constrained', literally 'hemmed in') until it is completed!' (Lk. 12:50).

So then, although he knew he must die, it was not because he was the helpless victim either of evil forces arrayed against him, or of any inflexible fate decreed for him, but because he freely embraced the purpose of his Father for the salvation of sinners, as it had been revealed in Scripture.

This was the perspective of Jesus on his death. Despite the great importance of his teaching, his example, and his works of compassion and power, none of these was central to his mission. What dominated his mind was not the living but the giving of his life. This final self-sacrifice was his 'hour', for which he had come into the world. And the four evangelists, who bear witness to him in the Gospels, show that they understand this by the disproportionate amount of space which they give to the story of his last few days on earth, his death and resurrection. It occupies between a third and a quarter of the three Synoptic Gospels, while John's Gospel has justly been described as having two parts, 'the Book of the Signs' and 'the Book of the Passion', since John spends an almost equal amount of time on each.

The apostles' emphasis

It is often asserted that in the book of Acts the apostles' emphasis was on the resurrection rather than the death of Jesus, and that in any case they gave no doctrinal explanation of his death. Neither of these arguments is sustained by the evidence. I am not of course wanting to claim that the apostles' sermons express a full doctrine of the atonement as it is later found in their letters. Luke's historical sense enables him to record what they said at the time, not what they might have said if they had been preaching several years later. Yet the seeds of the developed doctrine are there. Luke weaves his story round the two apostles Peter and Paul, and supplies five sample evangelistic sermons from each, in shorter or longer summaries. Thus we have Peter's sermons of the Day of Pentecost and in the Temple precincts, brief abstracts of what he said during

[30] Mk. 8:31; Lk. 24:44; Mt. 26:54; Lk. 24:26.

his two trials by the Sanhedrin, and a fairly full account of his message to the Gentile centurion Cornelius and his household.[31] Then, when Luke is recounting the missionary exploits of his hero Paul, he contrasts his address to Jews in the synagogue 'at Pisidian Antioch with that to pagans in the open air at Lystra, contrasts two more in the second missionary journey, namely to Thessalonian Jews and Athenian philosophers, and summarizes his teaching to the Jewish leaders in Rome.[32] In each sermon the approach is different. To Jews Paul spoke of the God of the covenant, the God of Abraham, Isaac and Jacob, but to Gentiles of the God of creation, who made the heavens, the earth and the sea and everything in them. Nevertheless, there was a core to the proclamation of both apostles, which might be reconstructed as follows:

'Jesus was a man who was accredited by God through miracles and anointed by the Spirit to do good and to heal. Despite this, he was crucified through the agency of wicked men, though also by God's purpose according to the Scriptures that the Messiah must suffer. Then God reversed the human verdict on Jesus by raising him from the dead, also according to the Scriptures, and as attested by the apostolic eyewitnesses. Next God exalted him to the place of supreme honour as Lord and Saviour. He now possesses full authority both to save those who repent, believe and are baptized in his name, bestowing on them the forgiveness of sins and the gift of the Spirit, and to judge those who reject him.'

Several important points emerge from this gospel core.

First, although the apostles attributed the death of Jesus to human wickedness, they declared that it was also due to a divine purpose.[33] Moreover, what God had foreknown, he had foretold. So the apostles repeatedly emphasized that the death and resurrection of Jesus happened 'according to the Scriptures'. Paul's own later summary of the gospel also stressed this: 'that Christ died for our sins according to the Scriptures, . . . that he was raised on the third day according to the Scriptures . . .' (1 Cor. 15:3–4). Only sometimes are actual biblical quotations recorded. Many more unrecorded ones must have been used, as when in the Thessalonian synagogue Paul 'reasoned with them from the Scriptures, explaining and proving that the Christ had to suffer and rise from the dead' (Acts 17:2–3). It seems likely that these were – or at

[31] Acts 2:14–39; 3:12–26; 4:8–12; 5:29–32 and 10:34–43.
[32] Acts 13:16–41; 14:15–17; 17:2–3 and 22–31; 28:23–31.
[33] E.g. Acts 2:23; 3:18; 4:28.

least included – the Scriptures which Jesus used, and therefore the doctrine which they expressed.

Secondly, although a full-scale atonement doctrine is missing, the apostolic preaching of the cross was not undoctrinal. Not only did they proclaim that Christ died according to the Scriptures, and so according to God's saving purpose, but they called the cross on which he died a 'tree'. Luke is careful to record this fact of both the leading apostles, Peter and Paul. Peter twice used the expression that the people 'killed him by hanging him on a tree', to the Jewish Sanhedrin and to the Gentile Cornelius. Similarly, Paul told the synagogue congregation in Pisidian Antioch that when the people and their rulers in Jerusalem 'had carried out all that was written about him, they took him down from the tree'.[34]

Now they were under no necessity to use this language. Peter also spoke of Jesus' 'crucifixion', and Paul of his 'sufferings' and 'execution'.[35] So why their references to the 'tree' and to his having been 'hanged' on it? The only possible explanation is to be found in Deuteronomy 21:22–23, where instructions were given for the body of a man, who had been executed for a capital offence by hanging, to be buried before nightfall, 'because anyone who is hung on a tree is under God's curse'. The apostles were quite familiar with this legislation, and with its implication that Jesus died under the divine curse. Yet, instead of hushing it up, they deliberately drew people's attention to it. So evidently they were not embarrassed by it. They did not think of Jesus as in any sense deserving to be accursed by God. They must, therefore, have at least begun to understand that it was our curse which he was bearing. Certainly both apostles stated this plainly in their later letters. Paul in Galatians, probably written very soon after his visit to Pisidian Antioch, wrote that 'Christ redeemed us from the curse of the law by becoming a curse for us, for it is written: "Cursed is everyone who is hanged on a tree" ' (3:13). And Peter wrote: 'He himself bore our sins in his body on the tree' (1 Pet. 2:24). If then Peter and Paul in their letters plainly saw the cross of Jesus in sin-bearing or curse-bearing terms, and both linked this fact with the verses in Deuteronomy about being hanged on a tree, is it not reasonable to suppose that already in their Acts speeches, in which they called the cross a tree, they had glimpsed the same truth? In this case there is more doctrinal teaching about the cross in the early sermons of the apostles than they are often credited with.

[34] Acts 5:30; 10:39; 13:29.
[35] Acts 2:23, 36; 4:10; 17:3 and 13:28.

34

Thirdly, we need to consider how the apostles presented the resurrection. Although they emphasized it, it would be an exaggeration to call their message an exclusively resurrection gospel. For in the nature of the case the resurrection cannot stand by itself. Since it is a resurrection from death, its significance is determined by the nature of this death. Indeed, the reason for emphasizing the resurrection may be rather to emphasize something about the death which it cancels and conquers. This proves to be the case. At its simplest their message was: 'you killed him, God raised him, and we are witnesses.'[36] In other words, the resurrection was the divine reversal of the human verdict. But it was more than this. By the resurrection God 'glorified' and 'exalted' the Jesus who had died.[37] Promoting him to the place of supreme honour at his right hand, in fulfilment of Psalm 110:1 and on account of the achievement of his death, God made the crucified and risen Jesus 'both Lord and Christ', both 'Prince and Saviour', with authority to save sinners by bestowing upon them repentance, forgiveness and the gift of the Spirit.[38] Moreover, this comprehensive salvation is specifically said to be due to his powerful 'Name' (the sum total of his person, death and resurrection), in which people must believe and into which they must be baptized, since there is 'no other name under heaven given to men' by which they must be saved.[39]

When we turn from the apostles' early sermons recorded in the Acts to the maturer utterances of their letters, the prominent place they give to the cross is even more marked. True, some of the shortest letters do not mention it (such as Paul's to Philemon, Jude's, and John's second and third), and it is not altogether surprising that James' largely ethical homily does not refer to it. Yet the three major letter-writers of the New Testament – Paul, Peter and John – are unanimous in witnessing to its centrality, as are also the letter to the Hebrews and the Revelation.

We begin with Paul. He found no anomaly in defining his gospel as 'the message of the cross', his ministry as 'we preach Christ crucified', baptism as initiation 'into his death' and the Lord's Supper as a proclamation of the Lord's death. He boldly declared that, though the cross seemed either foolishness or a 'stumbling block' to the self-confident, it was in fact the very essence of God's wisdom and power.[40] So convinced was he of this that he had deliberately resolved, he told the Corinthians, to renounce worldly

[36] *Cf.* Acts 2:23–24; 3:15; 4:10; 5:30; 10:39–40; 13:28–30.
[37] Acts 3:13 and 2:33.
[38] *Cf.* Acts 2:33–36; 3:26; 5:31–32; 10:43 and 13:38–39.
[39] Acts 2:38; 3:16; 4:10, 12; *cf.* Lk. 24:46–47.
[40] 1 Cor. 1:18–25; Rom. 6:3; 1 Cor. 11:26.

wisdom and instead to know nothing among them 'except Jesus Christ and him crucified' (1 Cor. 2:1–2). When later in the same letter he wished to remind them of his gospel, which he had himself received and had handed on to them, which had become the foundation on which they were standing and the good news by which they were being saved, what was 'of first importance' (he said) was 'that Christ died for our sins according to the Scriptures, that he was buried, that he was raised on the third day according to the Scriptures, and that he appeared . . .' (1 Cor. 15:1–5). And when a few years later he developed this outline into the full gospel manifesto which his letter to the Romans is, his emphasis is even more strongly on the cross. For having proved all humankind sinful and guilty before God, he explains that God's righteous way of putting the unrighteous right with himself operates 'through the redemption that came by Christ Jesus', whom 'God presented as a sacrifice of atonement, through faith in his blood' (Rom. 3:21–25). Consequently, we are 'justified by his blood' and 'reconciled to God through the death of his Son' (Rom. 5:9–10). Without Christ's sacrificial death for us salvation would have been impossible. No wonder Paul boasted in nothing except the cross (Gal. 6:14).

The apostle Peter's testimony is equally clear. He begins his first letter with the startling statement that his readers have been sprinkled with the blood of Jesus Christ. And a few verses later, he reminds them that the price of their redemption from their former empty way of life has not been 'perishable things such as silver or gold', but rather 'the precious blood of Christ, a lamb without blemish or defect' (1 Pet. 1:18–19). Although the remaining references in his letter to the death of Jesus relate it to the unjust sufferings of Christians ('glory through suffering' being the principle for them as for him), Peter nevertheless takes the opportunity to give some profound instruction about the Saviour's death. 'He himself bore our sins in his body on the tree' and 'Christ died for sins once for all, the righteous for the unrighteous, to bring you to God' (2:24; 3:18), in fulfilment of the prophecy of Isaiah 53. Because in the context Peter is emphasizing the cross as our example, it is all the more striking that he should at the same time write of Christ our sinbearer and substitute.

John's emphasis in his letters was on the incarnation. Because he was combating an early heresy which tried to sever Christ from Jesus, the divine Son from the human being, he insisted that Jesus was 'the Christ come in the flesh' and that anyone who denied this was Antichrist.[41] Nevertheless, he saw the incarnation as being

[41] *E.g.* 1 Jn. 2:22; 4:1–3; 2 Jn. 7.

with a view to the atonement. For God's unique love was seen not so much in the coming as in the dying of his Son, whom he 'sent . . . as an atoning sacrifice for our sins' and whose 'blood . . . purifies us from every sin'.[42]

The letter to the Hebrews, which is more a theological tract than a letter, was written to Jewish Christians who, under the pressure of persecution, were being tempted to renounce Christ and relapse into Judaism. The author's tactic was to demonstrate the supremacy of Jesus Christ, not only as Son over the angels and as Prophet over Moses, but in particular as Priest over the now obsolete Levitical priesthood. For the sacrificial ministry of Jesus, our 'great high priest' (4:14), is incomparably superior to theirs. He had no sins of his own for which to make sacrifice; the blood he shed was not of goats and calves, but his own; he had no need to offer the same sacrifices repeatedly, which could never take away sins, because he made 'one sacrifice for sins for ever'; and he has thus obtained an 'eternal redemption' and established an 'eternal covenant' which contains the promise, 'I will forgive their wickedness and will remember their sins no more.'[43]

Still more striking than all this, however, is the portraiture of Jesus in the last book of the Bible, the Revelation. He is introduced to us in its first chapter as 'the firstborn from the dead' (v.5) and 'the Living One', who was dead but now is alive for ever, and who holds the keys of death and Hades (v.18). An appropriate doxology is added: 'To him who loves us and has freed us from our sins by his blood, . . . to him be glory and power for ever and ever!' (vv.5–6).

John's commonest designation of Jesus, consonant with the symbolic imagery of the Revelation, is simply 'the Lamb'. The reason for this title, which is applied to him twenty-eight times throughout the book, has little to do with the meekness of his character (although once his qualities as both 'Lion' and 'Lamb' are deliberately contrasted (5:5–6)); it is rather because he has been slain as a sacrificial victim and by his blood has set his people free. In order to grasp the broad perspective from which John views the influence of the Lamb, it may be helpful to divide it into four spheres – salvation, history, worship and eternity.

The redeemed people of God (that 'great multitude that no-one could count'), who are drawn from every nation and language, and stand before God's throne, specifically attribute their salvation to God and the Lamb. They cry with a loud voice:

---

[42] 1 Jn. 3:16; 4:9, 14; 4:10 and *cf.* 2:1–2; 1:7.
[43] See especially Hebrews 8 – 10.

'Salvation belongs to our God,
who sits on the throne,
and to the Lamb.'

By a very dramatic figure of speech the robes they are wearing are said to have been 'washed . . . and made white in the blood of the Lamb'. In other words, they owe their righteous standing before God entirely to the cross of Christ, through which their sins have been forgiven and their defilement cleansed. Their salvation through Christ is also secure, for not only are their names written in the Lamb's book of life, but the Lamb's name is written on their foreheads.[44]

In John's vision, however, the Lamb is more than the Saviour of a countless multitude; he is depicted also as the lord of all history. To begin with, he is seen 'standing in the centre of the throne', that is, sharing in the sovereign rule of Almighty God. More than that, the occupant of the throne is holding in his right hand a seven-sealed scroll, which is generally identified as the book of history. At first John 'wept and wept' because no-one in the universe could open the scroll, or even look inside it. But then at last the Lamb is said to be worthy. He takes the scroll, breaks the seals one by one, and thus (it seems) unfolds history chapter by chapter. It is significant that what has qualified him to assume this role is his cross; for this is the key to history and the redemptive process it inaugurated. Despite their sufferings from war, famine, plague, persecution and other catastrophes, God's people can yet overcome the devil 'by the blood of the Lamb', and are assured that the final victory will be his and theirs, since the Lamb proves to be 'Lord of lords and King of kings'.[45]

It is not surprising to learn that the author of salvation and the lord of history is also the object of heaven's worship. In chapter 5 we listen as one choir after another is brought in to swell the praise of the Lamb. First, when he had taken the scroll, 'the four living creatures and the twenty-four elders' (probably representing the whole creation on the one hand and the whole church of both Testaments on the other) 'fell down before the Lamb . . . and sang a new song:

'You are worthy to take the scroll
and to open the seals,
because you were slain,

[44] Rev. 7:9–14, 16–17; 13:8; 21:27; 14:1ff.
[45] Rev. 5:1–6; 22:1, 3; 12:11; 17:14.

38

and with your blood you purchased men for God
from every tribe and language and people and nation . . . .'

Next, John heard the voice of a hundred million angels, or more,
who constituted the outer circle of those surrounding the throne.
They too sang with a loud voice:

'Worthy is the Lamb, who was slain,
to receive power and wealth and wisdom and strength
and honour and glory and praise!'

Then finally he 'heard every creature in heaven and on earth and
under the earth and on the sea, and all that is in them' – universal
creation – singing:

'To him who sits on the throne and to the Lamb
be praise and honour and glory and power,
    for ever and ever!'

To this the four living creatures responded with their 'Amen', and
the elders fell down and worshipped.[46]

Jesus the Lamb does more than occupy the centre of the stage
today, in salvation, history and worship; in addition, he will have
a central place when history ends and the curtain rises on eternity.
On the day of judgment those who have rejected him will try to
escape from him. They will call to the mountains and rocks to
engulf them: 'Fall on us and hide us from the face of him who sits
on the throne and from the wrath of the Lamb! For the great day
of their wrath has come, and who can stand?' For those who have
trusted and followed him, however, that day will be like a wedding
day and a wedding feast. For the final union of Christ with his
people is depicted in terms of the Lamb's marriage to his bride.
Changing the metaphor, the new Jerusalem will descend from
heaven. It will have no temple in it, 'because the Lord God
Almighty and the Lamb are its temple'; nor will it need either sun
or moon, 'for the glory of God gives it light, and the Lamb is its
lamp'.[47]

One cannot fail to notice, or to be impressed by, the seer's
repeated and uninhibited coupling of 'God and the Lamb'. The
person he places on an equality with God is the Saviour who died
for sinners. He depicts him as mediating God's salvation, sharing

[46] Rev. 5:8–9, 11–14.
[47] Rev. 6:15–17; 19:6–7; 21:9–10, 22–23.

God's throne, receiving God's worship (the worship due to him) and diffusing God's light. And his worthiness, which qualifies him for these unique privileges, is due to the fact that he was slain, and by his death procured our salvation. If (as may be) the book of life is said in 13:8 to belong to 'the Lamb that was slain from the creation of the world', then John is telling us nothing less than that from an eternity of the past to an eternity of the future the centre of the stage is occupied by the Lamb of God who was slain.

Persistence despite opposition

This survey leaves us in no doubt that the principal contributors to the New Testament believed in the centrality of the cross of Christ, and believed that their conviction was derived from the mind of the Master himself. The early post-apostolic church, therefore, had a firm double base – in the teaching of Christ and his apostles – for making a cross the sign and symbol of Christianity. Church tradition proved in this to be a faithful reflection of Scripture.

Moreover, we must not overlook their remarkable tenacity. They knew that those who had crucified the Son of God had subjected him to 'public disgrace' and that in order to endure the cross Jesus had had to humble himself to it and to 'scorn its shame'.[48] Nevertheless, what was shameful, even odious, to the critics of Christ, was in the eyes of his followers most glorious. They had learnt that the servant was not greater than the master, and that for them as for him suffering was the means to glory. More than that, suffering *was* glory, and whenever they were 'insulted because of the name of Christ', then 'the Spirit of glory' rested upon them.[49]

Yet the enemies of the gospel neither did nor do share this perspective. There is no greater cleavage between faith and unbelief than in their respective attitudes to the cross. Where faith sees glory, unbelief sees only disgrace. What was foolishness to Greeks, and continues to be to modern intellectuals who trust in their own wisdom, is nevertheless the wisdom of God. And what remains a stumbling-block to those who trust in their own righteousness, like the Jews of the first century, proves to be the saving power of God (1 Cor. 1:18–25).

One of the saddest features of Islam is that it rejects the cross, declaring it inappropriate that a major prophet of God should come to such an ignominious end. The Koran sees no need for the

[48] Heb. 6:6; Phil. 2:8; Heb. 12:2.
[49] Lk. 24:26; Jn. 12:23–24; 1 Pet. 1:11; 4:13; 5:1, 10; 4:14.

sin-bearing death of a Saviour. At least fives times it declares categorically that 'no soul shall bear another's burden'. Indeed, 'if a laden soul cries out for help, not even a near relation shall share its burden'. Why is this? It is because 'each man shall reap the fruits of his own deeds', even though Allah is merciful and forgives those who repent and do good. Denying the need for the cross, the Koran goes on to deny the fact. The Jews 'uttered a monstrous falsehood' when they declared 'we have put to death the Messiah Jesus the son of Mary, the apostle of Allah', for 'they did not kill him, nor did they crucify him, but they thought they did'.[50] Although Muslim theologians have interpreted this statement in different ways, the commonly held belief is that God cast a spell over the enemies of Jesus in order to rescue him, and that either Judas Iscariot[51] or Simon of Cyrene was substituted for him at the last moment. In the nineteenth century the Ahmadiya sect of Islam borrowed from different liberal Christian writers the notion that Jesus only swooned on the cross, and revived in the tomb, adding that he subsequently travelled to India to teach, and died there; they claim to be the guardians of his tomb in Kashmir.

But Christian messengers of the good news cannot be silent about the cross. Here is the testimony of the American missionary Samuel M. Zwemer (1867–1952), who laboured in Arabia, edited *The Muslim World* for forty years, and is sometimes called 'The Apostle to Islam':

> The missionary among Moslems (to whom the Cross of Christ is a stumbling-block and the atonement foolishness) is driven daily to deeper meditation on this mystery of redemption, and to a stronger conviction that here is the very heart of our message and our mission. . . .
>
> If the Cross of Christ is anything to the mind, it is surely everything – the most profound reality and the sublimest mystery. One comes to realize that literally all the wealth and glory of the gospel centres here. The Cross is the pivot as well as the centre of New Testament thought. It is the exclusive mark of the

[50] Quotations are from *The Koran*. The five rejections of the possibility of 'substitution' are on pages 114 (liii.38), 176 (xxv.18), 230 (xvii.15), 274 (xxxix.7) and 429 (vi.164).

[51] The spurious 'Gospel of Barnabas', written in Italian in the fourteenth or fifteenth century by a Christian convert to Islam, contains parts of the Koran as well as of the four canonical Gospels. It tells the fantastic tale that, when Judas came with the soldiers to arrest Jesus, he withdrew into a house. There angels rescued him through a window, while Judas 'was so changed in speech and in face to be like Jesus' that everybody was deceived, and Judas was crucified in Jesus' place.

Christian faith, the symbol of Christianity and its cynosure.

The more unbelievers deny its crucial character, the more do believers find in it the key to the mysteries of sin and suffering. We rediscover the apostolic emphasis on the Cross when we read the gospel with Moslems. We find that, although the offence of the Cross remains, its magnetic power is irresistible.[52]

'Irresistible' is the very word an Iranian student used when telling me of his conversion to Christ. Brought up to read the Koran, say his prayers and lead a good life, he nevertheless knew that he was separated from God by his sins. When Christian friends brought him to church and encouraged him to read the Bible, he learnt that Jesus Christ had died for his forgiveness. 'For me the offer was irresistible and heaven-sent,' he said, and he cried to God to have mercy on him through Christ. Almost immediately 'the burden of my past life was lifted. I felt as if a huge weight ... had gone. With the relief and sense of lightness came incredible joy. At last it had happened. I was free of my past. I *knew* that God had forgiven me, and I felt clean. I wanted to shout, and tell everybody.' It was through the cross that the character of God came clearly into focus for him, and that he found Islam's missing dimension, 'the intimate fatherhood of God and the deep assurance of sins forgiven'.

Muslims are not by any means the only people, however, who repudiate the gospel of the cross. Hindus also, though they can accept its historicity, reject its saving significance. Gandhi, for example, the founder of modern India, who while working in South Africa as a young lawyer was attracted to Christianity, yet wrote of himself while there in 1894:

I could accept Jesus as a martyr, an embodiment of sacrifice, and a divine teacher, but not as the most perfect man ever born. His death on the cross was a great example to the world, but that there was anything like a mysterious or miraculous virtue in it, my heart could not accept.[53]

Turning to the West, perhaps the most scornful rejection of the cross has come from the pen of the German philosopher and philologist, Friedrich Nietzsche (died 1900). Near the beginning of *The Anti-Christ* (1895) he defined the good as 'the will to power', the bad as 'all that proceeds from weakness', and happiness as 'the

[52] Samuel M. Zwemer, *Glory of the Cross*, p. 6.
[53] *Gandhi: An Autobiography*, p. 113.

feeling that power *increases* . . .', while 'what is more harmful than any vice' is 'active sympathy for the ill-constituted and weak – Christianity'. Admiring Darwin's emphasis on the survival of the fittest, he despised all forms of weakness, and in their place dreamt of the emergence of a 'superman' and a 'daring ruler race'. To him 'depravity' meant 'decadence', and nothing was more decadent than Christianity which 'has taken the side of everything weak, base, ill-constituted'. Being 'the religion of *pity*', it 'preserves what is ripe for destruction' and so 'thwarts the law of evolution' (pp. 115–118). Nietzsche reserved his bitterest invective for 'the Christian conception of God' as 'God of the sick, God as spider, God as spirit', and for the Christian Messiah whom he dismissed contemptuously as 'God on the Cross' (pp. 128, 168).

If Nietzsche rejected Christianity for its 'weakness', others have done so for its supposedly 'barbaric' teachings. Professor Sir Alfred Ayer, for example, the Oxford philosopher who is well known for his antipathy to Christianity, wrote in a recent newspaper article that, among religions of historical importance, there was quite a strong case for considering Christianity the worst. Why so? Because it rests 'on the allied doctrines of original sin and vicarious atonement, which are intellectually contemptible and morally outrageous'.[54]

How is it that Christians can face such ridicule without shifting their ground? Why do we 'cling to the old rugged cross' (in the words of a rather sentimental, popular hymn), and insist on its centrality, refusing to let it be pushed to the circumference of our message? Why must we proclaim the scandalous, and glory in the shameful? The answer lies in the single word 'integrity'. Christian integrity consists partly in a resolve to unmask the caricatures, but mostly in personal loyalty to Jesus, in whose mind the saving cross was central. Indeed, readers who have come without bias to the Scriptures all seem to have come to the same conclusion. Here is a sample from this century.

P. T. Forsyth, the English Congregationalist, wrote in *The Cruciality of the Cross* (1909):

> Christ is to us just what his cross is. All that Christ was in heaven or on earth was put into what he did there . . . Christ, I repeat, is to us just what his cross is. You do not understand Christ till you understand his cross (pp. 44–45).

And the following year (1910) in *The Work of Christ* he wrote:

[54] *The Guardian*, 30 August 1979.

On this interpretation of the work of Christ (*sc.* the Pauline doctrine of reconciliation) the whole Church rests. If you move faith from that centre, you have driven *the* nail into the Church's coffin. The Church is then doomed to death, and it is only a matter of time when she shall expire (p. 53).

Next, Emil Brunner, the Swiss theologian, whose book *The Mediator* was first published in German in 1927, sub-titled 'A study of the central doctrine of the Christian faith', defended his conviction with these words:

In Christianity faith in the Mediator is not something optional, not something about which, in the last resort, it is possible to hold different opinions, if we are only united on the 'main point'. For faith in the Mediator – in the event which took place once for all, a revealed atonement – *is* the Christian religion itself; it is the 'main point'; it is not something alongside of the centre; it is the substance and kernel, not the husk. This is so true that we may even say: in distinction from all other forms of religion, the Christian religion is faith in the one Mediator . . . And there is no other possibility of being a Christian than through faith in that which took place once for all, revelation and atonement through the Mediator (p. 40).

Later Brunner applauds Luther's description of Christian theology as a *theologia crucis*, and goes on:

The Cross is the sign of the Christian faith, of the Christian Church, of the revelation of God in Jesus Christ. . . . The whole struggle of the Reformation for the *sola fide*, the *soli deo gloria*, was simply the struggle for the right interpretation of the Cross. He who understands the Cross aright – this is the opinion of the Reformers – understands the Bible, he understands Jesus Christ (p. 435).

Again,

the believing recognition of this uniqueness, faith in the Mediator, is the sign of the Christian faith. Whoever considers this statement to be a sign of exaggeration, intolerance, harshness, non-historical thought, and the like, has not yet heard the message of Christianity (p. 507).

My final quotation comes from the Anglican scholar, Bishop

Stephen Neill:

> In the Christian theology of history, the death of Christ is the
> central point of history; here all the roads of the past converge;
> hence all the roads of the future diverge.[55]

The verdict of scholars has understandably percolated through
into popular Christian devotion. Allowances should be made for
Christians who at Christ's cross have found their pride broken,
their guilt expunged, their love kindled, their hope restored and
their character transformed, if they go on to indulge in a little
harmless hyperbole. Perceiving the cross to be the centre of history
and theology, they naturally perceive it also to be the centre of all
reality. So they see it everywhere, and have always done so. I give
two examples, one ancient and the other modern.

Justin Martyr, the second-century Christian apologist, confessed
that wherever he looked, he saw the cross. Neither the sea is
crossed nor the earth is ploughed without it, he writes, referring
to a ship's mast and yard, and to a plough's blade and yoke.
Diggers and mechanics do not work without cross-shaped tools,
alluding presumably to a spade and its handle. Moreover, 'the
human form differs from that of the irrational animals in nothing
else than in its being erect and having the arms extended'. And if
the torso and arms of the human form proclaim the cross, so do
the nose and eyebrows of the human face.[56] Fanciful? Yes, entirely,
and yet I find myself willing to forgive any such fancies which
glorify the cross.

My modern example is the most eloquent description I know of
the universality of the cross. It is Malcolm Muggeridge uncon-
sciously updating Justin Martyr. Brought up in a Socialist home,
and familiar with Socialist Sunday Schools and their 'sort of agnos-
ticism sweetened by hymns', he became uneasy about 'this whole
concept of a Jesus of good causes'. Then:

> I would catch a glimpse of a cross – not necessarily a crucifix;
> maybe two pieces of wood accidentally nailed together, on a
> telegraph pole, for instance – and suddenly my heart would
> stand still. In an instinctive, intuitive way I understood that
> something more important, more tumultuous, more passionate,
> was at issue than our good causes, however admirable they might
> be. . . .

[55] From the chapter entitled 'Jesus and History' in *Truth of God Incarnate*, ed. E. M. B. Green, p. 80.
[56] Justin Martyr's *First Apology*, Ch. lv, 'Symbols of the Cross'.

It was, I know, an obsessive interest . . . I might fasten bits of wood together myself, or doodle it. This symbol, which was considered to be derisory in my home, was yet also the focus of inconceivable hopes and desires. . . .

As I remember this, a sense of my own failure lies leadenly upon me. I should have worn it over my heart; carried it, a precious standard, never to be wrested out of my hands; even though I fell, still borne aloft. It should have been my cult, my uniform, my language, my life. I shall have no excuse; I can't say I didn't know. I knew from the beginning, and turned away.[57]

Later, however, he turned back, as each of us must who has ever glimpsed the reality of Christ crucified. For the only authentic Jesus is the Jesus who died on the cross.

But why did he die? Who was responsible for his death? That is the question to which we turn in the next chapter.

[57] Malcolm Muggeridge, *Jesus Rediscovered*, pp. 24–25.

2

Why did Christ die?

Why did Christ die? Who was responsible for his death?

Many people see no problem in these questions and therefore have no difficulty in answering them. The facts seem to them as plain as day. Jesus did not 'die', they say; he was killed, publicly executed as a felon. The doctrines he taught were felt to be dangerous, even subversive. The Jewish leaders were incensed by his disrespectful attitude to the law and by his provocative claims, while the Romans heard that he was proclaiming himself King of the Jews, and so challenging the authority of Caesar. To both groups Jesus appeared to be a revolutionary thinker and preacher, and some considered him a revolutionary activist as well. So profoundly did he disturb the *status quo* that they determined to do away with him. In fact, they entered into an unholy alliance with one another in order to do so. In the Jewish court a theological charge was brought against him, blasphemy. In the Roman court the charge was political, sedition. But whether his offence was seen to be primarily against God or against Caesar, the outcome was the same. He was perceived as a threat to law and order, which could not be tolerated. So he was liquidated. Why did he die? Ostensibly he died as a law-breaker, but in reality as the victim of small minds, and as a martyr to his own greatness.

One of the fascinating features of the Gospel writers' accounts of the trial of Jesus[1] is this blending of the legal and moral factors. They all indicate that in both Jewish and Roman courts a certain legal procedure was followed. The prisoner was arrested, charged

[1] For a recent scholarly defence by a lawyer of the historical accuracy of the trials, as described in the Gospels, see *Le Procès de Jésus* by Prof. Jean Imbert.

and cross-examined, and witnesses were called. The judge then reached his verdict and pronounced the sentence. Yet the evangelists also make it clear that the prisoner was not guilty of the charges laid, that the witnesses were false, and that the sentence of death was a gross miscarriage of justice. Further, the reason for this was the presence of personal, moral factors which influenced the course of the law. Caiaphas the Jewish high priest and Pilate the Roman procurator were not just officers of church and state, fulfilling their official roles; they were fallen and fallible human beings, swayed by the dark passions which rule us all. For our motives are always mixed. We may succeed in preserving a modicum of rectitude in the performance of our public duty, but behind this façade lurk violent and sinful emotions, which are always threatening to erupt. These secret sins the evangelists expose, as they tell their story of the arrest, custody, trial, sentence and execution of Jesus. It is one of the purposes of their narrative, for the material of the Gospels was used in the moral instruction of converts.

The Roman soldiers and Pilate

Those immediately responsible for the death of Jesus were of course the Roman soldiers who carried out the sentence. The actual process of crucifying him is not, however, described by any of the four evangelists.

If we had to rely exclusively on the Gospels, we would not have known what happened. But other contemporary documents tell us what a crucifixion was like.[2] The prisoner would first be publicly humiliated by being stripped naked. He was then laid on his back on the ground, while his hands were either nailed or roped to the horizontal wooden beam (the *patibulum*), and his feet to the vertical pole. The cross was then hoisted to an upright position and dropped into a socket which had been dug for it in the ground. Usually a peg or rudimentary seat was provided to take some of the weight of the victim's body and prevent it from being torn loose. But there he would hang, helplessly exposed to intense physical pain, public ridicule, daytime heat and night-time cold. The torture would last several days.

None of this is described by the Gospel writers. Piecing together what they do tell us, it seems that, according to known Roman custom, Jesus began by carrying his own cross to the place of execution. Presumably, however, he stumbled under its weight. For

[2] For a summary of available information about crucifixion see Martin Hengel's *Crucifixion*.

a man named Simon, from Cyrene in North Africa, who was at that moment coming into the city from the country, was stopped and forced to carry the cross for Jesus. When they arrived at 'the place called Golgotha (which means The Place of the Skull)', Jesus was offered some wine mixed with myrrh, which was a merciful gesture intended to dull the worst pain. But, although according to Matthew he tasted it, he refused to drink it. Next, all four evangelists write simply: 'and they crucified him'.[3] That is all. They have previously described in some detail how the soldiers mocked him in the Praetorium (the governor's residence): they dressed him in a purple robe, placed a crown of thorns on his head and a sceptre of reed in his right hand, blindfolded him, spat on him, slapped him in the face and struck him on the head, at the same time challenging him to identify who was hitting him. They also knelt down before him in mock homage. But the evangelists give no details of the crucifixion; they make no reference at all to hammer or nails or pain, or even blood.

All we are told is 'they crucified him'. That is, the soldiers carried out their gruesome task. There is no evidence that they enjoyed it, no suggestion that they were cruel or sadistical. They were just obeying orders. It was their job. They did what they had to do. And all the while, Luke tells us, Jesus kept praying out loud, 'Father, forgive them, for they do not know what they are doing' (23:34).

Although the Gospel writers seem to be implying that no particular blame attached to the Roman soldiers for crucifying Jesus (and they add that later the centurion in charge of them believed, or at least semi-believed), the case is quite different with the Roman procurator who ordered the crucifixion. 'Finally Pilate handed him over to them to be crucified. So the soldiers took charge of Jesus . . . they crucified him' (Jn. 19:16–18). Pilate was culpable. In fact, his guilt is written into our Christian creed, which declares that Jesus was 'crucified under Pontius Pilate'.

Pilate is known to have been appointed procurator (*i.e.* Roman governor) of the border province of Judea by the Emperor Tiberius, and to have served for 10 years from about AD 26 to 36. He acquired a reputation as an able administrator, with a typically Roman sense of fair play. But he was hated by the Jews because he was contemptuous of them. They did not forget his provocative act, at the beginning of his period of office, of exhibiting the Roman standards in Jerusalem itself. Josephus describes another of his follies, namely that he misappropriated some Temple money to

[3] Mt. 27:32–35; Mk. 15:21–25; Lk. 23:26–33; Jn. 19:17–18.

build an aqueduct.[4] Many think that it was in the ensuing riot that he had mixed the blood of certain Galileans with their sacrifices (Lk. 13:1). These are only samples of his hot temper, violence and cruelty. According to Philo, King Agrippa I described him in a letter to the Emperor Caligula as 'a man of a very inflexible disposition, and very merciless as well as very obstinate'.[5] His overriding aim was to maintain law and order, to keep those troublesome Jews firmly under control, and, if necessary for these ends, to be ruthless in the suppression of any riot or threat of one.

The portrait of Pontius Pilate in the Gospels tallies well with this external evidence. When the Jewish leaders brought Jesus to him with the words 'We have found this man subverting our nation', and added that 'he opposes the payment of taxes to Caesar and claims to be Christ, a king' (Lk. 23:2), Pilate could not fail to take notice. As his investigation proceeded, the evangelists emphasize two important points.

First, Pilate was convinced of Jesus' innocence. He was obviously impressed by the prisoner's noble bearing, self-control and political harmlessness. So three times he declared publicly that he could find no ground for charging him. The first was soon after daybreak on the Friday morning when the Sanhedrin referred the case to him. Pilate listened to them, asked Jesus a few questions, and after this preliminary hearing announced, 'I find no basis for a charge against this man.'[6]

The second occasion was when Jesus came back from being examined by Herod. Pilate said to the priests and people: 'You brought me this man as one who was inciting the people to rebellion. I have examined him in your presence and have found no basis for your charges against him. Neither has Herod, for he sent him back to us: as you can see, he has done nothing to deserve death.'[7] At this the crowd shouted, 'Crucify him! Crucify him!' But Pilate responded for the third time: 'Why? What crime has this man committed? I have found in him no grounds for the death penalty.'[8] Moreover, the procurator's personal conviction about the innocence of Jesus was confirmed by the message his wife sent him: 'Don't have anything to do with that innocent man, for I have suffered a great deal today in a dream because of him' (Mt. 27:19).

Pilate's repeated insistence on the innocence of Jesus is the essential background to the second point about him which the evangelists emphasize, namely his ingenious attempts to avoid having to

---

[4] *Antiquities* xviii.3.2.   [5] *Ad Gaium* 38, p. 165.
[6] Lk. 23:4; Jn. 18:38.   [7] Lk. 23:13–15; *cf.* Jn. 19:4–5.
[8] Lk. 23:22; Jn. 19:6.

come down clearly on one side or the other. He wanted to avoid sentencing Jesus (since he believed he was innocent) and at the same time avoid exonerating him (since the Jewish leaders believed he was guilty). How could he contrive to reconcile these irreconcilables? We watch him wriggling, as he attempts to release Jesus and pacify the Jews, *i.e.* be just and unjust simultaneously. He tried four evasions.

First, on hearing that Jesus was a Galilean, and therefore under Herod's jurisdiction, he sent him to Herod for trial, hoping to transfer to him the responsibility of decision. But Herod sent Jesus back unsentenced (Lk. 23:5–12).

Secondly, he tried half-measures: 'I will have him punished (*i.e.* scourged) and then release him' (Lk. 23:16, 22). He hoped the crowd might be satisfied by something less than the supreme penalty, and their blood-lust sated by the sight of his lacerated back. It was despicable. For if Jesus was innocent, he should have been immediately released, not flogged first.

Thirdly, he tried to do the right thing (release Jesus) for the wrong reason (because the crowd chose him for release). Remembering the procurator's established custom to grant a Passover amnesty to some prisoner, he hoped the people would select Jesus for this favour. Then he could release him as an act of clemency instead of as an act of justice. It was an astute idea, but inherently shameful, and the people thwarted it by demanding instead that the procurator's pardon be granted to a notorious criminal and murderer, Barabbas.

Fourthly, he tried to protest his innocence. He took water and washed his hands before the crowd, saying 'I am innocent of this man's blood' (Mt. 27:24). And then, before his hands were dry, he handed Jesus over to be crucified. How could he bring himself to incur this great guilt immediately after proclaiming his innocence?

It is easy to condemn Pilate and overlook our own equally devious behaviour. Anxious to avoid the pain of a whole-hearted commitment to Christ, we too search for convenient subterfuges. We either leave the decision to somebody else, or opt for a half-hearted compromise, or seek to honour Jesus for the wrong reason (*e.g.* as teacher instead of as Lord), or even make a public affirmation of loyalty while at the same time denying him in our hearts.

Three tell-tale expressions in Luke's narrative illumine what in the end Pilate did: 'their shouts prevailed', 'Pilate decided to grant their demand', and he 'surrendered Jesus to their will' (Lk. 23:23–25). *Their* shouts, *their* demand, *their* will: to these Pilate weakly capitulated. He was 'wanting to release Jesus' (Lk. 23:20), but he was also 'wanting to satisfy the crowd' (Mk. 15:15). The crowd won. Why? Because they said to him: 'If you let this man go, you are no friend of Caesar. Anyone who claims to be a king opposes Caesar' (Jn. 19:12). This clinched it. The choice was between honour and ambition, between principle and expediency. He had already been in trouble with Tiberius Caesar on two or three previous occasions. He could not afford another.

Sure, Jesus was innocent. Sure, justice demanded his release. But how could he champion innocence and justice if thereby he denied the will of the people, flouted the nation's leaders, and above all provoked an uprising, thereby forfeiting the imperial favour? His conscience was drowned by the loud voices of rationalization. He compromised because he was a coward.

The Jewish people and their priests

Although we cannot exonerate Pilate, we can certainly acknowledge that he was on the horns of a difficult dilemma, and that it was the Jewish leaders who impaled him there. For it was they who committed Jesus to him for trial, who accused him of subversive claims and teaching, and who stirred up the crowd to demand his crucifixion. Therefore, as Jesus himself said to Pilate, 'the one who handed me over to you is guilty of a greater sin' (Jn. 19:11). Perhaps, since he used the singular, he was referring to the high priest Caiaphas, but the whole Sanhedrin was implicated. Indeed, so were the people, as Peter boldly said to them soon after Pentecost: 'Men of Israel, . . . you handed him (Jesus) over to be killed, and you disowned him before Pilate, though he had decided to let him go. You disowned the Holy and Righteous One and asked that a murderer be released to you. You killed the author of life . . . ' (Acts 3:12–15). The very same crowds, it seems, who had given Jesus a tumultuous welcome into Jerusalem on Palm Sunday, were within five days screaming for his blood. Yet their leaders were even more to blame for inciting them.

Jesus had upset the Jewish establishment from the outset of his public ministry. To begin with, he was an irregular. Though he posed as a Rabbi, he had not entered by the correct door or climbed up by the right ladder. He had no credentials, no proper authorization. Next, he had courted controversy by his provocative behaviour, fraternizing with disreputable people, feasting instead of fasting, and profaning the sabbath by healing people on it. Not content with disregarding the traditions of the elders, he had actually rejected them wholesale, and criticized the Pharisees for exalting tradition above Scripture. They cared more for regulations than for persons, he had said, more for ceremonial cleansing than for moral purity, more for laws than for love. He had even denounced them as 'hypocrites', called them 'blind leaders of the blind', and likened them to 'whitewashed tombs, which look beautiful on the outside but on the inside are full of dead men's bones and everything unclean' (Mt. 23:27). These were intolerable accusations. Worse still, he was undermining their authority. And at the same time he was making outrageous claims to be lord of the sabbath, to know God uniquely as his Father, even to be equal with God. It was blasphemy. Yes, that's what it was, blasphemy.

So they were full of self-righteous indignation over Jesus. His doctrine was heretical. His behaviour was an affront to the sacred law. He was leading the people astray. And there were rumours that he was encouraging disloyalty to Caesar. So his ministry must be stopped before he did any further damage. They had good political, theological and ethical reasons for demanding that he be arrested, put on trial and silenced. Moreover when they had him in court, and put him on oath to testify, even then he made blasphemous claims for himself. They heard him with their own ears. No more witnesses were necessary. He was a self-confessed blasphemer. He deserved to die. It was absolutely clear. He was guilty. Their hands were clean.

And yet, and yet, there were flaws in the Jewish leaders' case. Leaving aside the fundamental question whether Jesus' claims were true or false, there was the matter of motivation. What was the fundamental reason for the priests' hostility to Jesus? Was it entirely that they were concerned for political stability, doctrinal truth and moral purity? Pilate did not think so. He was not taken in by their rationalizations, especially their pretence of loyalty to the Emperor. As H. B. Swete put it, 'he detected under their disguise the vulgar vice of envy'.[9] In Matthew's words, 'he knew it was out of envy that they had handed Jesus over to him'.[10] There is no reason to question Pilate's assessment. He was a shrewd judge of human character. Besides, the evangelists appear, by recording his judgment, to endorse it.

Envy! Envy is the reverse side of a coin called vanity. Nobody is ever envious of others who is not first proud of himself. And the Jewish leaders were proud, racially, nationally, religiously and morally proud. They were proud of their nation's long history of a special relationship with God, proud of their own leadership role in this nation, and above all proud of their authority. Their contest with Jesus was essentially an authority struggle. For he challenged

[9] H. B. Swete, *The Gospel According to St Mark*, p. 350.
[10] Mt. 27:18; *cf.* Mk. 15:10.

their authority, while at the same time possessing himself an authority which they manifestly lacked. When they came to him with their probing questions, 'By what authority are you doing these things? And who gave you authority to do this?' (Mk. 11:28), they thought they had nailed him. But instead they found themselves nailed by his counter-question: 'John's baptism – was it from heaven, or from men? Tell me!' (v.30). They were trapped. They could not answer 'from heaven' or he would want to know why they did not believe him. Nor could they answer 'from men', because they feared the people who were convinced that John was a true prophet. So they gave no reply. Their prevarication was a symptom of their insincerity. If they could not face the challenge of John's authority, they certainly could not face the challenge of Christ's. He claimed authority to teach about God, to drive out demons, to forgive sins, to judge the world. In all this he was utterly unlike them, for the only authority they knew was an appeal to other authorities. Besides, there was a self-evident genuineness about his authority. It was real, effortless, transparent, from God.

So they felt threatened by Jesus. He undermined their prestige, their hold over the people, their own self-confidence and self-respect, while leaving his intact. They were 'envious' of him, and therefore determined to get rid of him. It is significant that Matthew recounts two jealous plots to eliminate Jesus, the first by Herod the Great at the beginning of his life, and the other by the priests at its end. Both felt their authority under threat. So both sought to 'destroy' Jesus.[11] However outwardly respectable the priests' political and theological arguments may have appeared, it was envy which led them to 'hand over' Jesus to Pilate to be destroyed (Mk. 15:1, 10).

The same evil passion influences our own contemporary attitudes to Jesus. He is still, as C. S. Lewis called him, 'a transcendental interferer'.[12] We resent his intrusions into our privacy, his demand for our homage, his expectation of our obedience. Why can't he mind his own business, we ask petulantly, and leave us alone? To which he instantly replies that we are his business and that he will never leave us alone. So we too perceive him as a threatening rival, who disturbs our peace, upsets our *status quo*, undermines our authority and diminishes our self-respect. We too want to get rid of him.

[11] Mt. 2:13 and 27:20, AV.   [12] C. S. Lewis, *Surprised by Joy*, p. 163.

Judas Iscariot the traitor

Having seen how Jesus was handed over by the priests to Pilate, and by Pilate to the soldiers, we now have to consider how in the first place he was handed over to the priests by Judas. This 'handing over' is specifically termed a 'betrayal'. Indeed, Maundy Thursday will always be remembered as 'the night on which he was betrayed' (1 Cor. 11:23), and Judas as 'he who betrayed him'. This accusing epitaph is already attached to his name when it is first mentioned in the Gospels among the Twelve. All three Synoptic evangelists put him at the bottom of their list of the apostles.[13]

It is not unusual to hear people expressing sympathy for Judas. They feel he was given an unfair deal in his lifetime and has had an unfair press ever since. 'After all,' they say, 'if Jesus had to die, somebody had to betray him. So why blame Judas? He was but the tool of providence, the victim of predestination.' Well, the biblical narrative certainly indicates that Jesus foreknew the identity of his betrayer[14] and referred to him as 'doomed to destruction so that Scripture would be fulfilled'.[15] It is also true that Judas did what he did only after Satan first 'prompted' him and then actually 'entered into him'.[16]

Nevertheless, none of this exonerates Judas. He must be held responsible for what he did, having no doubt plotted it for some time previously. The fact that his betrayal was foretold in the Scriptures does not mean that he was not a free agent, any more than the Old Testament predictions of the death of Jesus mean that he did not die voluntarily. So Luke referred later to his 'wickedness' (Acts 1:18). However strong the Satanic influences upon him were, there must have been a time when he opened himself to them. Jesus seems clearly to have regarded him as responsible for his actions, for even at the last minute in the upper room he made a final appeal to him by dipping a piece of bread in the dish and giving it to him (Jn. 13:25–30). But Judas rejected Jesus' appeal, and his betrayal has always seemed the more odious because it was a flagrant breach of hospitality. In this it fulfilled another Scripture which said: 'Even my close friend, whom I trusted, he who shared my bread, has lifted up his heel against me' (Ps. 41:9). Judas' ultimate cynicism was to choose to betray his Master with a kiss, using this sign of friendship as a means to destroy it. So Jesus affirmed his guilt, saying, 'Woe to that man who betrays the Son of Man! It would be better for him if he had not been born'

---

[13] Mt. 10:4; Mk. 3:19; Lk. 6:16. [14] Jn. 6:64, 71; 13:11.
[15] Jn. 17:12. *Cf.* Acts 1:15–17, 25. [16] Jn. 13:2, 27. *Cf.* Lk. 22:3.

(Mk. 14:21). Not only did Jesus thus condemn him, but he came in the end to condemn himself. He acknowledged his crime in betraying innocent blood, returned the money for which he had sold Jesus, and committed suicide. Doubtless he was seized more with remorse than repentance, but at least he confessed his guilt.

The motive for Judas' crime has long occupied the curiosity and ingenuity of students. Some have been convinced that he was a Jewish zealot,[17] had joined Jesus and his followers in the belief that theirs was a national liberation movement, and finally betrayed him either out of political disillusion or as a ploy to force Jesus' hand and compel him to fight. Those who attempt a reconstruction of this kind think they find confirmatory evidence in his name 'Iscariot', although everybody admits that it is obscure. It is generally taken to indicate his origin as a 'man of Kerioth', a town in the southern territory of Judah which is mentioned in Joshua 15:25. But those who think Judas was a zealot suggest that 'Iscariot' is linked to the word *sikarios*, an assassin (from the Latin *sica* and Greek *sikarion*, a 'dagger'). Josephus refers to the *sikarioi*.[18]

Fired with a fanatical Jewish nationalism, they were determined to recover their country's independence from the colonial domination of Rome, and to this end did not shrink from assassinating their political enemies, whom they despised as collaborators. They are referred to once in the New Testament, namely when the Roman commander who had rescued Paul from being lynched in Jerusalem told him he had thought he was 'the Egyptian who started a revolt and led four thousand terrorists (*sikarioi*) out into the desert some time ago' (Acts 21:38).

Other commentators consider the basis for this reconstruction too flimsy, and attribute the defection of Judas to a moral fault rather than a political motivation, namely the greed which the fourth evangelist mentions. He tells us that Judas was the 'treasurer' (as we would say) of the apostolic band, having been entrusted with the common purse. The occasion of John's comment was the anointing of Jesus by Mary of Bethany. She brought an alabaster

[17] The founder of the zealot party was Judas' namesake, namely 'Judas the Galilean', who in AD 6 led an armed revolt against Rome (mentioned in Acts 5:37). The rebellion was crushed and Judas was killed, but his sons continued the struggle. Masada was the final stronghold of zealot resistance to Rome; it fell in AD 74. William Barclay is one of those who considered it 'more than likely' that Judas was a zealot, and that the kiss in the Garden of Gethsemane was 'no intended treachery', but rather a signal meant to provoke Jesus to abandon his wavering and launch his long-awaited campaign (*Crucified and Crowned*, pp. 36–38).

[18] See Josephus' *Antiquities* xx.163–165, 186–188 and *Jewish War* ii.254–257.

jar containing very expensive perfume ('pure nard' according to Mark and John), which she proceeded to pour over him as he was reclining at table, until the house was filled with the fragrant scent. It was a gesture of lavish, almost reckless devotion, which Jesus himself later called a 'beautiful thing'. But some present (of whom Judas was the spokesman) reacted in a totally different way. Watching her with incredulity, they 'snorted' (literally) with self-righteous indignation. 'What a waste!' they said. 'What wicked extravagance! The perfume could have been sold for more than a year's wages, and the money given to the poor.' But their comment was sick and insincere, as John goes on to say. Judas 'did not say this because he cared about the poor but because he was a thief; as keeper of the money bag, he used to help himself to what was put into it'. Indeed, having witnessed and denounced what he saw as Mary's irresponsible wastefulness, he seems to have gone straight to the priests to recoup some of the loss. 'What are you willing to give me if I hand him over to you?' he asked them. No doubt they then began to bargain, and in the end agreed on 30 silver coins, the ransom price of a common slave. The evangelists with their sense of high drama deliberately contrast Mary and Judas, her uncalculating generosity and his coldly calculated bargain. What other dark passions were seething in his heart we can only guess, but John insists that it was monetary greed which finally overwhelmed him. Incensed by the waste of a year's wages, he went and sold Jesus for barely a third that amount.[19]

It is not for nothing that Jesus tells us to 'beware of all covetousness', or that Paul declares the love of money to be 'a root of all kinds of evil'.[20] For in pursuit of material gain human beings have descended to deep depravity. Magistrates have perverted justice for bribes, like the judges of Israel of whom Amos said: 'They sell the righteous for silver, and the needy for a pair of sandals' (2:6). Politicians have used their power to give contracts to the highest bidder, and spies have sunk low enough to sell their country's secrets to the enemy. Businessmen have entered into shady transactions, jeopardizing the prosperity of others in order to get a better deal. Even supposedly spiritual teachers have been known to turn religion into a commercial enterprise, and some are still doing it today, so that a candidate for the pastorate is warned not to be 'a lover of money'.[21] The language of all such people is the same as that of Judas: 'what are you willing to give me, and I will hand him over to you?' For 'everybody has his price', the cynic

[19] Mt. 26:6–16; Mk. 14:3–11; Jn. 12:3–8 and 13:29.
[20] Lk. 12:15, RSV; 1 Tim. 6:10.
[21] 1 Tim. 3:3, 8; Tit. 1:7. *Cf.* Acts 8:18–23 and 20:33–34.

asserts, from the hired assassin, who is prepared to bargain over somebody's life, to the petty official who delays the issue of a permit or passport until his bribe has been paid. Judas was not exceptional. Jesus had said that it is impossible to serve God and money. Judas chose money. Many others have done the same.

Their sins and ours

We have looked at the three individuals – Pilate, Caiaphas and Judas – on whom the evangelists fasten the major blame for the crucifixion of Jesus, and at those associated with them, whether priests or people or soldiers. Of each person or group the same verb is used, *paradidōmi*, to 'hand over' or 'betray'. Jesus had predicted that he would be 'betrayed into the hands of men' or 'handed over to be crucified'.[22] And the evangelists tell their story in such a way as to show how his prediction came true. First, Judas 'handed him over' to the priests (out of greed). Next, the priests 'handed him over' to Pilate (out of envy). Then Pilate 'handed him over' to the soldiers (out of cowardice), and they crucified him.[23]

Our instinctive reaction to this accumulated evil is to echo Pilate's astonished question, when the crowd howled for his blood: 'Why? What crime has he committed?' (Mt. 27:23). But Pilate received no rational answer. The hysterical crowd only shouted all the louder, 'Crucify him!' But why?

> Why? What has my Lord done?
>   What makes this rage and spite?
> He made the lame to run
>   And gave the blind their sight.
>   Sweet injuries!
>   Yet they at these
>   Themselves displease,
>   And 'gainst him rise.

It is natural to make excuses for them, for we see ourselves in them and we would like to be able to excuse ourselves. Indeed, there were some mitigating circumstances. As Jesus himself said in praying for the forgiveness of the soldiers who were crucifying him, 'they do not know what they are doing'. Similarly, Peter said to a Jewish crowd in Jerusalem, 'I know that you acted in ignorance, as did your leaders.' Paul added that, if 'the rulers of this

[22] Mt. 17:22; 26:2.
[23] Mt. 26:14–16 (Judas); 27:18 (the priests); 27:26 (Pilate).

age' had understood, 'they would not have crucified the Lord of glory'.[24] Yet they knew enough to be culpable, to accept the fact of their guilt and to be condemned for their actions. Were they not claiming full responsibility when they cried out, 'Let his blood be on us and on our children!'?[25] Peter was quite outspoken on the Day of Pentecost: 'Let all Israel be assured of this: God has made this Jesus, *whom you crucified*, both Lord and Christ.' Moreover, far from disagreeing with his verdict, his hearers were 'cut to the heart' and asked what they should do to make amends (Acts 2:36–37). Stephen was even more direct in his speech to the Sanhedrin which led to his martyrdom. Calling the Council 'stiff-necked people, with uncircumcised hearts and ears', he accused them of resisting the Holy Spirit just like their ancestors. For their ancestors had persecuted the prophets and killed those who predicted the Messiah's coming, and now they had betrayed and murdered the Messiah himself (Acts 7:51–52). Paul was later to use similar language in writing to the Thessalonians about contemporary Jewish opposition to the gospel: they 'killed the Lord Jesus and the prophets and also drove us out'. Because they were trying to keep the Gentiles from salvation, God's judgment would fall upon them (1 Thes. 2:14–16).

This blaming of the Jewish people for the crucifixion of Jesus is extremely unfashionable today. Indeed, if it is used as a justification for slandering and persecuting the Jews (as it has been in the past), or for anti-semitism, it is absolutely indefensible. The way to avoid anti-semitic prejudice, however, is not to pretend that the Jews were innocent, but, having admitted their guilt, to add that others shared in it. This was how the apostles saw it. Herod and Pilate, Gentiles and Jews, they said, had together 'conspired' against Jesus (Acts 4:27). More important still, we ourselves are also guilty. If we were in their place, we would have done what they did. Indeed, we *have* done it. For whenever we turn away from Christ, we 'are crucifying the Son of God all over again and subjecting him to public disgrace' (Heb. 6:6). We too sacrifice Jesus to our greed like Judas, to our envy like the priests, to our ambition like Pilate. 'Were you there when they crucified my Lord?' the old negro spiritual asks. And we must answer, 'Yes, we were there.' Not as spectators only but as participants, guilty participants, plotting, scheming, betraying, bargaining, and handing him over to be crucified. We may try to wash our hands of responsibility like Pilate. But our attempt will be as futile as his. For there is blood on our hands. Before we can begin to see the cross as something

[24] Lk. 23:34; Acts 3:17; 1 Cor. 2:8.   [25] Mt. 27:25. *Cf.* Acts 5:28.

done *for* us (leading us to faith and worship), we have to see it as something done *by* us (leading us to repentance). Indeed, 'only the man who is prepared to own his share in the guilt of the cross', wrote Canon Peter Green, 'may claim his share in its grace'.[26]

Horatius Bonar (1808–89), who has been called 'the prince of Scottish hymn-writers', expressed it well:

> 'Twas I that shed the sacred blood;
>   I nailed him to the tree;
> I crucified the Christ of God;
>   I joined the mockery.
>
> Of all that shouting multitude
>   I feel that I am one;
> And in that din of voices rude
>   I recognize my own.
>
> Around the cross the throng I see,
>   Mocking the Sufferer's groan;
> Yet still my voice it seems to be,
>   As if I mocked alone.

The answer which we have so far given to the question 'Why did Christ die?' has sought to reflect the way in which the Gospel writers tell their story. They point to the chain of responsibility (from Judas to the priests, from the priests to Pilate, from Pilate to the soldiers), and they at least hint that the greed, envy and fear which prompted their behaviour also prompt ours. Yet this is not the complete account which the evangelists give. I have omitted one further and vital piece of evidence which they supply. It is this: that although Jesus was brought to his death by human sins, he did not die as a martyr. On the contrary, he went to the cross voluntarily, even deliberately. From the beginning of his public ministry he consecrated himself to this destiny.

In his baptism he identified himself with sinners (as he was to do fully on the cross), and in his temptation he refused to be deflected from the way of the cross. He repeatedly predicted his sufferings and death, as we saw in the last chapter, and steadfastly set himself to go to Jerusalem to die there. His constant use of the word 'must' in relation to his death expressed not some external compulsion, but his own internal resolve to fulfil what had been written of him. 'The good shepherd lays down his life for the sheep,' he said. Then, dropping the metaphor, 'I lay down my life

[26] Peter Green, *Watchers by the Cross*, p. 17.

. . . No-one takes it from me, but I lay it down of my own accord' (Jn. 10:11, 17–18).

Moreover, when the apostles took up in their letters the voluntary nature of the dying of Jesus, they several times used the very verb (*paradidōmi*) which the evangelists used of his being 'handed over' to death by others. Thus Paul could write 'the Son of God . . . loved me and gave (*paradontos*) himself for me'.[27] It was perhaps a conscious echo of Isaiah 53:12, which says that 'he poured out (LXX *paredothē*) his life unto death'. Paul also used the same verb when he looked behind the voluntary self-surrender of the Son to the Father's surrender of him. For example, 'he who did not spare his own Son, but gave him up (*paredōken*) for us all – how will he not also, along with him, graciously give us all things?'[28] Octavius Winslow summed it up in a neat statement: 'Who delivered up Jesus to die? Not Judas, for money; not Pilate, for fear; not the Jews, for envy; – but the Father, for love!'[29]

It is essential to keep together these two complementary ways of looking at the cross. On the human level, Judas gave him up to the priests, who gave him up to Pilate, who gave him up to the soldiers, who crucified him. But on the divine level, the Father gave him up, and he gave himself up, to die for us. As we face the cross, then, we can say to ourselves both '*I* did it, my sins sent him there' and '*he* did it, his love took him there'. The apostle Peter brought the two truths together in his remarkable statement on the Day of Pentecost, both that 'this man was handed over to you by God's set purpose and foreknowledge' and that 'you, with the help of wicked men, put him to death by nailing him to the cross'.[30] Peter thus attributed Jesus' death simultaneously to the plan of God and to the wickedness of men. For the cross which, as we have particularly considered in this chapter, is an exposure of human evil, is at the same time a revelation of the divine purpose to overcome the human evil thus exposed.

I come back at the end of this chapter to the question with which I began it: why did Jesus Christ die? My first answer was that he did not die; he was killed. Now, however, I have to balance this answer with its opposite. He was not killed; he died, giving himself

[27] Gal. 2:20. *Cf.* Eph. 5:2, 25 and also Lk. 23:46.
[28] Rom. 8:32; *cf.* 4:25.
[29] I am grateful to David Kingdon for drawing my attention to this quotation, which John Murray includes in his *Romans*, Vol. 1, p. 324, having taken it from Winslow's *No Condemnation in Christ Jesus* (1857).
[30] Acts 2:23; *cf.* 4:28. Later, in his first letter, Peter was to describe Jesus the Lamb as having been 'chosen before the creation of the world' (1 Pet. 1:19–20).

up voluntarily to do his Father's will.

In order to discern what the Father's will was, we have to go over the same events again, this time looking below the surface.

3

Looking below the surface

In the previous chapters I have sought to establish two facts about the cross. First, its central importance (to Christ, to his apostles and to his world-wide church ever since), and secondly its deliberate character (for, though due to human wickedness, it was also due to the set purpose of God, voluntarily accepted by Christ who gave himself up to death).

But why? We return to this basic puzzle. What was there about the crucifixion of Jesus which, in spite of its horror, shame and pain, makes it so important that God planned it in advance and Christ came to endure it?

An initial construction

It may be helpful to answer this question in four stages, beginning with the straightforward and the non-controversial, and gradually penetrating more deeply into the mystery.

First, *Christ died for us*. In addition to being necessary and voluntary, his death was altruistic and beneficial. He undertook it for our sake, not for his own, and he believed that through it he would secure for us a good which could be secured in no other way. The Good Shepherd, he said, was going to lay down his life 'for the sheep', for their benefit. Similarly, the words he spoke in the upper room when giving them the bread were, 'This is my body given for you.' The apostles picked up this simple concept and repeated it, sometimes making it more personal by changing it from the second person to the first: 'Christ died for us.'[1] There

[1] Jn. 10:11, 15; Lk. 22:19; Rom. 5:8; Eph. 5:2; 1 Thes. 5:10; Tit. 2:14. Professor Martin Hengel has shown with great erudition that the concept

is no explanation yet, and no identification of the blessing he died to procure for us, but at least we are agreed over the 'for you' and 'for us'.

Secondly, *Christ died for us that he might bring us to God* (1 Pet. 3:18). The beneficial purpose of his death focuses down on our reconciliation. As the Nicene Creed expresses it, 'for us (general) and for our salvation (particular) he came down from heaven . . .'. The salvation he died to win for us is variously portrayed. At times it is conceived negatively as redemption, forgiveness or deliverance. At other times it is positive – new or eternal life, or peace with God in the enjoyment of his favour and fellowship.[2] The precise vocabulary does not matter at present. The important point is that it is in consequence of his death that he is able to confer upon us the great blessing of salvation.

Thirdly, *Christ died for our sins.* Our sins were the obstacle preventing us from receiving the gift he wanted to give us. So they had to be removed before it could be bestowed. And he dealt with our sins, or took them away, by his death. This expression 'for our sins' (or very similar phrases) is used by most of the major New Testament authors; they seem to have been quite clear that – in some way still to be determined – Christ's death and our sins were related to each other. Here is a sample of quotations: 'Christ died for our sins according to the Scriptures' (Paul); 'Christ died for sins once for all' (Peter); 'he has appeared once for all . . . to do away with sin by the sacrifice of himself', and he 'offered for all time one sacrifice for sins' (Hebrews); 'the blood of Jesus, (God's) Son, purifies us from all sin' (John); 'to him who loves us and has freed us from our sins by his blood . . . be glory' (Revelation).[3] All these verses (and many more) link his death with our sins. What, then, is the link?

Fourthly, *Christ died our death,* when he died for our sins. That is to say, granted that his death and our sins are linked, the link is not merely that of consequence (he was the victim of our human brutality) but of penalty (he endured in his innocent person the penalty our sins had deserved). For, according to Scripture, death

---

of a person voluntarily dying for his city, family and friends, truth, or to pacify the gods, was widespread in the Graeco-Roman world. A special composite word *hyperapothnēskein* ('to die for') had been formed to express it. The gospel that 'Christ died for us' would, therefore, have been readily intelligible to first-century pagan audiences. (Martin Hengel, *Atonement*, pp. 1–32.)

[2] For the negative see, *e.g.*, Gal. 1:4; Eph. 1:7; Heb. 9:28. For the positive see, *e.g.*, Jn. 3:14–16; Eph. 2:16; Col. 1:20; 1 Thes. 5:10; 1 Pet. 3:18.

[3] 1 Cor. 15:3; 1 Pet. 3:18; Heb. 9:26; 10:12; 1 Jn. 1:7; Rev. 1:5–6.

is related to sin as its just reward: 'the wages of sin is death' (Rom. 6:23). The Bible everywhere views human death not as a *natural* but as a *penal* event. It is an alien intrusion into God's good world, and not part of his original intention for humankind. To be sure, the fossil record indicates that predation and death existed in the animal kingdom before the creation of man. But God seems to have intended for his human image-bearers a more noble end, akin perhaps to the 'translation' which Enoch and Elijah experienced, and to the 'transformation' which will take place in those who are alive when Jesus comes.[4] Throughout Scripture, then, death (both physical and spiritual) is seen as a divine judgment on human disobedience.[5] Hence the expressions of horror in relation to death, the sense of anomaly that man should have become 'like the beasts that perish', since 'the same fate awaits them both'.[6] Hence too the violent 'snorting' of indignation which Jesus experienced in his confrontation with death at the graveside of Lazarus.[7] Death was a foreign body. Jesus resisted it; he could not come to terms with it.

If, then, death is the penalty of sin, and if Jesus had no sin of his own in his nature, character or conduct, must we not say that he need not have died? Could he not instead have been translated? When his body became translucent on the occasion of his mountain-top transfiguration, were the apostles not given a preview of his resurrection body (hence his instruction to tell nobody about it until he had risen from the dead, Mk. 9:9)? Could he not at that point have stepped straight into heaven and escaped death? But he came back into our world in order to go *voluntarily* to the cross. No-one would take his life from him, he insisted; he was going to lay it down of his own accord. So when the moment of death came, Luke represented it as his own self-determined act. 'Father,' he said, 'into your hands I commit my spirit.'[8] All this means that the simple New Testament statement 'he died for our sins' implies much more than appears on the surface. It affirms that Jesus Christ, who being sinless had no need to die, died our death, the death our sins had deserved.

We shall need in subsequent chapters to penetrate further into the rationale, the morality and the efficacy of these statements. For

[4] See Gn. 5:24; 2 Ki. 2:1–11; 1 Cor. 15:50–54.
[5] *E.g.* Gn. 2:17; 3:3, 19, 23; Rom. 5:12–14; Rev. 20:14; 21:8.
[6] Ps. 49:12, 20; Ec. 3:19–21.
[7] See the occurrence of the verb *embrimaomai* in John 11:33, 38. Used of the snorting of horses, it was transferred to the strong human emotions of displeasure and indignation.
[8] Jn. 10:18; Lk. 23:46.

the time being we must be content with this preliminary fourfold construction, that Christ died for us, for our good; that the 'good' he died to procure for us was our salvation; that in order to procure it he had to deal with our sins; and that in dying for them it was our death that he died.

The question I want to ask now, and seek to answer during the rest of this chapter, is whether this preliminary theological construction fits the facts. Is it a rather complex theory imposed on the story of the cross, or does the evangelists' narrative itself supply evidence for it and even remain unintelligible without it? I shall argue the latter. Further, I shall seek to show that what the evangelists portray, although it is their witness, is not their invention. What they are doing is to allow us to enter a little way into the mind of Christ himself.

So we shall look at three of the main scenes of Jesus' last twenty-four hours on earth – the upper room, the Garden of Gethsemane and the place called Golgotha. As we do so, we shall be unable to limit ourselves to the mere telling of a poignant story, since each scene contains sayings of Jesus which demand explanation and cannot be swept under the carpet. Something deeper was happening than mere words and deeds, something below the surface. Theological truth keeps breaking through, even when we wish it would leave us alone. In particular, we feel obliged to ask questions about the institution of the Lord's Supper in the upper room, the 'agony' in the Garden of Gethsemane, and the 'cry of dereliction' on the cross.

Before we do so, however, there is a noteworthy fact which needs to delay us. It concerns Jesus' perspective throughout. Our story begins on the evening of Maundy Thursday. Jesus had already seen the sun set for the last time. Within about fifteen hours his limbs would be stretched out on the cross. Within twenty-four hours he would be both dead and buried. And he knew it. Yet the extraordinary thing is that he was thinking of his mission as still future, not past. He was a comparatively young man, almost certainly between thirty and thirty-five years of age. He had lived barely half the allotted span of human life. He was still at the height of his powers. At his age most people have their best years ahead of them. Mohammed lived until he was sixty, Socrates until he was seventy, and Plato and the Buddha were over eighty when they died. If death threatens to cut a person's life short, a sense of frustration plunges him or her into gloom. But not Jesus, for this simple reason: he did not regard the death he was about to die as bringing his mission to an untimely end, but as actually necessary to accomplish it. It was only seconds before he died (and not till that moment) that he would be able to shout, 'Finished!' So then, although it was his last evening, and although he had but a few more hours to live, Jesus was not looking *back* at a mission he had completed, still less that had failed; he was still looking *forward* to a mission which he was about to fulfil. The mission of a lifetime of thirty to thirty-five years was to be accomplished in its last twenty-four hours, indeed, its last six.

The Last Supper in the upper room

Jesus was spending his last evening on earth in quiet seclusion with his apostles. It was the first day of the Feast of Unleavened Bread, and they had met to eat the Passover meal together in a friend's house. The place is described as 'a large upper room, furnished and ready', and we can picture them round a low meal-table, reclining on cushions on the floor. Evidently no servant was in attendance, so that there had been no-one to wash their feet before the meal began. Nor was any of the apostles humble enough to undertake this menial task. It was to their intense embarrassment, therefore, that during supper Jesus put on a slave's apron, poured water into a basin, and went round washing their feet, thus doing what none of them had been willing to do. He then proceeded to tell them how authentic love always expresses itself in humble service and how the world would identify them as his disciples only if they loved one another. In contrast to the priority of sacrificial and serving love, he warned them that one of them was going to betray him. He also spoke much of his impending departure, of the coming of the Comforter to take his place, and of this Spirit of truth's varied ministry of teaching and witnessing.

Then, at some point while the meal was still in progress, they watched enthralled as he took a loaf of bread, blessed it (that is, gave thanks for it), broke it into pieces and handed it round to them with the words, 'This is my body, which is given for you; do this in remembrance of me.' In the same way, after supper had ended, he took a cup of wine, gave thanks for it, passed it round to them, and said either 'This cup is the new covenant in my blood' or 'This is my blood of the new covenant, which is poured out for many for the forgiveness of sins; do this, whenever you drink it, in remembrance of me'.[9]

These are tremendously significant deeds and words. It is a pity that we are so familiar with them that they tend to lose their

[9] The words of administration are recorded somewhat differently by Paul and the Synoptic evangelists. See 1 Cor. 11:23–25; Mt. 26:26–28; Mk. 14:22–24; Lk. 22:17–19.

impact. For they throw floods of light on Jesus' own view of his death. By what he did with the bread and wine, and by what he said about them, he was visibly dramatizing his death before it took place and giving his own authoritative explanation of its meaning and purpose. He was teaching at least three lessons.

The first lesson concerned *the centrality of his death*. Solemnly and deliberately, during his last evening with them, he was giving instructions for his own memorial service. It was not to be a single occasion, however, like our modern memorial services, the final tribute paid by friends and relatives. Instead, it was to be a regular meal or service or both. He specifically told them to repeat it: 'do this in remembrance of me'. What were they to do? They were to copy what he had done, both his acts and his words, namely to take, break, bless, identify and share bread and wine. What did the bread and wine signify? The words he had spoken explained. Of the bread he had said 'This is my body given for you', and of the wine 'This is my blood shed for you'. So his death spoke to them from both the elements. The bread did not stand for his living body, as he reclined with them at table, but his body as it was shortly to be 'given' for them in death. Similarly, the wine did not stand for his blood as it flowed in his veins while he spoke to them, but his blood which was shortly to be 'poured out' for them in death. The evidence is plain and irrefutable. The Lord's Supper, which was instituted by Jesus, and which is the only regular commemorative act authorized by him, dramatizes neither his birth nor his life, neither his words nor his works, but only his death. Nothing could indicate more clearly the central significance which Jesus attached to his death. It was by his death that he wished above all else to be remembered. There is then, it is safe to say, no Christianity without the cross. If the cross is not central to our religion, ours is not the religion of Jesus.

Secondly, Jesus was teaching about *the purpose of his death*. According to Paul and Matthew, Jesus' words about the cup referred not only to his 'blood' but to the 'new covenant' associated with his blood, and Matthew adds further that his blood was to be shed 'for the forgiveness of sins'. Here is the truly fantastic assertion that through the shedding of Jesus' blood in death God was taking the initiative to establish a new pact or 'covenant' with his people, one of the greatest promises of which would be the forgiveness of sinners. What did he mean?

Many centuries previously God had entered into a covenant with Abraham, promising to bless him with a good land and an abundant posterity. God renewed this covenant at Mount Sinai, after rescuing Israel (Abraham's descendants) from Egypt. He pledged himself to be their God and to make them his people. Moreover, this covenant was ratified with the blood of sacrifice: 'Moses . . . took the blood, sprinkled it on the people and said, "This is the blood of the covenant that the LORD has made with you in accordance with all these words." ' [10] Hundreds of years passed, in which the people forsook God, broke his covenant and provoked his judgment, until one day in the seventh century BC the word of the Lord came to Jeremiah, saying:

'The time is coming,' declares the LORD,
   'when I will make a new covenant
with the house of Israel
   and with the house of Judah.
It will not be like the covenant
   I made with their forefathers
when I took them by the hand
   to lead them out of Egypt,
because they broke my covenant,
    though I was a husband to them,'
                declares the LORD.
'This is the covenant that I will make
    with the house of Israel
after that time,' declares the LORD.
'I will put my law in their minds
   and write it on their hearts.
I will be their God,
   and they will be my people.
No longer will a man teach his neighbour,
   or a man his brother, saying, "Know the LORD,"
because they will all know me,
   from the least of them to the greatest,'
                declares the LORD.
'For I will forgive their wickedness
   and will remember their sins no more'
              (Je. 31:31–34).

More than six more centuries passed, years of patient waiting and growing expectancy, until one evening in an upper room in Jerusalem a Galilean peasant, carpenter by trade and preacher by vocation, dared to say in effect: 'this new covenant, prophesied in Jeremiah, is about to be established; the forgiveness of sins prom-

---

[10] Ex. 24:8. See also the covenant references in Is. 42:6; 49:8; Zc. 9:11 and Heb. 9:18–20.

ised as one of its distinctive blessings is about to become available; and the sacrifice to seal this covenant and procure this forgiveness will be the shedding of my blood in death.' Is it possible to exaggerate the staggering nature of this claim? Here is Jesus' view of his death. It is the divinely appointed sacrifice by which the new covenant with its promise of forgiveness will be ratified. He is going to die in order to bring his people into a new covenant relationship with God.

The third lesson Jesus was teaching concerned *the need to appropriate his death personally*. If we are right in saying that in the upper room Jesus was giving an advance dramatization of his death, it is important to observe what form the drama took. It did not consist of one actor on the stage, with a dozen in the audience. No, it involved them as well as him, so that they took part in it as well as he. True, he took, blessed and broke the bread, but then he explained its significance as he gave it to them to eat. Again he took and blessed the cup, but then he explained its meaning as he gave it to them to drink. Thus they were not just spectators of this drama of the cross; they were participants in it. They can hardly have failed to get the message. Just as it was not enough for the bread to be broken and the wine to be poured out, but they had to eat and drink, so it was not enough for him to die, but they had to appropriate the benefits of his death personally. The eating and drinking were, and still are, a vivid acted parable of receiving Christ as our crucified Saviour and of feeding on him in our hearts by faith. Jesus had already taught this in his great discourse on the Living Bread which followed his feeding of the five thousand:

'I tell you the truth, unless you eat the flesh of the Son of Man and drink his blood, you have no life in you. Whoever eats my flesh and drinks my blood has eternal life, and I will raise him up at the last day. For my flesh is real food and my blood is real drink' (Jn. 6:53–55).

His words on that occasion and his actions in the upper room both bear witness to the same reality. For him to give his body and blood in death was one thing; for us to make the blessings of his death our own is another. Yet many have not learnt this distinction. I can still remember what a revelation it was to me as a young man to be told that any action on my part was necessary. I used to imagine that because Christ had died, the world had been automatically put right. When someone explained to me that Christ had died for *me*, I responded rather haughtily 'everybody knows that', as if the fact itself or my knowledge of the fact had brought me salvation. But God does not impose his gifts on us willy-nilly; we have to receive them by faith. Of both the divine gift and the human reception the Lord's Supper remains the perpetual outward sign. It is intended to be 'a participation in the body and blood of Christ' (1 Cor. 10:16).

Here then are the lessons of the upper room about the death of Christ. First, it was central to his own thinking about himself and his mission, and he desired it to be central to ours. Secondly, it took place in order to establish the new covenant and procure its promised forgiveness. Thirdly, it needs to be appropriated individually if its benefits (the covenant and the forgiveness) are to be enjoyed. The Lord's Supper which Jesus instituted was not meant to be a slightly sentimental 'forget-me-not', but rather a service rich in spiritual significance.

What makes the events of the upper room and the significance of the Lord's Supper yet more impressive is that they belong to the context of the Passover. That Jesus thought of his death in terms of an Old Testament sacrifice we have already seen. But which sacrifice did he have in mind? Not only, it seems, the Mount Sinai sacrifice of Exodus 24, by which the covenant was decisively renewed, but also the Passover sacrifice of Exodus 12, which became an annual commemoration of God's liberation of Israel and covenant with them.

According to the Synoptic evangelists, the last supper was the Passover meal which followed the sacrificing of the Passover lambs. This is clear because the disciples asked Jesus where they should make preparations to 'eat the Passover', and Jesus himself referred to the meal as 'this Passover'.[11] According to John, however, the Passover meal would not be eaten until the Friday evening, which meant that Jesus was dying on the cross at the very time that the Passover lambs were being killed.[12] In his important book *The Eucharistic Words of Jesus*, Joachim Jeremias elaborated the three main attempts which have been made to harmonize these two chronologies (pp. 20–62). The best seems to be to declare both correct, each having been followed by a different group. Either the Pharisees and Sadducees were using alternative calendars, which differed from each other by a day, or there were so many pilgrims in Jerusalem for the festival (perhaps as many as 100,000) that the Galileans killed their lambs on the Thursday and ate them that evening, while the Judeans observed the celebration one day later.

However the two chronologies are to be reconciled, the Passover

---

[11] Mk. 14:12–16; Lk. 22:15.
[12] Jn. 18:28. *Cf.* Jn. 19:36 and Ex. 12:46.

context further enforces the three lessons that we have already considered. The central importance which Jesus attached to his death is underlined by the fact that he was actually giving instructions for the annual celebration of the Passover to be replaced by his own supper. For he spoke words of explanation over the bread and wine ('This is my body . . . this is my blood . . .'), just as the head of an Aramaic Jewish household did over the Passover food ('This is the bread of affliction which our fathers had to eat as they came out of Egypt', pp. 54–57).[13] Thus 'Jesus modelled his sayings upon the ritual of interpreting the Passover' (p. 61).

This further clarifies Jesus' understanding of the purpose of his death. He 'presupposes', wrote Jeremias, 'a slaying that has separated flesh and blood. In other words, *Jesus spoke of himself as a sacrifice*'. Indeed, he was 'most probably speaking of himself as the paschal lamb', so that the meaning of his last parable was: 'I go to death as the true Passover sacrifice' (pp. 222–224). The implications of this are far-reaching. For in the original Passover in Egypt each paschal lamb died instead of the family's first-born son, and the first-born was spared only if a lamb was slain in his place. Not only had the lamb to be slain, but also its blood had to be sprinkled on the front door and its flesh eaten in a fellowship meal. Thus the Passover ritual taught the third lesson too, that it was necessary for the benefits of Christ's sacrificial death to be personally appropriated.

The agony in the Garden of Gethsemane

Supper is now over, and Jesus has finished his instruction of the apostles. He has urged them to abide in him, as the branches abide in the vine. He has warned them of the opposition of the world, yet encouraged them to bear witness to him none the less, remembering that the Spirit of truth will be the chief witness. He has also prayed – first for himself that he may glorify his Father in the coming ordeal, then for them that they may be kept in truth, holiness, mission and unity, and lastly for all those of subsequent generations who would believe in him through their message. Probably now they sing a hymn, and then together they leave the upper room. They walk through the streets of the city in the stillness of the night, and in the soft light of the Paschal moon, cross the Kidron Valley, begin to climb the Mount of Olives, and turn off into an olive orchard, as its name 'Gethsemane' ('oil press') suggests. It is evidently a favourite retreat for Jesus, for John

[13] *Cf.* Ex. 12:26–27; 13:8; Dt. 16:3.

comments that he 'had often met there with his disciples' (18:2).
Here something takes place which, despite the sober way the evangelists describe it, simply cries out for an explanation, and begins
to disclose the enormous costliness of the cross to Jesus. We rightly
call it 'the agony in the garden'.

Leaving most of the apostles behind, and urging them to watch
and pray, he takes Peter, James and John – the intimate three – a
stone's throw farther into the olive grove with him, shares with
them that he feels 'overwhelmed with sorrow to the point of death',
and asks them to keep watch with him. He then goes on a little
farther alone, falls prostrate with his face to the ground and prays:
'My Father, if it is possible, may this cup be taken from me. Yet
not as I will, but as you will.' Returning to the apostles, he finds
them sleeping and remonstrates with them. Going away a second
time, he prays: 'My Father, if it is not possible for this cup to be
taken away unless I drink it, may your will be done.' Again he
finds the disciples sleeping. So he leaves them once more and prays
the third time, saying the same thing. After this third season of
prayer he returns to find them asleep again, for they cannot enter
into the fathomless mystery of his suffering. This is a path he has
to walk alone. At some point, Luke says, he was 'in anguish' (or
'agony'), and prayed yet more earnestly, so that 'his sweat was like
drops of blood falling to the ground'.[14]

As we approach this sacred scene, we should first consider the
forceful words which Jesus and the evangelists used to express his
strong emotions. We have been prepared for these a little by two
of his earlier statements. The first, which Luke records, was that
he had 'a baptism to undergo' and felt 'distressed' (or 'pressed',
even 'tormented', *synechō*) until it was completed. The second was
a saying which John records that his heart was 'troubled' (or
'agitated', *tarassō*), so that he even wondered if he should ask his
Father to save him from 'this hour'. It was an anticipation of
Gethsemane.[15]

B. B. Warfield wrote a careful study entitled 'On the Emotional
Life of Our Lord', in the course of which he referred to the terms
employed by the Synoptic evangelists in relation to Gethsemane.
Luke's word *agōnia* he defines as 'consternation, appalled reluctance'. Matthew and Mark share two expressions. The primary
idea of 'troubled' (*adēmoneō*), he suggests, is 'loathing aversion,

[14] Jesus' agony in the Garden of Gethsemane is described by Matthew
(26:36–46), Mark (14:32–42) and Luke (22:39–46). John does not refer
to it, although he does tell of the walk to the olive orchard at the foot of
the Mount of Olives where Jesus was betrayed and arrested (18:1–11).
[15] Lk. 12:50; Jn. 12:27.

perhaps not unmixed with despondency', while Jesus' self-description as 'overwhelmed with sorrow' (*perilypos*) 'expresses a sorrow, or perhaps we would better say, a mental pain, a distress, which hems him in on every side, from which there is therefore no escape'. Mark uses another word of his own, 'deeply distressed' (*ekthambeomai*), which has been rendered 'horror-struck'; it is 'a term', Warfield adds, 'which more narrowly defines the distress as consternation – if not exactly dread, yet alarmed dismay'.[16] Put together, these expressive words indicate that Jesus was feeling an acute emotional pain, causing profuse sweat, as he looked with apprehension and almost terror at his future ordeal.

This ordeal he refers to as a bitter 'cup' which he ardently prays may, if possible, be taken from him, so that he does not have to drink it. What is this cup? Is it physical suffering from which he shrinks, the torture of the scourge and the cross, together perhaps with the mental anguish of betrayal, denial and desertion by his friends, and the mockery and abuse of his enemies? Nothing could ever make me believe that the cup Jesus dreaded was any of these things (grievous as they were) or all of them together. His physical and moral courage throughout his public ministry had been indomitable. To me it is ludicrous to suppose that he was now afraid of pain, insult and death. Socrates in the prison cell in Athens, according to Plato's account, took his cup of hemlock 'without trembling or changing colour or expression'. He then 'raised the cup to his lips, and very cheerfully and quietly drained it'. When his friends burst into tears, he rebuked them for their 'absurd' behaviour and urged them to 'keep quiet and be brave'.[17] He died without fear, sorrow or protest. So was Socrates braver than Jesus? Or were their cups filled with different poisons?

Then there have been the Christian martyrs. Jesus had himself told his followers that when insulted, persecuted and slandered, they were to 'rejoice and be glad'. Did Jesus not practise what he preached? His apostles did. Leaving the Sanhedrin with backs bleeding from a merciless flogging, they were actually 'rejoicing because they had been counted worthy of suffering disgrace for the Name'. Pain and rejection were to them a joy and a privilege, not an ordeal to be shrunk from in dismay.[18]

In the post-apostolic period there was even a longing to be united with Christ in martyrdom. Ignatius, Bishop of Antioch in Syria at

---

[16] These particular Greek words occur in Mt. 26:37; Mk. 14:33 and Lk. 22:44. B. B. Warfield's essay is published in his *Person and Work*, pp. 93–145. His translations of these words occur on pp. 130–131.

[17] *Phaedo*, 117–118.

[18] Mt. 5:11–12; Acts 5:41; Phil. 1:29–30.

the beginning of the second century, on his way to Rome, begged the church there not to attempt to secure his release lest they should deprive him of this honour! 'Let fire and the cross,' he wrote, 'let the companies of wild beasts, let breaking of bones and tearing of limbs, let the grinding of the whole body, and all the malice of the devil, come upon me; be it so, if only I may gain Christ Jesus!'[19] A few years later, in the middle of the second century, Polycarp the eighty-six-year-old Bishop of Smyrna, having refused to escape death either by fleeing or by denying Christ, was burnt at the stake. Just before the fire was lit, he prayed, 'O Father, I bless thee that thou hast counted me worthy to receive my portion among the number of martyrs.'[20] As for Alban, the first known British Christian martyr during one of the severe persecutions of the third century, he was first 'cruelly beaten, yet suffered he the same patiently, nay rather joyfully, for the Lord's sake', and was then beheaded.[21] And so it has continued in every generation. 'O the joy that the martyrs of Christ have felt', cried Richard Baxter, 'in the midst of the scorching flames!' Although made of flesh and blood like us, he continued, their souls could rejoice even 'while their bodies were burning'.[22]

Of many examples which could be given from the present century I choose only those mentioned by Sadhu Sundar Singh, the Indian Christian mystic and evangelist. He told, for instance, of a Tibetan evangelist, flogged by tormentors who then rubbed salt into his wounds, whose 'face shone with peace and joy', and of another who, sewn into a damp yak skin and left in the sun for three days, 'was joyful all the time' and thanked God for the privilege of suffering for him. It is true that the Sadhu sometimes embellished or romanticized his stories, yet there seems no reason to doubt his testimony, from his own experience and others', that even in the midst of torture God gives his people a supernatural joy and peace.[23]

We turn back to that lonely figure in the Gethsemane olive orchard – prostrate, sweating, overwhelmed with grief and dread, begging if possible to be spared the drinking of the cup. The martyrs were joyful, but he was sorrowful; they were eager, but he was reluctant. How can we compare them? How could they have gained their inspiration from him if he had faltered when they did not? Besides, up till now he had been clear-sighted about the necessity of his sufferings and death, determined to fulfil his destiny, and vehement in opposing any who sought to deflect him.

[19] Quoted in Foxe's *Book of Martyrs*, p. 19.   [20] *Ibid.*, pp. 20–25.
[21] *Ibid.*, pp. 31–33.   [22] From *Saints' Everlasting Rest*, p. 393.
[23] Friedrich Heiler, *Gospel of Sadhu Sundar Singh*, pp. 173–178.

Had all that suddenly changed? Was he now after all, when the moment of testing came, a coward? No, no! All the evidence of his former teaching, character and behaviour is against such a conclusion.

In that case the cup from which he shrank was something different. It symbolized neither the physical pain of being flogged and crucified, nor the mental distress of being despised and rejected even by his own people, but rather the spiritual agony of bearing the sins of the world, in other words, of enduring the divine judgment which those sins deserved. That this is the correct understanding is strongly confirmed by Old Testament usage, for in both the Wisdom literature and the prophets the Lord's 'cup' was a regular symbol of his wrath. A wicked person was said to 'drink of the wrath of the Almighty' (Jb. 21:20). Through Ezekiel, Yahweh warned Jerusalem that she would shortly suffer the same fate as Samaria, which had been destroyed:

'You will drink your sister's cup,
  a cup large and deep;
it will bring scorn and derision,
  for it holds so much.
You will be filled with drunkenness and sorrow,
  the cup of ruin and desolation,
  the cup of your sister Samaria.
You will drink it and drain it dry; . . .'
(Ezk. 23:32–34).

Not long afterwards this prophecy of judgment came true, and then the prophets began to encourage the people with promises of restoration. Describing Jerusalem as 'you who have drunk from the hand of the LORD the cup of his wrath, you who have drained to its dregs the goblet that makes men stagger', Isaiah summoned her to wake up and to get up, for Yahweh had now taken the cup out of her hand and she would never have to drink it again. Nor was the cup of the Lord's wrath given only to his disobedient people. Psalm 75 is a meditation on the universal judgment of God: 'In the hand of the LORD is a cup full of foaming wine mixed with spices; he pours it out, and all the wicked of the earth drink it down to its very dregs.' Similarly, Jeremiah was told to take from God's hand a cup filled with the wine of his wrath and to make all the nations drink it to whom he was sent. The same figure of speech recurs in the book of Revelation, where the wicked 'will drink of the wine of God's fury, which has been poured full strength into the cup of his wrath', and the final judgment is depicted as the pouring out of 'the seven bowls of God's wrath on the earth'.[24]

This Old Testament imagery will have been well known to Jesus. He must have recognized the cup he was being offered as containing the wine of God's wrath, given to the wicked, and causing a complete disorientation of body (staggering) and mind (confusion) like drunkenness. Was he to become so identified with sinners as to bear their judgment? From this contact with human sin his sinless soul recoiled. From the experience of alienation from his Father which the judgment on sin would involve, he hung back in horror. Not that for even a single instant he rebelled. His vision had evidently become blurred, as a dreadful darkness engulfed his spirit, but his will remained surrendered. Each prayer began 'My Father, if it is possible, may this cup be taken from me', and each prayer ended 'yet not as I will, but as you will'. Although in theory 'everything is possible' to God, as Jesus himself affirmed in Gethsemane (Mk. 14:36), yet this was not possible. God's purpose of love was to save sinners, and to save them righteously; but this would be impossible without the sin-bearing death of the Saviour. So how could he pray to be saved from 'this hour' of death? 'No,' he had said, he would not, since 'it was for this very reason I came to this hour' (Jn. 12:27).

From his agony of dread, as he contemplated the implications of his coming death, Jesus emerged with serene and resolute confidence. So when Peter drew his sword in a frantic attempt to avert the arrest, Jesus was able to say: 'Shall I not drink the cup the Father has given me?' (Jn. 18:11). Since John has not recorded Jesus' agonized prayers for the cup to be removed, this reference to it is all the more important. Jesus knows now that the cup will not be taken away from him. The Father has given it to him. He will drink it. Moreover, bitter and painful though the draining of the cup will be, he will yet find that to do the will of the Father who sent him and to finish his work will be his 'meat and drink' (as we might say), deeply and completely satisfying to his thirst (Jn. 4:34).

The agony in the garden opens a window on to the greater agony of the cross. If to bear man's sin and God's wrath was so terrible in anticipation, what must the reality have been like?

> We may not know, we cannot tell,
> What pains he had to bear;

[24] Is. 51:17–22; Ps. 75:8; Je. 25:15–29 (*cf.* Hab. 2:16); 49:12; Rev. 14:10; 16:1ff. and 18:6.

But we believe it was for us
He hung and suffered there.

The cry of dereliction on the cross

We must now pass by the details of the betrayal and arrest of
Jesus, his trials before Annas and Caiaphas, Herod and Pilate,
Peter's denials, the cruel mockery by priests and soldiers, the spit-
ting and the scourging, and the hysteria of the mob who demanded
his death. We move on to the end of the story. Condemned to
death by crucifixion, 'he was led like a lamb to the slaughter, and
as a sheep before her shearers is silent, so he did not open his
mouth' (Is. 53:7). Carrying his own cross, until Simon of Cyrene
was compelled to carry it for him, he will have walked along the
via dolorosa, out of the city, to Golgotha, 'the place of the skull'.
'Here they crucified him', the evangelists write, declining to dwell
on the stripping, the clumsy hammering home of the nails, or the
wrenching of his limbs as the cross was hoisted and dropped into
its place. Even the excruciating pain could not silence his repeated
entreaties: 'Father, forgive them, for they do not know what they
are doing.' The soldiers gambled for his clothes. Some women
stood afar off. The crowd remained a while to watch. Jesus
commended his mother to John's care and John to hers. He spoke
words of kingly assurance to the penitent criminal crucified at his
side. Meanwhile, the rulers sneered at him, shouting: 'He saved
others, but he can't save himself!' Their words, spoken as an
insult, were the literal truth. He could not save himself and others
simultaneously. He chose to sacrifice himself in order to save the
world.

Gradually the crowd thinned out, their curiosity glutted. At last
silence fell and darkness came – darkness perhaps because no eye
should see, and silence because no tongue could tell, the anguish
of soul which the sinless Saviour now endured. 'At the birth of the
Son of God', Douglas Webster has written, 'there was brightness
at midnight; at the death of the Son of God there was darkness at
noon.'[25] What happened in the darkness is expressed by biblical
writers in a variety of ways:

. . . he was pierced for our transgressions,
     he was crushed for our iniquities;
the punishment that brought us peace was upon him,
     and by his wounds we are healed.

[25] Douglas Webster, *In Debt to Christ*, p. 46.

We all, like sheep, have gone astray,
  each of us has turned to his own way;
and the LORD has laid on him
  the iniquity of us all.

Look, the Lamb of God, who takes away the sin of the world!

The Son of Man came . . . to give his life as a ransom for many.

Christ was sacrificed once to take away the sins of many people.

He himself bore our sins in his body on the tree.

Christ died for sins once for all, the righteous for the unrighteous,
to bring you to God.

God made him who had no sin to be sin for us, so that in him
we might become the righteousness of God.

Christ redeemed us from the curse of the law by becoming a
curse for us.[26]

The fearful concept of Jesus 'bearing', even actually 'becoming',
our sin and curse, how it could be and what it could mean, we
will leave until the next chapters. Meanwhile, it seems that the
darkness of the sky was an outward symbol of the spiritual darkness which enveloped him. For what is darkness in biblical
symbolism but separation from God who is light and in whom
'there is no darkness at all' (1 Jn. 1:5)? 'Outer darkness' was one
of the expressions Jesus used for hell, since it is an absolute
exclusion from the light of God's presence. Into that outer darkness
the Son of God plunged for us. Our sins blotted out the sunshine
of his Father's face. We may even dare to say that our sins sent
Christ to hell – not to the 'hell' (*hadēs*, the abode of the dead) to
which the Creed says he 'descended' after death, but to the 'hell'
(*gehenna*, the place of punishment) to which our sins condemned
him before his body died.

The darkness seems to have lasted for three hours. For it was at
the third hour (9 a.m.) that he was crucified, at the sixth hour (12
noon) that the darkness came over the whole land, and at the ninth
hour (3 p.m.) that, emerging out of the darkness, Jesus cried out
in a loud voice in Aramaic: '*Eloi, Eloi, lama sabachthani?*'
meaning, 'My God, my God, why have you forsaken me?'[27] The
Greek speakers present misunderstood his words and thought he

[26] Is. 53:5–6; Jn. 1:29; Mk. 10:45; Heb. 9:28; 1 Pet. 2:24; 3:18;
2 Cor. 5:21; Gal. 3:13.
[27] Mk. 15:25, 33–34.

was calling for Elijah. What he said is still misunderstood by many today. Four main explanations of his terrible cry of 'dereliction' (desertion, abandonment) have been offered. All commentators agree that he was quoting Psalm 22:1. But they are not agreed as to why he did so. What was the significance of this quotation on his lips?

First, some suggest that it was *a cry of anger, unbelief or despair*. Perhaps he had clung to the hope that even at the last moment the Father would send angels to rescue him, or at least that in the midst of his utter obedience to the Father's will he would continue to experience the comfort of the Father's presence. But no, it was now clear to him that he had been abandoned, and he cried out with a heart-rending 'why?' of dismay or defiance. His faith failed him. But of course, these interpreters add, he was mistaken. He imagined he was forsaken, when he was not. Those who thus explain the cry of dereliction can scarcely realize what they are doing. They are denying the moral perfection of the character of Jesus. They are saying that he was guilty of unbelief on the cross, as of cowardice in the garden. They are accusing him of failure, and failure at the moment of his greatest and supremest self-sacrifice. Christian faith protests against this explanation.

A second interpretation, which is a modification of the first, is to understand the shout of dereliction as *a cry of loneliness*. Jesus, it is now maintained, knew God's promises never to fail or forsake his people.[28] He knew the steadfastness of God's covenant love. So his 'why?' was not a complaint that God had actually forsaken him, but rather that he had allowed him to *feel* forsaken. 'I have sometimes thought', wrote T. R. Glover, 'there never was an utterance that reveals more amazingly the distance between feeling and fact.'[29] Instead of addressing God as 'Father', he could now call him only 'my God', which is indeed an affirmation of faith in his covenant faithfulness, but falls short of declaring his fatherly loving-kindness. In this case Jesus was neither mistaken, nor unbelieving, but experiencing what the saints have called 'the dark night of the soul', and indeed doing so deliberately out of solidarity with us. In this condition, as Thomas J. Crawford puts it, the people of God 'derive no conscious satisfaction from the joys of his favour and the comforts of his fellowship'. They are granted 'no approving smile, no commending voice, no inward manifestation of the divine favour'.[30] This explanation is possible. It does not cast a slur on the character of Jesus like the first. Yet there seems to be

[28] *E.g.* Jos. 1:5, 9 and Is. 41:10.
[29] T. R. Glover, *Jesus of History*, p. 192.
[30] Thomas J. Crawford, *Doctrine of Holy Scripture*, pp. 137–138.

an insuperable difficulty in the way of adopting it, namely that the words of Psalm 22:1 express an experience of *being*, and not just *feeling*, God-forsaken.

A third quite popular interpretation is to say that Jesus was uttering *a cry of victory*, the exact opposite of the first explanation, the cry of despair. The argument now is that, although Jesus quoted only the first verse of Psalm 22, he did so to represent the whole Psalm which begins and continues with an account of appalling sufferings, but ends with great confidence, and even triumph: 'I will declare your name to my brothers; in the congregation I will praise you. You who fear the LORD, praise him! . . . For he has not despised or disdained the suffering of the afflicted one; he has not hidden his face from him but has listened to his cry for help' (vv. 22). This is ingenious but (it seems to me) far-fetched. Why should Jesus have quoted from the Psalm's beginning if in reality he was alluding to its end? It would seem rather perverse. Would anybody have understood his purpose?

The fourth explanation is simple and straightforward. It is to take the words at their face value and to understand them as *a cry of real dereliction*. I agree with Dale who wrote: 'I decline to accept any explanation of these words which implies that they do not represent the actual truth of our Lord's position.'[31] Jesus had no need to repent of uttering a false cry. Up to this moment, though forsaken by men, he could add, 'Yet I am not alone, for my Father is with me' (Jn. 16:32). In the darkness, however, he was absolutely alone, being now also God-forsaken. As Calvin put it, 'If Christ had died only a bodily death, it would have been ineffectual. . . . Unless his soul shared in the punishment, he would have been the Redeemer of bodies alone.' In consequence, 'he paid a greater and more excellent price in suffering in his soul the terrible torments of a condemned and forsaken man'.[32] So then an actual and dreadful separation took place between the Father and the Son; it was voluntarily accepted by both the Father and the Son; it was due to our sins and their just reward; and Jesus expressed this horror of great darkness, this God-forsakenness, by quoting the only verse of Scripture which accurately described it, and which he had perfectly fulfilled, namely, 'My God, my God, why have you forsaken me?' The theological objections and problems we shall

[31] R. W. Dale, *Atonement*, p. 61.

[32] Calvin's *Institutes*, II.xvi.10 and 12. It is true, and somewhat strange, that Calvin (following Luther) believed this to be the explanation of Jesus' 'descent into hell' after his death. What matters most is the fact that he experienced God-forsakenness for us, however, and not precisely *when* he did so.

come to later, although we already insist that the God-forsakenness of Jesus on the cross must be balanced with such an equally biblical assertion as 'God was reconciling the world to himself in Christ'. C. E. B. Cranfield is right to emphasize both the truth that Jesus experienced 'not merely a felt, but a real, abandonment by his Father' and 'the paradox that, while this God-forsakenness was utterly real, the unity of the Blessed Trinity was even then unbroken'.[33] At this point, however, it is enough to suggest that Jesus had been meditating on Psalm 22, which describes the cruel persecution of an innocent and godly man, as he was meditating on other Psalms which he quoted from the cross;[34] that he quoted verse 1 for the same reason that he quoted every other Scripture, namely that he believed he was fulfilling it; and that his cry was in the form of a question ('Why . . . ?'), not because he did not know its answer, but only because the Old Testament text itself (which he was quoting) was in that form.

Almost immediately after the cry of dereliction, Jesus uttered three more words or sentences in quick succession. First, 'I am thirsty', his great spiritual sufferings having taken their toll of him physically. Secondly, he called out, again (according to Matthew and Mark) in a loud voice, 'It is finished.' And thirdly the tranquil, voluntary, confident self-commendation, 'Father, into your hands I commit my spirit,' as he breathed his last breath.[35] The middle cry, the loud shout of victory, is in the Gospel text the single word *tetelestai*. Being in the perfect tense, it means 'it has been and will for ever remain finished'. We note the achievement Jesus claimed just before he died. It is not men who have finished their brutal deed; it is he who has accomplished what he came into the world to do. He has borne the sins of the world. Deliberately, freely and in perfect love he has endured the judgment in our place. He has procured salvation for us, established a new covenant between God and humankind, and made available the chief covenant blessing, the forgiveness of sins. At once the curtain of the Temple, which for centuries had symbolized the alienation of sinners from God, was torn in two from top to bottom, in order to demonstrate that the sin-barrier had been thrown down by God, and the way into his presence opened.

Thirty-six hours later God raised Jesus from the dead. He who had been condemned for us in his death, was publicly vindicated

[33] C. E. B. Cranfield, *Mark*, pp. 458–459.
[34] *E.g.* 'I am thirsty' (Jn. 19:28) is an allusion to Ps. 69:21 (*cf.* Ps. 22:15), and 'Into your hands I commit my spirit' (Lk. 23:46), a quotation of Ps. 31:5.
[35] Jn. 19:28, 30; Lk. 23:46.

in his resurrection. It was God's decisive demonstration that he had not died in vain.

All this presents a coherent and logical picture. It gives an explanation of the death of Jesus which takes into proper scientific account all the available data, without avoiding any. It explains the central importance which Jesus attached to his death, why he instituted his supper to commemorate it, and how by his death the new covenant has been ratified, with its promise of forgiveness. It explains his agony of anticipation in the garden, his anguish of dereliction on the cross, and his claim to have decisively accomplished our salvation. All these phenomena become intelligible if we accept the explanation given by Jesus and his apostles that 'he himself bore our sins in his body on the tree'.

In conclusion, the cross enforces three truths – about ourselves, about God and about Jesus Christ.

First, our sin must be extremely horrible. Nothing reveals the gravity of sin like the cross. For ultimately what sent Christ there was neither the greed of Judas, nor the envy of the priests, nor the vacillating cowardice of Pilate, but our own greed, envy, cowardice and other sins, and Christ's resolve in love and mercy to bear their judgment and so put them away. It is impossible for us to face Christ's cross with integrity and not to feel ashamed of ourselves. Apathy, selfishness and complacency blossom everywhere in the world except at the cross. There these noxious weeds shrivel and die. They are seen for the tatty, poisonous things they are. For if there was no way by which the righteous God could righteously forgive our unrighteousness, except that he should bear it himself in Christ, it must be serious indeed. It is only when we see this that, stripped of our self-righteousness and self-satisfaction, we are ready to put our trust in Jesus Christ as the Saviour we urgently need.

Secondly, God's love must be wonderful beyond comprehension. God could quite justly have abandoned us to our fate. He could have left us alone to reap the fruit of our wrongdoing and to perish in our sins. It is what we deserved. But he did not. Because he loved us, he came after us in Christ. He pursued us even to the desolate anguish of the cross, where he bore our sin, guilt, judgment and death. It takes a hard and stony heart to remain unmoved by love like that. It is more than love. Its proper name is 'grace', which is love to the undeserving.

Thirdly, Christ's salvation must be a free gift. He 'purchased' it for us at the high price of his own life-blood. So what is there left for us to pay? Nothing! Since he claimed that all was now 'finished', there is nothing for us to contribute. Not of course that we now have a licence to sin and can always count on God's forgiveness. On the contrary, the same cross of Christ, which is the ground of a free salvation, is also the most powerful incentive to a holy life. But this new life follows. First, we have to humble ourselves at the foot of the cross, confess that we have sinned and deserve nothing at his hand but judgment, thank him that he loved us and died for us, and receive from him a full and free forgiveness. Against this self-humbling our ingrained pride rebels. We resent the idea that we cannot earn – or even contribute to – our own salvation. So we stumble, as Paul put it, over the stumbling-block of the cross.[36]

[36] 1 Cor. 1:23; Gal. 5:11; *cf.* Mt. 11:6; Rom. 9:32; 1 Pet. 2:8.

84

Part Two

The heart of the cross

4

The problem of forgiveness

The last chapter's 'look below the surface' may well have provoked in some readers an impatient response. 'That simple supper in the upper room,' you may be saying, 'and even the confessedly agonized prayer in the garden and cry from the cross, all admit of much more straightforward explanations. Why must you complicate everything with your tortuous theologizing?' It is an understandable reaction.

In particular, our insistence that according to the gospel the cross of Christ is the only ground on which God forgives sins bewilders many people. 'Why should our forgiveness depend on Christ's death?' they ask. 'Why does God not simply forgive us, without the necessity of the cross?' As the French cynic put it, 'le bon Dieu me pardonnera; c'est son métier.'[1] 'After all,' the objector may continue, 'if we sin against one another, we are required to forgive one another. We are even warned of dire consequences if we refuse. Why can't God practise what he preaches and be equally generous? Nobody's death is necessary before we forgive each other. Why then does God make so much fuss about forgiving us and even declare it impossible without his Son's "sacrifice for sin"? It sounds like a primitive superstition which modern people should long since have discarded.'

It is essential to ask and to face these questions. Two answers may be given to them immediately, although we shall need the rest of the chapter in which to elaborate them. The first was supplied by Archbishop Anselm in his great book *Cur Deus Homo?* at the

[1] 'The good God will forgive me; that's his job (or his speciality).' Quoted by S. C. Neill in *Christian Faith Today*, p. 145. James Denney attributed the quotation to Heine in his *Death of Christ*, p. 186.

end of the eleventh century. If anybody imagines, he wrote, that God can simply forgive us as we forgive others, that person has 'not yet considered the seriousness of sin', or literally 'what a heavy weight sin is' (i.xxi). The second answer might be expressed similarly: 'You have not yet considered the majesty of God.' It is when our perception of God and man, or of holiness and sin, are askew that our understanding of the atonement is bound to be askew also.

The fact is that the analogy between our forgiveness and God's is far from being exact. True, Jesus taught us to pray: 'Forgive us our sins, as we forgive those who sin against us.' But he was teaching the impossibility of the unforgiving being forgiven, and so the obligation of the forgiven to forgive, as is clear from the Parable of the Unmerciful Servant; he was not drawing any parallel between God and us in relation to the *basis* of forgiveness.[2] For us to argue 'we forgive each other unconditionally, let God do the same to us' betrays not sophistication but shallowness, since it overlooks the elementary fact that we are not God. We are private individuals, and other people's misdemeanours are personal injuries. God is not a private individual, however, nor is sin just a personal injury. On the contrary, God is himself the maker of the laws we break, and sin is rebellion against him.

The crucial question we should ask, therefore, is a different one. It is not why God finds it *difficult* to forgive, but how he finds it *possible* to do so at all. As Emil Brunner put it, 'Forgiveness is the very opposite of anything which can be taken for granted. Nothing is less obvious than forgiveness.'[3] Or, in the words of Carnegie Simpson, 'forgiveness is to man the plainest of duties; to God it is the profoundest of problems'.[4]

The problem of forgiveness is constituted by the inevitable collision between divine perfection and human rebellion, between God as he is and us as we are. The obstacle to forgiveness is neither our sin alone, nor our guilt alone, but also the divine reaction in love and wrath towards guilty sinners. For, although indeed 'God is love', yet we have to remember that his love is 'holy love',[5] love which yearns over sinners while at the same time refusing to condone their sin. How, then, could God express his holy love? – his love in forgiving sinners without compromising his holiness, and his holiness in judging sinners without frustrating his love?

---

[2] Mt. 6:12–15; 18:21–35. [3] Emil Brunner, *Mediator*, p. 448.
[4] P. Carnegie Simpson, *Fact of Christ*, p. 109.
[5] For the emphasis on 'holy love' see P. T. Forsyth in both *Cruciality of the Cross* and *Work of Christ*, William Temple in *Christus Veritas*, e.g. pp. 257, 269, and Emil Brunner in *Mediator*.

Confronted by human evil, how could God be true to himself as holy love? In Isaiah's words, how could he be simultaneously 'a righteous God and a Saviour' (45:21)? For, despite the truth that God demonstrated his righteousness by taking action to save his people, the words 'righteousness' and 'salvation' cannot be regarded as simple synonyms. Rather his saving initiative was compatible with, and expressive of, his righteousness. At the cross in holy love God through Christ paid the full penalty of our disobedience himself. He bore the judgment we deserve in order to bring us the forgiveness we do not deserve. On the cross divine mercy and justice were equally expressed and eternally reconciled. God's holy love was 'satisfied'.

I am running on too fast, however. The reason why many people give the wrong answers to questions about the cross, and even ask the wrong questions, is that they have carefully considered neither the seriousness of sin nor the majesty of God. In order to do so now, we shall review four basic biblical concepts, namely the gravity of sin, human moral responsibility, true and false guilt, and the wrath of God. We shall thus see ourselves successively as sinful, responsible, guilty and lost. It will not be a pleasant exercise, and our integrity will be tested in the course of it.

The gravity of sin

The very word 'sin' has in recent years dropped from most people's vocabulary. It belongs to traditional religious phraseology which, at least in the increasingly secularized West, is now declared by many to be meaningless. Moreover, if and when 'sin' is mentioned, it is most likely to be misunderstood. What is it, then?

The New Testament uses five main Greek words for sin, which together portray its various aspects, both passive and active. The commonest is *hamartia*, which depicts sin as a missing of the target, the failure to attain a goal. *Adikia* is 'unrighteousness' or 'iniquity', and *ponēria* is evil of a vicious or degenerate kind. Both these terms seem to speak of an inward corruption or perversion of character. The more active words are *parabasis* (with which we may associate the similar *paraptōma*), a 'trespass' or 'transgression', the stepping over a known boundary, and *anomia*, 'lawlessness', the disregard or violation of a known law. In each case an objective criterion is implied, either a standard we fail to reach or a line we deliberately cross.

It is assumed throughout Scripture that this criterion or ideal has been established by God. It is, in fact, his moral law, which expresses his righteous character. It is not the law of his own being only, however; it is also the law of ours, since he has made us in his image and in so doing has written the requirements of his law in our hearts (Rom. 2:15). There is, thus, a vital correspondence between God's law and ourselves, and to commit sin is to commit 'lawlessness' (1 Jn. 3:4), offending against our own highest welfare as well as against the authority and love of God.

The emphasis of Scripture, however, is on the godless self-centredness of sin. Every sin is a breach of what Jesus called 'the first and great commandment', not just by failing to love God with all our being, but by actively refusing to acknowledge and obey him as our Creator and Lord. We have rejected the position of dependence which our createdness inevitably involves, and made a bid for independence. Worse still, we have dared to proclaim our self-dependence, our autonomy, which is to claim the position occupied by God alone. Sin is not a regrettable lapse from conventional standards; its essence is hostility to God (Rom. 8:7), issuing in active rebellion against him. It has been described in terms of 'getting rid of the Lord God' in order to put ourselves in his place in a haughty spirit of 'God-almightiness'. Emil Brunner sums it up well: 'Sin is defiance, arrogance, the desire to be equal with God, ... the assertion of human independence over against God, ... the constitution of the autonomous reason, morality and culture.' It is appropriate that he entitled the book from which this quotation is taken *Man In Revolt* (p. 129).

Once we have seen that every sin we commit is an expression (in differing degrees of self-consciousness) of this spirit of revolt against God, we shall be able to accept David's confession: 'Against you, you only, have I sinned and done what is evil in your sight' (Ps. 51:4). In committing adultery with Bathsheba, and in arranging to have her husband Uriah killed in battle, David had committed extremely serious offences against them and against the nation. Yet it was God's laws which he had broken and thereby ultimately against God that he had chiefly offended.

Perhaps it is a deep-seated reluctance to face up to the gravity of sin which has led to its omission from the vocabulary of many of our contemporaries. One acute observer of the human condition, who has noticed the disappearance of the word, is the American psychiatrist Karl Menninger. He has written about it in his book, *Whatever Became of Sin?* Describing the malaise of western society, its general mood of gloom and doom, he adds that 'one misses any mention of "sin" '. 'It was a word once in everyone's mind, but is now rarely if ever heard. Does that mean', he asks, 'that no sin is involved in all our troubles . . .? Has no-one committed any sins? Where, indeed, did sin go? What became of it?' (p. 13). Enquiring into the causes of sin's disappearance, Dr Menninger notes first that 'many former sins have become crimes', so that responsibility for dealing with them has passed from church to state, from priest to policeman (p. 50), while others have dissipated into sicknesses, or at least into symptoms of sickness, so that in their case punishment has been replaced by treatment (pp. 74ff.). A third convenient device called 'collective irresponsibility' has enabled us to transfer the blame for some of our deviant behaviour from ourselves as individuals to society as a whole or to one of its many groupings (pp. 94ff.).

Dr Menninger goes on to plead not only for the reinstatement of the word 'sin' in our vocabulary, but also for a recognition of the reality which the word expresses. Sin cannot be dismissed as merely a cultural taboo or social blunder. It must be taken seriously. He takes preachers to task for soft-pedalling it, and adds: 'The clergyman cannot minimize sin and maintain his proper role in our culture' (p. 198). For sin is 'an implicitly aggressive quality – a ruthlessness, a hurting, a breaking away from God and from the rest of humanity, a partial alienation, or act of rebellion. . . . Sin has a willful, defiant or disloyal quality: *someone* is defied or offended or hurt' (p. 19). To ignore this would be dishonest. To confess it would enable us to do something about it. Moreover, the reinstatement of sin would lead inevitably to 'the revival or reassertion of personal responsibility'. In fact the 'usefulness' of reviving sin is that responsibility would be revived with it (pp. 178f.).

Human moral responsibility

But is it fair to blame human beings for their misconduct? Are we really responsible for our actions? Are we not more often victims of other agencies than free agencies ourselves, and so more sinned against than sinning? A whole gamut of scapegoats is ready at hand – our genes, our chemistry (a temporary hormonal imbalance), our inherited temper and temperament, our parents' failures during our early childhood, our upbringing, our educational and social environment. Together these seem to constitute an infallible alibi.

Perhaps no more comprehensive attempt has been made to undermine the traditional concept of personal responsibility than Professor B. F. Skinner's book *Beyond Freedom and Dignity*. His thesis is that 'the terrifying problems that face us in the world today' (especially the threats of population overgrowth, nuclear war, famine, disease and pollution) could all be solved by 'a technology of human behaviour'. That is, 'vast changes in human

91

behaviour' could be secured by changes in the human environment. Man could be programmed to behave properly. What stands in the way, then? Answer: the concept of 'autonomous man', his supposed 'freedom' (in that he is held responsible for his actions) and his supposed 'dignity' (in that he is given credit for his achievements). But these things are an illusion, for 'a scientific analysis shifts both the responsibility and the achievement to the environment' (pp. 9–30). Man must have the courage to create a social environment or culture which adequately 'shapes and maintains the behaviour of those who live in it' (p. 141). This is essential for the survival of humankind, which is more important than the traditional, 'flattering' concept of our 'freedom and dignity' (p. 208). To be sure, C. S. Lewis called this 'the abolition of man'. What would be abolished, however, is only 'autonomous man, . . . the man defended by the literature of freedom and dignity'. Indeed, 'his abolition has been long overdue' (p. 196). Peering into the future, in which man creates an environment which controls him, and so performs 'a gigantic exercise in self-control', B. F. Skinner ends his book with the words: 'We have not yet seen what man can make of man' (p. 210). It is a chilling prospect of self-determined determinism.

The human spirit rebels against it, however. The concept of 'diminished responsibility' we certainly accept, but not the total dissolution of all responsibility, except in the most extreme circumstances. The parallel between moral responsibility and legal liability is instructive at this point. Generally speaking, the criminal law assumes that people have it in their power to choose whether they will obey or break the law, and it treats them accordingly. Nevertheless, responsibility for crime can be diminished, and even excluded, by certain 'excusing' conditions. In his essays in the philosophy of law entitled *Punishment and Responsibility*, H. L. A. Hart defines the principle as follows: 'In all advanced legal systems liability to conviction for serious crimes is made dependent, not only on the offender having done those outward acts which the law forbids, but on his having done them in a certain frame of mind or with a certain will' (p. 187).[6] This state of mind and will is known technically as *mens rea* which, though a literal translation would be 'a guilty mind', really refers to the person's 'intention'. For example, the distinction between intentional and unintentional homicide, that is, between murder and manslaughter, goes right back to the Mosaic law. The principle also has a wider bearing. If a person commits an offence while insane, under duress

[6] Similar statements appear on pp. 28 and 114.

or as an automaton, criminal liability cannot be established. Provocation may reduce murder to manslaughter. The plea of insanity has been accepted for centuries, and has been interpreted since the McNaghten Rules of 1843 as 'disease of the mind', leading to such 'a defect of reason' that the offender either did not know 'the nature and quality of the act he was doing' or, if he did know it, 'did not know he was doing what was wrong'.

The Rules were criticized, however, for concentrating on the ignorance of the offender, rather than on his lack of capacity for self-control. So the Infanticide Act of 1938 made provision for acts done by a woman when 'the balance of her mind was disturbed by reason of her not having fully recovered from the effect of giving birth . . .', and the Homicide Act of 1957 provided that a person 'shall not be convicted of murder if he was suffering from such abnormality of mind . . . as substantially impaired his mental responsibility for his acts . . .'. So, too, the British Parliament has decided that no child under ten years can be held guilty of an offence, while between the ages of ten and fourteen it has to be proved specifically that an offending child knew that what he or she was doing was seriously wrong.

Thus, legal liability depends on mental and moral responsibility, that is, on *mens rea*, the intention of mind and will. But pleas based on lack of consciousness or control will always need to be precisely defined, and exceptional. An accused person certainly cannot plead his genetic inheritance or social upbringing as an excuse for criminal behaviour, let alone personal negligence ('I simply wasn't thinking what I was doing'). No, generally speaking, the whole procedure of trying, convicting and sentencing in the courts rests on the assumption that human beings are free to make choices and are responsible for the choices they make.

It is the same in everyday situations. Admittedly we are conditioned by our genes and upbringing, but the human spirit (not to mention the Christian mind) protests against the reductionism which declares a human being to be nothing but a computer (programmed to perform and respond) or an animal (at the mercy of his instincts). Over against these concepts we appeal to the ineradicable sense which men and women have that within reasonable limits we are free agents, able to make up our own minds and decide our own actions. Faced with an alternative, we know we are able to choose. And when we make a wrong choice, we reproach ourselves, because we know we could have behaved differently. We also act on the assumption that other people are free and responsible, for we try to persuade them to our point of view, and 'we all praise or blame people from time to time'.[7]

Sir Norman Anderson is, I think, right to draw attention to this human sense of responsibility. On the one hand, he writes, we can speculate about the extent to which people are 'preconditioned by the constitution and condition of their brains, by the psychological make-up they have inherited or acquired, by the blind and inevitable course of "nature" or by the sovereignty of a Creator God, to behave in the way they do'. But on the other hand it is possible 'unequivocally to affirm that there is no reason whatever to suppose that ordinary men and women are mistaken in their firm conviction that they have, within limits, a genuine freedom of choice and action, and that this necessarily entails a corresponding measure of moral responsibility'.[8]

The three contributors to the 1982 London Lectures in Contemporary Christianity, entitled *Free to Be Different*, came to the same conclusion. Professor Malcolm Jeeves spoke and wrote as a psychologist, Professor Sam Berry as a geneticist, and Dr David Atkinson as a theologian. Together they investigated the respective influences on human behaviour of 'nature' (our genetic inheritance), 'nurture' (our social conditioning) and 'grace' (God's loving and transforming initiative). They agreed that these things evidently both shape and constrain our behaviour. Nevertheless, their lectures were a vigorous, interdisciplinary rejection of determinism and assertion of human responsibility. Although the whole subject is admittedly complex and it is not possible neatly to disentangle all the threads, yet the three contributors were able to express this common conclusion:

> We are not automata, able to do nothing but react mechanically to our genes, our environment or even God's grace. We are personal beings created by God for himself. . . . Moreover, what God has given us is not to be regarded as a static endowment. Our character can be refined. Our behaviour can change. Our convictions can mature. Our gifts can be cultivated. . . . We are indeed free to be different. . . .[9]

When we turn to the Bible, we find the same tension, of which we are aware in our personal experience, between the pressures which condition and even control us, and our abiding moral responsibility nonetheless. There is a strong biblical emphasis on

[7] Alec R. Vidler, *Essays in Liberality*, p. 45.
[8] J. N. D. Anderson, *Morality, Law and Grace*, p. 38.
[9] Malcolm Jeeves, R. J. Berry and David Atkinson, *Free to Be Different*, p. 155.

the influence of our inheritance, of what we are 'in Adam'. The doctrine of original sin means that the very nature we have inherited is tainted and twisted with self-centredness. It is, therefore, 'from within, out of men's hearts', Jesus taught, that evil thoughts and actions come (Mk. 7:21–23). It is not surprising that he also described the sinner as 'a slave to sin' (Jn. 8:34). We are, in fact, enslaved to the world (public fashion and opinion), the flesh (our fallen nature) and the devil (demonic forces). Even after Christ has liberated us and made us his slaves instead, we are not yet entirely rid of the insidious power of our fallenness, so that Paul can conclude his argument in Romans 7 with the summary: 'So then, I myself in my mind am a slave to God's law, but in the sinful nature a slave to the law of sin' (v. 25b).

Scripture recognizes the subtlety and strength of these forces, which indeed diminish our responsibility. It is because God 'knows how we are formed' and 'remembers that we are dust' that he is patient towards us, slow to anger, and 'does not treat us as our sins deserve' (Ps. 103:10, 14). Similarly, God's Messiah is gentle with the weak, refusing to break bruised reeds or to snuff out smouldering wicks.[10]

At the same time, the biblical recognition that our responsibility is diminished does not mean that it is destroyed. On the contrary, Scripture invariably treats us as morally responsible agents. It lays upon us the necessity of choice between 'life and good, death and evil', between the living God and idols.[11] It exhorts us to obedience and remonstrates with us when we disobey. Jesus himself pleaded with recalcitrant Jerusalem to acknowledge and welcome him. Often, he said, addressing the city in direct speech, 'I have longed to gather your children together, as a hen gathers her chicks under her wings, but you were not willing' (Mt. 23:37). He thus attributed Jerusalem's spiritual blindness, apostasy and coming judgment to her obstinacy. It is true that he also said 'no-one can come to me unless the Father ... draws him', but only after he had said 'you refuse to come to me'.[12] Why is it that people do not come to Christ? Is it that they cannot, or is it that they will not? Jesus taught both. And in this 'cannot' and 'will not' lies the ultimate antinomy between divine sovereignty and human responsibility. But however we state it, we must not eliminate either part. Our responsibility before God is an inalienable aspect of our human dignity. Its final expression will be on the day of judgment. Nobody

[10] Is. 42:1–3; Mt. 12:15–21. God also distinguishes between sins committed in ignorance and those committed knowingly and deliberately. See, *e.g.*, Lk. 23:34; Acts 3:17; 1 Tim. 1:13.

[11] Dt. 30:15–20; Jos. 24:15.   [12] Jn. 6:44; 5:40.

will be sentenced without trial. All people, great and small, irrespective of their social class, will stand before God's throne, not crushed or browbeaten, but given this final token of respect for human responsibility, as each gives an account of what he or she has done.

Emil Brunner is surely right to emphasize our responsibility as an indispensable aspect of our humanness. 'Today our slogan must be: no determinism, on any account! For it makes all understanding of man as man impossible.'[13] Man has to be seen as 'a thinking – willing being', responsive and responsible to his Creator, 'the creaturely counterpart of his divine self-existence'. Further, this human responsibility is in the first instance 'not . . . a task but a gift, . . . not law but grace'. It expresses itself in 'believing, responsive love' (p. 98). So then, 'one who has understood the nature of responsibility has understood the nature of man. Responsibility is not an attribute, it is the "substance" of human existence. It contains everything . . ., [it is] that which distinguishes man from all other creatures. . . .' (p. 50). Therefore 'if responsibility be eliminated, the whole meaning of human existence disappears' (p. 258).

But has not the Fall seriously weakened man's responsibility? Is he responsible for his actions any longer? Yes, he is. 'Man never sins purely out of weakness, but always also in the fact that he "lets himself go" in weakness. Even in the dullest sinner there is still a spark of decision', indeed of defiant rebellion against God. So man cannot shuffle off his responsibility for his own wickedness. 'No Fate, no metaphysical constitution, no weakness of his nature, but himself, man, in the centre of his personality is made responsible for his sin' (pp. 130–131).

True and false guilt

If human beings have sinned (which they have), and if they are responsible for their sins (which they are), then they are guilty before God. Guilt is the logical deduction from the premises of sin and responsibility. We have done wrong, by our own fault, and are therefore liable to bear the just penalty of our wrongdoing.

This is the argument of the early chapters of the letter to the Romans. Paul divides the human race into three major sections, and shows how each knows something of its moral duty, but has deliberately suppressed its knowledge in order to pursue its own sinful course. As John put it, 'This is the verdict: Light has come into the world, but men loved darkness instead of light because their deeds were evil' (Jn. 3:19). Nothing is more serious than this

[13] Emil Brunner, *Man In Revolt*, p. 257.

96

deliberate rejection of the light of truth and goodness. Paul begins with decadent Roman society. Its people have known God's power and glory from the creation, and his holiness from their conscience, but they have refused to live up to their knowledge. Instead, they have turned from worship to idolatry. So God has given them over to immorality and other forms of anti-social behaviour (Rom. 1:18–32).

The second section of humanity that Paul addresses is the self-righteous world, whose knowledge of God's law may be either in the Scriptures (Jews) or in their hearts (Gentiles). In either case they do not live up to their knowledge (2:1–16). The third section is the specifically Jewish world, whose members pride themselves on the knowledge they have and on the moral instruction they give to others. Yet the very law they teach they also disobey. This being so, their privileged status as God's covenant people will not render them immune to his judgment (2:17 – 3:8).

What, then, is the conclusion? Paul answers his own question. 'We have already made the charge that Jews and Gentiles alike are all under sin' (3:9). Old Testament Scripture confirms this verdict. We are all without excuse, since we have all known our duty, and none of us has done it. Every protest is silenced, and the whole world is guilty and accountable to God (3:19–20).

Is this a rather morbid viewpoint? Christians have often been criticized (not least evangelical Christians) for continuously harping on sin, for becoming obsessed with it in our own lives and, particularly in our evangelism, for trying to induce in others a sense of their guilt. Nietzsche, for example, bitterly complained that 'Christianity *needs* sickness. . . . *Making* sick is the true hidden objective of the Church's whole system of salvation procedures. . . . One is not "converted" to Christianity – one must be sufficiently sick for it'.[14] Nietzsche was partly correct, namely that Christianity is medicine for the sin-sick. After all, Jesus himself defended his concentration on 'tax collectors and sinners' by saying 'It is not the healthy who need a doctor, but the sick'. 'I have not come to call the righteous,' he added, 'but sinners' (Mk. 2:17). We vigorously deny, however, that it is the church's role to 'make' people sick in order to convert them. Instead, we have to make them aware of their sickness, so that they will turn to the Great Physician.

Yet the criticism persists that Christians are unhealthily preoccupied with sin. An eloquent contemporary spokesman of this viewpoint is the BBC's former Religious Affairs Correspondent, Gerald Priestland. One of his talks in the radio series *Priestland's*

[14] Friedrich Nietzsche, *The Anti-Christ*, pp. 167–168.

Progress was entitled 'Guilt-edged Religion'. He told us how at the age of ten he thought Christianity was about sin and that by the time he was fifteen he was having 'glimpses into the abyss of depression', accompanied by fears of divine vengeance for his 'unnameable secret crimes', fears which kept growing for the next thirty years. His Christianity gave him no help. 'When I looked at the Cross, with its suffering victim, its only message to me was: "You did this – and there is no health in you!".' His equivalent of a Damascus Road conversion came to him at last 'on the psychiatrist's couch', for that was where he learnt 'the missing element of forgiveness'. Since then he confesses to 'a fairly low level of personal guilt and relatively little interest in the matter of sin' (pp. 59–60).

That is not the whole of Gerald Priestland's story, but it is enough to illustrate the grievous damage done by half-truths. How could anyone imagine that Christianity is about sin rather than about the forgiveness of sin? How could anyone look at the cross and see only the shame of what we did to Christ, rather than the glory of what he did for us? The prodigal son had to 'come to himself' (acknowledge his self-centredness) before he could 'come to his father'. The humiliation of penitence was necessary before the joy of reconciliation. There would have been no ring, no robe, no kiss, no feast if he had remained in the far country or returned impenitent. A guilty conscience is a great blessing, but only if it drives us to come home.

This does not mean that our conscience is always a reliable guide. There is such a thing as a morbid, overscrupulous conscience, and it would be mischievous to seek deliberately to create one. Not all guilt feelings are pathological, however. On the contrary, those who declare themselves sinless and guiltless are suffering from an even worse sickness. For to manipulate, smother and even 'cauterize' (1 Tim. 4:2) the conscience, in order to escape the pain of its accusations, renders us impervious to our need for salvation.

Is it, then, healthy or unhealthy to insist on the gravity of sin and the necessity of atonement, to hold people responsible for their actions, to warn them of the peril of divine judgment, and to urge them to confess, repent and turn to Christ? It is healthy. For if there is 'false guilt' (feeling bad about evil we have *not* done), there is also 'false innocence' (feeling good about the evil we *have* done). If false contrition is unhealthy (an ungrounded weeping over guilt), so is false assurance (an ungrounded rejoicing over forgiveness). It may be, therefore, that it is not we who exaggerate, when we stress the seriousness of sin, but our critics, who underestimate it. God said of the false prophets in Old Testament days: 'They dress the wound of my people as though it were not serious. "Peace, peace," they say, when there is no peace.'[15] Superficial remedies are always due to a faulty diagnosis. Those who prescribe them have fallen victim to the deceiving spirit of modernity which denies the gravity of sin. To make a true diagnosis of our condition, however, grave as it is, could never be unhealthy, provided that we go on immediately to the remedy. So the law which condemns us is nevertheless God's good gift, because it sends us to Christ to be justified. And the Holy Spirit came to 'convict the world of guilt', but only in order that he might more effectively bear witness to Christ as the Saviour from guilt (Jn. 16:8; 15:26–27). There is no joy comparable to the joy of the forgiven.

It is here that some recent American psychologists and psychiatrists go wrong, for they go only half-way. They start right, however, even some who make no Christian profession, for they insist that we must take sin, responsibility and guilt seriously. This is certainly great gain, but to diagnose well without being able to prescribe well is to embrace a dangerous and disillusioning half-measure.

Dr Hobart Mowrer, who was Research Professor of Psychology at the University of Illinois when his critique of Freudian psychoanalysis *The Crisis in Psychiatry and Religion* was published (1961), rejected the notion that 'psychoneurosis implies no moral responsibility'. For 'just so long as we deny the reality of sin, we cut ourselves off ... from the possibility of radical redemption ("recovery")' (p. 40). Dr Mowrer created quite a stir within his profession by his use of the word 'sin'. But he persisted in teaching the fact of sin and the need for an acknowledgment of it.

> Just so long as a person lives under the shadow of real, unacknowledged, and unexpiated guilt, he *cannot* ... 'accept himself'. ... He will continue to hate himself and to suffer the inevitable consequences of self-hatred. But the moment he ... begins to accept his guilt and his sinfulness, the possibility of radical reformation opens up, and with this ... a new freedom of self-respect and peace (p. 54).

A few years later, also rebelling against the Freudian insistence that guilt is pathological, Dr William Glasser began in Los Angeles to develop a different approach in treating juvenile delinquents and others which he called 'Reality Therapy'. His thesis was that a person who is 'unable to fulfil his essential needs', especially

[15] Je. 6:14; 8:11.

99

love and self-worth, denies the reality of the world around him and acts irresponsibly. So the therapist seeks 'to make him face a truth he has spent his life trying to avoid: *he is responsible for his behaviour*'.[16] Dr Mowrer in his Foreword sums up the essence of Dr Glasser's therapeutic method as 'a psychiatric version of the three R's, namely reality, responsibility and right-and-wrong' (p. xii).

Similarly, 'sin must be dealt with in the private courts of the human heart', writes Karl Menninger.[17] Well and good. But how? Especially, he goes on, by 'repentance, reparation, restitution and atonement'. Karl Menninger here betrays his very partial grasp of the gospel. For those four words cannot be bracketed in this way. The first three do indeed belong together. Reparation (a general word for making amends) and restitution (the more particular restoration of what has been stolen) are both necessary to signify the genuineness of repentance. But 'atonement' is not something we can do; only God can atone for our sins, and indeed has done so through Christ.

It is true that Dr Menninger mentions the forgiveness of God once or twice in passing (though without any basis in Christ's cross). Dr Hobart Mowrer, however, studiously avoids both the word and the concept. Like Karl Menninger he concentrates on the acknowledging of faults and the making of restitution. He calls his therapy groups 'integrity groups' because their foundation is personal integrity in the acknowledgment of wrongdoing. Initiation into a group is by means of 'a complete unqualified self-disclosure' which he calls *exomologēsis*. When, during a personal conversation with Dr Mowrer at the University of Illinois in 1970, I mentioned that *exomologēsis* is the Greek word for 'confession', and that in the Christian tradition the purpose of confession is to receive forgiveness from the injured party, he immediately responded, 'Oh, we never talk about forgiveness.' His concept of sin is that in each case it is the breach of a contractual obligation for which the guilty person must make restitution. Forgiveness is therefore unnecessary, either by the injured person or even by God.

Although, as has been pointed out, Dr Menninger does not share Dr Mowrer's inhibition about mentioning forgiveness, neither of them ever refers to the cross, let alone regards it as the only and sufficient ground on which God forgives sins. To recover the concepts of human sin, responsibility, guilt and restitution, without simultaneously recovering confidence in the divine work of atone-

---

[16] William Glasser, *Reality Therapy*, pp. 5–41.
[17] Karl Menninger, *Whatever Became of Sin?*, p. 180.

ment, is tragically lopsided. It is diagnosis without prescription, the futility of self-salvation in place of the salvation of God, and the rousing of hope only to dash it to the ground again.

A full acknowledgment of human responsibility and therefore guilt, far from diminishing the dignity of human beings, actually enhances it. It presupposes that men and women, unlike the animals, are morally responsible beings, who know what they are, could be and should be, and do not make excuses for their poor performance. This is the thesis of Harvey Cox in his book *On Not Leaving it to the Snake*. Eve's sin in the Garden of Eden, he urges, was not so much her disobedience in eating the forbidden fruit as her feeble surrender of responsibility which preceded it, not her pride but her sloth. Although Dr Cox is surely mistaken in his refusal to accept the biblical view of sin as essentially pride, and is tainted with the 'man come-of-age' misconception, he nevertheless makes an important point when he says that 'apathy is the key form of sin in today's world. . . . For Adam and Eve apathy meant letting a snake tell them what to do. It meant abdicating . . . the exercise of dominion and control of the world' (p. xvii). But decision-making belongs to the essence of our humanness. Sin is not only the attempt to be God; it is also the refusal to be man, by shuffling off responsibility for our actions. 'Let's not let any snake tell us what to do' (p. xviii). The commonest defence of the Nazi war criminals was that they were merely following orders. But the court held them responsible all the same.

The Bible takes *sin* seriously because it takes *man* (male and female) seriously. As we have seen, Christians do not deny the fact – in some circumstances – of diminished responsibility, but we affirm that diminished responsibility always entails diminished humanity. To say that somebody 'is not responsible for his actions' is to demean him or her as a human being. It is part of the glory of being human that we are held responsible for our actions. Then, when we also acknowledge our sin and guilt, we receive God's forgiveness, enter into the joy of his salvation, and so become yet more completely human and healthy. What is unhealthy is every wallowing in guilt which does not lead to confession, repentance, faith in Jesus Christ and so forgiveness.

In his justly famous essay 'The Humanitarian Theory of Punishment', C. S. Lewis bemoans the modern tendency to abandon the notion of just retribution and replace it with humanitarian concerns both for the criminal (reform) and for society as a whole (deterrence). For this means, he argues, that every lawbreaker 'is deprived of the rights of a human being. The reason is this. The Humanitarian theory removes from punishment the concept of desert. But the concept of desert is the only connecting link between punishment and justice. It is only as deserved or undeserved that a sentence can be just or unjust.' Again, 'when we cease to consider what the criminal deserves and consider only what will cure him or deter others, we have tacitly removed him from the sphere of justice altogether; instead of a person, a subject of rights, we now have a mere object, a patient, a "case".' By what right may we use force to impose treatment on a criminal, either to cure him or to protect society, unless he *deserves* it?

> To be 'cured' against one's will, and cured of states which we may not regard as disease, is to be put on a level with those who have not yet reached the age of reason or those who never will; to be classed with infants, imbeciles, and domestic animals. But to be punished, however severely, because we have deserved it, because we 'ought to have known better', is to be treated as a human person made in God's image.[18]

God's holiness and wrath

We have considered the seriousness of sin as rebellion against God, the continuing responsibility of men and women for their actions, and their consequent guilt in God's sight and liability to punishment. But can we think of God as 'punishing' or 'judging' evil? Yes, we can and must. Indeed the essential background to the cross is not only the sin, responsibility and guilt of human beings but the just reaction of God to these things, in other words his holiness and wrath.

That God is holy is foundational to biblical religion. So is the corollary that sin is incompatible with his holiness. His eyes are 'too pure to look on evil' and he 'cannot tolerate wrong'. Therefore our sins effectively separate us from him, so that his face is hidden from us and he refuses to listen to our prayers.[19] In consequence, it was clearly understood by the biblical authors that no human being could ever set eyes on God and survive the experience. They might perhaps be permitted to see his 'back' but not his 'face', the sunshine but not the sun.[20] And all those who were granted even

---

[18] C. S. Lewis' essay 'The Humanitarian Theory of Punishment' has been published in several collections of his writings. I have used the text as it appears in *Churchmen Speak*, ed. Philip E. Hughes, pp. 39–44. See also C. S. Lewis' letter to T. S. Eliot on 25 May 1962 in *Letters of C. S. Lewis*, ed. W. H. Lewis, p. 304. He writes: 'It is vile tyranny to submit a man to compulsory "cure" . . . unless he *deserves* it'.
[19] Hab. 1:13; Is. 59:1ff.   [20] E.g. Ex. 33:20–23; Jdg. 13:22.

a glimpse of his glory were unable to endure the sight. Moses 'hid his face, because he was afraid to look at God'. When Isaiah had his vision of Yahweh enthroned and exalted, he was overwhelmed by the sense of his uncleanness. When God revealed himself personally to Job, Job's reaction was to 'despise' himself and to 'repent in dust and ashes'. Ezekiel saw only 'the appearance of the likeness of the glory of the LORD', in burning fire and brilliant light, but it was enough to make him fall prostrate to the ground. At a similar vision Daniel also collapsed and fainted, with his face to the ground. As for those who were confronted by the Lord Jesus Christ, even during his earthly life when his glory was veiled, they felt a profound discomfort. For example, he provoked in Peter a sense of his sinfulness and of his unfitness to be in his presence. And when John saw his ascended magnificence, he 'fell at his feet as though dead'.[21]

Closely related to God's holiness is his wrath, which is in fact his holy reaction to evil. We certainly cannot dismiss it by saying that the God of wrath belongs to the Old Testament, while the God of the New Testament is love. For God's love is clearly seen in the Old Testament, as is also his wrath in the New. R. V. G. Tasker correctly wrote: 'It is an axiom of the Bible that there is no incompatibility between these two attributes of the divine nature; and for the most part the great Christian theologians and preachers of the past have endeavoured to be loyal to both sides of the divine self-disclosure.'[22] Yet the concept of an angry God continues to raise problems in Christian minds. How can an emotion, they ask, which Jesus equated with murder, and which Paul declared to be one of the 'acts of the sinful nature' of which we must rid ourselves, possibly be attributed to the all-holy God?[23]

One attempted explanation is associated particularly with the name of C. H. Dodd, and with his commentary on *The Epistle of Paul to the Romans*. He pointed out that, although alongside references to God's love Paul also writes that he 'loved' us, yet alongside references to God's anger he never writes that he 'is angry' with us. In addition to this absence of the verb to 'be angry', the noun *orgē* (anger or wrath) is constantly used by Paul 'in a curiously impersonal way' (p. 21). He refers to 'wrath' or 'the wrath' without specifying whose wrath it is, and thus almost abso-

---

[21] Ex. 3:6; Is. 6:1–5; Jb. 42:5–6; Ezk. 1:28; Dn. 10:9; Lk. 5:8; Rev. 1:17.
[22] R. V. G. Tasker, *Biblical Doctrine of the Wrath of God*, p. vii. 'Wrath' is attributed to Jesus in Mk. 3:5 and (perhaps, following some manuscripts) Mk. 1:41.
[23] Mt. 5:21–26; Gal. 5:20; Eph. 4:31; Col. 3:8.

lutizes it. For example, he writes of 'the day of God's wrath', of how 'law brings wrath', and of how wrath 'has come upon' disbelieving Jews, while believers will be rescued from 'the coming wrath' through Jesus Christ.[24] Dodd's deduction from this evidence was that Paul retained the concept of wrath 'not to describe the attitude of God to man, but to describe an inevitable process of cause and effect in a moral universe' (p. 23).

Professor A. T. Hanson has elaborated C. H. Dodd's thesis in his comprehensive biblical survey *The Wrath of the Lamb*. Drawing attention to 'a marked tendency' among post-exilic biblical authors 'to speak of the divine wrath in a very impersonal manner', he defines it as 'the inevitable process of sin working itself out in history' (pp. 21 and 37). Coming to the New Testament, he writes: 'there can be little doubt that for Paul the impersonal character of the wrath was important; it relieved him of the necessity of attributing wrath directly to God, it transformed the wrath from an attribute of God into the name for a process, which sinners bring upon themselves.' For wrath is 'wholly impersonal' and 'does not describe an attitude of God but a condition of men' (pp. 69 and 110).

That expression 'relieved him of the necessity' is revealing. It suggests that Paul was uncomfortable with the notion of God's personal wrath, looked round for an escape from having to believe and teach it, and was 'relieved' of his burden by discovering that wrath was not a divine emotion, attribute or attitude, but an impersonal historical process affecting sinners. In this Professor Hanson seems to be projecting on to Paul his own dilemma, for he is candid enough to confess that he has just such an *a priori* problem himself. Towards the end of his discussion he writes: 'If we once allow ourselves to be led into thinking that a reference to the wrath of God in the New Testament means that God is conceived of as angry . . ., we cannot avoid maintaining that in some sense the Son endured the wrath of the Father, we cannot help thinking in forensic terms, with all the strain and violence to our God-given sense of moral justice that such a theory involves' (pp. 193–194). He seems to be saying that it is in order to overcome these 'appalling difficulties' that he has reinterpreted the wrath of God. To say that Christ bore 'wrath' on the cross, he maintains, means that he 'endured the consequences of men's sins', not their penalty (p. 194).

We must watch our presuppositions, therefore. It is perilous to begin with any *a priori*, even with a 'God-given sense of moral

---

[24] Rom. 2:5; 4:15; 1 Thes. 2:16; 1:10; Rom. 5:9.

justice' which then shapes our understanding of the cross. It is wiser and safer to begin inductively with a God-given doctrine of the cross, which then shapes our understanding of moral justice. I hope later to demonstrate that it is possible to hold a biblical and Christian concept of 'wrath' and 'propitiation' which, far from contradicting moral justice, both expresses and safeguards it.

The attempts by C. H. Dodd, A. T. Hanson and others to reconstruct 'wrath' as an impersonal process must be declared at least 'not proven'. To be sure, sometimes the word is used without explicit reference to God, and with or without the definite article, but the full phrase 'the wrath of God' is used as well, apparently without embarrassment, by both Paul and John. Without doubt also, Paul taught that God's wrath is being revealed in the present both through the moral deterioration of pagan society and through the State's administration of justice.[25] These processes are not identified with God's wrath, however, but declared to be manifestations of it. The truth that God's wrath (*i.e.* his antagonism to evil) is active through social and legal processes does not necessitate the conclusion that it is itself a purely impersonal continuum of cause and effect. Perhaps the reason for Paul's adoption of impersonal expressions is not to affirm that God is never angry, but to emphasize that his anger is void of any tinge of personal malice. After all Paul sometimes refers to *charis* (grace) without referring to God. He can write, for example, of grace 'increasing' and of grace 'reigning' (Rom. 5:20–21). Yet we do not on that account depersonalize grace and convert it into an influence or process. On the contrary, grace is the most personal of all words; grace is God himself acting graciously towards us. And just as *charis* stands for the gracious personal activity of God himself, so *orgē* stands for his equally personal hostility to evil.

How, then, shall we define anger? Writing particularly of righteous human anger, James Denney called it 'the instinctive resentment or reaction of the soul against anything which it regards as wrong or injurious' and 'the vehement repulsion of that which hurts'.[26] Similarly, God's wrath in the words of Leon Morris is his 'personal divine revulsion to evil' and his 'personal vigorous opposition' to it.[27] To speak thus of God's anger is a legitimate anthropomorphism, provided that we recognize it as no more than a rough and ready parallel, since God's anger is absolutely pure,

[25] Rom. 1:18–32 and 13:1–7. C. H. Dodd refers to these on pp. 26 and 204 of his commentary.

[26] James Denney, article 'Anger', pp. 60–62.

[27] Leon Morris, *Cross in the New Testament*, pp. 190–191. See also his *Apostolic Preaching*, pp. 161–166.

and uncontaminated by those elements which render human anger sinful. Human anger is usually arbitrary and uninhibited; divine anger is always principled and controlled. Our anger tends to be a spasmodic outburst, aroused by pique and seeking revenge; God's is a continuous, settled antagonism, aroused only by evil, and expressed in its condemnation. God is entirely free from personal animosity or vindictiveness; indeed, he is sustained simultaneously with undiminished love for the offender. Charles Cranfield's summary is that God's *orgē* is 'no nightmare of an indiscriminate, uncontrolled, irrational fury, but the wrath of the holy and merciful God called forth by, and directed against, men's *asebeia* (ungodliness) and *adikia* (unrighteousness)'.[28]

What is common to the biblical concepts of the holiness and the wrath of God is the truth that they cannot coexist with sin. God's holiness exposes sin; his wrath opposes it. So sin cannot approach God, and God cannot tolerate sin. Several vivid metaphors are used in Scripture to illustrate this stubborn fact.

The first is *height*. Frequently in the Bible the God of creation and covenant is called 'the Most High God', and is personally addressed in several Psalms as 'Yahweh Most High'.[29] His lofty exaltation expresses both his sovereignty over the nations, the earth and 'all gods',[30] and also his inaccessibility to sinners. True, his throne is called 'the throne of grace' and is encircled by the rainbow of his covenant promise. Nevertheless, it is 'high and exalted' and he himself is 'the high and lofty One', who does not live in man-made temples, since heaven is his throne and the earth his footstool; so sinners should not presume.[31] True again, he condescends to the contrite and lowly, who find security in his shadow. But proud sinners he knows only 'from afar', and he cannot stand the high and haughty looks of the arrogant.[32]

The 'high' exaltation of God is not literal, of course, and was never meant to be taken literally. The recent hue and cry about abandoning a God 'up there' was largely superfluous. The biblical writers used height as a symbol of transcendence, just as we do. It is more expressive than depth. 'The Ground of Being' may speak of ultimate reality to some people, but 'the high and lofty One' conveys God's otherness more explicitly. When thinking of the

[28] C. E. B. Cranfield, *Romans*, Vol. I, p. 111.
[29] *E.g.* Gn. 14:18–22; Pss. 7:17; 9:2; 21:7; 46:4; 47:2; 57:2; 83:18; 92:8; 93:4; 113:4; Dn. 3:26; 4:2, 17, 24–25, 32, 34; 5:18–21; 7:18–27; Ho. 7:16; 11:7; Mi. 6:6.
[30] *E.g.* Pss. 97:9 and 99:2.
[31] Heb. 4:16: Rev. 4:3; Is. 6:1; 57:15; Acts 7:48–49.
[32] Is. 57:15; Pss. 91:1, 9; 138:6; Pr. 21:4; Is. 10:12.

great and living God, it is better to look up than down, and outside than inside ourselves.

The second picture is that of *distance*. God is not only 'high above' us, but 'far away' from us also. We dare not approach too close. Indeed, many are the biblical injunctions to keep our distance. 'Do not come any closer,' God said to Moses out of the burning bush. So it was that the arrangements for Israel's worship expressed the complementary truths of his nearness to them because of his covenant and his separation from them because of his holiness. Even as he came down to them at Mount Sinai to reveal himself to them, he told Moses to put limits for the people around the base of the mountain and to urge them not to come near. Similarly, when God gave instructions for the building of the Tabernacle (and later the Temple), he both promised to live among his people and yet warned them to erect a curtain before the inner sanctuary as a permanent sign that he was out of reach to sinners. Nobody was permitted to penetrate the veil, on pain of death, except the high priest, and then only once a year on the Day of Atonement, and then only if he took with him the blood of sacrifice.[33] And when the Israelites were about to cross the Jordan into the promised land, they were given this precise command: 'Keep a distance of about a thousand yards between you and the ark; do not go near it' (Jos. 3:4). It is against the background of this plain teaching about God's holiness and about the perils of presumption that the story of Uzzah's death must be understood. When the oxen carrying the ark stumbled, he reached out and took hold of it. But 'the LORD's anger burned against Uzzah because of his irreverent act',[34] and he died. Commentators tend to protest at this 'primitive' Old Testament understanding of God's wrath as 'fundamentally an irrational and in the last resort inexplicable thing which broke out with enigmatic, mysterious and primal force' and which bordered closely on 'caprice'.[35] But no, there is nothing inexplicable about God's wrath: its explanation is always the presence of evil in some form or other. Sinners cannot approach the all-holy God with impunity. On the last day, those who have not found refuge and cleansing in Christ will hear those most terrible of all words: 'Depart from me.'[36]

[33] Ex. 3:5; 19:3–25 (*cf.* Heb. 12:18–21); 20:24; 25 – 40, especially 29:45–46; Lv. 16 (*cf.* Heb. 9:7–8).
[34] 2 Sa. 6:6–7. *Cf* 1 Sa. 6:19. Plain warnings had been given to the Levites, whose responsibility it was to dismantle, carry and reassemble the Tabernacle. See Nu. 1:51, 53.
[35] Johannes Fichtner in his article on *orgē*, pp. 401–402.
[36] *E.g.* Mt. 7:23; 25:41.

The third and fourth pictures of the holy God's unapproach-ability to sinners are those of *light* and *fire*: 'God is light', and 'our God is a consuming fire'. Both discourage, indeed inhibit, too close an approach. Bright light is blinding; our eyes cannot endure its brilliance, and in the heat of the fire everything shrivels up and is destroyed. So God 'lives in unapproachable light'; 'no-one has seen or can see' him. And those who deliberately reject the truth have 'only a fearful expectation of judgment and of raging fire that will consume the enemies of God. . . . It is a dreadful thing to fall into the hands of the living God.'[37]

The fifth metaphor is the most dramatic of all. It indicates that the holy God's rejection of evil is as decisive as the human body's rejection of poison by *vomiting*. Vomiting is probably the body's most violent of all reactions. The immoral and idolatrous practices of the Canaanites were so disgusting, it is written, that 'the land vomited out its inhabitants', and the Israelites were warned that if they committed the same offences, the land would vomit them out as well. Moreover what is said to be the land's repudiation of evil was in reality the Lord's. For in the same context he is represented as declaring that he 'abhorred' the Canaanites because of their evil doings. The identical Hebrew word is used of him in relation to the stubborn disobedience of Israel in the wilderness: 'For forty years I was angry with (literally 'loathed') that generation.' Here too the verb probably alludes to nauseating food, as it does in the statement, 'we detest this miserable food!' Our delicate upbringing may find this earthy metaphor distinctly embarrassing. Yet it continues in the New Testament. When Jesus threatens to 'spit' the lukewarm Laodicean church people out of his mouth, the Greek verb literally means to 'vomit' (*emeō*). The picture may be shocking, but its meaning is clear. God cannot tolerate or 'digest' sin and hypocrisy. They cause him not distaste merely, but disgust. They are so repulsive to him that he must rid himself of them. He must spit or vomit them out.[38]

All five metaphors illustrate the utter incompatibility of divine holiness and human sin. Height and distance, light, fire and vomiting all say that God cannot be in the presence of sin, and that if it approaches him too closely it is repudiated or consumed.

Yet these notions are foreign to modern man. The kind of God who appeals to most people today would be easygoing in his tolerance of our offences. He would be gentle, kind, accommo-dating, and would have no violent reactions. Unhappily, even in

[37] 1 Jn. 1:5; Heb. 12:29 (*cf.* Dt. 4:24); 1 Tim. 6:16; Heb. 10:27, 31.
[38] Lv. 18:25–28; 20:22–23; Ps. 95:10; Nu. 21:5; Rev. 3:16.

the church we seem to have lost the vision of the majesty of God. There is much shallowness and levity among us. Prophets and psalmists would probably say of us that 'there is no fear of God before their eyes'. In public worship our habit is to slouch or squat; we do not kneel nowadays, let alone prostrate ourselves in humility before God. It is more characteristic of us to clap our hands with joy than to blush with shame or tears. We saunter up to God to claim his patronage and friendship; it does not occur to us that he might send us away. We need to hear again the apostle Peter's sobering words: 'Since you call on a Father who judges each man's work impartially, live your lives . . . in reverent fear.'[39] In other words, if we dare to call our Judge our Father, we must beware of presuming on him. It must even be said that our evangelical emphasis on the atonement is dangerous if we come to it too quickly. We learn to appreciate the access to God which Christ has won for us only after we have first seen God's inaccessibility to sinners. We can cry 'Hallelujah' with authenticity only after we have first cried 'Woe is me, for I am lost'. In Dale's words, 'it is partly because sin does not provoke our own wrath, that we do not believe that sin provokes the wrath of God'.[40]

We must, therefore, hold fast to the biblical revelation of the living God who hates evil, is disgusted and angered by it, and refuses ever to come to terms with it. In consequence, we may be sure that, when he searched in his mercy for some way to forgive, cleanse and accept evil-doers, it was not along the road of moral compromise. It had to be a way which was expressive equally of his love and of his wrath. As Brunner put it, 'where the idea of the wrath of God is ignored, there also will there be no understanding of the central conception of the Gospel: the uniqueness of the revelation in the Mediator'.[41] Similarly, 'only he who knows the greatness of wrath will be mastered by the greatness of mercy'.[42]

All inadequate doctrines of the atonement are due to inadequate doctrines of God and man. If we bring God down to our level and raise ourselves to his, then of course we see no need for a radical salvation, let alone for a radical atonement to secure it. When, on the other hand, we have glimpsed the blinding glory of the holiness of God, and have been so convicted of our sin by the Holy Spirit that we tremble before God and acknowledge what we are, namely 'hell-deserving sinners', then and only then does the necessity of the cross appear so obvious that we are astonished we never saw it before.

[39] 1 Pet. 1:17. [40] R. W. Dale, *Atonement*, pp. 338–339.
[41] Emil Brunner, *Mediator*, p. 152.
[42] Gustav Stählin in his article on *orgē*, p. 425.

The essential background to the cross, therefore, is a balanced understanding of the gravity of sin and the majesty of God. If we diminish either, we thereby diminish the cross. If we reinterpret sin as a lapse instead of a rebellion, and God as indulgent instead of indignant, then naturally the cross appears superfluous. But to dethrone God and enthrone ourselves not only dispenses with the cross; it also degrades both God and man. A biblical view of God and ourselves, however, that is, of our sin and of God's wrath, honours both. It honours human beings by affirming them as responsible for their own actions. It honours God by affirming him as having moral character.

So we come back to where we began this chapter, namely that forgiveness is for God the profoundest of problems. As Bishop B. F. Westcott expressed it, 'nothing superficially seems simpler than forgiveness', whereas 'nothing if we look deeply is more mysterious or more difficult'.[43] Sin and wrath stand in the way. God must not only respect us as the responsible beings we are, but he must also respect himself as the holy God he is. Before the holy God can forgive us, some kind of 'satisfaction' is necessary. That is the subject of our next chapter.

---

[43] B. F. Westcott, *Historic Faith*, p. 130.

5

Satisfaction for sin

No two words in the theological vocabulary of the cross arouse more criticism than 'satisfaction' and 'substitution'. Yet it is in defence of these words that this chapter and the next are written. In combination ('satisfaction through substitution') they may even seem intolerable. How, people ask, can we possibly believe that God needed some kind of 'satisfaction' before he was prepared to forgive, and that Jesus Christ provided it by enduring as our 'substitute' the punishment we sinners deserved? Are not such notions unworthy of the God of the biblical revelation, a hangover from primitive superstitions, indeed frankly immoral?

Sir Alister Hardy, for example, formerly Linacre Professor of Zoology at Oxford, who was friendly to all kinds of religious experience because he spent a lifetime investigating it, nevertheless expressed his inability to come to terms with the 'crude' beliefs he thought 'so many orthodox churchmen' entertain. In his 1965 Gifford Lectures, published under the title *The Divine Flame*, he asked whether Jesus himself would be a Christian if he were to live today. 'I very much doubt it,' Sir Alister replied. 'I feel certain that he would not have preached to us of a God who would be appeased by the cruel sacrifice of a tortured body. . . . I cannot accept either the hypothesis that the appalling death of Jesus was a sacrifice in the eyes of God for the sins of the world, or that God, in the shape of his son, tortured himself for our redemption. I can only confess that, in my heart of hearts, I find such religious ideas to be amongst the least attractive in the whole of anthropology. To me they belong to quite a different philosophy – different psychology – from that of the religion that Jesus taught' (p. 218).

Sir Alister Hardy was right to say that Jesus would not (because he did not) explain his death in those crude terms, but wrong to suppose that 'many orthodox churchmen' do so. He caricatured the Christian understanding of the cross in order the more readily to condemn it. The real question is whether we can hold fast to the saving efficacy of the death of Jesus, and to its traditional vocabulary (including 'satisfaction' and 'substitution'), without denigrating God. I believe we can and must. To be sure, neither 'satisfaction' nor 'substitution' is a biblical word, and therefore we need to proceed with great caution. But each is a biblical concept. There is, in fact, a biblical revelation of 'satisfaction through substitution', which is uniquely honouring to God, and which should therefore lie at the very heart of the church's worship and witness. That is why Cranmer included a clear statement of it at the beginning of his Prayer of Consecration (1549). In consequence, for 400 years Anglicans have described Jesus Christ as having made on the cross, by his 'one oblation of himself once offered', 'a full, perfect, and sufficient sacrifice, oblation, and satisfaction for the sins of the whole world'.

But the way in which different theologians have developed the concept of satisfaction depends on their understanding of the obstacles to forgiveness which need first to be removed. What demands are being made which stand in the way until they are satisfied? And who is making them? Is it the devil? Or is it the law, or God's honour or justice, or 'the moral order'? All these have been proposed. I shall argue, however, that the primary 'obstacle' is to be found within God himself. He must 'satisfy himself' in the way of salvation he devises; he cannot save us by contradicting himself.

Satisfying the devil

The notion that it was the devil who made the cross necessary was widespread in the early church.[1] To be sure, Jesus and his apostles did speak of the cross as the means of the devil's overthrow (as we shall consider in a later chapter). But some of the early Fathers were extremely injudicious in the ways in which they represented both the devil's power and how the cross deprived him of it. They all recognized that since the Fall, and on account of it, mankind has been in captivity not only to sin and guilt but to the devil.

[1] For historical surveys of the different theories of the atonement see H. E. W. Turner, *Patristic Doctrine*, J. K. Mozley, *Doctrine of the Atonement*, Robert Mackintosh, *Historic Theories* and Robert S. Franks, *History of the Doctrine of the Work of Christ*.

112

They thought of him as the lord of sin and death, and as the major tyrant from whom Jesus came to liberate us.

But with the benefit of hindsight we may say that they made three mistakes. First, they credited the devil with more power than he has. Even though they portrayed him as a rebel, a robber and a usurper, they tended to speak as if he had acquired certain 'rights' over man which even God himself was under obligation to satisfy honourably. Gregory of Nazianzus in the fourth century was one of the few early theologians who vigorously repudiated this idea. He called it an 'outrage'.[2]

Secondly, they therefore tended to think of the cross as a divine transaction with the devil; it was the ransom-price demanded by him for the release of his captives, and paid to him in settlement of his rights. This was a very popular belief in the early centuries of the church.

Thirdly, some went further and represented the transaction in terms of a deception. Theologically, they pictured the devil as having over-reached himself. Although in the case of us sinners he 'holds the power of death' (Heb. 2:14), he had no such authority over the sinless Jesus, and in hounding him to death he shed innocent blood. Therefore, having thus abused his power, he was deprived of it. Some Fathers added at this point that he did not altogether realize what he was doing, either because he did not recognize who Jesus was, or because, seeing Godhead in human form, he thought he now had a unique opportunity to overpower him. But he was deceived. Origen was the first to teach unequivocally that the death of Jesus was both the ransom-price paid to the devil and the means of his deception and overthrow. Gregory of Nyssa, a shy Cappadocian scholar of the fourth century, further developed these ideas in his *Great Catechism* or *Catechetical Oration*, using vivid imagery:

> God, . . . in order to secure that the ransom in our behalf might be easily accepted by him (*sc.* the devil) who required it . . . was hidden under the veil of our nature, that so, as with ravenous fish, the hook of the Deity might be gulped down along with the bait of flesh, and thus, life being introduced into the house of death, . . . (the devil) might vanish.[3]

To us the analogy of the fish-hook is grotesque, as is also Augustine's sermonic use of mousetrap imagery. Peter Lombard was to

[2] *Orat.* xlv.22.
[3] *Catechetical Oration* 22 – 26. See A. S. Dunstone, *Atonement in Gregory of Nyssa*, p. 15, footnote 7.

use it centuries later, affirming that 'the cross was a mousetrap (*muscipula*) baited with the blood of Christ'.[4] To be sure, these theologians may well have developed such pictures as a concession to the popular mind, and the early Fathers saw a certain justice in the idea that he who had deceived the human race into disobedience should himself be deceived into defeat. But to attribute fraudulent action to God is unworthy of him.

What is of permanent value in these theories is first that they took seriously the reality, malevolence and power of the devil (the 'strong man, fully armed' of Lk. 11:21), and secondly that they proclaimed his decisive, objective defeat at the cross for our liberation (by the 'someone stronger' who attacked and overpowered him, Lk. 11:22).[5] Nevertheless, R. W. Dale was not exaggerating when he dubbed them 'intolerable, monstrous and profane'.[6] We deny that the devil has any rights over us which God is obliged to satisfy. Consequently, any notion of Christ's death as a necessary transaction with, let alone deception of, the devil is ruled out.

Satisfying the law

Another way of explaining the moral necessity of the divine 'satisfaction' at the cross has been to exalt the law. Sin is 'lawlessness' (1 Jn. 3:4), a disregard for God's law and a disobedience of it. But the law cannot be broken with impunity. Sinners therefore incur the penalty of their law-breaking. They cannot simply be let off. The law must be upheld, its dignity defended, and its just penalties paid. The law is thereby 'satisfied'.

A popular illustration of this truth is the story of King Darius in the book of Daniel (chapter 6). He appointed 120 satraps to rule Babylonia, and set three administrators over them, of whom Daniel was one. Further, such were Daniel's exceptional qualities and distinguished service that the king planned to promote him over all his colleagues. This aroused their jealousy, and they immediately began to plot his downfall. Watching him like hawks, they tried to find some inconsistency or inefficiency in his conduct of public affairs, so that they could lodge charges against him. But

---

[4] *Sentences*, Liber III, Distinctio xix.1.

[5] Nathaniel Dimock, while not accepting 'the unguarded language or misleading statements of *some* of the Fathers', since God does not trade with the devil, nevertheless believes that in over-reaction 'undue condemnation has been bestowed on the Patristic view of this subject'. He therefore salvages some biblical truths from it in his Additional Note B, 'on Christ's Redemption as viewed in relation to the dominion and works of the devil'. See his *Doctrine of the Death of Christ*, pp. 121–136.

[6] R. W. Dale, *Atonement*, p. 277.

they failed, 'because he was trustworthy and neither corrupt nor negligent' (v.4). So they turned their scrutiny upon his private life; their only hope, they reckoned, was to find him guilty of some technical fault in connection with his regular religious devotion. They managed to persuade the king to 'issue an edict and enforce the decree that anyone who prays to any god or man during the next thirty days', except to the king himself, would be thrown into the lions' den (v.7). With incredible naivety the king fell into their trap. By putting the decree into writing he even made it unalterable, 'in accordance with the laws of the Medes and Persians, which cannot be repealed' (vv.8-9).

The publication of the decree reached Daniel's ears, but did not lead him to change his routine. On the contrary, he continued three times a day to pray to his God. His practice was to do so kneeling in his upstairs room, whose windows opened towards Jerusalem. There he was visible to passers-by, and there his enemies duly saw him. They went back to the king immediately, and reported Daniel's flagrant breach of the royal decree. 'When the king heard this, he was greatly distressed; he was determined to rescue Daniel and made every effort until sundown to save him' (v.14). But he could find no solution to the legal problem he had created for himself. His administrators and satraps reminded him that 'according to the law of the Medes and Persians no decree or edict that the king issues can be changed' (v.15). So Darius reluctantly bowed to the inevitable and gave the order for Daniel to be thrown into the lions' den. The law had triumphed.

Many are the preachers (myself among them) who have used this story to highlight the divine dilemma. Darius respected Daniel and laboured long to find some way of saving him, but the law must take its course and not be tampered with. So God loves us sinners and longs to save us, but cannot do so by violating the law which has justly condemned us. Hence the cross, in which the penalty of the law was paid and its sanctity vindicated. As one recent exponent of this view, I cite Henry Wace, Dean of Canterbury from 1903 to 1924:

A law which has no sanction, in the technical sense of that expression – in other words, a law which can be broken without an adequate penalty, is no law at all; and it is inconceivable that God's moral law can be violated without entailing consequences of the most terrible kind. The mere violation of one of his physical laws may entail, whether men intend the violation or not, the most lasting and widespread misery; and can it reasonably be supposed that the most flagrant and wilful violation of the highest of all laws – those of truth and righteousness – should entail no such results?[7]

Again, 'God cannot abolish that moral constitution of things which he has established'. It is true that Dean Wace went on to qualify these statements, by reminding us that the moral world is not 'a kind of moral machine in which laws operate as they do in physical nature', and that 'we have to do not simply with an established order but with a living personality, with a living God'. Nevertheless, he refers again to 'the penalty necessarily involved in the violation of the Divine law'.[8]

I am not wanting to disagree with this language, and indeed I continue to use it myself. It has, in fact, good scriptural warrant. For Paul quotes Deuteronomy with approval to the effect that every law-breaker is 'cursed', and then goes on to affirm that 'Christ redeemed us from the curse of the law by becoming a curse for us' (Gal. 3:10, 13). If therefore Paul was not afraid to use an impersonal expression like 'the curse of the law', we should not be either.

The fourth-century Latin Fathers such as Ambrose and Hilary regularly expounded the cross in these terms. Going further than Tertullian, who was the first to use the legal terms 'merit' and 'satisfaction' of the Christian's relation to God, they interpreted texts such as Galatians 3:13 in the light of 'the *satisfactio* of the Roman public law, which means the endurance of the law's sentence'.[9] The sixteenth-century Reformers developed this further. They rightly emphasized that Jesus Christ's personal submission to the law was indispensable to our rescue from its condemnation. They also taught that his submission took two forms, his perfect obedience to it in his life and his bearing of its penalty in his death. They called the first his 'active' and the second his 'passive' obedience. These adjectives are inexact, however, since Jesus' obedience unto death on the cross was just as 'active' (*i.e.* voluntary and determined) as his obedient submission to the moral law. His obedience to the Father's will is one and the same, whether in his conduct or mission, his life or death. The value of continuing to speak of Christ's 'double' obedience is that we then distinguish between his fulfilling the demands of the law and his enduring the condemnation of the law. Both kinds of submission to the law were essential to the efficacy of the cross.

Nevertheless, we need to be alert to the dangers of law-language

---

[7] Henry Wace, *Sacrifice of Christ*, p. 16.   [8] *Ibid.*, pp. 22, 28–29, 36.
[9] Robert S. Franks, *Work of Christ*, p. 135.

and to the inadequacy of likening God's moral law either to the civil laws of the country or to the physical laws of the universe. True, a part of the glory of a constitutional monarchy is that even the monarch is not above the law but under it, being required to obey its provisions and (if in breach of them) to bear its penalties. Darius provides a good example of this. Yet the decree he made was rash and foolish, since it contained no religious conscience clause, and so led to the punishment of a righteous man for a righteous deed which the king had never intended his decree to make a punishable offence. We cannot think of God as caught in a technical legal muddle of this kind. Nor is it wise to liken God's moral laws to his physical laws and then declare them equally inflexible. For example, 'if you put your hand in the fire it will be burnt, and if you break the ten commandments you will be punished'. There is truth in the analogy, but the concept of mechanical penalties is misleading. It may be true of the laws of nature, even though strictly they are not 'laws' which bind God's action but a description of the normal uniformity of his action which human beings have observed. The real reason why disobedience of God's moral laws brings condemnation is not that God is their prisoner, but that he is their creator.

As R. W. Dale put it, God's connection with the law is 'not a relation of subjection but of identity. . . . In God the law is *alive*; it reigns on his throne, sways his sceptre, is crowned with his glory'.[10] For the law is the expression of his own moral being, and his moral being is always self-consistent. Nathaniel Dimock captures this truth well in the following words:

> There can be nothing . . . in the demands of the law, and the severity of the law, and the condemnation of the law, and the death of the law, and the curse of the law, which is not a reflection (in part) of the perfections of God. Whatever is due to the law is due to the law because it is the law of God, and is due therefore to God himself.[11]

Satisfying God's honour and justice

If the early Greek Fathers represented the cross primarily as a 'satisfaction' of the devil, in the sense of being the ransom-price demanded by him and paid to him, and the early Latin Fathers saw it as a satisfaction of God's law, a fresh approach was made

[10] R. W. Dale, *Atonement*, p. 372.
[11] Nathaniel Dimock, *Doctrine of the Death of Christ*, p. 32, footnote 1.

by Anselm of Canterbury in the eleventh century, who in his
Cur Deus Homo? made a systematic exposition of the cross as a
satisfaction of God's offended honour. His book was 'epoch-
making in the whole history of our doctrine', wrote R. S. Franks,
'in that it for the first time in a thoroughgoing and consistent
way applies to the elucidation of the subject the conceptions of
satisfaction and merit'.[12] James Denney went further and called it
'the truest and greatest book on the atonement that has ever been
written'.[13]

Anselm was a godly Italian, who first settled in Normandy,
and then in 1093 following the Norman Conquest was appointed
Archbishop of Canterbury. He has been described as the first
representative of medieval 'scholasticism', which was an attempt
to reconcile philosophy and theology, Aristotelian logic and biblical
revelation. Although he included in his writings a number of
biblical quotations, however, and referred to Holy Scripture as 'a
firm foundation', his overriding concern was to be 'agreeable to
reason' (ii.xi). As his imaginary interlocutor Boso put it, 'the way
by which you lead me is so walled in by reasoning on each side
that I do not seem able to turn out of it either to the right hand
or the left' (ii.ix).

In *Cur Deus Homo?*, Anselm's great treatise on the relationship
between the incarnation and the atonement, he agrees that the
devil needed to be overcome, but rejects the patristic ransom-
theories on the ground that 'God owed nothing to the devil but
punishment' (ii.xix). Instead, man owed something to God, and
this is the debt which needed to be repaid. For Anselm defines sin
as 'not rendering to God what is his due' (i.xi), namely the
submission of our entire will to his. To sin is, therefore, to 'take
away from God what is his own', which means to steal from him
and so to dishonour him. If anybody imagines that God can simply
forgive us in the same way that we are to forgive others, he has not
yet considered the seriousness of sin (i.xxi). Being an inexcusable
disobedience of God's known will, sin dishonours and insults him,
and 'nothing is less tolerable . . . than that the creature should take
away from the Creator the honour due to him, and not repay what
he takes away' (i.xiii). God cannot overlook this. 'It is not proper
for God to pass by sin thus unpunished' (i.xii). It is more than
improper; it is impossible. 'If it is not becoming to God to do
anything unjustly or irregularly, it is not within the scope of his
liberty or kindness or will to let go unpunished the sinner who

[12] Robert S. Franks, *Work of Christ*, p. 126.
[13] James Denney, *Atonement*, p. 116.

does not repay to God what he has taken away' (i.xii). 'God upholds nothing more justly than he doth the honour of his own dignity' (i.xiii).

So what can be done? If we are ever to be forgiven, we must repay what we owe. Yet we are incapable of doing this, either for ourselves or for other people. Our present obedience and good works cannot make satisfaction for our sins, since these are required of us anyway. So we cannot save ourselves. Nor can any other human being save us, since 'one who is a sinner cannot justify another sinner' (i.xxiii). Hence the dilemma with which Book i ends: 'man the sinner owes to God, on account of sin, what he cannot repay, and unless he repays it he cannot be saved' (i.xxv).

Near the beginning of Book ii, the only possible way out of the human dilemma is unfolded: 'there is no-one . . . who *can* make this satisfaction except God himself. . . . But no-one *ought* to make it except man; otherwise man does not make satisfaction.' Therefore, 'it is necessary that one who is God-man should make it' (ii.vi). A being who is God and not man, or man and not God, or a mixture of both and therefore neither man nor God, would not qualify. 'It is needful that the very same Person who is to make this satisfaction be perfect God and perfect man, since no-one *can* do it except one who is truly God, and no-one *ought* to do it except one who is truly man' (ii.vii). This leads Anselm to introduce Christ. He was (and is) a unique Person, since in him 'God the Word and man meet' (ii.ix). He also performed a unique work, for he gave himself up to death – not as a debt (since he was sinless and therefore under no obligation to die) but freely for the honour of God. It was also reasonable that man, 'who by sinning stole himself away from God as completely as he possibly could do so, should, in making satisfaction, surrender himself to God as completely as he can do so', namely by his voluntary self-offering unto death. Serious as human sin is, yet the life of the God-man was so good, so exalted and so precious that its offering in death 'outweighs the number and greatness of all sins' (ii.xiv), and due reparation has been made to the offended honour of God.

The greatest merits of Anselm's exposition are that he perceived clearly the extreme gravity of sin (as a wilful rebellion against God in which the creature affronts the majesty of his Creator), the unchanging holiness of God (as unable to condone any violation of his honour), and the unique perfections of Christ (as the God-man who voluntarily gave himself up to death for us). In some places, however, his scholastic reasoning took him beyond the boundaries of the biblical revelation, as when he speculated whether Christ's payment was exactly what sinners owed or more, and whether the number of redeemed humans would exceed the number of fallen angels. Moreover, his whole presentation reflects the feudal culture of his age, in which society was rigidly stratified, each person stood on the dignity which had been accorded him, the 'proper' or 'becoming' conduct of inferiors to superiors (and especially to the king) was laid down, breaches of this code were punished, and all debts must be honourably discharged.

When God is portrayed, however, in terms reminiscent of a feudal overlord who demands honour and punishes dishonour, it is questionable whether this picture adequately expresses the 'honour' which is indeed due to God alone. We must certainly remain dissatisfied whenever the atonement is presented as a necessary satisfaction either of God's 'law' or of God's 'honour' in so far as these are objectified as existing in some way apart from him.

It was during the twelfth century that three distinct interpretations of the death of Christ were clarified. Anselm (died 1109), as we have seen, emphasized the objective satisfaction to the honour of God which had been paid by the God-man Jesus, while his younger contemporary Peter Abelard of Paris (died 1142) (Abelard's teaching is considered in greater detail on pp. 217ff.) emphasized the subjective moral influence which the cross has on believers. Meanwhile, Bernard of Clairvaux (died 1153), the mystic theologian, continued to teach that a ransom-price had been paid to the devil. It was the Anselmian view, however, which prevailed, for careful students of Scripture were unable to eliminate from it the notion of satisfaction. So the 'scholastics' or 'schoolmen' (so-called because they taught in the recently founded medieval European 'schools', *i.e.* universities) further developed Anselm's position – both the 'Thomists' who were Dominicans looking to Thomas Aquinas (died 1274) and the 'Scotists' who were Franciscans looking to Duns Scotus (died 1308). Although these two groups of 'schoolmen' differed in details, they both taught that the demands of divine justice were satisfied by Christ's cross.

With the Reformation, and the Reformers' emphasis on justification, it is understandable that they stressed the justice of God and the impossibility of a way of salvation which did not satisfy his justice. For, as Calvin wrote in the *Institutes*, 'there is a perpetual and irreconcilable disagreement between righteousness and unrighteousness' (II.xvi.3). It was necessary therefore for Christ 'to undergo the severity of God's vengeance, to appease his wrath and satisfy his just judgment'.[14] Thomas Cranmer in his 'Homily of Salvation' explained that three things had to go together in our

---

[14] *Institutes*, II.xvi.10. Cf. II.xii.3.

justification: on God's part 'his great mercy and grace', on Christ's part 'the satisfaction of God's justice', and on our part 'true and lively faith'. He concluded the first part of the homily: 'It pleased our heavenly Father, of his infinite mercy, without any our desert or deserving, to prepare for us the most precious jewels of Christ's body and blood, whereby our ransom might be fully paid, the law fulfilled, and his justice fully satisfied.'[15]

This same teaching can be found in Luther's works. After his death, however, the Protestant 'scholastics' systematized the doctrine of the death of Christ into a double satisfaction, namely of God's law and of God's justice. God's law was satisfied by Christ's perfect obedience in his life, and God's justice by his perfect sacrifice for sin, bearing its penalty in his death. This is rather too neat a formulation, however. Since God's law is an expression of his justice, the two cannot be precisely separated.

Then was God's concern to satisfy the 'moral order'? This concept, like that of 'law', is an expression of the justice or moral character of God. It is perhaps at once more general and more broad than 'law', since it embraces not only moral standards but a built-in system of sanctions. It rests on the belief that the holy God who rules the world rules it morally. He has established an order in which the good is to be approved and rewarded, while the evil is to be condemned and punished. To approve the evil or to condemn the good would subvert this moral order. In such a world the unprincipled forgiveness of sins would be equally subversive.

The beginnings of this concept in relation to the death of Christ may be seen in Hugo Grotius (died 1645), the Dutch lawyer and statesman, who deplored Christian controversies and divisions, and dreamt of a reunited, reformed Christendom. His understanding of the atonement was something of a compromise between Anselm and Abelard. Sometimes he taught an almost Abelardian view of the subjective influence of the cross, which leads sinners to repentance and so enables God to forgive them. Usually, however, he preserved the objectivity of the cross, and saw it as a satisfaction of God's justice. In addition, he had a jurist's concern for public morality, both the preventing of crime and the upholding of law. He saw God neither as the offended party, nor as creditor, nor even as judge, but as the Supreme Moral Governor of the world.

[15] Thomas Cranmer, *First Book of Homilies*, p. 130. The Westminster Confession of Faith (1647) also declares that the Lord Jesus, by his perfect obedience and self-sacrifice, has 'fully satisfied the justice of his Father' (VIII.5). Indeed, it was 'a proper, real, and full satisfaction to his Father's justice' on behalf of the justified (XI.3).

So public justice was more important to him than retributive justice, and it was this in particular which he believed was satisfied at the cross. To be sure, Christ died for our sins in our place. But what part or office did God occupy in this? he asked. 'The right of inflicting punishment does not belong to the injured party as injured' but rather 'to the ruler as ruler'.[16] Again, 'to inflict punishment ... is only the prerogative of the ruler as such, ... for example, of a father in a family, of a king in a state, of God in the universe' (p. 51). So Grotius developed his 'rectoral' or 'governmental' interpretation of the cross. He taught that God ordained it 'for the order of things and for the authority of his own law' (p. 137). He was preoccupied with the public vindication of God's justice. 'God was unwilling to pass over so many sins, and so great sins, without a distinguished example', that is, of his serious displeasure with sin (p. 106). 'God has ... most weighty reasons for punishing', but chief among them in Grotius' mind was the resolve to uphold the established order of law, so that we might 'estimate the magnitude and multitude of sins' (p. 107).

Several twentieth-century theologians have taken up Grotius' vision of God as 'the moral governor of the world' and developed it further in relation to the atonement. P. T. Forsyth, for example, wrote of 'this cosmic order of holiness', and added: 'God's moral order demands atonement wherever moral ideas are taken with final seriousness, and man's conscience re-echoes the demand.'[17]

Another example is B. B. Warfield, who drew attention to the universal sense of guilt among human beings. It is a 'deep moral self-condemnation which is present as a primary factor in all truly religious experience. It cries out for satisfaction. No moral deduction can persuade it that forgiveness of sins is a necessary element in the moral order of the world. It knows on the contrary that indiscriminate forgiveness of sin would be precisely the subversion of the moral order of the world. . . . It cries out for expiation'.[18]

But the most striking statement of the inviolability of the moral order has been made by Emil Brunner in his famous book *The Mediator*. Sin is more than 'an attack on God's honour', he wrote (p. 444); it is an assault on the moral world order which is an expression of God's moral will.

The law of his divine Being, on which all the law and order in the world is based, . . . the logical and reliable character of all

[16] Hugo Grotius, *Defence of the Catholic Faith*, p. 57.
[17] P. T. Forsyth, *Cruciality of the Cross*, pp. 137–138. See also his *Work of Christ*, pp. 122–129. [18] B. B. Warfield, *Person and Work*, p. 292.

that happens, the validity of all standards, of all intellectual, legal and moral order, the Law itself, in its most profound meaning, demands the divine reaction, the divine concern about sin, the divine resistance to this rebellion and this breach of order. . . . If this were not true, then there would be no seriousness in the world at all; there would be no meaning in anything, no order, no stability; the world order would fall into ruins; chaos and desolation would be supreme. All order in the world depends upon the inviolability of his (*sc.* God's) honour, upon the certitude that those who rebel against him will be punished (pp. 444–445).

Later Brunner drew an analogy between natural law and moral law, asserting that neither can be infringed with impunity. Forgiveness without atonement would be a contravention of logic, law and order more serious and vast 'than the suspension of the laws of nature' (p. 447). How is forgiveness possible, then, if 'punishment is the expression of the divine law and order, of the inviolability of the divine order of the world' (p. 449)? Since law is 'the expression of the will of the Lawgiver, of the personal God' (p. 459), then, if it is broken, it cannot and does not heal by itself. Sin has caused a 'break in the world order', a disorder so deep-seated that reparation or restitution is necessary, that is, 'Atonement' (p. 485).

God satisfying himself

Here, then, are five ways in which theologians have expressed their sense of what is necessary before God is able to forgive sinners. One speaks of the overthrow of the devil by 'satisfying' his demands, others of 'satisfying' God's law, honour or justice, and the last of 'satisfying the moral order of the world'. In differing degrees all these formulations are true. The limitation they share is that, unless they are very carefully stated, they represent God as being subordinate to something outside and above himself which controls his actions, to which he is accountable, and from which he cannot free himself. 'Satisfaction' is an appropriate word, providing we realize that it is he himself in his inner being who needs to be satisfied, and not something external to himself. Talk of law, honour, justice and the moral order is true only in so far as these are seen as expressions of God's own character. Atonement is a 'necessity' because it 'arises from within God himself'.[19]

[19] Ronald S. Wallace, *Atoning Death*, p. 113.

To be sure, 'self-satisfaction' in fallen human beings is a particularly unpleasant phenomenon, whether it refers to the satisfying of our instincts and passions or to our complacency. Since we are tainted and twisted with selfishness, to say 'I must satisfy myself' lacks self-control, while to say 'I am satisfied with myself' lacks humility. But there is no lack of self-control or humility in God, since he is perfect in all his thoughts and desires. To say that he must 'satisfy himself' means that he must be himself and act according to the perfection of his nature or 'name'. The necessity of 'satisfaction' for God, therefore, is not found in anything outside himself but within himself, in his own immutable character. It is an inherent or intrinsic necessity. The law to which he must conform, which he must satisfy, is the law of his own being. Negatively, he 'cannot disown himself' (2 Tim. 2:13); he cannot contradict himself; he 'never lies' (Tit. 1:2, RSV: *apseudēs*, 'free from all deceit'), for the simple reason that 'it is impossible for God to lie' (Heb. 6:18); he is never arbitrary, unpredictable or capricious; he says 'I will not . . . be false to my faithfulness' (Ps. 89:33, RSV). Positively, he is 'a faithful God who does no wrong' (Dt. 32:4). That is, he is true to himself; he is always invariably himself.

Scripture has several ways of drawing attention to God's self-consistency, and in particular of emphasizing that when he is obliged to judge sinners, he does it because he must, if he is to remain true to himself.

The first example is *the language of provocation*. Yahweh is described (and indeed describes himself) as 'provoked' by Israel's idolatry to anger or jealousy or both. For example, 'they made him jealous with their foreign gods and angered him with their detestable idols'.[20] The exilic prophets, such as Jeremiah and Ezekiel, were constantly employing this vocabulary.[21] They did not mean that Yahweh was irritated or exasperated, or that Israel's behaviour had been so 'provocative' that his patience had run out. No, the language of provocation expresses the inevitable reaction of God's perfect nature to evil. It indicates that there is within God a holy intolerance of idolatry, immorality and injustice. Wherever these occur, they act as stimuli to trigger his response of anger or indignation. He is never provoked without reason. It is evil alone which provokes him, and necessarily so since God must be (and behave like) God. If evil did *not* provoke him to anger he would forfeit our respect, for he would no longer be God.

[20] Dt. 32:16, 21. *Cf.* Jdg. 2:12; 1 Ki. 15:30; 21:22; 2 Ki. 17:17; 22:17; Ps. 78:58.
[21] *E.g.* Je. 32:30–32; Ezk. 8:17; Ho. 12:14.

Secondly, there is *the language of burning*. Under this heading may be mentioned the verbs which depict God's anger as a fire and speak of its 'kindling', 'burning', 'quenching' and 'consuming'. It is true that human beings are also said to 'burn with anger'.[22] But this vocabulary is much more frequently applied in the Old Testament to Yahweh, who 'burns with anger' whenever he sees his people disobeying his law and breaking his covenant.[23] In fact, it is precisely when he is 'provoked' to anger that he is said to 'burn' with it,[24] or his anger is said to 'break out and burn like fire'.[25] In consequence, we read of 'the fire of his anger' or 'the fire of his jealousy'; indeed God himself unites them by referring to 'the fire of my jealous anger'.[26] As with the provocation of Yahweh to anger, so with the fire of his anger, a certain inevitability is implied. In the dry heat of a Palestinian summer fires were easily kindled. It was the same with Yahweh's anger. Never from caprice, however; always only in response to evil. Nor was his anger ever uncontrolled. On the contrary, in the early years of Israel's national life 'time after time he restrained his anger and did not stir up his full wrath'.[27] But when he 'could no longer endure' his people's stubborn rebellion against him, he said: 'The time has come for me to act. I will not hold back; I will not have pity, nor will I relent. You will be judged according to your conduct and your actions, declares the Sovereign LORD.'[28]

If a fire was easy to kindle during the Palestinian dry season, it was equally difficult to put out. So with God's anger. Once righteously aroused, he 'did not turn away from the heat of his fierce anger, which burned against Judah'. Once kindled, it was not readily 'quenched'.[29] Instead, when Yahweh's anger 'burned' against people, it 'consumed' them. That is to say, as fire leads to destruction, so Yahweh's anger leads to judgment. For Yahweh is 'a consuming fire'.[30] The fire of his anger was 'quenched', and so 'subsided' or 'ceased', only when the judgment was complete,[31] or

---

[22] *E.g.* Gn. 39:19; Ex. 32:19; 1 Sa. 11:6; 2 Sa. 12:5; Est. 7:10.

[23] *E.g.* Jos. 7:1; 23:16; Jdg. 3:8; 2 Sa. 24:1; 2 Ki. 13:3; 22:13; Ho. 8:5.

[24] *E.g.* Dt. 29:27–28; 2 Ki. 22:17; Ps. 79:5.

[25] *E.g.* Je. 4:4; 21:12.   [26] *E.g.* Ezk. 36:5–6; 38:19; Zp. 1:18; 3:8.

[27] Ps. 78:38. *Cf.* Is. 48:9; La. 3:22; and in the New Testament Rom. 2:4 and 2 Pet. 3:9.

[28] Je. 44:22; Ezk. 24:13–14; *cf.* Ex. 32:10.

[29] 2 Ki. 23:26; 22:17; 2 Ch. 34:25; Je. 21:12.

[30] Dt. 4:24, quoted in Heb. 12:29. Some examples of the portrayal of God's judgment as a devouring fire are: Nu. 11:1; Dt. 6:15; Ps. 59:13; Is. 10:17; 30:27; La. 2:3; Ezk. 22:31; Zp. 1:18.

[31] *E.g.* Jos. 7:26; Ezk. 5:13; 16:42; 21:17.

when a radical regeneration had taken place, issuing in social justice.[32]

The imagery of fire endorses what is taught by the vocabulary of provocation. There is something in God's essential moral being which is 'provoked' by evil, and which is 'ignited' by it, proceeding to 'burn' until the evil is 'consumed'.

Thirdly, there is *the language of satisfaction itself*. A cluster of words seems to affirm the truth that God must be himself, that what is inside him must come out, and that the demands of his own nature and character must be met by appropriate action on his part. The chief word is *kālah*, which is used particularly by Ezekiel in relation to God's anger. It means 'to be complete, at an end, finished, accomplished, spent'. It occurs in a variety of contexts in the Old Testament, nearly always to indicate the 'end' of something, either because it has been destroyed, or because it has been finished in some other way. Time, work and life all have an end. Tears are exhausted by weeping, water used up and grass dried up in drought, and our physical strength is spent. So through Ezekiel Yahweh warns Judah that he is about to 'accomplish' (AV), 'satisfy' (RSV) or 'spend' (NIV) his anger 'upon' or 'against' them.[33] They have refused to listen to him and have persisted in their idolatry. So now at last 'the time has come, the day is near. . . . I am about to pour out my wrath on you and spend my anger against you' (Ezk. 7:7–8). It is significant that the 'pouring out' and the 'spending' go together, for what is poured out cannot be gathered again, and what is spent is finished. The same two images are coupled in Lamentations 4:11, 'The LORD has given full vent (*kālah*) to his wrath; he has poured out his fierce anger.' Indeed, only when Yahweh's wrath is 'spent' does it 'cease'. The same concept of inner necessity is implied by these verbs. What exists within Yahweh must be expressed; and what is expressed must be completely 'spent' or 'satisfied'.

To sum up, God is 'provoked' to jealous anger over his people by their sins. Once kindled, his anger 'burns' and is not easily quenched. He 'unleashes' it, 'pours' it out, 'spends' it. This three-fold vocabulary vividly portrays God's judgment as arising from within him, out of his holy character, as wholly consonant with it, and therefore as inevitable.

So far the picture has been one-sided, however. Because of the history of Israel's apostasy, the prophets concentrated on Yahweh's anger and consequent judgment. But the reason why this threat of national destruction is so poignant is that it was uttered against

[32] *E.g.* Je. 4:4; 21:12.   [33] Ezk. 5:13; 6:12; 7:8; 13:15; 20:8, 21.

the background of God's love for Israel, his choice of them and his covenant with them. This special relationship with Israel, which God had initiated and sustained, and which he promised to renew, had also arisen out of his character. He had acted 'for the sake of his name'. He had not set his love upon Israel and chosen them because they were more numerous than other peoples, for they were the fewest. No, he had set his love upon them only because he loved them (Dt. 7:7–8). No explanation of his love for them could be given, except his love for them.

So there is a fourth way in which Scripture emphasizes the self-consistency of God, namely by using *the language of the Name*. God always acts 'according to his name'. To be sure, this is not the only criterion of his activity. He also deals with us 'according to our works'. By no means invariably, however. Indeed, if he did, we would be destroyed. So 'he does not treat us as our sins deserve or repay us according to our iniquities'.[34] For he is 'the compassionate and gracious God, slow to anger, abounding in love and faithfulness' (Ex. 34:6). Although he does not always treat us 'according to our works', however, he always does 'according to his name', that is, in a manner consistent with his revealed nature.[35] The contrast is deliberately drawn in Ezekiel 20:44: 'You will know that I am the LORD, when I deal with you for my name's sake and not according to your evil ways and your corrupt practices, O house of Israel, declares the Sovereign LORD.'

Jeremiah 14 expresses with emphatic thoroughness the recognition that Yahweh is and always will be true to his name, that is to himself. The situation was one of devastating drought: the cisterns were empty, the ground cracked, the farmers dismayed and the animals disorientated (vv.1–6). In their extremity Israel cried to God: 'Although our sins testify against us, O LORD, do something for the sake of your name' (v.7). In other words, 'although we cannot appeal to you to act on the ground of who *we* are, we can and do on the ground of who *you* are'. Israel remembered that they were God's chosen people, and begged him to act in a way which would be consistent with his gracious covenant and steadfast character, for, they added, 'we bear your name' (vv. 8–9). In contrast to the pseudo-prophets, who were preaching a lopsided message of peace without judgment (vv. 13–16), Jeremiah prophesied 'sword, famine and plague' (v.12). But he also looked beyond judgment to restoration, convinced that

[34] Ps. 103:10. For God's forbearance, the restraining of his anger and the delaying of his judgment, see also Ne. 9:31; La. 3:22; Rom. 2:4–16; 3:25; 2 Pet. 3:9. Contrast, for example, Ezk. 7:8–9, 27.
[35] E.g. Pss. 23:3; 143:11.

Yahweh would act, he said to him, 'for the sake of your name' (v.21).

The same theme was further developed in Ezekiel 36. There Yahweh promised his people restoration after judgment, but was disconcertingly candid about his reasons. 'It is not for your sake, O house of Israel, that I am going to do these things, but for the sake of my holy name' (v.22). They had profaned it, caused it to be despised and even blasphemed by the nations. But Yahweh would take pity on his great name and once more demonstrate its holiness, its uniqueness, before the world. For then the nations would know that he was the Lord, the Living One (vv.21, 23). When God thus acts 'for the sake of his name', he is not just protecting it from misrepresentation; he is determining to be true to it. His concern is less for his reputation than for his consistency.

In the light of all this biblical material about the divine self-consistency, we can understand why it is impossible for *God* to do what Christ commanded *us* to do. He told us to 'deny ourselves', but 'God cannot deny himself'.[36] Why is that? Why is it that God will not do, indeed cannot do, what he tells us to do? It is because God is God and not man, let alone fallen man. We have to deny or disown everything within us which is false to our true humanity. But there is nothing in God which is incompatible with his true deity, and therefore nothing to deny. It is in order to be our true selves that we have to deny ourselves; it is because God is never other than his true self that he cannot and will not deny himself. He can empty himself of his rightful glory and humble himself to serve. Indeed, it is precisely this that he has done in Christ (Phil. 2:7–8). But he cannot repudiate any part of himself, because he is perfect. He cannot contradict himself. This is his integrity. As for us, we are constantly aware of our human inconsistencies; they usually arouse a comment. 'It's so uncharacteristic of him', we say, or 'you are not yourself today', or 'I've come to expect something better from you'. But can you imagine saying such things to or about God? He is always himself and never inconsistent. If he were ever to behave 'uncharacteristically', in a way that is out of character with himself, he would cease to be God, and the world would be thrown into moral confusion. No, God is God; he never deviates one iota, even one tiny hair's breadth, from being entirely himself.

---

[36] Mk. 8:34; 2 Tim. 2:13, RSV.

The holy love of God

What has this to do with the atonement? Just that the way God chooses to forgive sinners and reconcile them to himself must, first and foremost, be fully consistent with his own character. It is not only that he must overthrow and disarm the devil in order to rescue his captives. It is not even only that he must satisfy his law, his honour, his justice or the moral order: it is that he must satisfy himself. Those other formulations rightly insist that at least one expression of himself must be satisfied, either his law or honour or justice or moral order; the merit of this further formulation is that it insists on the satisfaction of God himself in *every* aspect of his being, including both his justice and his love.

But when we thus distinguish between the attributes of God, and set one over against another, and even refer to a divine 'problem' or 'dilemma' on account of this conflict, are we not in danger of going beyond Scripture? Was P. T. Forsyth correct in writing that 'there is nothing in the Bible about the strife of attributes'?[37] I do not think he was. To be sure, talk about 'strife' or 'conflict' in God is very anthropomorphic language. But then the Bible is not afraid of anthropomorphisms. All parents know the costliness of love, and what it means to be 'torn apart' by conflicting emotions, especially when there is a need to punish the children. Perhaps the boldest of all human models of God in Scripture is the pain of parenthood which is attributed to him in Hosea, chapter 11. He refers to Israel as his 'child', his 'son' (v.1), whom he had taught to walk, taking him in his arms (v.3) and bending down to feed him (v.4). Yet his son proved wayward and did not recognize his Father's tender love. Israel was determined to turn from him in rebellion (vv.5–7). He therefore deserved to be punished. But can his own father bring himself to punish him? So Yahweh soliloquizes:

> How can I give you up, Ephraim?
>   How can I hand you over, Israel?
> How can I treat you like Admah?
>   How can I make you like Zeboiim?
> My heart is changed within me;
>   all my compassion is aroused.
> I will not carry out my fierce anger,
>   nor devastate Ephraim again.
> For I am God, and not man –

[37] P. T. Forsyth, *The Work of Christ*, p. 118.

the Holy One among you.
I will not come in wrath (Ho. 11:8–9).

Here surely is a conflict of emotions, a strife of attributes, within God. The four questions beginning with the words 'how can I . . .?' bear witness to a struggle between what Yahweh *ought* to do because of his righteousness and what he *cannot* do because of his love. And what is the 'change of heart' within him but an inner tension between his 'compassion' and his 'fierce anger'?

The Bible includes a number of other phrases which in different ways express this 'duality' within God. He is 'the compassionate and gracious God. . . . Yet he does not leave the guilty unpunished'; in him 'love and faithfulness meet together; righteousness and peace kiss each other'; he announces himself as 'a righteous God and a Saviour', besides whom there is no other; and in wrath he remembers mercy. John describes the Word made flesh, the Father's one and only Son, as 'full of grace and truth'; and Paul, contemplating God's dealings with both Jews and Gentiles, invites us to consider 'the kindness and sternness of God'. In relation to the cross and to salvation Paul also writes of God demonstrating his justice 'so as to be just and the one who justifies the man who has faith in Jesus', and he finds nothing anomalous about juxtaposing references to God's 'wrath' and God's 'love', while John assures us that, if we confess our sins, God will be 'faithful and just' to forgive us.[38] Here are nine couplets, in each of which two complementary truths about God are brought together, as if to remind us that we must beware of speaking of one aspect of God's character without remembering its counterpart.

Emil Brunner in *The Mediator* did not hesitate to write of God's 'dual nature' as 'the central mystery of the Christian revelation' (p. 519). For 'God is not simply Love. The nature of God cannot be exhaustively stated in one single word' (pp. 281–282). Indeed, modern opposition to forensic language in relation to the cross is mainly 'due to the fact that the idea of the Divine Holiness has been swallowed up in that of the Divine love; this means that the biblical idea of God, in which the decisive element is this twofold nature of holiness and love, is being replaced by the modern, unilateral, monistic idea of God' (p. 467). Yet 'the dualism of holiness and love, . . . of mercy and wrath cannot be dissolved, changed into *one* synthetic conception, without at the same time destroying the seriousness of the biblical know-

[38] Ex. 34:6–7; Ps. 85:10; Is. 45:21; Hab. 3:2; Mi. 7:18; Jn. 1:14; Rom. 11:22; 3:26; Eph. 2:3–4; 1 Jn. 1:9.

ledge of God, the reality and the mystery of revelation and atonement. . . . Here arises the "dialectic" of all genuine Christian theology, which simply aims at expressing in terms of thought the indissoluble nature of this dualism' (p. 519, footnote). So then, the cross of Christ 'is the event in which God makes known his holiness and his love simultaneously, in one event, in an absolute manner' (p. 450). 'The cross is the only place where the loving, forgiving merciful God is revealed in such a way that we perceive that his holiness and his love are equally infinite' (p. 470). In fact, 'the objective aspect of the atonement . . . may be summed up thus: it consists in the combination of inflexible righteousness, with its penalties, and transcendent love' (p. 520).

At the same time, we must never think of this duality within God's being as irreconcilable. For God is not at odds with himself, however much it may appear to us that he is. He is 'the God of peace', of inner tranquillity not turmoil. True, we find it difficult to hold in our minds simultaneously the images of God as the Judge who must punish evil-doers and of the Lover who must find a way to forgive them. Yet he is both, and at the same time. In the words of G. C. Berkouwer, 'in the cross of Christ God's justice and love are *simultaneously* revealed',[39] while Calvin, echoing Augustine, was even bolder. He wrote of God that 'in a marvellous and divine way he loved us even when he hated us'.[40] Indeed, the two are more than simultaneous, they are identical, or at least alternative expressions of the same reality. For 'the wrath of God is the love of God', Brunner wrote in a daring sentence, 'in the form in which the man who has turned away from God and turned against God experiences it'.[41]

One theologian who has struggled with this tension is P. T. Forsyth, who coined – or at least popularized – the expression 'the holy love of God'.

Christianity (he wrote) is concerned with God's holiness before all else, which issues to man as love. . . . This starting-point of the supreme holiness of God's love, rather than its pity, sympathy or affection, is the watershed between the Gospel and . . . theological liberalism. . . . My point of departure is that Christ's first concern and revelation was not simply the forgiving love of God, but the holiness of such love.

[39] G. C. Berkouwer, *Work of Christ*, p. 277.
[40] *Institutes*, II.xvi.4. *Cf.* II.xvii.2.
[41] Emil Brunner, *Man in Revolt*, p. 187.

Again,

> If we spoke less about God's love and more about his holiness, more about his judgment, we should say much more when we did speak of his love.[42]

Yet again,

> Without a holy God there would be no problem of atonement. It is the holiness of God's love that necessitates the atoning cross. . . .[43]

This vision of God's holy love will deliver us from caricatures of him. We must picture him neither as an indulgent God who compromises his holiness in order to spare and spoil us, nor as a harsh, vindictive God who suppresses his love in order to crush and destroy us. How then can God express his holiness without consuming us, and his love without condoning our sins? How can God satisfy his holy love? How can he save *us* and satisfy *himself* simultaneously? We reply at this point only that, in order to satisfy himself, he sacrificed – indeed substituted – himself for us. What that meant will be our concern in the next chapter to understand.

> Beneath the cross of Jesus
> I fain would take my stand –
> The shadow of a mighty rock
> Within a weary land. . . .
>
> O safe and happy shelter!
> O refuge tried and sweet!
> O trysting-place, where heaven's love
> And heaven's justice meet!

---

[42] P. T. Forsyth, *Cruciality of the Cross*, pp. 5–6 and 73.
[43] P. T. Forsyth, *Work of Christ*, p. 80. He also uses the expression 'holy love' in *The Justification of God*, especially pp. 124–131 and 190–195. William Temple picked it up in *Christus Veritas*, especially pp. 257–260.

6

The self-substitution of God

We have located the problem of forgiveness in the gravity of sin and the majesty of God, that is, in the realities of who we are and who he is. How can the holy love of God come to terms with the unholy lovelessness of man? What would happen if they were to come into collision with each other? The problem is not outside God; it is within his own being. Because God never contradicts himself, he must be himself and 'satisfy' himself, acting in absolute consistency with the perfection of his character. 'It is the recognition of this divine necessity, or the failure to recognise it,' wrote James Denney, 'which ultimately divides interpreters of Christianity into evangelical and non-evangelical, those who are true to the New Testament and those who cannot digest it.'[1]

Moreover, as we have seen, this inward necessity does not mean that God must be true to only a part of himself (whether his law or honour or justice), nor that he must express one of his attributes (whether love or holiness) at the expense of another, but rather that he must be completely and invariably himself in the fullness of his moral being. T. J. Crawford stressed this point: 'It is altogether an error ... to suppose that God acts at one time according to one of his attributes, and at another time according to another. He acts in conformity with all of them at all times. . . . As for the divine justice and the divine mercy in particular, the end of his (sc. Christ's) work was not to bring them into harmony, as if they had been at variance with one another, but jointly to manifest and glorify them in the redemption of sinners. It is a case of *combined action*, and not of *counteraction*, on the part of these attributes,

[1] James Denney, *Atonement*, p. 82.

133

that is exhibited on the cross.'[2]

How then could God express simultaneously his holiness in judgment and his love in pardon? Only by providing a divine substitute for the sinner, so that the substitute would receive the judgment and the sinner the pardon. We sinners still of course have to suffer some of the personal, psychological and social consequences of our sins, but the penal consequence, the deserved penalty of alienation from God, has been borne by Another in our place, so that we may be spared it. I have not come across a more careful statement of the substitutionary nature of the atonement than that made by Charles E. B. Cranfield in his commentary on *Romans*. Although it summarizes the conclusion towards which this chapter will argue, it may be helpful to quote it near the beginning, so that we know the direction in which we are heading. The quotation is part of Dr Cranfield's comment on Romans 3:25. He writes:

> God, because in his mercy he willed to forgive sinful men, and, being truly merciful, willed to forgive them righteously, that is, without in any way condoning their sin, purposed to direct against his own very self in the person of his Son the full weight of that righteous wrath which they deserved (p. 217).

The vital questions which must now occupy us are these: who is this 'Substitute'? And how are we to understand and justify the notion of his substituting himself for us? The best way to approach these questions is to consider the Old Testament sacrifices, since these were the God-intended preparation for the sacrifice of Christ.

Sacrifice in the Old Testament

'The interpretation of Christ's death as a sacrifice is imbedded in every important type of the New Testament teaching.'[3] Sacrificial vocabulary and idiom are widespread. Sometimes the reference is unambiguous, as when Paul says Christ 'gave himself up for us as a fragrant offering (*prosphora*) and sacrifice (*thysia*) to God' (Eph. 5:2). At other times the allusion is less direct, simply that Christ 'gave himself' (*e.g.* Gal. 1:4) or 'offered himself' (*e.g.* Heb. 9:14) for us, but the background of thought is still the Old Testament sacrificial system. In particular, the statement that he died 'for sin' or 'for sins' (*e.g.* Rom. 8:3, RSV and 1 Pet. 3:18) self-consciously

---

[2] Thomas J. Crawford, *Doctrine of Holy Scripture*, pp. 453–454.
[3] From the article 'Sacrifice' by W. P. Paterson, p. 343.

borrows the Greek translation of the 'sin offering' (*peri hamartias*). Indeed, the letter to the Hebrews portrays the sacrifice of Jesus Christ as having perfectly fulfilled the Old Testament 'shadows'. For he sacrificed himself (not animals), once and for all (not repeatedly), and thus secured for us not only ceremonial cleansing and restoration to favour in the covenant community but the purification of our consciences and restoration to fellowship with the living God.

What did the Old Testament sacrifices signify, however? And did they have a substitutionary meaning? In order to answer these questions, we must not make the mistake of turning first to anthropological studies. To be sure, priests, altars and sacrifices seem to have been a universal phenomenon in the ancient world, but we have no right to assume *a priori* that Hebrew and pagan sacrifices had an identical meaning. They may well have had a common origin in God's revelation to our earliest ancestors. But it would be more consonant with a recognition of the special status of Scripture to say that the Israelites (despite their backslidings) preserved the substance of God's original purpose, whereas pagan sacrifices were degenerate corruptions of it.

Sacrifices were offered in a wide variety of circumstances in the Old Testament. They were associated, for example, with penitence and with celebration, with national need, covenant renewal, family festivity and personal consecration. This diversity warns us against imposing on them a single or simple significance. Nevertheless, there do seem to have been two basic and complementary notions of sacrifice in God's Old Testament revelation, each being associated with particular offerings. The first expressed the sense human beings have of belonging to God by right, and the second their sense of alienation from God because of their sin and guilt. Characteristic of the first were the 'peace' or 'fellowship' offering which was often associated with thanksgiving (Lv. 7:12), the burnt offering (in which everything was consumed) and the ritual of the three annual harvest festivals (Ex. 23:14–17). Characteristic of the second were the sin offering and the guilt offering, in which the need for atonement was clearly acknowledged. It would be incorrect to distinguish these two kinds of sacrifice as representing respectively man's approach to God (offering gifts, let alone bribes to secure his favour) and God's approach to man (offering forgiveness and reconciliation). For both kinds of sacrifice were essentially recognitions of God's grace and expressions of dependence upon it. It would be better to distinguish them, as B. B. Warfield did, by seeing in the former 'man conceived merely as creature' and in the latter 'the needs of man as sinner'. Or, to elaborate the same distinction, in the first the human being is 'a creature claiming protection', and in the second 'a sinner craving pardon'.[4]

Then God is revealed in the sacrifices on the one hand as the Creator on whom man depends for his physical life, and on the other as simultaneously the Judge who demands and the Saviour who provides atonement for sin. Of these two kinds of sacrifice it was further recognized that the latter is the foundation of the former, in that reconciliation to our Judge is necessary even before worship of our Creator. It is therefore significant that in Hezekiah's purification of the Temple, the sin offering 'to atone for all Israel' was sacrificed before the burnt offering (2 Ch. 29:20–24). Further, it may be that we can discern the two kinds of offering in the sacrifices of Cain and Abel, although both are termed *minha*, a gift offering. The reason why Cain's was rejected, we are told, was that he did not respond in faith like Abel to God's revelation (Heb. 11:4). In contrast to God's revealed will, either he put worship before atonement or he distorted his presentation of the fruits of the soil from a recognition of the Creator's gifts into an offering of his own.

The notion of substitution is that one person takes the place of another, especially in order to bear his pain and so save him from it. Such an action is universally regarded as noble. It is good to spare people pain; it is doubly good to do so at the cost of bearing it oneself. We admire the altruism of Moses in being willing for his name to be blotted out of Yahweh's book if only thereby Israel might be forgiven (Ex. 32:32). We also respect an almost identical wish expressed by Paul (Rom. 9:1–4), and his promise to pay Philemon's debts (Phm. 18–19). Similarly in our own century we cannot fail to be moved by the heroism of Father Maximilian Kolbe, the Polish Franciscan, in the Auschwitz concentration camp. When a number of prisoners were selected for execution, and one of them shouted that he was a married man with children, 'Father Kolbe stepped forward and asked if he could take the condemned man's place. His offer was accepted by the authorities, and he was placed in an underground cell, where he was left to die of starvation'.[5]

So it is not surprising that this commonly understood principle of substitution should have been applied by God himself to the sacrifices. Abraham 'sacrificed . . . as a burnt offering instead of his son' the ram which God had provided (Gn. 22:13). Moses enacted that, in the case of an unsolved murder, the town's elders

---

[4] From the essay 'Christ our Sacrifice' by B. B. Warfield, published in *Biblical Doctrines*, pp. 401–435; especially p. 411.
[5] The story is told by Trevor Beeson in *Discretion and Valour*, p. 139.

should first declare their own innocence and then sacrifice a heifer in place of the unknown murderer (Dt. 21:1–9). Micah evidently understood the substitutionary principle well, for he soliloquized about how he should come before Yahweh, and wondered if he should bring burnt offerings, animals, rivers of oil or even 'my firstborn for my transgression, the fruit of my body for the sin of my soul'. The fact that he gave himself a moral instead of a ritual answer, and especially that he rejected the horrific thought of sacrificing his own child in place of himself, does not mean that he rejected the substitutionary principle which was built into the Old Testament sacrificial system (Mi. 6:6–8).

This elaborate system provided for daily, weekly, monthly, annual and occasional offerings. It also included five main types of offering, which are detailed in the early chapters of Leviticus, namely the burnt, cereal, peace, sin and guilt offerings. Because the cereal offering consisted of grain and oil, rather than flesh and blood, it was atypical and was therefore made in association with one of the others. The remaining four were blood sacrifices and, although there were some differences between them (relating to their proper occasion, and the precise use to which the flesh and blood were put), they all shared the same basic ritual involving worshipper and priest. It was very vivid. The worshipper brought the offering, laid his hand or hands on it and killed it. The priest then applied the blood, burnt some of the flesh, and arranged for the consumption of what was left of it. This was significant symbolism, not meaningless magic. By laying his hand(s) on the animal, the offerer was certainly identifying himself with it and 'solemnly' designating 'the victim as standing for him'.[6] Some scholars go further and see the laying-on of hands as 'a symbolic transferral of the sins of the worshipper to the animal',[7] as was explicitly so in the case of the scapegoat, to be considered later. In either case, having taken his place, the substitute animal was killed in recognition that the penalty for sin was death, its blood (symbolizing that the death had been accomplished) was sprinkled, and the offerer's life was spared.

The clearest statement that the blood sacrifices of the Old Testament ritual had a substitutionary significance, however, and that this was why the shedding and sprinkling of blood was indispensable to atonement, is to be found in this statement by God

[6] F. D. Kidner, *Sacrifice in the Old Testament*, p. 14. See also the article 'Sacrifice and Offering' by R. J. Thompson and R. T. Beckwith, and the additional note on 'Old Testament sacrifice' by G. J. Wenham in his *Commentary on Numbers*, pp. 202–205.

[7] Leon Morris, *Atonement*, p. 47.

explaining why the eating of blood was prohibited:

> For the life of a creature is in the blood, and I have given it to you to make atonement for yourselves on the altar; it is the blood that makes atonement for one's life (Lv. 17:11).

Three important affirmations about blood are made in this text. First, blood is the symbol of life. This understanding that 'blood is life' seems to be very ancient. It goes back at least to Noah, whom God forbade to eat meat which had its 'lifeblood' still in it (Gn. 9:4), and was later repeated in the formula 'the blood is the life' (Dt. 12:23). The emphasis, however, was not on blood flowing in the veins, the symbol of life being lived, but on blood shed, the symbol of life ended, usually by violent means.

Secondly, blood makes atonement, and the reason for its atoning significance is given in the repetition of the word 'life'. It is only because 'the life of a creature is in the blood' that 'it is the blood that makes atonement for one's life'. One life is forfeit; another life is sacrificed instead. What makes atonement 'on the altar' is the shedding of substitutionary lifeblood. T. J. Crawford expressed it well: 'The text, then, according to its plain and obvious import, teaches the *vicarious* nature of the rite of sacrifice. *Life was given for life*, the life of the victim for the life of the offerer', indeed 'the life of the innocent victim for the life of the sinful offerer'.[8]

Thirdly, blood was given by God for this atoning purpose. 'I have given it to you', he says, 'to make atonement for yourselves on the altar.' So we are to think of the sacrificial system as God-given, not man-made, and of the individual sacrifices not as a human device to placate God but as a means of atonement provided by God himself.

This Old Testament background helps us to understand two crucial texts in the letter to the Hebrews. The first is that 'without the shedding of blood there is no forgiveness' (9:22), and the second that 'it is impossible for the blood of bulls and goats to take away sins' (10:4). No forgiveness without blood meant no atonement without substitution. There had to be life for life or blood for blood. But the Old Testament blood sacrifices were only shadows; the substance was Christ. For a substitute to be effective, it must be an appropriate equivalent. Animal sacrifices could not atone for human beings, because a human being is 'much more valuable . . . than a sheep', as Jesus himself said (Mt. 12:12). Only 'the precious blood of Christ' was valuable enough (1 Pet. 1:19).

[8] T. J. Crawford, *Doctrine of Holy Scripture*, pp. 237, 241.

The Passover and 'sin-bearing'

We turn now from the principle of substitution, as it is seen in what the Old Testament says about blood sacrifices in general, to two particular examples of it, namely the Passover and the concept of 'sin-bearing'.

It is right for two reasons to start with the Passover. The first is that the original Passover marked the beginning of Israel's national life. 'This month is to be for you the first month,' God had said to them, 'the first month of your year' (Ex. 12:2). It was to inaugurate their annual calendar because in it God redeemed them from their long and oppressive Egyptian bondage, and because the exodus led to the renewal of God's covenant with them at Mount Sinai. But before the exodus and the covenant came the Passover. That day they were to 'commemorate for the generations to come'; they were to 'celebrate it as a festival to the LORD – a lasting ordinance' (12:14, 17).

The second reason for beginning here is that the New Testament clearly identifies the death of Christ as the fulfilment of the Passover, and the emergence of his new and redeemed community as the new exodus. It is not only that John the Baptist hailed Jesus as 'the Lamb of God, who takes away the sin of the world' (Jn. 1:29, 36),[9] nor only that according to John's chronology of the end Jesus was hanging on the cross at the precise time when the Passover lambs were being slaughtered,[10] nor even that in the book of Revelation he is worshipped as the slain Lamb who by his blood has purchased men for God.[11] It is specially that Paul categorically declares: 'Christ, our Passover lamb, has been sacrificed. Therefore let us keep the Festival . . .' (1 Cor. 5:7–8).

What then happened at the first Passover? And what does this tell us about Christ, our Passover lamb?

The Passover story (Ex. 11 – 13) is a self-disclosure of the God of Israel in three roles. First, Yahweh revealed himself as the Judge. The background was the threat of the final plague. Moses was to warn Pharaoh in the most solemn terms that at midnight Yahweh

[9] Scholarly debate continues as to whether John the Baptist's 'Lamb of God' was a reference to the Passover lamb, the *tamid* (the lamb of the daily sacrifice), the binding of Isaac (Gn. 22), the horned lamb of Jewish apocalyptic, or the suffering servant of Isaiah 53. For a competent summary of the arguments, in the light of the Fourth Evangelist's use of the Old Testament, see George L. Carey's lecture 'Lamb of God', pp. 97–122.

[10] *E.g.* Jn. 13:1; 18:28; 19:14, 31.

[11] Rev. 5:6, 9, 12; 12:11. Jesus is identified as 'the Lamb' twenty-eight times in the book of Revelation.

himself was going to pass through Egypt and strike down every firstborn. There would be no discrimination either between human beings and animals, or between different social classes. Every firstborn male would die. There would be only one way of escape, by God's own devising and provision.

Secondly, Yahweh revealed himself as the Redeemer. On the tenth day of the month each Israelite household was to choose a lamb (a year-old male without defect), and on the fourteenth evening to kill it. They were then to take some of the lamb's blood, dip a branch of hyssop in it and sprinkle it on the lintel and side-posts of their front door. They were not to go out of their house at all that night. Having shed and sprinkled the blood, they must shelter under it. For Yahweh, who had already announced his intention to 'pass through' Egypt in judgment, now added his promise to 'pass over' every blood-marked house in order to shield it from his threatened destruction.

Thirdly, Yahweh revealed himself as Israel's covenant God. He had redeemed them to make them his own people. So when he had saved them from his own judgment, they were to commemorate and celebrate his goodness. On Passover night itself they were to feast on the roasted lamb, with bitter herbs and unleavened bread, and they were to do so with their cloak tucked into their belt, their sandals on their feet and their staff in their hand, ready at any moment for their rescue. Some features of the meal spoke to them of their former oppression (*e.g.* the bitter herbs), and others of their future liberation (*e.g.* their dress). Then on each anniversary the festival was to last seven days, and they were to explain to their children what the whole ceremony meant: 'It is the Passover sacrifice to the LORD, who passed over the houses of the Israelites in Egypt and spared our homes when he struck down the Egyptians.' In addition to the celebration in which the whole family would share, there was to be a special ritual for the firstborn males. It was they who had been personally rescued from death by the death of the Passover lambs. Thus redeemed, they belonged in a special way to Yahweh who had purchased them by blood, and they were therefore to be consecrated to his service.

The message must have been absolutely clear to the Israelites; it is equally clear to us who see the fulfilment of the Passover in the sacrifice of Christ. First, the Judge and the Saviour are the same person. It was the God who 'passed through' Egypt to judge the firstborn, who 'passed over' Israelite homes to protect them. We must never characterize the Father as Judge and the Son as Saviour. It is one and the same God who through Christ saves us from himself. Secondly, salvation was (and is) by substitution. The only firstborn males who were spared were those in whose families a firstborn lamb had died instead. Thirdly, the lamb's blood had to be sprinkled after it had been shed. There had to be an individual appropriation of the divine provision. God had to 'see the blood' before he would save the family. Fourthly, each family rescued by God was thereby purchased for God. Their whole life now belonged to him. So does ours. And consecration leads to celebration. The life of the redeemed is a feast, ritually expressed in the Eucharist, the Christian festival of thanksgiving, as we shall consider more fully in chapter 10.

The second major illustration of the principle of substitution is the notion of 'sin-bearing'. In the New Testament we read of Christ that 'he himself bore our sins in his body on the tree' (1 Pet. 2:24) and similarly that he 'was once offered to bear the sins of many' (Heb. 9:28, AV). But what does it mean to 'bear sin'? Must it be understood in terms of the bearing of sin's penalty, or can it be interpreted in other ways? And is 'substitution' necessarily involved in 'sin-bearing'? If so, what kind of substitution is in mind? Can it refer only to the innocent, God-provided substitute taking the place of the guilty party and enduring the penalty instead of him? Or are there alternative kinds of substitution?

During the last one hundred years a number of ingenious attempts have been made to retain the vocabulary of 'substitution', while rejecting 'penal substitution' ('penal' being derived from *poena*, a penalty or punishment). Their origin can be traced back to Abelard's protest against Anselm in the twelfth century, and even more to Socinus' scornful rejection of the Reformers' doctrine in the sixteenth. In his book *De Jesu Christo Servatore* (1578) Faustus Socinus denied not only the deity of Jesus but any idea of 'satisfaction' in his death. The notion that guilt can be transferred from one person to another,[12] he declaimed, was incompatible with both reason and justice. It was not only impossible, but unnecessary. For God is perfectly capable of forgiving sinners without it. He leads them to repentance, and so makes them forgivable.

John McLeod Campbell's *The Nature of the Atonement* (1856) stands in the same general tradition. Christ came to do God's will, he wrote, and in particular to bear men's sins. Not in the traditional

---

[12] Calvin had written: 'This is our acquittal: the guilt that held us liable for punishment has been transferred to the head of the Son of God (Is. 53:12). We must, above all, remember this substitution, lest we tremble and remain anxious throughout life', that is, in fear of God's judgment (*Institutes*, II.xvi.5).

sense, however, but in two others. First, in dealing with men on behalf of God, Christ's sufferings were not 'penal sufferings endured in meeting a demand of divine justice', but 'the sufferings of divine love suffering from our sins according to its own nature' (pp. 115–116). Secondly, in dealing with God on behalf of men, the 'satisfaction' due to divine justice took the form of 'a perfect confession of our sins'. In this way Christ acknowledged the justice of God's wrath against sin, 'and in that perfect response he absorbs it' (pp. 117–118). He was so much one with God as to be 'filled with the sense of the Father's righteous condemnation of our sin', and so much one with us as to 'respond with a perfect Amen to that condemnation' (p. 127). In this way 'sin-bearing' has dissolved into sympathy, 'satisfaction' into sorrow for sin, and 'substitution' into vicarious penitence, instead of vicarious punishment.

Ten years later *The Vicarious Sacrifice* was published, by Horace Bushnell, the American Congregationalist.[13] Like McLeod Campbell he rejected 'penal' substitution. Yet the death of Jesus was 'vicarious' or 'substitutionary' in the sense that he bore our pain rather than our penalty. For 'love is itself an essentially vicarious principle' (p. 11). Consequently, God's love entered through the incarnation and public ministry of Jesus (not only his death) into our sorrows and sufferings, and 'bore' them in the sense of identifying with them and feeling burdened by them. 'There is a cross in God before the wood is seen upon Calvary' (p. 35). This loving sacrifice of God in Christ – expressed in his birth, life and death – is 'the power of God unto salvation' because of its inspiring influence upon us. Christ is now able 'to bring us out of our sins . . . and so out of their penalties' (p. 7). It is thus that the Lamb of God takes away our sins. 'Atonement . . . is a change wrought in us, a change by which we are reconciled to God' (p. 450). But the 'subjective atoning' (*i.e.* the change in us) comes first, and only then 'God is objectively propitiated' (p. 448).

R. C. Moberly developed similar ideas in his *Atonement and Personality* (1901). He rejected all forensic categories in relation to the cross, and in particular any idea of retributive punishment. He taught that penitence (worked in us by the Spirit of the Crucified One) makes us first 'forgivable' and then holy. Christ may be said to take our place only in terms of vicarious penitence, not of

[13] Horace Bushnell somewhat modified his views in his later publication, *Forgiveness and Law*. While still repudiating the traditional doctrine, he nevertheless affirmed that there was in the cross an objective propitiation of God, and that he was 'incarnated into the curse', in order to rescue us from it. He added, however, that Christ consciously suffered the curse or shame of our sin throughout his life.

vicarious penalty.

The attempt by these theologians to retain the language of substitution and sin-bearing, while changing its meaning, must be pronounced a failure. It creates more confusion than clarity. It conceals from the unwary that there is a fundamental difference between 'penitent substitution' (in which the substitute offers what we could not offer) and 'penal substitution' (in which he bears what we could not bear). Here is Dr J. I. Packer's definition of the latter. It is the notion

> that Jesus Christ our Lord, moved by a love that was determined to do everything necessary to save us, endured and exhausted the destructive divine judgment for which we were otherwise inescapably destined, and so won us forgiveness, adoption and glory. To affirm penal substitution is to say that believers are in debt to Christ specifically for this, and that this is the mainspring of all their joy, peace and praise both now and for eternity.[14]

The essential question, however, concerns how the biblical authors themselves employ 'sin-bearing' language.

It is clear from Old Testament usage that to 'bear sin' means neither to sympathize with sinners, nor to identify with their pain, nor to express their penitence, nor to be persecuted on account of human sinfulness (as others have argued), nor even to suffer the consequences of sin in personal or social terms, but specifically to endure its penal consequences, to undergo its penalty. The expression comes most frequently in the books of Leviticus and Numbers. It is written of those who sin by breaking God's laws that they 'will bear their iniquity (or sin)' (AV and RSV). That is, they 'will be held responsible' or 'will suffer for their sins' (NIV). Sometimes the matter is put beyond question by the fact that the penalty is specified: the offender is to be 'cut off from his people' (*i.e.* excommunicated) and even, for example in the case of blasphemy, put to death.[15]

It is in this context of sin-bearing that the possibility is envisaged of somebody else bearing the penalty of the sinner's wrongdoing. For example, Moses told the Israelites that their children would have to wander in the desert, 'suffering for your unfaithfulness' (Nu. 14:34); if a married man failed to nullify a foolish vow or pledge made by his wife, then (it was written) 'he is responsible for her guilt' (Nu. 30:15, NIV) or more simply 'he shall bear her

---

[14] J. I. Packer, 'What Did the Cross Achieve?', p. 25.
[15] Some examples of 'sin-bearing' expressions are Ex. 28:43; Lv. 5:17; 19:8; 22:9; 24:15 and Nu. 9:13; 14:34 and 18:22.

iniquity' (RSV); again, after the destruction of Jerusalem in 586 BC the remnant who stayed in the otherwise deserted ruins said: 'Our fathers sinned and are no more, and we bear their punishment' (La. 5:7).

These are examples of involuntary vicarious sin-bearing. In each case innocent people found themselves suffering the consequences of others' guilt. The same phraseology was used, however, when the vicarious sin-bearing was intended. Then the notion of deliberate substitution was introduced, and God himself was said to provide the substitute, as when he instructed Ezekiel to lie down, and in dramatic symbolism to 'bear the sin of the house of Israel' (Ezk. 4:4–5). The sin offering was also referred to in terms of sin-bearing. Moses said of it to the sons of Aaron: 'it was given to you to take away the guilt of the community by making atonement for them before the LORD' (Lv. 10:17). Clearer still was the ritual of the annual Day of Atonement. The high priest was to 'take two male goats for a sin offering' in order to atone for the sins of the Israelite community as a whole (Lv. 16:5). One goat was to be sacrificed and its blood sprinkled in the usual way, while on the living goat's head the high priest was to lay both his hands, 'and confess over it all the wickedness and rebellion of the Israelites – all their sins – and put them on the goat's head' (v. 21). He was then to drive the goat away into the desert, and it would 'carry on itself all their sins to a solitary place' (v. 22). Some commentators make the mistake of driving a wedge between the two goats, the sacrificed goat and the scapegoat, overlooking the fact that the two together are described as 'a sin offering' in the singular (v. 5). Perhaps T. J. Crawford was right to suggest that each embodied a different aspect of the same sacrifice, 'the one exhibiting the means, and the other the results, of the atonement'.[16] In this case the public proclamation of the Day of Atonement was plain, namely that reconciliation was possible only through substitutionary sin-bearing. The author of the letter to the Hebrews has no inhibitions about seeing Jesus both as 'a merciful and faithful high priest' (2:17) and as the two victims, the sacrificed goat whose blood was taken into the inner sanctuary (9:7, 12) and the scapegoat which carried away the people's sins (9:28).

Although the sin offering and the scapegoat both in their different ways had a sin-bearing role, at least the more spiritually minded Israelites must have realized that an animal cannot be a satisfactory substitute for a human being. So, in the famous 'servant songs' in

[16] T. J. Crawford, *Doctrine of Holy Scripture*, p. 225. See also chapter 3, 'The Day of Atonement' in Leon Morris' *Atonement*, pp. 68–87.

the second part of Isaiah, the prophet began to delineate one whose mission would embrace the nations, and who, in order to fulfil it, would need to suffer, to bear sin and to die. Matthew applies to Jesus the first song about the quietness and gentleness of the servant in his ministry,[17] and Peter in his early speeches is recorded four times as calling Jesus God's 'servant' or 'holy servant'.[18]

But it is particularly the fifty-third chapter of Isaiah, describing the servant's suffering and death, which is applied consistently to Jesus Christ. 'No other passage from the Old Testament', Joachim Jeremias has written, 'was as important to the Church as Isaiah 53.'[19] The New Testament writers quote eight specific verses as having been fulfilled in Jesus. Verse 1 ('who has believed our message?') is applied to Jesus by John (12:38). Matthew sees the statement of verse 4 ('he took up our infirmities and carried our diseases') as fulfilled in Jesus' healing ministry (8:17). That we have gone astray like sheep (v. 6), but that by his wounds we have been healed (v. 5) are both echoed by Peter (1 Pet. 2:22–25), and so in the same passage are verse 9 ('nor was any deceit in his mouth') and verse 11 ('he will bear their iniquities'). Then verses 7 and 8, about Jesus being led like a sheep to the slaughter and being deprived of justice and of life, were the verses the Ethiopian eunuch was reading in his chariot, which prompted Philip to share with him 'the good news about Jesus' (Acts 8:30–35). Thus verses 1, 4, 5, 6, 7, 8, 9 and 11 – eight verses out of the chapter's twelve – are all quite specifically referred to Jesus.

Careful students of the Gospels have detected numerous references by Jesus himself, sometimes only in a single word, to Isaiah 53. For example, he said he would be 'rejected',[20] 'taken away'[21] and 'numbered with the transgressors'.[22] He would also be 'buried' like a criminal without any preparatory anointing, so that (he explained) Mary of Bethany gave him an advance anointing, 'to prepare for my burial'.[23] Other allusions may well be his description of the stronger man who 'divides up the spoils',[24] his deliberate silence before his judges,[25] his intercession for the transgressors[26] and his laying down his life for others.[27] If these be accepted, then

[17] Is. 42:1–4; *cf*. Mt. 12:17–21. [18] Acts 3:13, 26; 4:27, 30.
[19] J. Jeremias, *Eucharistic Words*, p. 228. See also his *Servant of God* and the article on *pais theou* ('servant of God') by Jeremias and Zimmerli, pp. 712 ff. Compare chapter 3, 'Jesus the Suffering Servant of God', in Oscar Cullmann's *Christology of the New Testament*.
[20] Mk. 9:12; *cf*. Is. 53:3. [21] Mk. 2:20; *cf*. Is. 53:8.
[22] Lk. 22:37; *cf*. Is. 53:12. [23] Mk. 14:8; *cf*. Is. 53:9.
[24] Lk. 11:22; *cf*. Is. 53:12.
[25] Mk. 14:61; 15:5; Lk. 23:9 and Jn. 19:9; *cf*. Is. 53:7.
[26] Lk. 23:34; *cf*. Is. 53:12. [27] Jn. 10:11, 15, 17; *cf*. Is. 53:10.

every verse of the chapter except verse 2 ('he had no beauty or majesty to attract us to him') is applied to Jesus in the New Testament, some verses several times. Indeed, there is good evidence that his whole public career, from his baptism through his ministry, sufferings and death to his resurrection and ascension, is seen as a fulfilment of the pattern foretold in Isaiah 53. Oscar Cullmann has argued that at his baptism he deliberately made himself one with those whose sins he had come to bear, that his resolve to 'fulfil all righteousness' (Mt. 3:15) was a determination to be God's 'righteous servant', who by his sin-bearing death would 'justify many' (Is. 53:11), and that the Father's voice from heaven, declaring himself 'well pleased' with his Son, also identified him as the servant (Is. 42:1).[28] Similarly, Vincent Taylor pointed out that already in the very first apostolic sermon in Acts 2 'the dominating conception is that of the Servant, humiliated in death and exalted . . .'.[29] More recently, Professor Martin Hengel of Tübingen has reached the same conclusion, arguing that this use of Isaiah 53 must go back to the mind of Jesus himself.[30]

So far my purpose in relation to Isaiah 53 has been to show how foundational the chapter is to the New Testament's understanding of Jesus. I have left to the last his two most important sayings, which focus on the sin-bearing nature of his death. The first is the 'ransom saying': 'for even the Son of Man did not come to be served, but to serve, and to give his life as a ransom for many' (Mk. 10:45). Here Jesus unites the divergent 'Son of man' and 'Servant' prophecies. The Son of Man would 'come with the clouds of heaven' and all peoples would 'serve him' (Dn. 7:13–14), whereas the Servant would not be served but serve, and complete his service by suffering, specially by laying down his life as a ransom instead of many. It was only by serving that he would be served, only by suffering that he would enter into his glory. The second text belongs to the institution of the Lord's Supper, when Jesus declared that his blood would be 'poured out for many',[31] an echo of Isaiah 53:12, 'he poured out his life unto death'.[32] Moreover both texts say that he would either give his life or pour

[28] Oscar Cullmann, *Baptism in the New Testament*, p. 18.
[29] Vincent Taylor, *Atonement*, p. 18.
[30] Martin Hengel, *Atonement*, pp. 33–75.
[31] Mk. 14:24; *cf.* Mt. 26:28.
[32] In his thorough study, *Atonement*, Professor Martin Hengel argues convincingly that behind Paul's statements that Christ 'died for our sins' (1 Cor. 15:3) and 'was given up for our sins' (Rom. 4:25) there lie the 'ransom-saying' and 'supper-sayings' of Jesus, recorded by Mark (10:45; 14:22–25); and that behind these there lies Isaiah 53 and Jesus' own understanding of it (pp. 33–75).

out his blood 'for many', which again echoes Isaiah 53:12, 'he bore the sin of many'. Some have been embarrassed by the apparently restrictive nature of this expression. But Jeremias has argued that, according to the pre-Christian Jewish interpretation of it, 'the many' were 'the godless among both the Jews and the Gentiles'. The expression therefore is 'not exclusive ("many, but not all") but, in the Semitic manner of speech, inclusive ("the totality, consisting of many")', which was 'a (Messianic) concept unheard of in contemporary rabbinical thought'.[33]

It seems to be definite beyond doubt, then, that Jesus applied Isaiah 53 to himself and that he understood his death in the light of it as a sin-bearing death. As God's 'righteous servant' he would be able to 'justify many', because he was going to 'bear the sin of many'. This is the thrust of the whole chapter, not just that he would be despised and rejected, oppressed and afflicted, led like a lamb to the slaughter and cut off from the land of the living, but in particular that he would be pierced for our transgressions, that the Lord would lay on him the iniquity of us all, that he would thus be numbered with the transgressors, and that he would himself bear their iniquities. 'The song makes twelve distinct and explicit statements', wrote J. S. Whale, 'that the servant suffers the *penalty* of other men's sins: not only vicarious suffering but penal substitution is the plain meaning of its fourth, fifth and sixth verses.'[34]

In the light of this evidence about the sin-bearing nature of Jesus' death, we now know how to interpret the simple assertion that 'he died for us'. The preposition 'for' can translate either *hyper* ('on behalf of') or *anti* ('instead of'). Most of the references have *hyper*. For example, 'while we were still sinners, Christ died for us' (Rom. 5:8), and again 'one died for all' (2 Cor. 5:14). *Anti* comes only in the ransom verses, namely in Mark 10:45 (literally 'to give his life as a ransom instead of many') and in 1 Timothy 2:6 ('who gave himself as a ransom for all men', where 'for' is again *hyper*, but the preposition *anti* is in the noun, *antilytron*).

The two prepositions do not always adhere to their dictionary definitions, however. Even the broader word *hyper* ('on behalf of') is many times shown by its context to be used in the sense of *anti* ('instead of'), as, for example, when we are said to be 'ambassadors for Christ' (2 Cor. 5:20), or when Paul wanted to keep Onesimus in Rome to serve him 'on behalf of' his master Philemon, that is,

---

[33] Joachim Jeremias, *Eucharistic Words*, pp. 228–229. Elsewhere Jeremias interprets Jesus' two sayings as referring to 'a vicarious dying for the countless multitude . . . of those who lay under the judgment of God'. See also his *Central Message*, pp. 45–46.

[34] J. S. Whale, *Victor and Victim*, pp. 69–70.

in his place (Phm. 13). The same is clear in the two most outspoken statements of the meaning of Christ's death in Paul's letters. One is that 'God made him who had no sin to be sin for us' (2 Cor. 5:21), and the other that Christ has 'redeemed us from the curse of the law by becoming a curse for us' (Gal. 3:13). Some commentators have found these assertions difficult to accept. Karl Barth called the first 'almost unbearably severe'[35] and A. W. F. Blunt described the language of the second as 'almost shocking'.[36] It will be observed that in both cases what happened to Christ on the cross ('made sin', 'becoming a curse') is said by Paul to have been intended 'for us', on our behalf or for our benefit. But what exactly did happen? The sinless one was 'made sin for us', which must mean that he bore the penalty of our sin instead of us, and he redeemed us from the law's curse by 'becoming a curse for us', which must mean that the curse of the law lying upon us for our disobedience was transferred to him, so that he bore it instead of us.

Both verses go beyond these negative truths (that he bore our sin and curse to redeem us from them) to a positive counterpart. On the one hand he bore the curse in order that we might inherit the blessing promised to Abraham (Gal. 3:14), and on the other, God made the sinless Christ to be sin for us, in order that 'in him we might become the righteousness of God' (2 Cor. 5:21). Both verses thus indicate that when we are united to Christ a mysterious exchange takes place: he took our curse, so that we may receive his blessing; he became sin with our sin, so that we may become righteous with his righteousness. Elsewhere Paul writes of this transfer in terms of 'imputation'. On the one hand, God declined to 'impute' our sins to us, or 'count' them against us (2 Cor. 5:19), with the implication that he imputed them to Christ instead. On the other, God has imputed Christ's righteousness to us.[37] Many are offended by this concept, considering it both artificial and unjust on God's part to arrange such a transfer. Yet the objection is due to a misunderstanding, which Thomas Crawford clears up for us. Imputation, he writes, 'does not at all imply the transference of one person's moral qualities to another'. Such a thing would be impossible, and he goes on to quote John Owen to the effect that 'we ourselves have done nothing of what is imputed to us, nor Christ anything of what is imputed to him'. It would be absurd

[35] Karl Barth, *Church Dogmatics*, vol. IV, 'The Doctrine of Reconciliation', p. 165.
[36] A. W. F. Blunt, *Galatians*, p. 96. See the last chapter for a fuller quotation.
[37] Rom. 4:6; 1 Cor. 1:30; Phil. 3:9.

and unbelievable to imagine, Crawford continues, 'that the moral turpitude of our sins was transferred to Christ, so as to make him personally sinful and ill-deserving; and that the moral excellence of his righteousness is transferred to us, so as to make us personally upright and commendable'. No, what was transferred to Christ was not moral qualities but legal consequences: he voluntarily accepted liability for our sins. That is what the expressions 'made sin' and 'made a curse' mean. Similarly, 'the righteousness of God' which we become when we are 'in Christ' is not here righteousness of character and conduct (although that grows within us by the working of the Holy Spirit), but rather a righteous standing before God.[38]

When we review all this Old Testament material (the shedding and sprinkling of blood, the sin offering, the Passover, the meaning of 'sin-bearing', the scapegoat and Isaiah 53), and consider its New Testament application to the death of Christ, we are obliged to conclude that the cross was a substitutionary sacrifice. Christ died for us. Christ died instead of us. Indeed, as Jeremias put it, this use of sacrificial imagery 'has the intention of expressing the fact that Jesus died without sin in substitution for our sins'.[39]

Who is the substitute?

The key question we now have to address is this: exactly who was our substitute? Who took our place, bore our sin, became our curse, endured our penalty, died our death? To be sure, 'while we were still sinners, Christ died for us' (Rom. 5:8). That would be the simple, surface answer. But who was this Christ? How are we to think of him?

Was he just a man? If so, how could one human being possibly – or justly – stand in for other human beings? Was he then simply God, seeming to be a man, but not actually being the man he seemed? If so, how could he represent humankind? Besides this, how could he have died? In that case, are we to think of Christ neither as man alone, nor as God alone, but rather as the one and only God-man who because of his uniquely constituted person was uniquely qualified to mediate between God and man? Whether the concept of substitutionary atonement is rational, moral, plausible, acceptable, and above all biblical, depends on our answers to these questions. The possibility of substitution rests on the identity of the substitute. We need therefore to examine in greater depth the

[38] See T. J. Crawford, *Doctrine of Holy Scripture*, pp. 444–445.
[39] Joachim Jeremias, *Central Message*, p. 36.

three explanations which I have sketched above.

The first proposal is that the substitute was *the man Christ Jesus*, viewed as a human being, and conceived as an individual separate from both God and us, an independent third party. Those who begin with this *a priori* lay themselves open to gravely distorted understandings of the atonement and so bring the truth of substitution into disrepute. They tend to present the cross in one or other of two ways, according to whether the initiative was Christ's or God's. In the one case Christ is pictured as intervening in order to pacify an angry God and wrest from him a grudging salvation. In the other, the intervention is ascribed to God, who proceeds to punish the innocent Jesus in place of us the guilty sinners who had deserved the punishment. In both cases God and Christ are sundered from one another: either Christ persuades God or God punishes Christ. What is characteristic of both presentations is that they denigrate the Father. Reluctant to suffer himself, he victimizes Christ instead. Reluctant to forgive, he is prevailed upon by Christ to do so. He is seen as a pitiless ogre whose wrath has to be assuaged, whose disinclination to act has to be overcome, by the loving self-sacrifice of Jesus.

Such crude interpretations of the cross still emerge in some of our evangelical illustrations, as when we describe Christ as coming to rescue us from the judgment of God, or when we portray him as the whipping-boy who is punished instead of the real culprit, or as the lightning conductor to which the lethal electric charge is deflected. Even some of our time-honoured hymns express this view:

> Jehovah lifted up his rod;
> O Christ, it fell on thee!
> Thou wast sore stricken of thy God;
> There's not one stroke for me.

There is, of course, some justification in Scripture for both kinds of formulation, or they would never have been developed by Christians whose desire and claim are to be biblical.

Thus, Jesus Christ is said to be the 'propitiation' for our sins and our 'advocate' with the Father (1 Jn. 2:2, AV), which at first sight suggests that he died to placate God's anger and is now pleading with him in order to persuade him to forgive us. But other parts of Scripture forbid us to interpret the language of propitiation and advocacy in that way, as we shall see in the next chapter. The whole notion of a compassionate Christ inducing a reluctant God to take action on our behalf founders on the fact of God's love.

There was no *Umstimmung* in God, no change of mind or heart secured by Christ. On the contrary, the saving initiative originated in him. It was 'because of the tender mercy of our God' (Lk. 1:78) that Christ came, 'because of his great love for us',[40] because of 'the grace of God that brings salvation' (Tit. 2:11).

As for the other formulation (that God punished Jesus for our sins), it is true that the sins of Israel were transferred to the scapegoat, that 'the Lord laid on him', his suffering servant, all our iniquity (Is. 53:6), that 'it was the Lord's will to crush him' (Is. 53:10), and that Jesus applied to himself Zechariah's prophecy that God would 'strike the shepherd'.[41] It is also true that in the New Testament God is said to have 'sent' his Son to atone for our sins (1 Jn. 4:9–10), 'delivered him up' for us,[42] 'presented him as a sacrifice of atonement' (Rom. 3:25), 'condemned sin' in his flesh (Rom. 8:3), and 'made him . . . to be sin for us' (2 Cor. 5:21). These are striking statements. But we have no liberty to interpret them in such a way as to imply either that God compelled Jesus to do what he was unwilling to do himself, or that Jesus was an unwilling victim of God's harsh justice. Jesus Christ did indeed bear the penalty of our sins, but God was active in and through Christ doing it, and Christ was freely playing his part (*e.g.* Heb. 10:5–10).

We must not, then, speak of God punishing Jesus or of Jesus persuading God, for to do so is to set them over against each other as if they acted independently of each other or were even in conflict with each other. We must never make Christ the object of God's punishment or God the object of Christ's persuasion, for both God and Christ were subjects not objects, taking the initiative together to save sinners. Whatever happened on the cross in terms of 'God-forsakenness' was voluntarily accepted by both in the same holy love which made atonement necessary. It was 'God in our nature forsaken of God'.[43] If the Father 'gave the Son', the Son 'gave himself'. If the Gethsemane 'cup' symbolized the wrath of God, it was nevertheless 'given' by the Father (Jn. 18:11) and voluntarily 'taken' by the Son. If the Father 'sent' the Son, the Son 'came' himself. The Father did not lay on the Son an ordeal he was reluctant to bear, nor did the Son extract from the Father a salvation he was reluctant to bestow. There is no suspicion anywhere in the New Testament of discord between the Father and the Son, 'whether by the Son wresting forgiveness from an unwilling Father or by the Father demanding a sacrifice from an

---

40 Eph. 2:4; *cf.* Jn. 3:16; 1 Jn. 4:9–10.
41 Zc. 13:7; Mk. 14:27. 42 Acts 2:23; Rom. 8:32.
43 John Murray, *Redemption Accomplished*, p. 77.

unwilling Son'.[44] There was no unwillingness in either. On the contrary, their wills coincided in the perfect self-sacrifice of love.

If then our substitute was not Christ alone as a third party independent of God, is the truth that *God alone* took our place, bore our sin and died our death? If we may not so exalt the initiative of Christ as virtually to eliminate the contribution of the Father, may we reverse their roles, ascribing the whole initiative and achievement to the Father, thus virtually eliminating Christ? For if God has himself done everything necessary for our salvation, does that not make Christ redundant?

This proposed solution to the problem is at first sight attractive theologically, for it avoids all the distortions which arise when Jesus is conceived as a third party. As we saw in the last chapter, it is God who must satisfy himself as holy love. He was unwilling to act in love at the expense of his holiness or in holiness at the expense of his love. So we may say that he satisfied his holy love by himself dying the death and so bearing the judgment which sinners deserved. He both exacted and accepted the penalty of human sin. And he did it 'so as to be just and the one who justifies the man who has faith in Jesus' (Rom. 3:26). There is no question now either of the Father inflicting punishment on the Son or of the Son intervening on our behalf with the Father, for it is the Father himself who takes the initiative in his love, bears the penalty of sin himself, and so dies. Thus the priority is neither 'man's demand on God' nor 'God's demand on men', but supremely 'God's demand on God, God's meeting his own demand'.[45]

Many theologians ancient and modern, representing different traditions, have seen the necessity of emphasizing that God himself was there on the cross, and have therefore expressed their understanding of the atonement in these terms. In the Old English poem 'The Dream of the Rood', which may date from as early as the seventh or eighth century, the author tells how in 'the most treasured of dreams' he saw 'the strangest of trees':

> Lifted aloft in the air, with light all around it,
> Of all beams the brightest. It stood as a beacon,
> Drenched in gold; gleaming gems were set
> Fair around its foot . . . .

Then in the dream the cross spoke, telling its own story. Having been cut from the forest, it was carried up the hill. Then it saw

[44] I. H. Marshall, *Work of Christ*, p. 74.
[45] P. T. Forsyth, *Justification of God*, p. 35.

what its destiny was to be:

> The King of all mankind coming in great haste,
> With courage keen, eager to climb me.

> Then the young hero – it was God Almighty –
> Strong and stedfast, stripped himself for battle;
> He climbed up on the high gallows, constant in his purpose,
> Mounted it in sight of many, mankind to ransom.

At the end of the poem, having seen God dying for him, the dreamer prays to 'that blessed beam' and, putting his trust in it, declares: 'My refuge is the Rood.'[46]

'God dying for man', wrote P. T. Forsyth. 'I am not afraid of that phrase; I cannot do without it. God dying for men; and for such men – hostile, malignantly hostile men.'[47] Again, because 'the holiness of God . . . is meaningless without judgment', the one thing God could not do in the face of human rebellion was nothing. 'He must either inflict punishment or assume it. And he chose the latter course, as honouring the law while saving the guilty. He took his own judgment.'[48]

It was 'God himself' giving himself for us. Karl Barth did not shrink from using those words. 'God's own heart suffered on the cross', he added. 'Noone else but God's own Son, and hence the eternal God himself. . . .'[49] Similarly, Bishop Stephen Neill wrote: 'If the crucifixion of Jesus . . . is in some way, as Christians have believed, the dying of God himself, then . . . we can understand what God is like.'[50] And hymns of popular devotion have echoed it, like this phrase from Charles Wesley's 'And can it be':

> Amazing love! How can it be
> That thou, my God, should'st die for me?

The reason why both scholarly and simple Christians have felt able to use this kind of language is of course that Scripture permits it. When the apostles wrote of the cross, they often indicated by a tell-tale expression who it was who died there and gave it its

---

[46] The quotations are from Helen Gardner's translation. 'Rood', from the old English word *rōd*, was used for the gallows, and especially for Christ's cross.

[47] P. T. Forsyth, *Work of Christ*, p. 25.

[48] P. T. Forsyth, *Cruciality of the Cross*, pp. 205–206.

[49] Karl Barth, *Church Dogmatics*, II.1, pp. 446 ff. See also pp. 396–403.

[50] S. C. Neill, *Christian Faith Today*, p. 159.

efficacy. Thus, he who humbled himself even to death on a cross was none other than he who 'being in very nature God' made himself nothing in order to become human and to die (Phil. 2:6–8). It was 'the Lord of glory' whom the rulers of this age crucified (1 Cor. 2:8). And the blood by which the robes of the redeemed have been washed clean is that of the Lamb who shares the centre of God's throne (Rev. 5:6, 9; 7:9). Moreover, the logic of the letter to the Hebrews requires us to say that it is God who died. It plays on the similarity between a 'covenant' and a 'will'. The terms of a will come into force only after the death of the testator. So he who makes promises in his will has to die before the legacies can be received. Since, then, the promises in question are God's promises, the death must be God's death (Heb. 9:15–17).

There is one other verse which we must not overlook. It occurs in Paul's farewell speech at Miletus to the elders of the Ephesian church. The flock over which the Holy Spirit has made them overseers and shepherds, he says, is nothing less than 'the church of God, which he bought with his own blood' (Acts 20:28). It is true that the text is uncertain (some manuscripts read 'the church of the Lord', referring to Christ, instead of 'the church of God'), and so is the translation (it might mean 'the church of God which he bought with the blood of his own', referring again to Christ). Nevertheless, the context seems to demand the readings 'the church of God' and 'his own blood'. For Paul's purpose is to remind the elders of the precious value of the church they have been called to serve. It is God's church. God's Spirit has appointed them elders over it, and the price paid for its purchase is actually 'God's blood' – an almost shocking phrase which was used by some of the church Fathers such as Ignatius and Tertullian,[51] and which medieval churchmen continued to use, albeit often as an oath.

In spite of this biblical justification, however, no verse specifically declares that 'God himself' died on the cross. Scripture bears witness to the deity of the person who gave himself for us, but it stops short of the unequivocal affirmation that 'God died'. The reasons for this are not far to seek. First, immortality belongs to God's essential being ('God . . . alone is immortal', 1 Tim. 6:16), and therefore he cannot die. So he became man, in order to be

---

[51] Ignatius refers to 'the blood of God' and to 'the suffering of my God' in the shorter versions of his Letters to the Ephesians (ch. I) and the Romans (ch. VI) respectively. In his *De Carne Christi* Tertullian is even more explicit. 'Was not God really crucified?' he asks. In fact it is he who first used the startling expression 'a crucified God' (ch. V). Another example is Gregory of Nazianzus, who wrote of 'the precious and lordly blood of our God . . .' (*Orat.* xlv. 22).

able to do so: 'Since the children have flesh and blood, he too shared in their humanity so that by his death he might destroy him who holds the power of death – that is, the devil' (Heb. 2:14). Similarly, he became man in order to be the 'one mediator between God and men' (1 Tim. 2:5).

The second reason why it is misleading to say that 'God died' is that 'God' in the New Testament frequently means 'the Father' (*e.g.* 'God sent his Son'), and the person who died on the cross was not the Father but the Son. At the beginning of the third century AD some denied this. They had difficulties with the doctrine of the Trinity and could not see how to believe in the Father, the Son and the Spirit without thereby becoming tritheists. So they began by emphasizing the unity of God, and then spoke of Father, Son and Spirit not as three eternally distinct 'persons' within the Godhead, but rather as three temporal 'modes' in which God successively revealed himself. Hence their name 'Modalists'. The Father became the Son, they taught, and then the Son became the Spirit. They were also referred to as 'Sabellians' because Sabellius was one of their leaders. Another was Praxeas, whose teaching is known to us through Tertullian's powerful refutation of it. Praxeas taught (or, according to Tertullian, the devil taught through him) 'that the Father himself came down into the virgin, was himself born of her, himself suffered, indeed was himself Jesus Christ'. Because Praxeas also opposed the Montanists, who have been loosely described as the charismatics of that era, Tertullian continued, 'Praxeas did a twofold service for the devil at Rome; he drove away prophecy and he brought in heresy; he put to flight the Paraclete, and he crucified the Father'.[52] The droll notion that the Father was crucified led the critics of Praxeas' followers to give them the nickname 'Patripassians' (those who taught that the Father suffered). Over against this Tertullian urged: 'Let us be content with saying that Christ died, the Son of the Father; and *let this suffice*, because the Scriptures have told us so much.'[53]

A somewhat similar deviation arose in the sixth century in Constantinople, which came to be known as 'theopaschitism' (the belief that God suffered). Its adherents rejected the definition of the Council of Chalcedon (AD 451) that Jesus, though one person, had two natures, being both truly God and truly man. Instead, they were 'Monophysites', teaching that Christ had only one composite nature (*physis*, 'nature'), which was essentially divine. Thus underplaying the humanity of Jesus, they naturally emphasized that God suffered in and through him.

---

[52] Tertullian, *Adversus Praxean*, ch. I. [53] *Ibid.*, ch. XXIV.

Although these controversies seem very remote to us in the twentieth century, we need to take warning from them. An over-emphasis on the sufferings of God on the cross may mislead us either into confusing the persons of the Trinity and denying the eternal distinctness of the Son, like the Modalists or Patripassians, or into confusing the natures of Christ, and denying that he was one person in two natures, like the Monophysites or Theopaschites. It is true that, since Jesus was both God and man, the Council of Ephesus (AD 431) declared it correct to refer to the virgin Mary as *theotokos* ('mother of God', literally 'God-bearer'). Similarly, and for the same reason, it seems permissible to refer to God suffering on the cross. For if God could be born, why could he not also die? The value of these expressions is that they eliminate the possibility of thinking of Jesus as an independent third party. Nevertheless, the words 'theotokos' and 'theopaschite' are misleading, even if technically legitimate, because they emphasize the deity of the person who was born and died, without making any comparable reference to his humanity. It would be wiser instead to say what the New Testament authors said, faithfully echoed by the Apostles' Creed, namely that he who 'was conceived by the Holy Spirit, born of the Virgin Mary, suffered under Pontius Pilate, was crucified, died and was buried' was not 'God', still less the Father, but 'Jesus Christ, his only Son, our Lord'. The apostles further clarify this by stressing the Son's willing obedience to the Father.[54]

God in Christ

Our substitute, then, who took our place and died our death on the cross, was neither Christ alone (since that would make him a third party thrust in between God and us), nor God alone (since that would undermine the historical incarnation), but *God in Christ*, who was truly and fully both God and man, and who on that account was uniquely qualified to represent both God and man and to mediate between them. If we speak only of Christ suffering and dying, we overlook the initiative of the Father. If we speak only of God suffering and dying, we overlook the mediation of the Son. The New Testament authors never attribute the atonement either to Christ in such a way as to disassociate him from the Father, or to God in such a way as to dispense with Christ, but rather to God and Christ, or to God acting in and through Christ with his whole-hearted concurrence.

The New Testament evidence for this is plain. In surveying it, it

[54] *E.g.* Rom. 5:12–19; Gal. 4:4; Phil. 2:7–8; Heb. 5:8.

seems logical to begin with the announcement of the Messiah's birth. The names he was given were Jesus ('divine Saviour' or 'God saves') and Emmanuel ('God with us'). For in and through his birth God himself had come to the rescue of his people, to save them from their sins (Mt. 1:21–23). Similarly, according to Luke, the Saviour who had been born was not just, in the familiar expression, the Christ of the Lord, the Lord's anointed, but actually 'Christ the Lord', himself both Messiah and Lord (Lk. 2:11).

When Jesus' public ministry began, his personal self-consciousness confirmed that God was at work in and through him. For though he did speak of 'pleasing' the Father (Jn. 8:29) and 'obeying' him (Jn. 15:10), of doing his will and finishing his work,[55] yet this surrender was entirely voluntary, so that his will and the Father's were always in perfect harmony.[56] More than that, according to John he spoke of a mutual 'indwelling', he in the Father and the Father in him, even of a 'union' between them.[57]

This conviction that Father and Son cannot be separated, especially when we are thinking about the atonement, since the Father was taking action through the Son, comes to its fullest expression in some of Paul's great statements about reconciliation. For example, 'all this is from God' (referring to the work of the new creation, 2 Cor. 5:17–18), who 'reconciled us to himself through Christ' and 'was reconciling the world to himself in Christ' (vv. 18–19). It does not seem to matter much where, in translating the Greek, we place the expressions 'through Christ' and 'in Christ'. What matters is that God and Christ were together active in the work of reconciliation, indeed that it was in and through Christ that God was effecting the reconciliation.

Two other important Pauline verses forge an indissoluble link between Christ's person and work, and so indicate that he was able to do what he did only because he was who he was. Both speak of God's 'fullness' dwelling in him and working through him (Col. 1:19–20 and 2:9). This work is variously portrayed, but it is all attributed to the fullness of God residing in Christ – reconciling all things to himself, making peace by the blood of the cross, resurrecting us with Christ, forgiving all our sins, cancelling the written code that was against us, taking it away, nailing it to the cross, and disarming the principalities and powers, triumphing over them either 'by it' (the cross) or 'in him' (Christ).

Anselm was right that only *man should* make reparation for his sins, since it is he who has defaulted. And he was equally right

---

[55] E.g. Jn. 4:34; 6:38–39; 17:4; 19:30.
[56] E.g. Jn. 10:18; Mk. 14:36; Heb. 10:7 (Ps. 40:7–8).
[57] E.g. Jn. 14:11; 17:21–23; 10:30.

that only *God could* make the necessary reparation, since it is he who has demanded it. Jesus Christ is therefore the only Saviour, since he is the only person in whom the 'should' and the 'could' are united, being himself both God and man. The weakness of Anselm's formulation, due probably to his cultural background in medieval feudalism, is that he overemphasized the humanity of Christ, since man the sinner must pay the debt he has incurred and repair the damage he has done. But the New Testament emphasis is more on the initiative of God, who 'sent' or 'gave' or 'delivered up' his Son for us,[58] and who therefore suffered in his Son's sufferings.

George Buttrick wrote of a picture which hangs in an Italian church, although he did not identify it. At first glance it is like any other painting of the crucifixion. As you look more closely, however, you perceive the difference, because 'there's a vast and shadowy Figure behind the figure of Jesus. The nail that pierces the hand of Jesus goes through to the hand of God. The spear thrust into the side of Jesus goes through into God's'.[59]

We began by showing that God must 'satisfy himself', responding to the realities of human rebellion in a way that is perfectly consonant with his character. This internal necessity is our fixed starting-point. In consequence, it would be impossible for us sinners to remain eternally the sole objects of his holy love, since he cannot both punish and pardon us at the same time. Hence the second necessity, namely substitution. The only way for God's holy love to be satisfied is for his holiness to be directed in judgment upon his appointed substitute, in order that his love may be directed towards us in forgiveness. The substitute bears the penalty, that we sinners may receive the pardon. Who, then, is the substitute? Certainly not Christ, if he is seen as a third party. Any notion of penal substitution in which three independent actors play a role – the guilty party, the punitive judge and the innocent victim – is to be repudiated with the utmost vehemence. It would not only be unjust in itself but would also reflect a defective Christology. For Christ is not an independent third person, but the eternal Son of the Father, who is one with the Father in his essential being.

What we see, then, in the drama of the cross is not three actors but two, ourselves on the one hand and God on the other. Not God as he is in himself (the Father), but God nevertheless, God-made-man-in-Christ (the Son). Hence the importance of those New

[58] *E.g.* Gal. 4:4; 1 Jn. 4:14; Jn. 3:16; Rom. 8:32.
[59] George A. Buttrick, *Jesus Came Preaching*, p. 207.

Testament passages which speak of the death of Christ as the death of God's Son: for example, 'God so loved the world that he gave his one and only Son', 'he . . . did not spare his own Son', and 'we were reconciled to God through the death of his Son'.[60] For in giving his Son he was giving himself. This being so, it is the Judge himself who in holy love assumed the role of the innocent victim, for in and through the person of his Son he himself bore the penalty which he himself inflicted. As Dale put it, 'the mysterious unity of the Father and the Son rendered it possible for God at once to endure and to inflict penal suffering'.[61] There is neither harsh injustice nor unprincipled love nor Christological heresy in that; there is only unfathomable mercy. For in order to save us in such a way as to satisfy himself, God through Christ substituted himself for us. Divine love triumphed over divine wrath by divine self-sacrifice. The cross was an act simultaneously of punishment and amnesty, severity and grace, justice and mercy.

Seen thus, the objections to a substitutionary atonement evaporate. There is nothing even remotely immoral here, since the substitute for the law-breakers is none other than the divine Lawmaker himself. There is no mechanical transaction either, since the self-sacrifice of love is the most personal of all actions. And what is achieved through the cross is no merely external change of legal status, since those who see God's love there, and are united to Christ by his Spirit, become radically transformed in outlook and character.

We strongly reject, therefore, every explanation of the death of Christ which does not have at its centre the principle of 'satisfaction through substitution', indeed divine self-satisfaction through divine self-substitution. The cross was not a commercial bargain with the devil, let alone one which tricked and trapped him; nor an exact equivalent, a *quid pro quo* to satisfy a code of honour or technical point of law; nor a compulsory submission by God to some moral authority above him from which he could not otherwise escape; nor a punishment of a meek Christ by a harsh and punitive Father; nor a procurement of salvation by a loving Christ from a mean and reluctant Father; nor an action of the Father which bypassed Christ as Mediator. Instead, the righteous, loving Father humbled himself to become in and through his only Son flesh, sin and a curse for us, in order to redeem us without compromising his own character. The theological words 'satisfaction' and 'substitution' need to be carefully defined and safeguarded, but they cannot in any circumstances be given up. The biblical gospel of atonement

[60] Jn. 3:16; Rom. 8:32 and 5:10. [61] R. W. Dale, *Atonement*, p. 393.

is of God satisfying himself by substituting himself for us.

The concept of substitution may be said, then, to lie at the heart of both sin and salvation. For the essence of sin is man substituting himself for God, while the essence of salvation is God substituting himself for man. Man asserts himself against God and puts himself where only God deserves to be; God sacrifices himself for man and puts himself where only man deserves to be. Man claims prerogatives which belong to God alone; God accepts penalties which belong to man alone.

If the essence of the atonement is substitution, at least two important inferences follow, the first theological and the second personal. The theological inference is that it is impossible to hold the historic doctrine of the cross without holding the historic doctrine of Jesus Christ as the one and only God-man and Mediator. As we have seen, neither Christ alone as man nor the Father alone as God could be our substitute. Only God in Christ, God the Father's own and only Son made man, could take our place. At the root of every caricature of the cross there lies a distorted Christology. The person and work of Christ belong together. If he was not who the apostles say he was, then he could not have done what they say he did. The incarnation is indispensable to the atonement. In particular, it is essential to affirm that the love, the holiness and the will of the Father are identical with the love, the holiness and the will of the Son. God was in Christ reconciling the world to himself.

Perhaps no twentieth-century theologian has seen this more clearly, or expressed it more vigorously, than Karl Barth.[62] Christology, he insisted, is the key to the doctrine of reconciliation. And Christology means confessing Jesus Christ the Mediator, he repeated several times, as 'very God, very man, and very God-man'. There are thus 'three Christological aspects' or 'three perspectives' for understanding the atonement. The first is that 'in Jesus Christ we have to do with very God. The reconciliation of man with God takes place as God himself actively intervenes' (p. 128). The second is that 'in Jesus Christ we have to do with a true man. . . . He is altogether man, just as he is altogether God. . . . That is how he is the reconciler between God and man' (p. 130). The third is that, although very God and very man, 'Jesus Christ himself is one. He is the God-man' (p. 135). Only when this biblical account of Jesus Christ is affirmed can the uniqueness of his atoning sacrifice be understood. The initiative lay with 'the eternal God himself, who has given himself in his Son to be man,

[62] Karl Barth, *Church Dogmatics*, IV.1.

and as man to take upon himself this human passion. . . . It is the Judge who in this passion takes the place of those who ought to be judged, who in this passion allows himself to be judged in their place' (p. 246). 'The passion of Jesus Christ is the judgment of God, in which the Judge himself was the judged' (p. 254).

The second inference is personal. The doctrine of substitution affirms not only a fact (God in Christ substituted himself for us) but its necessity (there was no other way by which God's holy love could be satisfied and rebellious human beings could be saved). Therefore, as we stand before the cross, we begin to gain a clear view both of God and of ourselves, especially in relation to each other. Instead of inflicting upon us the judgment we deserved, God in Christ endured it in our place. Hell is the only alternative. This is the 'scandal', the stumbling-block, of the cross. For our proud hearts rebel against it. We cannot bear to acknowledge either the seriousness of our sin and guilt or our utter indebtedness to the cross. Surely, we say, there must be something we can do, or at least contribute, in order to make amends? If not, we often give the impression that we would rather suffer our own punishment than the humiliation of seeing God through Christ bear it in our place.

George Bernard Shaw, who had considerable insight into the subtleties of human pride, dramatized this in his comedy about the Salvation Army entitled *Major Barbara* (1905). Bill Walker, 'a rough customer of about 25', arrives at the Army's West Ham shelter one cold January morning drunk and infuriated because his girl-friend Mog has not only been converted but 'got another bloke'. Bill's rival is Todger Fairmile, a champion music hall wrestler in Canning Town, who has also been converted. Accusing Jenny Hill, a young Salvation Army lass, of having set his girl-friend against him, Bill first seizes her by the hair until she screams and then strikes her with his fist in the face, cutting her lip. The bystanders mock him for his cowardice. He attacks a girl, they say, but he would not have the courage to hit Todger Fairmile. Gradually Bill's conscience and pride nag him, until he can no longer bear the insult. He determines to do something to redeem his reputation and expiate his guilt. He says in broad Cockney:

'Aw'm gowin to Kennintahn, to spit in Todger Fairmawl's eye. Aw beshed Jenny Ill's fice; an nar Aw'll git me aown fice beshed . . . Ee'll itt me ardern Aw itt er. Thatll mike us square. . . .'

But Todger refuses to co-operate, so Bill returns shamefaced:

'Aw did wot Aw said Aw'd do. Aw spit in is eye. E looks ap at the skoy and sez, "Ow that Aw should be fahnd worthy to be spit upon for the gospel's sike!" . . . an Mog sez "Glaory Allelloolier!".'

Jenny Hill says she is sorry and that he did not really hurt her, which makes him angrier still:

'Aw downt want to be forgive be you, or be ennybody. Wot Aw did Aw'll py for. Aw trawd to gat me aown jawr browk to settisfaw you –' Because that way has failed, however, he tries another ruse. He offers to pay a fine which one of his mates has just incurred, and produces a sovereign.

'Eahs the manney. Tike it; and lets ev no more o your forgivin an pryin an your Mijor jawrin me. Let wot Aw dan be dan an pide for; and let there be a end of it. . . . This bloomin forgivin an neggin an jawrin . . . mikes a menn thet sore that iz lawf's a burdn to im. Aw wownt ev it, Aw tell yer. . . . Awve offered to py. Aw can do no more. Tike it or leave it. There it is', – and he throws the sovereign down.

The proud human heart is there revealed. We insist on paying for what we have done. We cannot stand the humiliation of acknowledging our bankruptcy and allowing somebody else to pay for us. The notion that this somebody else should be God himself is just too much to take. We would rather perish than repent, rather lose ourselves than humble ourselves.

Moreover, only the gospel demands such an abject self-humbling on our part, for it alone teaches divine substitution as the only way of salvation. Other religions teach different forms of self-salvation. Hinduism, for example, makes a virtue of refusing to admit to sinfulness. In a lecture before the Parliament of Religions in Chicago in 1893, Swami Vivekananda said: 'The Hindu refuses to call you sinners. Ye are the children of God; the sharers of immortal bliss, holy and perfect beings. Ye divinities on earth, sinners? It is a sin to call a man a sinner. It is a standing libel on human nature.' Besides, if it has to be conceded that human beings do sin, then Hinduism insists that they can save themselves.[63]

As Brunner put it, 'all other forms of religion – not to mention philosophy – deal with the problem of guilt apart from the intervention of God, and therefore they come to a "cheap" conclusion. In them man is spared the final humiliation of knowing that the Mediator must bear the punishment instead of him. To this yoke he need not submit. He is not stripped absolutely naked.'[64]

But we cannot escape the embarrassment of standing stark naked before God. It is no use our trying to cover up like Adam and Eve in the garden. Our attempts at self-justification are as ineffectual as their fig-leaves. We have to acknowledge our nakedness, see the

[63] From *Speeches and Writings* by Swami Vivekananda, pp. 38–39. *Cf.* p. 125. See also *Crises of Belief* by S. C. Neill, p. 100.
[64] Emil Brunner, *Mediator*, p. 474.

divine substitute wearing our filthy rags instead of us, and allow him to clothe us with his own righteousness.[65] Nobody has ever put it better than Augustus Toplady in his immortal hymn 'Rock of Ages':

> Nothing in my hand I bring,
> Simply to your Cross I cling;
> Naked, come to you for dress;
> Helpless, look to you for grace;
> Foul, I to the fountain fly;
> Wash me, Saviour, or I die.

[65] *Cf.* Rev. 3:17–18.

Part Three

The achievement of the cross

7

The salvation of sinners

Moved by the perfection of his holy love, God in Christ substituted himself for us sinners. That is the heart of the cross of Christ. It leads us to turn now from the event to its consequences, from what happened on the cross to what was achieved by it. Why did God take our place and bear our sin? What did he accomplish by his self-sacrifice, his self-substitution?

The New Testament gives three main answers to these questions, which may be summed up in the words 'salvation', 'revelation' and 'conquest'. What God in Christ has done through the cross is to rescue us, disclose himself and overcome evil. In this chapter we shall focus on salvation through the cross.

It would be hard to exaggerate the magnitude of the changes which have taken place as a result of the cross, both in God and in us, especially in God's dealings with us and in our relations with him. Truly, when Christ died and was raised from death, a new day dawned, a new age began.

This new day is 'the day of salvation' (2 Cor. 6:2), and the blessings of 'such a great salvation' (Heb. 2:3) are so richly diverse that they cannot be neatly defined. Several pictures are needed to portray them. Just as the church of Christ is presented in Scripture as his bride and his body, the sheep of God's flock and the branches of his vine, his new humanity, his household or family, the temple of the Holy Spirit and the pillar and buttress of the truth, so the salvation of Christ is illustrated by the vivid imagery of terms like 'propitiation', 'redemption', 'justification' and 'reconciliation', which are to form the theme of this chapter. Moreover, as the images of the church are visually incompatible (one cannot envisage the body and the bride of Christ simultaneously), yet underlying them all is the truth that God is calling out a people for himself, so the images of salvation are incompatible (justification and redemption conjure up respectively the divergent worlds of law and commerce), yet underlying them all is the truth that God in Christ has borne our sin and died our death to set us free from sin and death. Such images are indispensable aids to human understanding of doctrine. And what they convey, being God-given, is true. Yet we must not deduce from this that to have understood the images is to have exhausted the meaning of the doctrine. For beyond the images of the atonement lies the mystery of the atonement, the deep wonders of which, I guess, we shall be exploring throughout eternity.

'Images' of salvation (or of the atonement) is a better term than 'theories'. For theories are usually abstract and speculative concepts, whereas the biblical images of the atoning achievement of Christ are concrete pictures and belong to the data of revelation. They are not alternative explanations of the cross, providing us with a range to choose from, but complementary to one another, each contributing a vital part to the whole. As for the imagery, 'propitiation' introduces us to rituals at a shrine, 'redemption' to transactions in a market-place, 'justification' to proceedings in a lawcourt, and 'reconciliation' to experiences in a home or family. My contention is that 'substitution' is not a further 'theory' or 'image' to be set alongside the others, but rather the foundation of them all, without which each lacks cogency. If God in Christ did not die in our place, there could be neither propitiation, nor redemption, nor justification, nor reconciliation. In addition, all the images begin their life in the Old Testament, but are elaborated and enriched in the New, particularly by being directly related to Christ and his cross.

Propitiation

Western Christians of earlier generations were quite familiar with the language of 'propitiation' in relation to the death of Christ. For the Authorized (King James') Version of the Bible, on which they were brought up, contained three explicit affirmations of it by Paul and John:

> Paul: '... Christ Jesus, whom God hath set forth to be a propitiation through faith in his blood' (Rom. 3:24–25).
> John: 'We have an advocate with the Father, Jesus Christ the righteous: and he is the propitiation for our sins.' Again, 'Herein is love, not that we loved God, but that he loved us,

and sent his Son to be the propitiation for our sins' (1 Jn. 2:1–2; 4:10).

Although this language was well known to our forebears, they were not necessarily comfortable in using it. To 'propitiate' somebody means to appease or pacify his anger. Does God then get angry? If so, can offerings or rituals assuage his anger? Does he accept bribes? Such concepts sound more pagan than Christian. It is understandable that primitive animists should consider it essential to placate the wrath of gods, spirits or ancestors, but are notions like these worthy of the Christian God? Should we not have grown out of them? In particular, are we really to believe that Jesus by his death propitiated the Father's anger, inducing him to turn from it and to look upon us with favour instead?

Crude concepts of anger, sacrifice and propitiation are indeed to be rejected. They do not belong to the religion of the Old Testament, let alone of the New. This does not mean, however, that there is no biblical concept of these things at all. What is revealed to us in Scripture is a pure doctrine (from which all pagan vulgarities have been expunged) of God's holy wrath, his loving self-sacrifice in Christ and his initiative to avert his own anger. It is obvious that 'wrath' and 'propitiation' (the placating of wrath) go together. It is when the wrath is purged of unworthy ideas that the propitiation is thereby purged. The opposite is also true. It is those who cannot come to terms with any concept of the wrath of God who repudiate any concept of propitiation. Here, for example, is Professor A. T. Hanson: 'If you think of the wrath as an attitude of God, you cannot avoid some theory of propitiation. But the wrath in the New Testament is never spoken of as being propitiated, because it is not conceived of as being an attitude of God.'[1]

It is this discomfort with the doctrines of wrath and propitiation, which has led some theologians to re-examine the biblical vocabulary. They have concentrated on a particular word-group which the Authorized Version translated in 'propitiatory' terms, namely the noun *hilasmos* (1 Jn. 2:2; 4:10), the adjective *hilastērios* (Rom. 3:25, where it may be used as a noun) and the verb *hilaskomai* (Heb. 2:17; also Lk. 18:13 in the passive, which should perhaps be rendered 'be propitiated – or propitious – to me, a sinner'). The crucial question is whether the object of the atoning action is God or man. If the former, then the right word is 'propitiation' (appeasing God); if the latter, the right word is 'expiation' (dealing

[1] A. T. Hanson, *Wrath of the Lamb*, p. 192.

with sin and guilt).

The British theologian who led the way in this attempted re-
interpretation was C. H. Dodd.[2] Here is his comment on Romans
3:25: 'the meaning conveyed . . . is that of expiation, not that of
propitiation. Most translators and commentators are wrong.'[3] He
expresses a similar opinion in relation to 1 John 2:2, namely that
the translation 'propitiation for our sins' is 'illegitimate here as
elsewhere'.[4] Since C. H. Dodd was director of the panels which
produced the New English Bible (New Testament 1961), it is not
surprising that his view was reflected in its rendering of the verses
just referred to. Romans 3:25 is translated 'God designed him to
be the means of expiating sin by his sacrificial death', while in
1 John 2:2 and 4:10 the key phrase is rendered 'he is himself the
remedy for the defilement of our sins'. The RSV, whose New Testament was published a few years earlier (1946), has 'expiation' in
all three verses.

C. H. Dodd's argument, developed with his customary erudition,
was linguistic. He acknowledged that in pagan Greek (both
classical and popular) the regular meaning of the verb *hilaskomai*
was to 'propitiate' or 'placate' an offended person, especially a
deity. But he denied that this was its meaning either in Hellenistic
Judaism, as evidenced in the Septuagint (LXX), or, on that account,
in the New Testament. He argued that in the LXX *kipper* (the
Hebrew verb for 'atone') was sometimes translated by Greek words
other than *hilaskomai*, which mean to 'purify' or 'cancel'; that
hilaskomai in the LXX sometimes translates other Hebrew words
than *kipper*, which mean to 'cleanse' or 'forgive'; and that when
hilaskomai does translate *kipper* the meaning is expiation or the
removal of defilement. This is how he sums up: 'Hellenistic
Judaism, as represented by the LXX, does not regard the cultus as
a means of pacifying the displeasure of the Deity, but as a means
of delivering man from sin.'[5] Indeed, it was generally believed in
antiquity that 'the performance of prescribed rituals . . . had the
value, so to speak, of a powerful disinfectant'.[6] Therefore, he
concludes, the New Testament occurrences of the *hilaskomai* word-

[2] C. H. Dodd contributed an article on *hilaskesthai* to the *Journal of
Theological Studies*, which was subsequently re-published in his *Bible and
the Greeks*. The same attempt to reinterpret 'propitiation' as 'expiation'
is also expressed in his two Moffatt New Testament Commentaries on
Romans and the *Johannine Epistles*.

[3] C. H. Dodd, *Bible and the Greeks*, p. 94. See also his *Romans*,
pp. 54–55.

[4] C. H. Dodd, *Johannine Epistles*, p. 25.

[5] C. H. Dodd, *Bible and the Greeks*, p. 93.

[6] C. H. Dodd, *Johannine Epistles*, pp. 25–26.

group should be interpreted in the same way. By his cross Jesus Christ expiated sin; he did not propitiate God.

Professor Dodd's reconstruction, although accepted by many of his contemporaries and successors, was subjected to a rigorous critique by others, in particular by Dr Leon Morris[7] and Dr Roger Nicole.[8] Both showed that his conclusions rested on either incomplete evidence or questionable deductions. For example, his assessment of the meaning of the *hilaskomai* group in Hellenistic Judaism makes no reference either (1) to the books of the Maccabees, although they belong to the LXX and contain several passages which speak of 'the wrath of the Almighty' being averted, or (2) to the writings of Josephus and Philo, although in them, as Friedrich Büchsel shows, the meaning to 'placate' prevails.[9] As for the New Testament understanding of these words, F. Büchsel points out what C. H. Dodd overlooks, that in both Clement's First Letter (end of the first century) and the Shepherd of Hermas (beginning of the second) *hilaskomai* is plainly used of propitiating God. So then, for C. H. Dodd's theory about the LXX and New Testament usage to be correct, he would have to maintain that they 'form a sort of linguistic island with little precedent in former times, little confirmation from the contemporaries, and no following in after years!'.[10]

But we have to declare his thesis incorrect. Even in the Old Testament canon itself there are numerous instances in which *kipper* and *hilaskomai* are used of propitiating the anger either of men (like Jacob pacifying Esau with gifts and a wise man appeasing a king's wrath[11]) or of God (like Aaron and Phinehas who turned God's anger away from the Israelites[12]). Even in passages where the natural translation is to 'make atonement for sin', the context often contains explicit mention of God's wrath, which implies that the human sin can be atoned for only by the divine anger being turned away.[13] These instances, Roger Nicole points out, are

---

[7] Leon Morris wrote an article on *hilaskesthai* in *The Expository Times*, and then expanded his thesis in his *Apostolic Preaching*. He has also produced a further development and simplification of this book in *Atonement*.

[8] Dr Roger R. Nicole's article entitled 'C. H. Dodd and the Doctrine of Propitiation' appeared in the *Westminster Theological Journal*, xvii.2 (1955), pp. 117–157. He acknowledges some indebtedness to Leon Morris, although it is an independent study.

[9] See the article on the *hilaskomai* word-group by F. Büchsel and J. Hermann in Kittel's *Theological Dictionary of the New Testament*, vol. III, pp. 300–323.

[10] Roger Nicole, 'C. H. Dodd', p. 132.   [11] Gn. 32:20; Pr. 16:14.

[12] Nu. 16:41–50 and 25:11–13. *Cf.* also Zc. 7:2; 8:22; Mal. 1:9.

[13] *E.g.* Ex. 32:30 (*cf.* v. 10); Dt. 21:1–9; 1 Sa. 3:14; 26:19.

consistent with 'the predominant use in classical and *koinē* Greek, in Josephus and Philo, in patristic writers and in the Maccabees'.[14] Leon Morris' conclusion in regard to the Old Testament is that, although *hilaskomai* is 'a complex word', yet 'the averting of anger seems to represent a stubborn substratum of meaning from which all the usages can be naturally explained'.[15]

The same is true of the New Testament occurrences. The description of Jesus as the *hilasmos* in relation to our sins (1 Jn. 2:2; 4:10) could be understood as meaning simply that he took them away or cancelled them. But he is also named our 'advocate with the Father' (2:1), which implies the displeasure of the One before whom he pleads our cause. As for the passage in Romans 3, the context is determinative. Whether we translate *hilastērion* in verse 25 'the place of propitiation' (*i.e.* the mercy-seat, as in Heb. 9:5) or 'the means of propitiation' (*i.e.* a propitiatory sacrifice), the Jesus who is so described is set forth by God as the remedy for universal human guilt under his wrath, which Paul has taken two and a half chapters to demonstrate. As Leon Morris justly comments, 'wrath has occupied such an important place in the argument leading up to this section that we are justified in looking for some expression indicative of its cancellation in the process which brings about salvation'.[16] It is true that in Hebrews 2:17 *hilaskomai* is a transitive verb, with 'the sins of the people' as its object. It could therefore be translated 'expiate' (NEB) or 'make atonement for' (NIV). This meaning is not indubitable, however. The NIV margin renders it 'that he might turn aside God's wrath, taking away' the people's sins.

If we grant that C. H. Dodd's linguistic argument has been lost, or at the very least that his case is 'not proven', and that the *hilaskomai* word-group means 'propitiation' not 'expiation', we still have to decide how to portray God's anger and its averting. It would be easy to caricature them in such a way as to dismiss them with ridicule. This William Neil has done in the following passage:

> It is worth noting that the 'fire and brimstone' school of theology who revel in ideas such as that Christ was made a sacrifice to appease an angry God, or that the cross was a legal transaction

---

[14] R. Nicole, 'C. H. Dodd', p. 134.

[15] L. Morris, *Apostolic Preaching*, p. 155.

[16] *Ibid.*, p. 169. In his large survey, *Cross in the New Testament*, Leon Morris writes: 'Throughout Greek literature, biblical and non-biblical alike *hilasmos* means "propitiation". We cannot now decide that we like another meaning better' (p. 349).

in which an innocent victim was made to pay the penalty for the crimes of others, a propitiation of a stern God, find no support in Paul. These notions came into Christian theology by way of the legalistic minds of the medieval churchmen; they are not biblical Christianity.[17]

But of course this is neither the Christianity of the Bible in general, nor of Paul in particular. It is doubtful if anybody has ever believed such a crude construction. For these are pagan notions of propitiation with but a very thin Christian veneer. If we are to develop a truly biblical doctrine of propitiation, it will be necessary to distinguish it from pagan ideas at three crucial points, relating to why a propitiation is necessary, who made it and what it was.

First, the reason why a propitiation is necessary is that sin arouses the wrath of God. This does not mean (as animists fear) that he is likely to fly off the handle at the most trivial provocation, still less that he loses his temper for no apparent reason at all. For there is nothing capricious or arbitrary about the holy God. Nor is he ever irascible, malicious, spiteful or vindictive. His anger is neither mysterious nor irrational. It is never unpredictable, but always predictable, because it is provoked by evil and by evil alone. The wrath of God, as we considered more fully in chapter 4, is his steady, unrelenting, unremitting, uncompromising antagonism to evil in all its forms and manifestations. In short, God's anger is poles apart from ours. What provokes our anger (injured vanity) never provokes his; what provokes his anger (evil) seldom provokes ours.

Secondly, who makes the propitiation? In a pagan context it is always human beings who seek to avert the divine anger either by the meticulous performance of rituals, or by the recitation of magic formulae, or by the offering of sacrifices (vegetable, animal or even human). Such practices are thought to placate the offended deity. But the gospel begins with the outspoken assertion that nothing we can do, say, offer or even contribute can compensate for our sins or turn away God's anger. There is no possibility of persuading, cajoling or bribing God to forgive us, for we deserve nothing at his hands but judgment. Nor, as we have seen, has Christ by his sacrifice prevailed upon God to pardon us. No, the initiative has been taken by God himself in his sheer mercy and grace.

This was already clear in the Old Testament, in which the sacrifices were recognized not as human works but as divine gifts.

[17] William Neil, *Apostle Extraordinary*, pp. 89–90.

They did not make God gracious; they were provided by a gracious God in order that he might act graciously towards his sinful people. 'I have given it to you', God said of the sacrificial blood, 'to make atonement for yourselves on the altar' (Lv. 17:11). And this truth is yet more plainly recognized in the New Testament, not least in the main texts about propitiation. God himself 'presented' (NIV) or 'put forward' (RSV) Jesus Christ as a propitiatory sacrifice (Rom. 3:25). It is not that we loved God, but that he loved us and sent his Son as a propitiation for our sins (1 Jn. 4:10). It cannot be emphasized too strongly that God's love is the source, not the consequence, of the atonement. As P. T. Forsyth expressed it, 'the atonement did not procure grace, it flowed from grace'.[18] God does not love us because Christ died for us; Christ died for us because God loved us. If it is God's wrath which needed to be propitiated, it is God's love which did the propitiating. If it may be said that the propitiation 'changed' God, or that by it he changed himself, let us be clear he did not change from wrath to love, or from enmity to grace, since his character is unchanging. What the propitiation changed was his dealings with us. 'The distinction I ask you to observe', wrote P. T. Forsyth, 'is between a change of feeling and a change of treatment . . . . God's feeling toward us never needed to be changed. But God's treatment of us, God's practical relation to us – that had to change.'[19] He forgave us and welcomed us home.

Thirdly, what was the propitiatory sacrifice? It was neither an animal, nor a vegetable, nor a mineral. It was not a thing at all, but a person. And the person God offered was not somebody else, whether a human person or an angel or even his Son considered as somebody distinct from or external to himself. No, he offered himself. In giving his Son, he was giving himself. As Karl Barth wrote repeatedly, 'it was the Son of God, *i.e.* God himself'. For example, 'the fact that it was God's Son, that it was God himself, who took our place on Golgotha and thereby freed us from the divine anger and judgment, reveals first the full implication of the wrath of God, of his condemning and punishing justice'. Again, 'because it was the Son of God, *i.e.* God himself, who took our place on Good Friday, the substitution could be effectual and procure our reconciliation with the righteous God . . . . Only God, our Lord and Creator, could stand surety for us, could take our place, could suffer eternal death in our stead as the consequence

---

[18] P. T. Forsyth, *Cruciality of the Cross*, p. 78. Compare Calvin's statement: 'The work of atonement derives from God's love; therefore it did not establish it' (*Institutes*, II.xvi.4).

[19] P. T. Forsyth, *The Work of Christ*, p. 105.

of our sin in such a way that it was finally suffered and overcome'.[20] And all this, Barth makes clear, was an expression not only of God's holiness and justice, but of 'the perfections of the divine loving', indeed of God's 'holy love'.

So then, God himself is at the heart of our answer to all three questions about the divine propitiation. It is God himself who in holy wrath needs to be propitiated, God himself who in holy love undertook to do the propitiating, and God himself who in the person of his Son died for the propitiation of our sins. Thus God took his own loving initiative to appease his own righteous anger by bearing it his own self in his own Son when he took our place and died for us. There is no crudity here to evoke our ridicule, only the profundity of holy love to evoke our worship.

In seeking thus to defend and reinstate the biblical doctrine of propitiation, we have no intention of denying the biblical doctrine of expiation. Although we must resist every attempt to replace propitiation by expiation, we welcome every attempt to see them as belonging together in salvation. Thus F. Büchsel wrote that '*hilasmos* . . . is the action in which God is propitiated and sin expiated'.[21] Dr David Wells has elaborated this succinctly:

> In Pauline thought, man is alienated from God by sin and God is alienated from man by wrath. It is in the substitutionary death of Christ that sin is overcome and wrath averted, so that God can look on man without displeasure and man can look on God without fear. Sin is expiated and God is propitiated.[22]

Redemption

We now move on from 'propitiation' to 'redemption'. In seeking to understand the achievement of the cross, the imagery changes from temple court to market-place, from the ceremonial realm to the commercial, from religious rituals to business transactions. For at its most basic to 'redeem' is to buy or buy back, whether as a purchase or a ransom. Inevitably, then, the emphasis of the redemption image is on our sorry state – indeed our captivity – in sin which made an act of divine rescue necessary. 'Propitiation' focuses on the wrath of God which was placated by the cross; 'redemption' on the plight of sinners from which they were ransomed by the cross.

And 'ransom' is the correct word to use. The Greek words *lytroō*

[20] Karl Barth, *Church Dogmatics*, Vol. II, Part 1, pp. 398 and 403.
[21] F. Büchsel, '*hilaskomai*', p. 317.
[22] David F. Wells, *Search for Salvation*, p. 29.

(usually translated 'redeem') and *apolytrōsis* ('redemption') are derived from *lytron* ('a ransom' or 'price of release'), which was almost a technical term in the ancient world for the purchase or manumission of a slave. In view of 'the unwavering usage of profane authors', namely that this word-group refers to 'a process involving release by payment of a ransom price',[23] often very costly, wrote Leon Morris, we have no liberty to dilute its meaning into a vague and even cheap deliverance. We have been 'ransomed' by Christ, not merely 'redeemed' or 'delivered' by him. B. B. Warfield was right to point out that we are 'assisting at the death bed of a word. It is sad to witness the death of any worthy thing – even of a worthy word. And worthy words do die, like any other worthy thing – if we do not take good care of them'. Sadder still is 'the dying out of the hearts of men of the things for which the words stand'.[24] He was referring to his generation's loss of a sense of gratitude to him who paid our ransom.

In the Old Testament property, animals, persons and the nation were all 'redeemed' by the payment of a price. The right (even the duty) to play the role of 'kinsman redeemer' and buy back a property which had been alienated, in order to keep it in the family or tribe, was illustrated in the case of both Boaz and Jeremiah.[25] As for animals, the firstborn males of all livestock belonged by right to Yahweh; donkeys and unclean animals, however, could be redeemed (*i.e.* bought back) by the owner.[26] In the case of individual Israelites, each had to pay 'a ransom for his life' at the time of the national census; firstborn sons (who since the first Passover belonged to God), and especially those in excess of the number of Levites who replaced them, had to be redeemed; the owner of a notoriously dangerous bull, which gored a man to death, was himself to be put to death, unless he redeemed his life by the payment of an adequate fine; and an impoverished Israelite compelled to sell himself into slavery could later either redeem himself or be redeemed by a relative.[27] In all these cases of 'redemption' there was a decisive and costly intervention. Somebody paid the price necessary to free property from mortgage, animals from

[23] Leon Morris, *Apostolic Preaching*, p. 10. See also chapter 5, 'Redemption', in his *Atonement*, pp. 106–131.
[24] From an article on 'Redemption' by B. B. Warfield, first published in *The Princeton Theological Review* (Vol. xiv, 1916), and reprinted in his *Person and Work*, pp. 345 and 347.
[25] Lv. 25:25–28; Ru. 3 and 4; Je. 32:6–8. *Cf.* Lv. 27 for redeeming land which had been dedicated to the Lord by a special vow.
[26] Ex. 13:13; 34:20; Nu. 18:14–17.
[27] Ex. 30:12–16; 13:13; 34:20 and Nu. 3:40–51; Ex. 21:28–32; Lv. 25:47–55.

slaughter, and persons from slavery, even death.

What about the nation? Certainly the vocabulary of redemption was used to describe Yahweh's deliverance of Israel both from slavery in Egypt[28] and from exile in Babylon.[29] But in this case, since the redeemer was not a human being but God himself, can we still maintain that to 'redeem' is to 'ransom'? What price did Yahweh pay to redeem his people? Bishop B. F. Westcott seems to have been the first to suggest an answer: 'the idea of the exertion of a mighty force, the idea that the "redemption" costs much, is everywhere present.'[30] Warfield enlarged on this: 'the idea that the redemption from Egypt was the effect of a great expenditure of the divine power and in that sense cost much, is prominent in the allusions to it, and seems to constitute the central idea sought to be conveyed.'[31] For God redeemed Israel 'with an outstretched arm' and 'with a mighty hand'.[32] We conclude that redemption *always* involved the payment of a price, and that Yahweh's redemption of Israel was not an exception. Even here, Warfield sums up, 'the conception of price-paying intrinsic in *lutrousthai* is preserved . . . . A redemption without a price paid is as anomalous a transaction as a sale without money passing'.[33]

When we enter the New Testament and consider its teaching about redemption, two changes immediately strike us. Although it is still inherent in the concept both that those needing redemption are in a bad plight and that they can be redeemed only by the payment of a price, yet now the plight is moral rather than material, and the price is the atoning death of God's Son. This much is already evident in Jesus' famous 'ransom-saying', which is foundational to the New Testament doctrine of redemption: 'The Son of Man did not come to be served, but to serve, and to give his life as a ransom for many' (Mk. 10:45). The imagery implies that we are held in a captivity from which only the payment of a ransom can set us free, and that the ransom is nothing less than the Messiah's own life. Our lives are forfeit; his life will be sacrificed instead. F. Büchsel is surely correct that the saying 'undoubtedly implies substitution'. This is made plain by the combination of the two adjectives in the Greek expression *antilytron hyper pollōn* (literally, 'a ransom in place of and for the sake of many'). 'The

---

[28] *E.g.* Ex. 6:6; Dt. 7:8; 15:15; 2 Sa. 7:23.
[29] *E.g.* Is. 43:1–4; 48:20; 51:11; Je. 31:11.
[30] B. F. Westcott, *Epistle to the Hebrews*, p. 298.
[31] B. B. Warfield, *Person and Work*, p. 448. Leon Morris makes the same point in his *Apostolic Preaching*, pp. 14–17 and 19–20.
[32] *E.g.* Ex. 6:6; Dt. 9:26; Ne. 1:10; Ps. 77:15.
[33] B. B. Warfield, *Person and Work*, pp. 453–454.

death of Jesus means that there happens to him what would have had to happen to the many. Hence he takes their place.'[34] A parallel expression (perhaps an echo of it) occurs in 1 Timothy 2:5–6, 'Christ Jesus . . . gave himself as a ransom for all men.'

It is instructive that the Jewish historian Josephus used similar language when he described the Roman general Crassus' visit to the Temple in Jerusalem in 54–53 BC, intent on plundering the sanctuary. A priest named Eleazar, who was guardian of the sacred treasures, gave him a large bar of gold (worth 10,000 shekels) as *lytron anti pantōn*, 'a ransom instead of all'. That is, the gold bar was offered as a substitute for the Temple treasures.[35]

What then, first, is the human plight, from which we cannot extricate ourselves and which makes it necessary for us to be redeemed? We have seen that in the Old Testament people were redeemed from a variety of grave social situations such as debt, captivity, slavery, exile and liability to execution. But it is a moral bondage from which Christ has ransomed us. This is described now as our 'transgressions' or 'sins' (since in two key verses 'redemption' is a synonym for 'the forgiveness of sins'[36]), now as 'the curse of the law' (namely the divine judgment which it pronounces on law-breakers),[37] and now as 'the empty way of life handed down to you from your forefathers'.[38] Yet even our release from these captivities does not complete our redemption. There is more to come. For Christ 'gave himself for us to redeem us from all wickedness',[39] to liberate us from *all* the ravages of the Fall. This we have not yet experienced. Just as the Old Testament people of God, though already redeemed from their Egyptian and Babylonian exiles, were yet waiting for the promise of a fuller redemption, 'looking forward to the redemption of Jerusalem',[40] so the New Testament people of God, though already redeemed from guilt and judgment, are yet waiting for 'the day of redemption' when we shall be made perfect. This will include 'the redemption of our bodies'. At that point the whole groaning creation will be liberated from its bondage to decay and be brought to share in the freedom of the glory of God's children. Meanwhile, the indwelling Holy Spirit is himself the seal, the guarantee and the firstfruits of our final redemption.[41] Only then will Christ have redeemed us (and the universe) from all sin, pain, futility and decay.

[34] F. Büchsel, '*hilaskomai*', p. 343.
[35] Josephus, *Antiquities* xiv. 107.
[36] Eph. 1:7 and Col. 1:14. *Cf.* Heb. 9:15.   [37] Gal. 3:13; 4:5.
[38] 1 Pet. 1:18.   [39] Tit. 2:14. The noun is *anomia*, 'lawlessness'.
[40] Lk. 2:38. *Cf.* 1:68; 24:21.
[41] Lk. 21:28; Eph. 1:14; 4:30; Rom. 8:18–23.

Secondly, having considered the plight *from* which, we need to consider the price *with* which, we have been redeemed. The New Testament never presses the imagery to the point of indicating to whom the ransom was paid, but it leaves us in no doubt about the price: it was Christ himself. To begin with, there was the cost of the incarnation, of entering into our condition in order to reach us. Certainly we are told that when God sent his Son, he was 'born under law, to redeem those under law' (Gal. 4:4–5). Jeremias wonders if Paul was alluding to 'the dramatic act of entering into slavery in order to redeem a slave', just as the giving of the body to be burnt (1 Cor. 13:3) may refer to being 'branded with the slave-mark'.[42] Beyond the incarnation, however, lay the atonement. To accomplish this he gave 'himself' (1 Tim. 2:6; Tit. 2:14) or his 'life' (his *psychē*, Mk.10:45), dying under the law's curse to redeem us from it (Gal. 3:13).

When indicating the costly price paid by Christ to ransom us, however, the commonest word used by the New Testament authors was neither 'himself' nor his 'life' but his 'blood'. It was 'not with perishable things such as silver or gold', wrote Peter, 'that you were redeemed . . ., but with the precious blood of Christ, a lamb without blemish or defect' (1 Pet. 1:18–19). The writer to the Hebrews, steeped as he was in sacrificial imagery, emphasized that Christ was victim as well as priest, since 'he entered the Most Holy Place once for all by his own blood'.[43]

But what is meant by Christ's 'blood'? Everybody agrees that it alludes to his death, but in what sense? Picking on the threefold assertion in Leviticus 17:11–14 that 'the life of a creature is in the blood' or 'the life of every creature is its blood', and the even more straightforward statement of Deuteronomy 12:23 that 'the blood is the life', a strangely popular theory was developed by British theologians at the end of the last century that Christ's blood stands not for his death but for his life, which is released through death and so made available for us. Vincent Taylor, C. H. Dodd and even P. T. Forsyth were among those who developed this idea. Its origin is usually traced back, however, to Bishop B. F. Westcott's *Commentary on the Epistles of John* (1883), in which he wrote:

> By the outpouring of the Blood the life which was in it was not destroyed, though it was separated from the organism which it had before quickened . . . . Thus two distinct ideas were included in the sacrifice of a victim, the death of the victim by the shedding

[42] Jeremias, *Central Message*, pp. 37–38. *Cf.* I Clem. lv.
[43] Heb. 9:12. See also the references to Christ's blood in relation to our redemption in both Rom. 3:24–25 and Eph. 1:7.

of its blood, and the liberation, so to speak, of the principle of life by which it had been animated, so that this life became available for another end.[44]

Just so, Christ's blood was his life first given *for* us and then given *to* us.

In his later commentary on the Epistle to the Hebrews Westcott was still teaching the same concept. Blood is life 'regarded as still living', and 'the blood poured out is the energy . . . made available for others'.[45]

James Denney was outspoken in his rejection of this thesis. In his book *The Death of Christ* (1902) he urged his readers not to adopt 'the strange caprice which fascinated Westcott', who distinguished in the blood of Christ between his death and his life, his blood shed and offered, his life laid down and liberated for men. 'I venture to say', he continued, 'that a more groundless fancy never haunted and troubled the interpretation of any part of Scripture' (p. 149).

Then in 1948 Alan Stibbs' excellent Tyndale monograph was published, *The Meaning of the Word 'Blood' in Scripture*, which should have laid this ghost to rest for ever. He makes a thorough examination of the occurrences of 'blood' in both Old and New Testaments, and has no difficulty in demonstrating that it is 'a word-symbol for death'. True, 'the blood is the life of the flesh'. But 'this means that if the blood is separated from the flesh, whether in man or beast, the present physical life in the flesh will come to an end. Blood shed stands, therefore, not for the release of life from the burden of the flesh, but for the bringing to an end of life in the flesh. It is a witness to physical death, not an evidence of spiritual survival'. To 'drink Christ's blood', therefore, describes 'not participation in his life but appropriation of the benefits of his life laid down'.[46] We cannot do better than conclude as he does with a quotation from Johannes Behm's article on 'blood' in Kittel's

[44] B. F. Westcott, *Epistles of John*. Additional Note on 1 John 1:7, 'The Idea of Christ's Blood in the New Testament', pp. 34 ff.

[45] B. F. Westcott, *Epistle to the Hebrews*. Additional Note on Hebrews 9:9, pp. 283 ff.

[46] Alan M. Stibbs, *Meaning of the Word 'Blood' in Scripture*, pp. 10, 12, 16 and 30. Leon Morris has a chapter entitled 'The Blood' in his *Apostolic Preaching* (pp. 108–124), and in his *Cross in the New Testament* writes: 'the Hebrews understood "blood" habitually in the sense of "violent death" ' (p. 219). F. D. Kidner also criticizes Westcott's thesis in his *Sacrifice in the Old Testament*, and points out that the prohibition of the use of blood in food 'is consistent with the idea of its preciousness, but hardly with that of its potency' (p. 24).

Dictionary: ' "Blood of Christ" is (like "Cross") only another, clearer expression for the death of Christ in its salvation meaning' or 'redemptive significance'.[47]

The 'redemption' image has a third emphasis. In addition to the plight from which, and the price with which, we are ransomed, it draws attention to the person of the redeemer who has proprietary rights over his purchase. Thus Jesus' lordship over both church and Christian is attributed to his having bought us with his own blood. Presbyters, for example, are summoned to conscientious oversight of the church on the ground that God in Christ has bought it with his own blood (Acts 20:28). If the church was worth his blood, is it not worth our labour? The privilege of serving it is established by the preciousness of the price paid for its purchase. That seems to be the argument. Again, the redeemed community in heaven are singing a new song which celebrates the worthiness of the Lamb:

> You are worthy to take the scroll
> and to open its seals,
> because you were slain,
> and with your blood you purchased men for God
> from every tribe and language and people and nation.[48]

A remembrance that Jesus Christ has bought us with his blood, and that in consequence we belong to him, should motivate us as individual Christians to holiness, just as it motivates presbyters to faithful ministry and the heavenly host to worship. We detect a note of outrage in Peter's voice when he speaks of false teachers who by their shameful behaviour are 'denying the sovereign Lord who bought them' (2 Pet. 2:1). Since he bought them, they are his. They should therefore acknowledge and not deny him. Paul's urgent summons to us to 'flee from sexual immorality' is based on the doctrine of the human body and who owns it. On the one hand, 'Don't you know', he asks incredulously, 'that your body is a temple of the Holy Spirit, who is in you, whom you have received from God?' On the other, 'You are not your own; you were bought at a price. Therefore honour God with your body.'[49] Our body has not only been created by God and will one day be resurrected by him, but it has been bought by Christ's blood and is indwelt by his Spirit. Thus it belongs to God three times over, by creation, redemption and indwelling. How then, since it does not belong to

---

[47] Johannes Behm, '*haima*', p. 173.
[48] Rev. 5:9; *cf.* 1:5–6 and 14:3–4. [49] 1 Cor. 6:18–20; *cf.* 7:23.

us, can we misuse it? Instead, we are to honour God with it, by obedience and self-control. Bought by Christ, we have no business to become the slaves of anybody or anything else. Once we were the slaves of sin; now we are the slaves of Christ, and his service is the true freedom.

Justification

The two pictures we have so far considered have led us into the temple precincts (propitiation) and the market-place (redemption). The third image (justification) will take us into the lawcourt. For justification is the opposite of condemnation (*e.g.* Rom. 5:18; 8:34), and both are verdicts of a judge who pronounces the accused either guilty or not guilty. There is logic in the order in which we are reviewing these great words which describe the achievement of the cross. Propitiation inevitably comes first, because until the wrath of God is appeased (that is, until his love has found a way to avert his anger), there can be no salvation for human beings at all. Next, when we are ready to understand the meaning of salvation, we begin negatively with redemption, meaning our rescue at the high price of Christ's blood from the grim captivity of sin and guilt. Justification is its positive counterpart. True, some scholars have denied this. Sanday and Headlam wrote that justification 'is simply forgiveness, free forgiveness',[50] and more recently Jeremias has asserted that 'justification is forgiveness, nothing but forgiveness'.[51] The two concepts are surely complementary, however, not identical. Forgiveness remits our debts and cancels our liability to punishment; justification bestows on us a righteous standing before God.

The sixteenth-century Reformers, whom God enlightened to rediscover the biblical gospel of 'justification by faith', were convinced of its central importance. Luther called it 'the principal article of all Christian doctrine, which maketh true Christians indeed'.[52] And Cranmer wrote:

This faith the holy Scripture teacheth: this is the strong rock and foundation of Christian religion: this doctrine all old and ancient authors of Christ's church do approve: this doctrine advanceth and setteth forth the true glory of Christ, and beateth down the vain glory of man: this whosoever denieth is not to be counted

[50] Sanday and Headlam, *Romans*, p. 36.
[51] Jeremias, *Central Message*, p. 66.
[52] Martin Luther, *Galatians*, p. 143 (on Gal. 2:16). *Cf.* p. 101 (on Gal. 2:4–5).

for a true Christian man . . . but for an adversary of Christ. . . .[53]

Let me add a statement by some contemporary Anglican Evangelicals:

> Justification by Faith appears to us, as it does to all evangelicals, to be the heart and hub, the paradigm and essence, of the whole economy of God's saving grace. Like Atlas, it bears a world on its shoulders, the entire evangelical knowledge of God's love in Christ towards sinners.[54]

Despite the paramount importance of this truth, there have been many objections to it. First, there are those who have a strong antipathy to legal categories in all talk about salvation, on the ground that they represent God as Judge and King, not as Father, and therefore cannot adequately portray either his personal dealings with us or our personal relationship with him. This objection would be sustained if justification were the only image of salvation. But its juridical flavour is balanced by the more personal imagery of 'reconciliation' and 'adoption' (in which God is Father, not Judge), which we shall consider next. Other critics, secondly, attempt to dismiss the doctrine as a Pauline idiosyncrasy, originating in his peculiarly forensic mind. We should not hesitate to dismiss this dismissal, however, since what is Pauline is apostolic and therefore authoritative. In any case the statement is false. The concept of justification was not invented by Paul. It goes back to Jesus, who said that the tax collector in his parable 'went home justified before God', rather than the Pharisee (Lk. 18:14). Indeed, it goes further back still to the Old Testament, in which God's righteous and suffering servant 'will justify many', because 'he will bear their iniquities' (Is. 53:11).

Thirdly, we need to look at the reasons for the Roman Catholic rejection of the Reformers' teaching on justification by faith. We might not unfairly sum up the Council of Trent's doctrine under three headings which concern the nature of justification, what precedes and occasions it, and what follows it. First, the Council taught that justification takes place at baptism and includes both forgiveness and renewal. The baptized person is cleansed from all original and actual sins, and is simultaneously infused with a new and supernatural righteousness. Secondly, before baptism God's

[53] From Cranmer's 'Sermon on Salvation' in the *First Book of Homilies*, pp. 25–26.
[54] R. T. Beckwith, G. E. Duffield and J. I. Packer, *Across the Divide*, p. 58.

prevenient grace predisposes people 'to convert themselves to their own justification by freely assenting to and co-operating with that grace'. Thirdly, post-baptismal sins (if 'mortal', causing the loss of grace) are not included within the scope of justification. They have to be purged by contrition, confession and penance (also, if any remain at death, by purgatory), so that these and other post-baptismal good works may be said to 'merit' eternal life.[55]

The Protestant churches had good reason to be deeply disturbed by this teaching. At the same time, neither side was listening carefully to the other, and both were marked by the acrimonious and polemical spirit of their age. Today the basic issue, which is the way of salvation, remains crucial. Very much is at stake. Yet the atmosphere has changed. Also Hans Küng's astonishing monograph on Karl Barth's doctrine of justification[56] has opened up fresh possibilities for dialogue. So has the Second Vatican Council of the early 1960s.[57]

Hans Küng's book is in two parts. Concerning the first, which expounds 'Karl Barth's Theology of Justification', Barth himself wrote to Hans Küng: 'You have fully and accurately reproduced my views as I myself understand them . . . . You have me say what I actually do say and . . . I mean it in the way you have me say it' (p.xvii). Concerning the second part, which offers 'An Attempt at a Catholic Response', and in its conclusion claims 'a fundamental agreement between Catholic and Protestant theology, precisely in the theology of justification' (p. 271), Barth wrote: 'If this is the teaching of the Roman Catholic Church, then I must certainly admit that my view of justification agrees with the Roman Catholic view, if only for the reason that the Roman Catholic teaching would then be most strikingly in accord with mine!' He then asks how this agreement 'could remain hidden so long and from so many', and mischievously enquires whether Hans Küng discovered it before, during or after his reading of the *Church Dogmatics* (pp. xvii-xviii)!

Hans Küng certainly makes some remarkable statements, although perhaps it is a pity that his thesis seeks to demonstrate

[55] See Council of Trent, Session VI, and its Decrees on Original Sin, on Justification and on Penance.

[56] Hans Küng, *Justification* (1957).

[57] For sympathetic but critical Protestant assessments of recent Roman Catholic thinking see *Revolution in Rome* by David F. Wells; *Across the Divide* by R. T. Beckwith, G. E. Duffield and J. I. Packer; *Justification Today: The Roman Catholic and Anglican Debate* by R. G. England; George Carey's contribution entitled 'Justification by Faith in Recent Roman Catholic Theology' to *Great Acquittal*; and James Atkinson's *Rome and Reformation Today*.

Trent's accord with Barth, rather than with Luther for whom he appears to have less sympathy. In chapter 27 he defines grace according to Scripture as 'graciousness', God's 'favour' or 'generous kindness'. 'The issue is not *my having* grace, but *his being* gracious' (pp. 189–190). In chapter 28 he writes that justification 'must be defined as a *declaring just by court order*', and that in the New Testament 'the association with a juridical situation is never absent' (p. 200). Again, it is 'a judicial event', 'a wonderfully gracious saving justice' (pp. 205–206). Then in chapter 31 Hans Küng strongly affirms the truth of *sola fide* (by faith alone), and says that Luther was entirely correct and orthodox to add the word 'alone' to the text of Romans 3:28, since it was 'not Luther's invention', it had already appeared in several other translations, and Trent had not intended to contradict it (p. 237). So 'we have to acknowledge a fundamental agreement', he writes, 'in regard to the *sola fides* formula . . . Man is justified by God on the basis of faith alone' (p. 246). Moreover, 'justification through "faith alone" bespeaks the complete incapacity and incompetence of man for any sort of self-justification' (p. 301). 'Thus man is justified through God's grace alone; man achieves nothing; there is no human activity. Rather man simply submits to the justification of God; he does not do works; he believes' (p. 240).

Professor Küng does not stop there, however. Despite his emphasis on the judicial nature of justification as a divine declaration, he insists that God's Word is always efficacious, so that whatever God pronounces comes into being. Therefore, when God says 'you are just', 'the sinner *is* just, really and truly, outwardly and inwardly, wholly and completely. His sins *are* forgiven, and man is just in his heart . . . . In brief, God's *declaration* of justice is . . . at the same time and in the same act a *making just*' (p. 204). Justification is 'the single act which simultaneously declares just and makes just' (p. 210).

But there is a dangerous ambiguity here, especially in the rhetorical sentence about the justified sinner being 'wholly and completely' just. What does this imply?

If 'just' here means 'forgiven, accepted, right with God', then indeed we become immediately, wholly and completely what God declares us to be; we enjoy the righteous status which he has conferred upon us. This is the true meaning of 'justification'.

If 'just' is used to signify 'made new, made alive', then again God's creative word immediately makes us what he declares. This would be a misuse of the word 'just', however, for what is being described now is not justification, but regeneration.

If 'just' means 'having a righteous character' or 'being conformed to the image of Christ', then God's declaration does not immediately secure it, but only initiates it. For this is not justification but sanctification, and is a continuous, lifelong process.

Even Hans Küng's explanatory Excursus II, 'Justification and Sanctification in the New Testament', does not disclose unambiguously what he means by God 'making' the sinner 'just'. He recognizes the problem that the language of 'sanctification' is used in the New Testament in two distinct senses. Sometimes it is almost a synonym for justification, because it denotes the holiness of our *status*, not our character. In this sense, at the very moment of our justification we become 'saints', for we have been 'sanctified in Christ Jesus', set apart to belong to the holy people of God.[58] At other times 'sanctification' describes the process of growing in holiness and becoming Christlike.[59]

The confusion seems to arise because Hans Küng does not maintain this distinction consistently. He refers to justification and sanctification now as happening together instantaneously ('God simultaneously justifies and sanctifies', p. 308) and now as being together capable of growth (Trent spoke of 'the necessity of . . . growth in justification', p. 228). This is very misleading, however. In the debate about justification it would be wise to reserve the word sanctification for its distinctive meaning of 'growing in holiness'. For then we can affirm that justification (God declaring us righteous through his Son's death) is instantaneous and complete, admitting no degrees, while sanctification (God making us righteous through his Spirit's indwelling), though begun the moment we are justified, is gradual and throughout this life incomplete, as we are being transformed into the likeness of Christ 'from one degree of glory to another' (2 Cor. 3:18, RSV).

In desiring a greater clarification at this point, I am not wishing to belittle Hans Küng's *tour de force*. At the same time, more than a quarter of a century has passed since the publication of his book, and one is not conscious of any widespread proclamation in the Roman Catholic Church of the gospel of justification by grace alone through faith alone.

Risking the danger of oversimplification, one may say that Evangelicals and Roman Catholics together teach that God by his grace is the only Saviour of sinners, that self-salvation is impossible, and that the death of Jesus Christ as a propitiatory sacrifice is the ultimate ground of justification. But precisely what justification is, how it relates to other aspects of salvation, and how it takes place

---

[58] *E.g.* Acts 20:32; 1 Cor. 1:2; 6:11; Heb. 10:29; 13:12.
[59] *E.g.* Rom. 6:19; 2 Cor. 7:1; 1 Thes. 4:3, 7; 5:23; Heb. 12:14.

– these are areas of continuing and anxious debate.

Evangelicals feel the need to press Roman Catholics about sin, grace, faith and works. Roman Catholics are uncomfortable when we talk about 'total depravity' (that every part of our humanness has been twisted by the Fall), which lies behind our insistence on the need both for a radical salvation and for non-contributory grace. They find this a pessimistic view of the human condition, involving an inadequate doctrine of creation. They add that human beings have not lost their free will, and are therefore able to co-operate with grace and contribute to salvation. We, however, see the need to underline the New Testament antitheses regarding salvation. 'It is by grace you have been saved, through faith – and this not from yourselves, it is the gift of God – not of works, so that no-one can boast.' 'We . . . know that a man is not justified by observing the law, but by faith in Jesus Christ.' Again, 'he saved us, not because of righteous things we had done, but because of his mercy'.[60] We cannot avoid the stark alternative which such texts put before us. Not works, but grace. Not law, but faith. Not our righteous deeds but his mercy. There is no co-operation here between God and us, only a choice between two mutually exclusive ways, his and ours. Moreover, the faith which justifies is emphatically not another work. No, to say 'justification by faith' is merely another way of saying 'justification by Christ'. Faith has absolutely no value in itself; its value lies solely in its object. Faith is the eye that looks to Christ, the hand that lays hold of him, the mouth that drinks the water of life. And the more clearly we see the absolute adequacy of Jesus Christ's divine-human person and sin-bearing death, the more incongruous does it appear that anybody could suppose that we have anything to offer. That is why justification by faith alone, to quote Cranmer again, 'advances the true glory of Christ and beats down the vain glory of man'.

If we desire to press Roman Catholics on these points, however, we need also to respond to their pressures upon us. The chief might be a series of questions like the following. 'Do you still insist that when God justifies sinners he "pronounces" but does not "make" them righteous? that justification is a legal declaration, not a moral transformation? that righteousness is "imputed" to us, but neither "infused" in us nor even "imparted" to us? that we put on Christ's righteousness like a cloak, which conceals our continuing sinfulness? that justification, while changing our status, leaves our character and conduct unchanged? that every justified Christian, as the Reformers taught, is *simul justus et peccator* (at one and the

---

[60] Eph. 2:8–9; Gal. 2:16; Tit. 3:5.

same time a righteous person and a sinner)? If so, is not justification a legal fiction, even a giant hoax, a phoney transaction external to yourself, which leaves you inwardly unrenewed? Are you not claiming to be changed when in fact you are not changed? Is not your doctrine of "justification by faith alone" a thinly disguised free licence to go on sinning?'

These are searching questions. In one way or another, I have heard all of them asked. And there is no doubt that we Evangelicals, in our zeal to emphasize the utter freeness of salvation, have sometimes been incautious in our phraseology, and have given the impression that good works are of no importance. But then the apostle Paul could evidently be incautious too, since his critics flung exactly the same charge at him, which led him to cry: 'What shall we say, then? Shall we go on sinning, so that grace may increase?' (Rom. 6:1). His indignant riposte to his own rhetorical question was to remind his readers of their baptism. Did they not know that, when they were baptized into Christ Jesus, they were baptized into his death? Having thus died with him to sin, how could they possibly live in it any longer? (vv. 2–3).

What Paul was doing by this response was to show that justification is not the only image of salvation. It would be entirely mistaken to make the equation 'salvation equals justification'. 'Salvation' is the comprehensive word, but it has many facets which are illustrated by different pictures, of which justification is only one. Redemption, as we have seen, is another, and bears witness to our radical deliverance from sin as well as guilt. Another is re-creation, so that 'if anyone is in Christ, he is a new creation' (2 Cor. 5:17). Yet another is regeneration or new birth, which is the inward work of the Holy Spirit, who then remains as a gracious indwelling presence, transforming the believer into the image of Christ, which is the process of sanctification. All these belong together. Regeneration is not an áspect of justification, but both are aspects of salvation, and neither can take place without the other. Indeed, the great affirmation 'he saved us' is broken down into its component parts, which are 'the washing of rebirth and renewal by the Holy Spirit' on the one hand and being 'justified by his grace' on the other (Tit. 3:5–7). The justifying work of the Son and the regenerating work of the Spirit cannot be separated. It is for this reason that good works of love follow justification and new birth as their necessary evidence. For salvation, which is never 'by works', is always 'unto works'. Luther used to illustrate the correct order of events by reference to the tree and its fruit: 'The tree must be first, and then the fruit. For the apples make not the tree, but the tree makes the apples. So faith first makes the person, who afterwards brings forth works.'[61]

Once we hold fast that the work of the Son for us and the work of the Spirit in us, that is to say, justification and regeneration, are inseparable twins, it is quite safe to go on insisting that justification is an external, legal declaration that the sinner has been put right with God, forgiven and reinstated. This is plain from the popular use of the word. As Leon Morris has pointed out, 'when we speak of justifying an opinion or an action, we do not mean that we change or improve it. Rather we mean that we secure a verdict for it, we vindicate it'.[62] Similarly, when Luke says that everybody, on hearing Jesus' teaching, 'justified God', what he means is that they 'acknowledged that God's way was right' (Lk. 7:29).

The vocabulary of justification and condemnation occurs regularly in the Old Testament. Moses gave instructions to the Israelite judges that they were to decide cases referred to them, 'acquitting (*i.e.* justifying) the innocent and condemning the guilty' (Dt. 25:1). Everybody knew that Yahweh would never 'acquit (justify) the guilty' (Ex. 23:7), and that 'acquitting the guilty and condemning the innocent – the LORD detests them both' (Pr. 17:15). The prophet Isaiah pronounced a fierce woe against magistrates who 'acquit the guilty for a bribe, but deny justice to the innocent' (5:23). To condemn the righteous and justify the unrighteous would be to turn the administration of justice on its head. It is against this background of accepted judicial practice that Paul must have shocked his Roman readers when he wrote that 'God . . . justifies the wicked' (Rom. 4:5). How could God conceivably do such a thing? It was outrageous that the Divine Judge should practise what – in the very same Greek words – he had forbidden human judges to do. Besides, how could the Righteous One declare the unrighteous righteous? The very thought was preposterous.

In order to summarize Paul's defence of the divine justification of sinners, I will select four of his key phrases, which relate successively to justification's source, ground, means and effects. First, the *source* of our justification is indicated in the expression *justified by his grace* (Rom. 3:24), that is, by his utterly undeserved favour. Since it is certain that 'there is no-one righteous, not even one' (Rom. 3:10), it is equally certain that no-one can declare himself to be righteous in God's sight.[63] Self-justification is a sheer impossibility (Rom. 3:20). Therefore, 'it is God who justifies' (Rom. 8:33); only he can. And he does it 'freely' (Rom. 3:24, *dōrean*, 'as a free gift, gratis'), not because of any works of ours, but because of his

---

[61] Martin Luther, *Epistle to the Galatians*, p. 247, on Gal. 3:10.
[62] L. Morris, *Cross in the New Testament*, p. 242.
[63] Ps. 143:2. *Cf.* Pss. 51:4; 130:3; Jb. 25:4.

own grace. In Tom Wright's neat epigram, 'no sin, no need for justification: no grace, no possibility of it'.[64]

Grace is one thing, however; justice is another. And justification has to do with justice. To say that we are 'justified by his grace' tells us the source of our justification, but says nothing about a righteous basis of it, without which God would contradict his own justice. So another key expression of Paul's, which introduces us to the *ground* of our justification, is *justified by his blood* (Rom. 5:9). Justification is not a synonym for amnesty, which strictly is pardon without principle, a forgiveness which overlooks – even forgets (*amnēstia* is 'forgetfulness') – wrongdoing and declines to bring it to justice. No, justification is an act of justice, of gracious justice. Its synonym is 'the righteousness of God' (Rom. 1:17; 3:21), which might for the moment be explained as his 'righteous way of righteoussing the unrighteous'. Dr J. I. Packer defines it as 'God's gracious work of bestowing upon guilty sinners a justified justification, acquitting them in the court of heaven without prejudice to his justice as their Judge'.[65] When God justifies sinners, he is not declaring bad people to be good, or saying that they are not sinners after all; he is pronouncing them legally righteous, free from any liability to the broken law, because he himself in his Son has borne the penalty of their law-breaking. That is why Paul is able to bring together in a single sentence the concepts of justification, redemption and propitiation (Rom. 3:24–25). The reasons why we are 'justified freely by God's grace' are that Christ Jesus paid the ransom-price and that God presented him as a propitiatory sacrifice. In other words, we are 'justified by his blood'. There could be no justification without atonement.

Thirdly, the *means* of our justification is indicated in Paul's favourite expression *justified by faith*.[66] Grace and faith belong indissolubly to one another, since faith's only function is to receive what grace freely offers. We are not, therefore, justified 'by' our faith, as we are justified 'by' God's grace and 'by' Christ's blood. God's grace is the source and Christ's blood the ground of our justification; faith is only the means by which we are united to Christ. As Richard Hooker put it with his usual precision: 'God doth justify the believing man, yet not for the worthiness of his belief, but for his worthiness who is believed.'[67]

---

[64] From his essay 'Justification: The Biblical Basis and its Relevance for Contemporary Evangelicalism', in *Great Acquittal*, p. 16.

[65] From his article 'Justification' in *New Bible Dictionary*, p. 647.

[66] *E.g.* Rom. 3:28; 5:1; Gal. 2:16; Phil. 3:9.

[67] From Hooker's 'Definition of Justification', being Chapter xxxiii of his *Ecclesiastical Polity*, which began to be published in 1593.

Further, if faith is only the means, it is also the only means. Although the word 'only' does not occur in the Greek of Romans 3:28, it was a right instinct of Luther's, as we have seen, and indeed a correct translation, to render Paul's expression 'we maintain that a man is justified by faith only, apart from observing the law'. The point of his writing 'by faith apart from works of law' was to exclude law-works altogether, leaving faith as the sole means of justification. And Paul has already given his reason in the previous verse, namely to exclude boasting. For unless all human works, merits, co-operation and contributions are ruthlessly excluded, and Christ's sin-bearing death is seen in its solitary glory as the only ground of our justification, boasting cannot be excluded. Cranmer saw this clearly: 'This saying, that we be justified by faith only, freely, and without works, is spoken for to take away clearly all merit of our works, as being unable to deserve our justification at God's hands, . . . and thereby wholly for to ascribe the merit and deserving of our justification unto Christ only and his most precious bloodshedding . . . . And this form of speaking we use in the humbling of ourselves to God, and to give all the glory to our Saviour Christ, who is best worthy to have it.'[68]

Fourthly, what are the *effects* of our justification? I think we can deduce them from another, and sometimes neglected, Pauline expression, namely that we are *justified in Christ*.[69] To say that we are justified 'through Christ' points to his historical death; to say that we are justified 'in Christ' points to the personal relationship with him which by faith we now enjoy. This simple fact makes it impossible for us to think of justification as a purely external transaction; it cannot be isolated from our union with Christ and all the benefits which this brings. The first is membership of the Messianic community of Jesus. If we are in Christ and therefore justified, we are also the children of God and the true (spiritual) descendants of Abraham. Further, no racial, social or sexual barrier can come between us. This is the theme of Galatians 3:26–29. Tom Wright is surely correct in his emphasis that 'justification is not an individualist's charter, but God's declaration that we belong to the covenant community'.[70] Secondly, this new community, to create which Christ gave himself on the cross, is to be 'eager to do what is good', and its members are to devote themselves to good

[68] From Cranmer's 'Sermon on Salvation' in the *First Book of Homilies*, pp. 25 and 29.
[69] Gal. 2:17. *Cf.* Rom. 8:1; 2 Cor. 5:21; Eph. 1:6.
[70] Tom Wright, 'Justification: The Biblical Basis' from *Great Acquittal*, p. 36.

works.[71] So there is no ultimate conflict between Paul and James. They may have been using the verb 'justify' in different senses. They were certainly writing against different heresies, Paul against the self-righteous legalism of the Judaizers and James against the dead orthodoxy of the intellectualizers. Yet both teach that an authentic faith works, Paul stressing the faith that issues in works, and James the works that issue from faith.[72]

The new community of Jesus is an eschatological community which lives already in the new age he inaugurated. For justification is an eschatological event. It brings forward into the present the verdict which belongs to the last judgment. That is why the church is a community of hope, which looks with humble confidence into the future. To be sure, we can say with Paul that the law condemned us. But 'there is now no condemnation for those who are in Christ Jesus'. Why not? Because God has done for us what the law could not do. By sending his own Son in the likeness of our sinful nature to be a sin offering, he actually condemned our sin in the human Jesus. It is only because he was condemned that we could be justified. What then have we to fear? 'Who will bring any charge against those whom God has chosen? It is God who justifies. Who is he that condemns? Christ Jesus, who died – more than that, who was raised to life – is at the right hand of God and is also interceding for us.' That is why, once we have been justified, nothing can separate us from the love of God that is in Christ Jesus our Lord.[73]

Reconciliation

The fourth image of salvation, which illustrates the achievement of the cross, is 'reconciliation'. It is probably the most popular of the four because it is the most personal. We have left behind us the temple precincts, the slave-market and the lawcourts; we are now in our own home with our family and friends. True, there is a quarrel, even 'enmity', but to reconcile means to restore a relationship, to renew a friendship. So an original relationship is presupposed which, having been broken, has been recovered by Christ.

A second reason why people feel at ease with this imagery is that reconciliation is the opposite of alienation, and many people nowadays refer to themselves as 'alienated'. Marxists continue to speak of the economic alienation of workers from the product of

[71] Tit. 2:14; 3:8. [72] *E.g.* Gal. 5:6; 1 Thes. 1:3; Jas. 2:14–26.
[73] Rom. 7:7–25; 8:1, 3, 33–34, 39.

their labour. Others talk of political alienation, a sense of power-lessness to change society. But for many more 'alienation' encapsulates the modern mood. They do not feel at home in the materialism, emptiness and superficiality of the western world. On the contrary, they feel unfulfilled and disorientated, unable to find themselves, their identity or their freedom. To them talk of reconciliation sounds like the good news it is.

The first thing that has to be said about the biblical gospel of reconciliation, however, is that it begins with reconciliation to God, and continues with a reconciled community in Christ. Reconciliation is not a term the Bible uses to describe 'coming to terms with oneself', although it does insist that it is only through losing ourselves in love for God and neighbour that we truly find ourselves.

Reconciliation with God, then, is the beginning. This is the meaning of 'atonement'. It alludes to the event through which God and human beings, previously alienated from one another, are made 'at one' again. The word occurs only once in the New Testament's Authorized (King James') Version, namely in the statement that through Christ 'we have now received the atonement' (Rom. 5:11), that is to say, 'the reconciliation'. It is significant that in Romans 5:9–11, which is one of the four great passages on reconciliation in the New Testament, to be reconciled and to be justified are parallels. 'Since we have now been justified by his blood' is balanced by 'if, when we were God's enemies, we were reconciled to him through the death of his Son'. The two states, though both effected by the cross, are not identical, however. Justification is our legal standing before our Judge in the court; reconciliation is our personal relationship with our Father in the home. Indeed, the latter is the sequel and fruit of the former. It is only when we have been justified by faith that we have peace with God (Rom. 5:1), which is reconciliation.

Two other New Testament terms confirm this emphasis that reconciliation means peace with God, namely 'adoption' and 'access'. With regard to the former, it was Jesus himself who always addressed God intimately as 'Abba, Father', who gave us permission to do the same, approaching him as 'our Father in heaven'. The apostles enlarged on it. John, who attributes our being children of God to our being born of God, expresses his sense of wonder that the Father should have loved us enough to call us, and indeed make us, his children.[74] Paul, on the other hand, traces our status as God's children rather to our adoption than to

[74] Jn. 1:12–13; 1 Jn. 3:1–10.

our new birth, and emphasizes the privileges we have in being sons
instead of slaves, and therefore God's heirs as well.[75]

'Access' (*prosagōgē*) to God is another blessing of reconciliation.
It seems to denote the active communion with God, especially in
prayer, which his reconciled children enjoy. Twice Paul brackets
'access to God' and 'peace with God', the first time attributing
them to our justification rather than our reconciliation (Rom.
5:1–2), and the second time explaining 'access' as a Trinitarian
experience, in that we have access to the Father through the Son
by the Spirit (Eph. 2:17–18), and 'we may approach God with
freedom and confidence' (3:12). Peter uses the cognate verb, declaring that it was in order to 'bring' us to God (*prosagō*) that Christ
died for us once for all, the righteous instead of the unrighteous
(1 Pet. 3:18). And the writer to the Hebrews borrows from the
Day of Atonement ritual, in order to convey the nearness to God
which Christ by his sacrifice and priesthood has made possible.
'Since we have confidence to enter the Most Holy Place by the
blood of Jesus,' he writes, 'let us draw near to God with a sincere
heart in full assurance of faith . . .' (10:19–22).

Thus, reconciliation, peace with God, adoption into his family
and access into his presence all bear witness to the same new
relationship into which God has brought us.

But reconciliation has a horizontal as well as a vertical plane.
For God has reconciled us to one another in his new community,
as well as to himself. A second great New Testament passage (Eph.
2:11–22) focuses on this, and in particular on the healing of the
breach between Jews and Gentiles, so that sometimes it is not clear
which reconciliation Paul is referring to. He reminds his Gentile
Christian readers that formerly they were on the one hand
'excluded from citizenship in Israel and foreigners to the covenants
of promise' and on the other 'separate from Christ . . . and without
God in the world' (v. 12). So they were 'far away' from both God
and Israel, doubly alienated; 'but now in Christ Jesus', he goes on,
'you who once were far away have been brought near through the
blood of Christ' – near to God and near to Israel (v. 13). In fact
Christ, who 'himself is our peace', has broken down the barrier
between these two halves of the human race, and 'made the two
one' (v. 14). He has both 'abolished' the law's regulations which
kept them apart and 'created' in himself 'one new man out of the
two, thus making peace' (v. 15). Knowing the mutual bitterness
and contempt which Jews and Gentiles felt for each other, this
reconciliation was a miracle of God's grace and power. It has

[75] E.g. Rom. 8:14–17; Gal. 3:26–29; 4:1–7.

resulted in the emergence of a single, new, unified humanity, whose members through the cross have been reconciled both to God and to one another. Formerly enemies, they have had their reciprocal hostility put to death. They are now fellow citizens in God's kingdom, brothers and sisters in God's family (v. 19), fellow members of Christ's body and sharers together in the Messianic promise (3:6). This complete equality of Jew and Gentile in the new community is the 'mystery' which for centuries had been kept secret, but which now God had revealed to the apostles, especially to Paul, the apostle to the Gentiles (3:4–6).

Even this does not complete the reconciliation which God has achieved through Christ. In *Colossians*, which is a sister epistle to *Ephesians* because the two contain many parallels, Paul adds a cosmic dimension to the work of Christ. Whether the great Christological passage (Col. 1:15–20) is an early Christian hymn, as many scholars believe, or an original composition of Paul's, it is a sublime statement of the absolute supremacy of Jesus Christ in creation and redemption, in the universe and the church. At the same time, it is aptly addressed to the Colossian heretics who seem to have taught the existence of angelic intermediaries ('thrones, powers, rulers, authorities') between the Creator and the material creation, and may have suggested that Jesus was one of them. Paul will not have it. His emphasis is on 'all things', an expression he uses five times, which usually means the cosmos, but here evidently includes the principalities and powers. All things were created by God 'in', 'through' and 'for' Christ (v. 16). He is 'before' all things in time and rank, and 'in' him all things are sustained and integrated (v. 17). Since all things exist in, through, for and under Christ, he is the supreme lord by right. In addition, he is the head of the body, the church, being the firstborn from among the dead, so that he might be pre-eminent in everything (v. 18). And this second sphere of his supremacy is due to the fact that God was pleased for his fullness both to dwell in him (v. 19) and to do his work of reconciliation through him, making peace through his blood shed on the cross. This time what is reconciled is again called 'all things', which are further described as 'things on earth or things in heaven' (v. 20).

We cannot be sure to what Paul was alluding. The presumption is that the 'all things' reconciled (v. 20) have the same identity as the 'all things' created (vv. 16–17). But if what was created through Christ needed later to be reconciled through Christ, something must have gone wrong in between. As Peter O'Brien puts it, 'the presupposition is that the unity and harmony of the cosmos have suffered a considerable dislocation, even a rupture, thus requiring reconciliation'.[76] If this is a reference to the natural order, then pehaps its 'reconciliation' is the same as the 'liberation from its bondage to decay' (Rom. 8:21), although this is a future event. If, on the other hand, the reference is to evil cosmic intelligences or fallen angels, there is no New Testament warrant for expecting that they have been (or will be) savingly reconciled to God. It seems more probable, therefore, that the principalities and powers have been 'reconciled' in the sense of the next chapter, namely that they have been 'disarmed' by Christ, who 'made a public spectacle of them, triumphing over them by the cross' (Col. 2:15). It is admittedly a strange use of the word 'reconciled', but, since Paul also describes this as 'making peace' (1:20), perhaps F. F. Bruce is right that he is thinking of a 'pacification' of cosmic beings 'submitting against their wills to a power which they cannot resist'.[77] In this case the same situation may be in mind which is elsewhere described as every knee bowing to Jesus and every tongue confessing his lordship (Phil. 2:9–11), and all things being placed by God under his feet until the day when they are brought together 'under one head, even Christ' (Eph. 1:10, 22).

So far we have been investigating the objects of God's reconciling work through Christ. He has reconciled sinners to himself, Jews and Gentiles to one another, and even the cosmic powers in the sense of disarming and pacifying them. We need now to consider how the reconciliation has taken place, and what in the great drama of reconciliation are the respective roles played by God, Christ and ourselves. For light on these questions we turn to the fourth reconciliation passage, 2 Corinthians 5:18–21.

> All this is from God, who reconciled us to himself through Christ and gave us the ministry of reconciliation: that God was reconciling the world to himself in Christ, not counting men's sins against them. And he has committed to us the message of reconciliation. We are therefore Christ's ambassadors, as though God were making his appeal through us – we implore you on Christ's behalf: Be reconciled to God. God made him who had no sin to be sin for us, so that in him we might become the righteousness of God.

The first truth this passage makes clear is that *God is the author of the reconciliation*. In fact, this is the principal emphasis throughout. 'All (*ta panta*, 'all things') is from God.' Perhaps the

[76] Peter T. O'Brien, *Colossians*, p. 53.
[77] E. K. Simpson and F. F. Bruce, *Ephesians and Colossians*, p. 210. Peter O'Brien follows F. F. Bruce in this interpretation (*Colossians*, p. 56).

'all things' look back to the 'new things' of the new creation with which the previous verse ended. God is the Creator; the new creation comes from him. Eight verbs follow in this paragraph which have God as their subject. They describe God's gracious initiative – God reconciling, God giving, God appealing, God making Christ to be sin for us. As the New English Bible translates the first sentence in verse 18: 'From first to last this has been the work of God.'

Therefore no explanation of the atonement is biblical which takes the initiative from God, and gives it instead either to us or to Christ. The initiative is certainly not ours. We have nothing to offer, to contribute, to plead. In William Temple's memorable phrase, 'all is of God; the only thing of my very own which I contribute to my redemption is the sin from which I need to be redeemed'. Nor has the primary initiative been Christ's. No interpretation of the atonement will do which attributes the initiative to Christ *in such a way as to take it from the Father*. Christ did indeed take the initiative to come, but only in the sense that he could say, 'Here I am . . . I have come to do your will, O God' (Heb. 10:7). The initiative of the Son was in submission to the initiative of the Father. There was no reluctance on the part of the Father. There was no intervention on the part of Christ as a third party. No, the reconciliation was conceived and born in the love of God. 'God so loved the world that he gave his one and only Son.'

We note here that wherever the verb 'to reconcile' occurs in the New Testament, either God is the subject (he reconciled us to himself) or, if the verb is passive, we are (we were reconciled to him). God is never the object. It is never said that 'Christ reconciled the Father to us'. Formally, linguistically, this is a fact. But we must be careful not to build too much on it theologically. For if we were right to say that God propitiated his own wrath through Christ, we could certainly say that he reconciled himself to us through Christ. If he needed to be propitiated, he equally needed to be reconciled. In other words, it is a mistake to think that the barrier between God and us, which necessitated the work of reconciliation, was entirely on our side, so that we needed to be reconciled and God did not. True, we were 'God's enemies', hostile to him in our hearts.[78] But the 'enmity' was on both sides. The wall or barrier between God and us was constituted both by our rebellion against him and by his wrath upon us on account of our

[78] For references to human hostility to God see Rom. 5:10; 8:7; Eph. 2:14, 16; Col. 1:21; Jas. 4:4.

rebellion. Three arguments support this contention.

First, the *language*. The very words 'enemy', 'enmity' and 'hostility' imply reciprocity. For example, in Romans 11:28 the word 'enemies' must be passive, since it is contrasted with the passive word 'loved'. Also the 'hostility' between Jews and Gentiles in Ephesians 2:14 was reciprocal, suggesting that the other 'hostility' (between God and sinners) was reciprocal too. So F. Büchsel writes that we should not interpret enemies 'unilaterally', as meaning only 'hostile to God', but as including 'standing under the wrath of God'.[79] The second argument concerns the *context*, both of each passage and of the whole Bible. In or near each major reconciliation passage there is a reference to God's wrath. The most striking is Romans 5, where 'saved from God's wrath' (v. 9) is immediately followed by 'we were God's enemies' (v. 10). Then there is the wider biblical context. Leon Morris particularly underlines this: 'there is, on the scriptural view, a definite hostility on the part of God to everything that is evil . . . . Thus, quite apart from details of interpretation of particular passages, there is strong and consistent teaching to the effect that God is active in his opposition to all that is evil.'[80] Thirdly, there is the *theology*. Paul's logic was that God had acted objectively in reconciliation *before* the message of reconciliation was proclaimed. So the 'peace' which evangelists preach (Eph. 2:17) cannot be that *our* enmity has been overcome (they are rather preaching in order that it may be), but that God has turned aside from *his* enmity because of Christ's cross. He has reconciled himself to us; we must now be reconciled to him.

Emil Brunner expressed himself forthrightly on this matter:

> Reconciliation presupposes enmity between two parties. To put it still more exactly: reconciliation, real reconciliation, an objective act of reconciliation, presupposes enmity on both sides; that is, that man is the enemy of God and that God is the enemy of man.[81]

Brunner goes on to explain that our enmity towards God is seen in our restlessness, ranging from frivolity to open renunciation and hatred of God, while his enmity to us is his wrath. Moreover, 'God is present in this anger, it is actually *his* anger' (p. 517).

---

[79] From the article on *allassō* and *katallassō* by F. Büchsel, p. 257.

[80] L. Morris, *Apostolic Preaching*, p. 196. See Dr Morris' chapters on 'Reconciliation' in both *Apostolic Preaching*, pp. 186–223 and *Atonement*, pp. 132–150.

[81] E. Brunner, *Mediator*, p. 516.

Secondly, if God is the author, *Christ is the agent of the reconciliation*. This is crystal clear in 2 Corinthians 5:18 and 19. 'God . . . reconciled us to himself through Christ' and 'God was reconciling the world to himself in Christ'. Both statements tell us that God took the initiative to reconcile, and that he did it in and through Christ. In this respect the sentences are identical. But the beneficiaries change from 'us' to 'the world', to show the universal scope of the reconciliation, and the preposition changes from 'through' to 'in', to show that God was not working through Christ as his agent at a distance but was actually present in him as he did the work.

We have now to notice the past tenses, especially the aorist ('reconciled', v. 18). Both verbs indicate that God was doing, indeed did, something in Christ. Let James Denney draw out the implication of this:

> The work of reconciliation, in the sense of the New Testament, is a work which is *finished*, and which we must conceive to be finished, *before the gospel is preached* . . . . Reconciliation . . . is not something which is being done; it is something which is done. No doubt there is a work of Christ which is in process, but it has as its basis a finished work of Christ. It is in virtue of something already consummated on his cross that Christ is able to make the appeal to us which he does, and to win the response in which we *receive* the reconciliation.[82]

A few years later P. T. Forsyth pungently expressed the same truth:

> 'God was in Christ reconciling', actually reconciling, finishing the work. It was not a tentative, preliminary affair . . . . Reconciliation was finished in Christ's death. Paul did not preach a gradual reconciliation. He preached what the old divines used to call the finished work . . . . He preached something done once for all – a reconciliation which is the base of every soul's reconcilement, not an invitation only.[83]

What, then, was it which God did or accomplished in and through Christ? Paul answers this question in two complementary ways, negative and positive. Negatively, God declined to reckon our transgressions against us (v. 19b). Of course we deserved to

---

[82] James Denney, *Death of Christ*, pp. 85–86. *Cf.* also p. 128.
[83] P. T. Forsyth, *Work of Christ*, p. 86.

have them counted against us. But if he were to bring us into judgment, we would die. 'If you, O LORD, kept a record of sins, O Lord, who could stand?' (Ps. 130:3). So God in his mercy refused to reckon our sins against us or require us to bear their penalty. What then has he done with them? For he cannot condone them. No, the positive counterpart is given in verse 21: 'God made him who had no sin to be sin for us, so that in him we might become the righteousness of God.' It is surely one of the most startling statements in the Bible, yet we must not on that account evade it. James Denney was not exaggerating when he wrote of it: 'Mysterious and awful as this thought is, it is the key to the whole of the New Testament.'[84] For our sake God actually made the sinless Christ to be sin with our sins. The God who refused to reckon our sins to us reckoned them to Christ instead. Indeed, his personal sinlessness uniquely qualified him to bear our sins in our place.

Moreover, Christ became sin for us, in order that 'in him we might become the righteousness of God'. In other words, our sins were imputed to the sinless Christ, in order that we sinners, by being united to him, might receive as a free gift a standing of righteousness before God. Christian disciples down the centuries have meditated on this exchange between the sinless Christ and sinners, and have marvelled at it. The first example is probably in the second-century *Epistle to Diognetus*, chapter 9: 'O sweet exchange! O unsearchable operation! O benefits surpassing all expectation! that the wickedness of many should be hid in a single Righteous One, and that the righteousness of One should justify many transgressors.' Then here is Luther writing to a monk in distress about his sins: 'Learn to know Christ and him crucified. Learn to sing to him and say "Lord Jesus, you are my righteousness, I am your sin. You took on you what was mine; yet set on me what was yours. You became what you were not, that I might become what I was not".'[85]

Half a century or so later (in 1585) Richard Hooker said in a sermon on Habakkuk 1:4:

Such we are in the sight of God the Father, as is the very Son of God himself. Let it be counted folly or frenzy or fury or whatsoever. It is our wisdom and our comfort; we care for no knowledge in the world but this, that man hath sinned and God has suffered; that God hath made himself the sin of men, and

[84] James Denney, *Death of Christ*, p. 88.
[85] Luther, *Letters of Spiritual Counsel*, p. 110.

that men are made the righteousness of God.[86]

As an example from this century let me choose Emil Brunner's epigram: 'Justification means this miracle: that Christ takes our place and we take his.'[87]

Looking back over the paragraph we are studying, it is important to note the paradox constituted by the first and last statements. On the one hand, God was in Christ reconciling. On the other, God made Christ to be sin for us. How God can have been in Christ when he made him to be sin is the ultimate mystery of the atonement. But we must hold both affirmations tenaciously, and never expound either in such a way as to contradict the other.

Thirdly, if God is the author and Christ is the agent, *we are the ambassadors of the reconciliation*. In considering verses 18 and 19 we have so far looked only at the first part of each sentence. But each is in two parts, the first stating the achievement of the reconciliation (God was in Christ reconciling the world to himself) and the second its announcement (he has committed to us the ministry and the message of reconciliation). Moreover this ministry of reconciliation is itself in two stages. It begins as a proclamation that God was in Christ reconciling and that he made Christ to be sin for us. It continues with an appeal to people to 'be reconciled to God', that is, 'avail yourselves of the offered terms of reconciliation with God' (*cf*. Mt. 5:24), or simply 'receive it' (*cf*. Rom. 5:11).[88] We must keep these things distinct. God finished the work of reconciliation at the cross, yet it is still necessary for sinners to repent and believe and so 'be reconciled to God'. Again, sinners need to 'be reconciled to God', yet we must not forget that on God's side the work of reconciliation has already been done. If these two things are to be kept distinct, they will also in all authentic gospel preaching be kept together. It is not enough to expound a thoroughly orthodox doctrine of reconciliation if we never beg people to come to Christ. Nor is it right for a sermon to consist of an interminable appeal, which has not been preceded by an exposition of the gospel. The rule should be 'no appeal without a proclamation, and no proclamation without an appeal'.

In issuing this appeal, 'we are . . . Christ's ambassadors' (v. 20). This was particularly true of Paul and his fellow apostles. They were the personal envoys and representatives of Jesus Christ. Yet in a secondary sense it is true of all Christian witnesses and preachers, who are heralds of the gospel: we speak in Christ's

---

[86] Hooker's 'Sermon on Habakkuk i.4', pp. 490f.
[87] E. Brunner, *Mediator*, p. 524.
[88] T. J. Crawford, *Doctrine of Holy Scripture*, p. 75.

name and on his behalf. Then, as we issue our appeal, another voice is often heard, for it is 'as though God were making his appeal through us'. It is a remarkable truth that the same God who worked 'through Christ' to achieve the reconciliation now works 'through us' to announce it.

We have examined four of the principal New Testament images of salvation, taken from the shrine, the market, the lawcourt and the home. Their pictorial nature makes it impossible to integrate them neatly with one another. Temple sacrifices and legal verdicts, the slave in the market and the child in the home all clearly belong to different worlds. Nevertheless, certain themes emerge from all four images.

First, each highlights a different aspect of our human need. Propitiation underscores the wrath of God upon us, redemption our captivity to sin, justification our guilt, and reconciliation our enmity against God and alienation from him. These metaphors do not flatter us. They expose the magnitude of our need.

Secondly, all four images emphasize that the saving initiative was taken by God in his love. It is he who has propitiated his own wrath, redeemed us from our miserable bondage, declared us righteous in his sight, and reconciled us to himself. Relevant texts leave us in no doubt about this: 'God . . . loved us, and sent his Son to be the propitiation for our sins.' 'God . . . has come and has redeemed his people.' 'It is God who justifies.' 'God . . . reconciled us to himself through Christ.'[89]

Thirdly, all four images plainly teach that God's saving work was achieved through the bloodshedding, that is, the substitutionary sacrifice of Christ. With regard to the blood of Christ the texts are again unequivocal. 'God presented him as a propitiatory sacrifice, through faith in his blood.' 'In him we have redemption through his blood.' 'We have now been justified by his blood.' 'You who once were far away have been brought near (*i.e.* reconciled) through the blood of Christ.'[90] Since Christ's blood is a symbol of his life laid down in violent death, it is also plain in each of the four images that he died in our place as our substitute. The death of Jesus was the atoning sacrifice because of which God averted his wrath from us, the ransom-price by which we have been redeemed, the condemnation of the innocent that the guilty might be justified, and the sinless One being made sin for us.[91]

So substitution is not a 'theory of the atonement'. Nor is it even

[89] 1 Jn. 4:10, AV; Lk. 1:68; Rom. 8:33; 2 Cor. 5:18.
[90] Rom. 3:25; Eph. 1:7; Rom. 5:9; Eph. 2:13 (*cf.* Col. 1:20).
[91] Rom. 3:25; 1 Pet. 1:18–19; Rom. 8:3, 33; 2 Cor. 5:21.

an additional image to take its place as an option alongside the others. It is rather the essence of each image and the heart of the atonement itself. None of the four images could stand without it. I am not of course saying that it is necessary to understand, let alone articulate, a substitutionary atonement before one can be saved. Yet the responsibility of Christian teachers, preachers and other witnesses is to seek grace to expound it with clarity and conviction. For the better people understand the glory of the divine substitution, the easier it will be for them to trust in the Substitute.

8

The revelation of God

The achievement of Christ's cross must be seen in terms of revelation as well as salvation. To borrow some current jargon, it was a 'revelatory' as well as a 'salvific' event. For through what God did there for the world he was also speaking to the world. Just as human beings disclose their character in their actions, so God has showed himself to us in the death of his Son. The purpose of this chapter is to investigate in what way the cross was a word as well as a work, and to listen attentively to it.

The glory of God

According to John's Gospel Jesus referred to his death as a 'glorification', the event through which he and his Father would be supremely 'glorified' or manifested. This comes to many people as a surprise. In the Old Testament God's glory or splendour was revealed in nature and history, that is, in the created universe and in the redeemed nation. On the one hand, heaven and earth were filled with his glory, including (Jesus added) the flowers of a Galilean spring, whose glory exceeded even Solomon's.[1] On the other hand, God showed his glory in delivering Israel from their Egyptian and Babylonian captivities, and in revealing to them his character of mercy and justice.[2] Thus God displayed his majesty in his world and in his people.

It is not in the least surprising that, when the New Testament opens, glory should be associated with Jesus Christ. As Lord

[1] Pss. 19:1; 29:9; Is. 6:3; Mt. 6:29.
[2] Nu. 14:22; Ps. 97:2–6; Is. 35:2; 40:5; Ex. 33:18 – 34:7.

Ramsey of Canterbury has written, 'in so far as *doxa* is the divine splendour, Jesus Christ *is* that splendour'.[3] According to the Synoptic Gospels, however, although Jesus' glory was glimpsed at his transfiguration, its full manifestation would not take place until his Parousia and the kingdom which would then be consummated.[4] It would be a revelation of 'power and glory'. What is striking about John's presentation is that, although his glory was manifested powerfully in his miracles or 'signs',[5] it was above all to be seen in his present weakness, in the self-humiliation of his incarnation. 'The Word became flesh and lived for a while among us. We have seen his glory, the glory of the one and only Son, who came from the Father, full of grace and truth' (Jn. 1:14). One must not miss the Old Testament allusions. God's glory which overshadowed and filled the tabernacle in the wilderness was now displayed in him who 'lived for a while' (*eskēnōsen*, 'tabernacled') among us. And as Yahweh showed Moses his glory by declaring his name to be both merciful and righteous, so the glory we have seen in Jesus Christ was 'full of grace and truth'. More important still is the deliberate antithesis between 'flesh' and 'glory', and so 'the fundamental *paradox* of the glory of the divine humiliation'.[6]

The self-humiliation of the Son of God, which began in the incarnation, culminated in his death. Yet in that very abasement of himself he was 'lifted up', not just physically raised on to the cross, but spiritually exalted before the eyes of the world.[7] Indeed, he was 'glorified'. The cross which appeared to be 'shame' was in fact 'glory'. Whereas in the Synoptic Gospels suffering is the path to future glory,[8] to John it is also the arena in which the glorification actually takes place.[9] On three separate occasions Jesus referred to his coming death as the hour of his glorification. First, in response to the request of some Greeks to see him, Jesus said 'the hour has come for the Son of Man to be glorified', and went on immediately to speak of his death in terms both of a kernel of wheat falling to the ground and of the Father's glorifying his own

[3] A. M. Ramsey, *Glory of God*, p. 28.
[4] For the transfiguration glory see Lk. 9:32 and 2 Pet.1:16; for the glory at the Parousia see Mk. 13:26, and for the glory of the final kingdom see Mk. 10:37; Mt. 25:31.
[5] Jn. 2:11; 11:4, 40.   [6] F. Donald Coggan, *Glory of God*, p. 52.
[7] John does not use the verb 'crucified' until chapter 19, where it occurs ten times. Before this he three times uses the term 'lifted up', with its deliberate *double entendre* (3:14; 8:28; 12:32).
[8] Lk. 24:26. *Cf* 1 Pet. 4:13; 5:1, 10 and Rom. 8:17–18.
[9] I write 'also' because clearly John thinks of Christ being glorified in other ways too, *e.g.* by the work of the Spirit (16:14), in the church (17:10) and in heaven (17:5, 24).

name. Secondly, as soon as Judas had left the upper room and gone out into the night, Jesus said, 'Now is the Son of Man glorified and God is glorified in him.' Thirdly, he began his great prayer, which terminated their evening in the upper room, with the words: 'Father, the time has come. Glorify your Son, that your Son may glorify you.'[10] What is notable about all three passages is first that each is introduced by either 'now' or 'the time has come', making the reference to the cross indisputable, and secondly that the glorification will be of the Father and the Son together.

So Father and Son are revealed by the cross. But what is it which they reveal of themselves? Certainly the self-humbling and self-giving of love are implicit there. But what about the holiness of that love, which made it necessary for the Lamb of God to take away the world's sin and for the Good Shepherd to lay down his life for his sheep, and which made it more expedient (as Caiaphas correctly prophesied) 'that one man die for the people than that the whole nation perish'?[11] These statements were integral to John's understanding of the death by which the Father and Son would be glorified. The glory which radiates from the cross is that same combination of divine qualities which God revealed to Moses as mercy and justice, and which we have seen in the Word made flesh as 'grace and truth'.[12] This is God's 'goodness', which Calvin saw displayed in the 'theatre' of the cross:

> For in the cross of Christ, as in a splendid theatre, the incomparable goodness of God is set before the whole world. The glory of God shines, indeed, in all creatures on high and below, but never more brightly than in the cross . . . .

> If it be objected that nothing could be less glorious than Christ's death . . ., I reply that in that death we see a boundless glory which is concealed from the ungodly.[13]

When we turn from John to Paul the concept that God has revealed himself in and through the cross is yet more explicit. What in John is the manifestation of God's glory in Paul is the demonstration, indeed the vindication, of his character of justice and love. It may be helpful, before we study the two key texts separately, to look at them side by side. They both occur in the letter to the Romans:

[10] Jn. 12:20–28; 13:30–32; 17:1.
[11] Jn. 1:29; 10:11; 11:49–52 and 18:14.　[12] Ex. 34:6; Jn. 1:14, 17.
[13] Calvin's *St John*, p. 68 (on Jn. 13:31) and p. 135 (on Jn. 17:1).

God . . . did this (*sc.* present Christ as an atoning sacrifice) to demonstrate his justice, because in his forbearance he had left the sins committed beforehand unpunished – he did it to demonstrate his justice at the present time, so as to be just and the one who justifies the man who has faith in Jesus (3:25–26).

But God demonstrates his own love for us in this: While we were still sinners, Christ died for us (5:8).

The Greek verbs rendered 'demonstrate' in chapters 3 and 5 respectively are different. But it was a true instinct of the NIV translators to use the same English verb. For they mean the same thing, and Paul is declaring that in the death of Christ God has given us a clear, public demonstration of both his justice and his love. We have already seen how God 'satisfied' his wrath and love, justice and mercy, by giving himself in Christ to bear our sin and condemnation. Now we are to see how, in satisfying these divine attributes in the cross, he displayed and demonstrated them.

The justice of God

Men and women of moral sensitivity have always been perplexed by the seeming injustice of God's providence. This is far from being a modern problem. Ever since Abraham, indignant that God intended in the destruction of Sodom and Gomorrah to kill the righteous with the wicked, uttered his anguished cry, 'Will not the Judge of all the earth do right?' (Gn. 18:25), the characters and authors of the Bible have struggled with this question. It is one of the recurring themes of the Wisdom Literature and dominates the book of Job. Why do the wicked flourish and the innocent suffer? 'Sin and death', human transgression and divine judgment, are said to be bracketed, even riveted together, so why do we not more frequently see sinners overwhelmed? Instead, more often than not, they seem to escape with impunity. The righteous, on the other hand, are frequently overtaken by disaster. Not only does God not protect them, he does not answer their prayers or even seem to care about their fate. So there is evidently a need for a 'theodicy', a vindication of the justice of God, a justification to humankind of the apparently unjust ways of God.

The Bible responds to this need in two complementary ways, first by looking on to the final judgment and secondly (from the perspective of New Testament believers) by looking back to the decisive judgment which took place at the cross. As to the first, this was the standard Old Testament answer to the problem, for example in Psalm 73. Evil people prosper. They are healthy and wealthy. In spite of their violence, their arrogance and their impudent defiance of God, they get away with it. No thunderbolt from heaven strikes them down. The psalmist admits that by envying their freedom to sin and their immunity to suffering, he had almost turned away from God, for his thoughts were more those of a 'brute beast' than of a godly Israelite. He failed to come to any satisfactory understanding until he 'entered the sanctuary of God'. But then he 'understood their final destiny'. The place on which they stand so self-confidently is more slippery than they realize, and one day they will fall, ruined by the righteous judgment of God.

This same certainty of ultimate judgment, when the imbalances of justice will be redressed, is several times repeated in the New Testament. Paul tells the Athenian philosophers that God has over-looked idolatry in the past only because 'he has set a day when he will judge the world with justice by the man he has appointed', and he warns his readers in Rome not to presume on the riches of God's 'kindness, tolerance and patience', which are giving them space in which to repent. Peter addresses the same message to 'scoffers' who ridicule the notion of a future day of judgment; the reason for its non-arrival is that God in his patience is holding the door of opportunity open a while longer, 'not wanting anyone to perish, but everyone to come to repentance'.[14]

If the first part of the biblical theodicy is to warn of future and final judgment, the second is to declare that the judgment of God has already taken place at the cross. That is why sins were allowed, as it were, to accumulate in Old Testament days without being either punished (as they deserved) or pardoned (since 'it is impossible for the blood of bulls and goats to take away sins'). But now, says the writer to the Hebrews, Christ 'has died as a ransom to set them free from the sins committed under the first covenant'.[15] In other words, the reason for God's previous inaction in the face of sin was not moral indifference but personal forbearance until Christ should come and deal with it on the cross. The classical passage on this theme is Romans 3:21–26, to which we now turn.

But now a righteousness from God, apart from law, has been made known, to which the Law and the Prophets testify. This righteousness from God comes through faith in Jesus Christ to all who believe. There is no difference, for all have sinned and fall short of the glory of God, and are justified freely by his

[14] Acts 17:30–31; Rom. 2:4; 2 Pet. 3:3–9. [15] Heb. 10:4 and 9:15.

grace through the redemption that came by Christ Jesus. God presented him as a sacrifice of atonement, through faith in his blood. He did this to demonstrate his justice, because in his forbearance he had left the sins committed beforehand unpunished – he did it to demonstrate his justice at the present time, so as to be just and the one who justifies the man who has faith in Jesus.

Charles Cranfield has described these six verses as 'the centre and heart' of the whole letter to the Romans. In order to understand them, we shall have to begin with at least a brief discussion of that enigmatic phrase in verse 21, 'But now a righteousness from God ... has been made known'. The wording is almost identical with 1:17 ('for ... a righteousness from God is revealed'), except that the verbs are in the past and present tenses respectively. Whatever the 'righteousness from God' may be, it is clear that the revelation of it is in the gospel. It was revealed there when the gospel first came to be formulated, and it continues to be revealed there whenever the gospel is preached. To be sure, this is not the only revelation Paul mentions. He has already affirmed that God's power and deity are revealed in the creation (1:19–20), and that to the ungodly who suppress the truth God's wrath is revealed from heaven (1:18), particularly in the moral disintegration of society. But the same God who has revealed his power in creation and his wrath in society has also revealed his righteousness in the gospel.

The meaning of 'the (or 'a') righteousness of God' has been endlessly debated. Three main explanations have been given. First, according to the medieval tradition, it was said to be the divine attribute of righteousness or justice, as in verses 25 and 26 where God is said to 'demonstrate' it. The trouble with this interpretation is that God's justice normally issues in judgment (*e.g.* Rev. 19:11), which is hardly the 'good news' revealed in the gospel. Luther held this view at first, and it almost drove him to despair. Of course, if God's justice could be shown in certain circumstances to issue in justification rather than in judgment, that would be a different matter. But I am anticipating.

Secondly, according to the Reformers the phrase meant a righteous status which is 'of God' (genitive) in the sense that it is 'from God' (as the NIV renders it), *i.e.* bestowed by him. It is 'apart from law' (v. 21), because the function of the law is to condemn not to justify, although 'the Law and the Prophets testify' to it, because it is an Old Testament doctrine. Since we are all ourselves unrighteous (3:10) and cannot establish our own righteousness

209

(3:20; 10:3), God's righteousness is a free gift (5:17), which we 'submit to' (10:3), 'receive' (9:30), 'have' (Phil. 3:9) and so even 'become' (2 Cor. 5:21). 'God's righteousness', being a gift to the unrighteous received by faith in Christ alone (v. 22), is in fact nothing other than justification.

Thirdly, a number of scholars in recent years have drawn attention to the Old Testament passages, especially in the Psalms and Isaiah, in which 'God's righteousness' and 'God's salvation' are synonyms, and refer to God's initiative in coming to the rescue of his people and vindicating them when oppressed.[16] In this case the 'righteousness of God' is neither his attribute of justice, nor his gift of the justified status, but his dynamic, saving activity. The main objection to this interpretation is that Paul, although declaring that the law and the prophets testify to God's righteousness, does not quote any of the appropriate verses.

The second of the three interpretations best fits each context in which the expression occurs, and seems almost certainly correct. On the other hand, it may not be necessary altogether to reject the other two. For if the righteousness of God is the righteous standing he gives to those who believe in Jesus, it is by his dynamic saving activity that such a gift is available and bestowed, and the whole operation is fully consonant with his justice. The 'righteousness of God', then, might be defined as 'God's righteous way of righteoussing the unrighteous'; it is the righteous status which he bestows on sinners whom he justifies. Moreover, as we saw in the last chapter, his free and gracious act of justifying is 'through the redemption that came by Christ Jesus' (v. 24), whom 'God presented (some think 'purposed') as a propitiatory sacrifice' (v. 25). If God in Christ on the cross had not paid the price of our ransom and propitiated his own wrath against sin, he could not have justified us.

Now the reason why 'he did this', namely presented Christ as a sacrifice of atonement, was 'to demonstrate his justice'. So important is this divine objective that the apostle states it twice in virtually identical words, although each time he adds a different explanation. The first time he looks back to the past, and says that God demonstrated his justice at the cross 'because in his forbearance he had left the sins committed beforehand unpunished' (v. 25). The second time he looks on from the cross to the present and future, and says that God demonstrated (indeed goes on demonstrating) his justice 'at the present time, so as to be just and the

---

[16] *E.g.* Pss. 71:15; 98:2; Is. 45:21 ('a righteous God and a Saviour'); 46:13; 51:5–6; 56:1. See, for example, C. H. Dodd in *Romans*, pp. 10–13.

one who justifies the man who has faith in Jesus' (v. 26).

By his past forbearance towards sinners God had created a problem for himself. Sin, guilt and judgment are supposed to be inexorably linked in his moral world. Why, then, had he not judged sinners according to their works? A theodicy was needed to vindicate his justice. Although in self-restraint he might postpone his judgment, he could not allow the backlog of human sins to mount up indefinitely, let alone cancel the judgment altogether. If God does not justly punish sin, he would be 'unjust to himself', as Anselm put it, or, in James Denney's words, he would 'not do justice to himself' but rather 'do himself an injustice'.[17] In fact he would destroy both himself and us. He would cease to be God and we would cease to be fully human. He would destroy himself by contradicting his divine character as righteous Lawgiver and Judge, and he would destroy us by contradicting our human dignity as morally responsible persons created in his image. It is inconceivable that he should do either. So, although in his forbearance he temporarily left sins unpunished, now in justice he has punished them, by condemning them in Christ. He has thus demonstrated his justice by executing it. And he has done it publicly (which some think is the emphasis of the verb 'presented'), in order not only to be just but also to be seen to be just. Because of his past appearance of injustice in not punishing sins, he has given a present and visible proof of justice in bearing the punishment himself in Christ.

No-one can now accuse God of condoning evil, and so of moral indifference or injustice. The cross demonstrates with equal vividness both his justice in judging sin and his mercy in justifying the sinner. For now, as a result of the propitiatory death of his Son, God can be 'just and the justifier' of those who believe in him. He is able to bestow a righteous status on the unrighteous, without compromising his own righteousness.

We should see more clearly now the relation between the achievement of the cross (illustrated in the four images examined in the last chapter) and the revelation of God. By bearing himself in Christ the fearful penalty of our sins, God not only propitiated his wrath, ransomed us from slavery, justified us in his sight, and reconciled us to himself, but thereby also defended and demonstrated his own justice. By the way he justified us, he also justified himself. This is the theme of P. T. Forsyth's book *The Justification of God*, which, being published in 1916, he subtitled 'lectures for wartime on a Christian theodicy'. 'There is no theodicy for the

---

[17] Anselm, *Cur Deus Homo?*, I. xiii, and James Denney, *Death of Christ*, p. 188.

world', he wrote, 'except in a theology of the Cross. The only final theodicy is that self-justification of God which was fundamental to his justification of men. No reason of man can justify God in a world like this. He must justify himself, and he did so in the cross of his Son.'[18]

The love of God

It is not only the justice of God which seems to be incompatible with the prevailing injustices of the world, but also his love. Personal tragedies, floods and earthquakes, accidents which cost hundreds of lives, hunger and poverty on a global scale, the cold vastness of the universe, the ferocities of nature, tyranny and torture, disease and death, and the sum total of the misery of the centuries – how can these horrors be reconciled with a God of love? Why does God allow them?

Christianity offers no glib answers to these agonized questions. But it does offer evidence of God's love, just as historical and objective as the evidence which seems to deny it, in the light of which the world's calamities need to be viewed. This evidence is the cross. Let me begin with two verses from John's first letter.

First, 'this is how we know what love is: Jesus Christ laid down his life for us' (3:16). Most people would have no difficulty in telling us what they think love is. They may know that whole books have been written with the purpose of distinguishing between different kinds of love, like Anders Nygren's *Agape and Eros* (1930) and C. S. Lewis' *The Four Loves* (1960). Nevertheless, they would claim that the meaning of love is self-evident. John would disagree with them, however. He dares to say that, apart from Christ and his cross, the world would never have known what true love is. Of course all human beings have experienced some degree and quality of love. But John is saying that only one act of pure love, unsullied by any taint of ulterior motive, has ever been performed in the history of the world, namely the self-giving of God in Christ on the cross for undeserving sinners. That is why, if we are looking for a definition of love, we should look not in a dictionary, but at Calvary.

John's second verse is more precise still. 'This is love: not that we loved God, but that he loved us and sent his Son as an atoning sacrifice (*hilasmos*) for our sins' (4:10). In the Romans 3 passage we have just been studying, Paul takes the propitiatory nature of

[18] P. T. Forsyth, *Justification of God*, pp. 124–125. Barth also wrote that the justification of man is the self-justification of God (*Church Dogmatics*, V.1, pp. 559–564).

the cross (*hilastērion*) as the demonstration of God's justice; here John takes it as the manifestation of God's love. It is both equally. True love is God's love, not ours, and he showed it among us (v. 9) by sending his one and only Son into the world that he might die for us and we might live through him. The two words 'live' (v. 9) and 'propitiation' (v. 10) both betray the extremity of our need. Because we were sinners, we deserved to die under the righteous anger of God. But God sent his only Son, and in sending him came himself, to die that death and bear that wrath instead of us. It was an act of sheer, pure, unmerited love.

We learn from John, then, that although in this world our attention is constantly arrested by the problems of evil and pain, which seem to contradict God's love, we will be wise not to allow it to be deflected from the cross, where God's love has been publicly and visibly made manifest. If the cross may be called a 'tragedy', it was a tragedy which illumines all other tragedies.

Paul also writes about the love of God in the first half of Romans 5. He refers to it twice, and thereby supplies us with two complementary ways of becoming assured of its reality. The first is that 'God has poured out his love into our hearts by the Holy Spirit, whom he has given us' (v. 5). The second is that 'God demonstrates his own love for us in this: While we were still sinners, Christ died for us' (v. 8). One of the most satisfying aspects of the gospel is the way in which it combines the objective and the subjective, the historical and the experimental, the work of God's Son and the work of God's Spirit. We may know that God loves us, Paul says, both because he has proved his love in history through the death of his Son, and because he continuously pours it into our hearts through the indwelling of his Spirit. And although we shall concentrate, as Paul does, on the objective demonstration of God's love at the cross, we shall not forget that the Holy Spirit confirms that historical witness by his own inward and personal witness, as he floods our hearts with the knowledge that we are loved. It is similar to our experience of the Holy Spirit testifying with our spirit that we are God's children – a witness he bears when, as we pray, he enables us to cry '*Abba*, Father', because we then know ourselves to be God's justified, reconciled, redeemed and beloved children (Rom. 8:15–16).

Because of the cross, however, 'God demonstrates his own love for us' (Rom. 5:8). It is his very own, *sui generis*, for there is no other love like it. In what does the demonstration consist? It has three parts, which together build a convincing case.

First, God gave *his Son* for us. True, in verse 8 Paul affirms simply that 'Christ' died for us. But the context tells us who this

Anointed One, this Messiah, was. For according to verse 10 the death of Christ was 'the death of his Son'. If God had sent a man to us, as he had sent the prophets to Israel, we would have been grateful. If he had sent an angel, as he did to Mary at the annunciation, we would have counted it a great privilege. Yet in either case he would have sent us a third party, since men and angels are creatures of his making. But in sending his own Son, eternally begotten from his own Being, he was not sending a creature, a third party, but giving himself. The logic of this is inescapable. How could the Father's love have been demonstrated if he had sent somebody else to us? No, since love is in its essence self-giving, then if God's love was seen in giving his Son, he must thereby have been giving himself. 'God so loved the world that he gave his one and only Son' (Jn. 3:16). Again, God 'did not spare his own Son, but gave him up for us all' (Rom. 8:32). P. T. Forsyth quite correctly added the gloss, 'he spared not his own Son, *i.e.* his own Self'.[19] It is because of the ultimacy of that self-giving love that Paul added his conviction that along with Christ God will 'graciously give us all things'. All lesser gifts are comprehended within 'his indescribable gift' of his Son (2 Cor. 9:15).

Secondly, God gave his Son *to die* for us. It would still have been wonderful if God had given his Son, and so himself, only to become flesh for us, to live and give and serve for us on earth. But the incarnation was but the beginning of his self-giving. Having 'emptied himself' of his glory and taken the nature of a servant, he then 'humbled himself' and became 'obedient to death – even death on a cross!' (Phil. 2:7–8). This was to give himself to the uttermost, to the torture of crucifixion and to the horror of sin-bearing and God-forsakenness. 'Christ died for us.' His body died and, as we have seen, his soul died, died the death of separation from God. Sin and death are inseparable, but, whereas usually the one who sins and the one who dies are the same person, on this occasion they were not, since it was *we* who sinned, but *he* who died for our sins. This is love, holy love, inflicting the penalty for sin by bearing it. For the Sinless One to be made sin, for the Immortal One to die – we have no means of imagining the terror or the pain involved in such experiences.

Thirdly, God gave his Son to die *for us*, that is to say, for undeserving sinners like us. 'Sinners' is the first word Paul uses to describe us, failures who have missed the target and who invariably 'fall short of the glory of God' (3:23). Next, we were 'ungodly' (v. 6), for we had not given God the glory due to his name, and

---

[19] P. T. Forsyth, *Justification*, p. 154.

there was no fear of God before our eyes (3:18). Paul's third descriptive epithet is 'enemies' (v. 10). That is, we were 'God's enemies', as the NIV explains, for we had rebelled against his authority, rebuffed his love and been defiant of his law (8:7). The fourth and last word is 'powerless' (v. 6): it was 'when we were still powerless' that Christ died for us. For we had no power to save ourselves; we were helpless. These four words make an ugly cluster of adjectives. Very rarely, Paul argues in verse 7, somebody may be willing to die for a 'righteous' man (whose righteousness is cold, austere, forbidding), though for a 'good' man (whose goodness is warm, friendly and attractive) someone might possibly dare to die. 'But God demonstrates his own love for us' – his unique love – in this, that he died for sinful, godless, rebellious and helpless people like us.

The value of a love-gift is assessed both by what it costs the giver and by the degree to which the recipient may be held to deserve it. A young man who is in love, for example, will give his beloved expensive presents, often beyond what he can afford, as symbols of his self-giving love, because he considers she deserves them, and more. Jacob served seven years for Rachel because of his love for her. But God in giving his Son gave himself to die for his enemies. He gave everything for those who deserved nothing from him. 'And that is God's own proof of his love towards us' (Rom. 5:8, NEB).

Canon William Vanstone has a chapter in his book *Love's Endeavour, Love's Expense* which is entitled 'The Phenomenology of Love' (pp. 39–54). His thesis is that all human beings, even those who have been deprived of love from childhood, are able to discern authentic love instinctively. He then suggests that 'if we can describe the form of authentic love, we can hardly look elsewhere for a description of the love of God' (p. 42). Although this conflicts with what I wrote earlier about God's love defining ours, rather than *vice versa*, I know what he means and do not want to quarrel with it. He lists three marks of false love, by which its falsity is exposed. They are the mark of limitation (something is withheld), the mark of control (manipulating people), and the mark of detachment (we remain self-sufficient, unimpaired, unhurt). By contrast, authentic love is characterized by limitless self-giving, risk-taking with no certainty of success, and a vulnerability which is easily hurt. I happened to be reading Canon Vanstone's book while I was writing this chapter, and could hardly fail to observe the parallel (even though it is not exact) between his three marks of authentic love and the three marks of God's love unfolded by Paul in Romans 5:8. Here is Canon Vanstone's final summary

(p. 115). God's love is 'expended in self-giving, wholly expended, without residue or reserve, drained, exhausted, spent'. That is, in giving his Son, he gave himself. Next, God's love is 'expended in precarious endeavour, ever poised upon the brink of failure . . .'. For he gave his Son to die, taking the risk of yielding up control over himself. Thirdly, God's love is seen 'waiting in the end, helpless before that which it loves, for the response which shall be its tragedy or its triumph'. For in giving his Son to die for sinners, God made himself vulnerable to the possibility that they would snub him and turn away.

Professor Jürgen Moltmann goes even further than this in his attempt to explain how God disclosed his love in the cross. He picks up Luther's striking expression 'the crucified God' (which Luther had himself borrowed from late medieval theology), and like Luther affirms both that God defines himself, and that we come to know him, at the cross. Luther's *theologia crucis*, therefore, 'is not a single chapter in theology, but the key signature for all Christian theology'.[20] No theology is genuinely Christian which does not arise from and focus on the cross. In particular, by 'the cross' Professor Moltmann means more than anything else the cry of dereliction. It shows, he writes, that Jesus was not only rejected by the Jews as a blasphemer and executed by the Romans as a rebel, but actually condemned and abandoned by his Father (pp. 149–152). It therefore prompts the question: 'Who is God in the cross of the Christ who is abandoned by God?' 'All Christian theology and all Christian life is basically an answer to the question which Jesus asked as he died' (p. 4). That is why theology has to be developed 'within earshot of the dying cry of Jesus' (p. 201). What, then, do we understand of God when we see the crucified Jesus and hear his derelict cry? We certainly see his willingness in love to identify with human rejects. For 'the symbol of the cross in the church points to the God who was crucified not between two candles on an altar, but between two thieves in the place of the skull, where the outcasts belong, outside the gates of the city' (p. 40). And in that awful experience which 'divides God from God to the utmost degree of enmity and distinction' (p. 152) we have to recognize that both Father and Son suffer the cost of their surrender, though differently. 'The Son suffers dying, the Father suffers the death of the Son. The grief of the Father here is just as important as the death of the Son. The Fatherlessness of the Son is matched by the Sonlessness of the Father' (p. 243). It is an arresting phrase. My own wish, I confess, is that Professor

---

[20] Jürgen Moltmann, *Crucified God*, p. 72.

Moltmann had emphasized more strongly that it was with the *spiritually* outcast, not just the *socially* outcast, that is to say, with sinners not just criminals, that Jesus identified on the cross. He could then have clarified both the nature and the cause of the terrible God-forsakenness. Nevertheless, his outspoken acceptance that the dereliction was real, and is the greatest evidence of God's love, is moving.

The 'moral influence' theory

The cross remains such an evident display and demonstration of God's love that several theologians, in different eras of church history, have tried to find its atoning value there. To them the power of the cross lies not in any objective, sin-bearing transaction but in its subjective inspiration, not in its legal efficacy (changing our status before God) but in its moral influence (changing our attitudes and actions).

The most famous exponent of this view, it is usually claimed, was the French philosopher-theologian Peter Abelard (1079–1142). He is best known for his passionate attachment to Heloïse (whom he secretly married after the birth of their son), which had such tragic consequences for them both. In his public academic life, however, his scintillating lectures and debates attracted large audiences. A younger contemporary of Anselm, he agreed with him in repudiating the notion that Christ's death was a ransom paid to the devil. But he violently disagreed with his teaching that it was a satisfaction for sin. 'How cruel and wicked it seems', he wrote, 'that anyone should demand the blood of an innocent person as the price for anything, or that it should in any way please him that an innocent man should be slain – still less that God should consider the death of his Son so agreeable that by it he should be reconciled to the whole world!'[21]

Instead, Abelard depicted Jesus as having been primarily our Teacher and Example. Although he continued to use traditional phrases like 'redeemed by Christ', 'justified in his blood', and 'reconciled to God', he interpreted the efficacy of Christ's death in exclusively subjective terms. The voluntary self-sacrifice of the Son of God moves us to grateful love in response, and so to contrition and repentance.

Redemption is that greatest love kindled in us by Christ's

[21] Abelard's Commentary on Romans 3:19–26, in *A Scholastic Miscellany*, ed. Eugene Fairweather, p. 283.

passion, a love which not only delivers us from the bondage of sin, but also acquires for us the true freedom of children, where love instead of fear becomes the ruling affection.[22]

In support of his thesis Abelard quoted Jesus' words: 'her sins are forgiven because she loved much' (Lk. 7:47). But he misunderstood the text, making love the ground of forgiveness instead of its result. Forgiveness to him was indeed the result of Christ's death, but indirectly, namely that the cross evokes our love for Christ, and when we love him, we are forgiven. 'Justification' has become for Abelard a divine infusion of love. As Robert Franks put it, 'he has reduced the whole process of redemption to one single clear principle, viz. the manifestation of God's love to us in Christ, which awakens an answering love in us'.[23]

Peter Lombard, who became Bishop of Paris in 1159 and could be described as a disciple of Abelard, wrote in his famous *Book of Sentences*:

So great a pledge of love having been given us, we are both moved and kindled to love God who did such great things for us; and by this we are justified, that is, being loosed from our sins we are made just. The death of Christ therefore justifies us, inasmuch as through it charity is stirred up in our hearts.[24]

By the beginning of the twelfth century, then, a theological debate of immense importance had clarified, whose chief protagonists were Anselm and Abelard. Anselm taught that the death of Jesus Christ was an objective satisfaction for sin, Abelard that its efficacy was largely subjective in the moral influence it exerts on us. The ground on which God forgives our sins was to Anselm the

---

[22] *Ibid.*, p. 284. *Cf.* James Orr, *Progress of Dogma*, pp. 229–230.

[23] Robert S. Franks, *Work of Christ*, p. 146. After writing these paragraphs my attention has been drawn to a penetrating article by Dr Alister McGrath, entitled 'The Moral Theory of the Atonement: An Historical and Theological Critique'. He maintains that to call the 'moral influence' theory 'Abelardian' is mistaken; that the mistake arose from regarding 'a single, small portion of Abelard's *Expositio in Epistolam ad Romanos* as representative of his teaching as a whole' (p. 208); and that the imitation of Christ he emphasized was not the means, but rather the result, of our redemption. Nevertheless, the passage in his commentary on the Letter to the Romans is quite explicit, so that I do not see how one can fairly eliminate this element from Abelard's view. At all events, the leaders of the German Enlightenment certainly taught the 'moral influence' theory as Dr McGrath shows. So did Hastings Rashdall, to whom I come soon.

[24] Peter Lombard's *Book of Sentences*, iii, Dist. xix.1 (quoted by Rashdall, pp. 371, 438).

propitiatory death of Christ; but to Abelard it was our own love, penitence and obedience which are aroused in us as we contemplate the death of Christ.

The most outspoken champion in this century of the 'moral influence' theory has probably been Dr Hastings Rashdall, whose 1915 Bampton Lectures were published under the title *The Idea of Atonement in Christian Theology*. He insisted that a choice had to be made between Anselm's objective and Abelard's subjective understandings of the atonement, and there was no question in his mind that Abelard was correct. For according to Jesus, Rashdall maintained, the only condition of salvation was repentance: 'the truly penitent man who confesses his sins to God receives instant forgiveness' (p. 26). 'God is a loving Father who will pardon sin upon the sole condition of true repentance', and the death of Jesus Christ 'operates by actually helping to produce that repentance' (p. 48). More than that, 'God can only be supposed to forgive by making the sinner better, and thereby removing any demand for punishment' (p. 359). In other words, it is *our* repentance and *our* conversion, produced within us as we contemplate the cross, which enable God to forgive us. The significance of the cross is not that it expressed God's love in dealing with our sins, but that it has evoked our love and so made any divine dealing with sins unnecessary. Good works of love, instead of being the evidence of salvation, become the ground on which it is bestowed.

There are three reasons why the 'moral influence' or 'exemplarist' theory must be confidently declared to be untenable, at least by those who take Scripture seriously. The first is that those who hold this view tend not take it seriously themselves. Rashdall rejected every text which was incompatible with his theory. Jesus' ransom-saying (Mk. 10:45) he declared to be a 'doctrinally coloured insertion', and his eucharistic words about the blood of the new covenant and the forgiveness of sins similarly secondary. On what ground? Simply that 'our Lord never taught that his death was necessary for the forgiveness of sins' (p. 45), which is a notable example of circular reasoning, assuming what he wishes to prove. He is more candid when he says that our belief in biblical inspiration must not prevent us from 'boldly rejecting any formulae which . . . seem to say that sin cannot be forgiven without a vicarious sacrifice' (p. 207). In other words, first construct your atonement theory, then defend it against all objections, and do not allow a little matter like divine inspiration to stand in your way. Instead, simply maintain that the pure message of Jesus was corrupted by pre-Pauline Christianity, based on Isaiah 53, and that Paul completed the process.

Secondly, we need to quote against Abelard and Rashdall the words of Anselm, 'you have not yet considered the seriousness of sin'. The 'moral influence' theory offers a superficial remedy because it has made a superficial diagnosis. It appeals to Enlightenment man because it has boundless confidence in human reason and human ability. It entirely lacks the profound biblical understanding of man's radical rebellion against God, of God's wrath as his outraged antagonism to human sin, and of the indispensable necessity of a satisfaction for sin which satisfies God's own character of justice and love. James Orr was right that Abelard's 'view of atonement is defective precisely on the side on which Anselm's was strong',[25] namely in his analysis of sin, wrath and satisfaction.

Thirdly, the moral influence theory has a fatal flaw in its own central emphasis. Its focus is on the love of Christ, which both shines from the cross and elicits our responsive love. On these two truths we desire to lay an equal stress. We too know that it is because Christ loved us that he gave himself for us.[26] We too have found that his love awakens ours. In John's words, 'we love because he first loved us' (1 Jn. 4:19). We agree with Denney when he wrote: 'I do not hesitate to say that the sense of debt to Christ is the most profound and pervasive of all emotions in the New Testament.'[27] So far then we are agreed. The cross is the epitome of Christ's love and the inspiration of ours. But the question we desire to press is this: just *how* does the cross display and demonstrate Christ's love? What is there in the cross which reveals love? True love is purposive in its self-giving; it does not make random or reckless gestures. If you were to jump off the end of a pier and drown, or dash into a burning building and be burnt to death, and if your self-sacrifice had no saving purpose, you would convince me of your folly, not your love. But if I were myself drowning in the sea, or trapped in the burning building, and it was in attempting to rescue me that you lost your life, then I would indeed see love not folly in your action. Just so the death of Jesus on the cross cannot be seen as a demonstration of love in itself, but only if he gave his life in order to rescue ours. His death must be seen to have had an objective, before it can have an appeal. Paul and John saw love in the cross because they understood it respectively as a death for sinners (Rom. 5:8) and as a propitiation for sins (1 Jn. 4:10). That is to say, the cross can be seen as a proof of God's love only when it is at the same time seen as a proof of his justice.

[25] James Orr, *Progress of Dogma*, p. 229.
[26] *E.g.* Gal. 2:20; Eph. 5:2, 25; 1 Jn. 3:16.
[27] James Denney, *Death of Christ*, p. 158.

Hence the need to keep these two demonstrations together in our minds, as Berkouwer has insisted: 'In the cross of Christ God's justice and love are *simultaneously* revealed, so that we can speak of his love only in connection with the reality of the cross.'[28] Again, 'God's graciousness and justice are revealed only in the real substitution, in the radical sacrifice, in the reversing of roles' (p. 311). Similarly, Paul wrote in 2 Corinthians 5:14–15,

> Christ's love compels us (literally 'grips us' and so leaves us no choice), because we are convinced that one died for all, and therefore all died. And he died for all, that those who live should no longer live for themselves but for him who died for them and was raised again.

The constraint of Christ's love, Paul says, rests upon a conviction. It is because we are convinced of the purpose and costliness of the cross, namely that we owe our life to his death, that we feel his love tightening its grip upon us and leaving us no alternative but to live for him.

R. W. Dale's great book *The Atonement* was written in order to prove that Christ's death on the cross was objective before it could be subjective, and that 'unless the great Sacrifice is conceived under objective forms, the subjective power will be lost' (p.li). The cross is the supreme revelation in history of the love of God. But 'the revelation consists essentially in a redemption, rather than the redemption in a revelation'.[29]

We should not, therefore, allow Anselm and Abelard to occupy opposite poles. In general terms, Anselm was right to understand the cross as a satisfaction for sin, but he should have laid more emphasis on God's love. Abelard was right to see the cross as a manifestation of love, but wrong to deny what Anselm affirmed. Anselm and Abelard need each other's positive witness, the one to God's justice and the other to his love. For it was precisely in making a just satisfaction for sin that the manifestation of love took place.

Even after these arguments have been deployed, however, the advocates of the 'moral influence' theory consider that they have a trump card left. It is that Jesus himself, in at least three of his parables, taught forgiveness without atonement, on the basis of repentance alone. In the Parable of the Pharisee and the Tax Collector, the latter cried 'God, have mercy on me, a sinner', and

[28] G. C. Berkouwer, *Work of Christ*, pp. 277–278.
[29] H. W. Robinson, *Suffering Human and Divine*.

was immediately 'justified' (Lk. 18:9–14). In the Parable of the Unmerciful Servant, the king freely forgave him, cancelling his debt without insisting on its repayment (Mt. 18:23–35). And in the Parable of the Lost Son the father welcomed the young man home and reinstated him, when he returned in penitence; no punishment was exacted (Lk. 15:11–24). All three parables illustrate God's forgiving mercy, it is said, and contain no hint of the need for an atoning sacrifice. Three points may be made in reply, however.

First, the parables in question make no allusion to Christ either. Are we to deduce from this that not only his cross, but he himself, is unnecessary for our forgiveness? No. Parables are not allegories; we have no right to expect an exact correspondence, point by point, between the story and its message.

Secondly, each of the three parables contains two actors who are deliberately contrasted with each other – two worshippers in the temple (the self-righteous Pharisee and the self-humbling tax collector), two servants in the royal household (one freely forgiven by his king and the other refused forgiveness by his fellow servant), and two sons in the home (the one unrighteous but penitent, the other righteous but arrogant). The parables highlight, through this contrast, the condition of forgiveness, not its ground. They tell us what we must do, but say nothing directly about what God has done, for our forgiveness.

Nevertheless, thirdly, Christians see the cross in all three parables, because the forgiving mercy shown to the humble tax collector, the bankrupt servant and the prodigal son received its supreme historical demonstration in the self-giving love of God-in-Christ, who died that sinners might be forgiven.

Of these three parables it is that of the Prodigal Son which has seemed to many to teach most clearly a 'gospel' of forgiveness without atonement. This was the argument of Hastings Rashdall in his 1915 Bampton Lectures, mentioned above. Jesus taught, he said, that God is a loving Father who pardons all sinners who repent. This is the 'simple teaching about the forgiveness of God which is taught in the Parable of the Prodigal Son', and which the early church proceeded to corrupt (p. 27). A few years later Douglas White maintained the same thesis: 'Jesus taught ... that God loves us and longs for us to be reconciled to him. If he ever taught anything at all, it was the freedom of forgiveness .... There was no question of penance or punishment; only love and forgiveness. Its great illustration was the prodigal son .... According to this teaching, there is no pre-requisite to God's forgiveness, save the spirit of repentance.' It was Paul who perverted this simple message, making the cross necessary for salvation, using 'repugnant' phraseology, and thereby 'obscuring the doctrine of Jesus as to the unconditioned freedom of God's forgiveness'.[30]

Dr Kenneth Bailey has explained how this interpretation of the parable is common in the Muslim world:

> Islam claims that in this story the boy is saved without a saviour. The prodigal returns. The father forgives him. There is no cross, no suffering, and no saviour. If man seeks forgiveness, says Islam, God is merciful and will forgive. The incarnation, the cross, and the resurrection are all quite unnecessary. If God is truly great, he can forgive without these things. The story of the prodigal son is for them proof that Christians have sadly perverted Christ's own message.[31]

So in his book *The Cross and the Prodigal* Dr Bailey, who has for many years taught New Testament at the Near East School of Theology in Beirut, takes a fresh look at Luke 15 'through the eyes of Middle Eastern peasants'. He explains that the whole village would know that the returning prodigal was in disgrace, and that punishment of some kind was inevitable, if only to preserve the father's honour. But the father bears the suffering instead of inflicting it. Although 'a man of his age and position *always* walks in a slow, dignified fashion', and although 'he has not run *anywhere* for any purpose for 40 years', he yet 'races' down the road like a teenager to welcome his home-coming son. Thus risking the ridicule of the street urchins, 'he takes upon himself the shame and humiliation due to the prodigal'. 'In this parable', Kenneth Bailey continues, 'we have a father who leaves the comfort and security of his home and exposes himself in a humiliating fashion in the village street. The coming down and going out to his boy hints at the incarnation. The humiliating spectacle in the village street hints at the meaning of the cross' (pp. 54–55). Thus 'the cross and the incarnation are implicitly yet dramatically present in the story', for 'the suffering of the cross was not primarily the physical torture but rather the agony of rejected love'. What was essential for the prodigal's reconciliation was a 'physical demonstration of self-emptying love in suffering . . . . Is not this the story of the way of God with man on Golgotha?' (pp. 56–57).

We conclude, then, that the cross was an unparalleled manifest-

---

[30] Douglas White, 'Nature of Punishment', pp. 6–9.
[31] Kenneth E. Bailey, *Cross and the Prodigal*, p. 56.

ation of God's love; that he showed his love in bearing our penalty and therefore our pain, in order to be able to forgive and restore us, and that the Parable of the Prodigal Son, far from contradicting this, implicitly expresses it. I think T. J. Crawford was right to put it in this way, that before we can see in the sufferings of Christ any proof of the Father's love for us, 'some good must accrue to us from them, not otherwise to be obtained, or some evil must be averted from us by them, not otherwise to be removed or remedied'.[32] This 'otherwise unavoidable evil' is the fearful judgment of God, and this 'otherwise unattainable good' is his adoption of us into his family (p. 375). By securing such great blessings for us at the cost of such great sufferings, God has given us an unequalled demonstration of his love.

The wisdom and power of God

When Paul has finished his magisterial exposition of the gospel in the first eleven chapters of Romans, how God presented Christ as a propitiatory sacrifice, justifies sinners through faith in Christ, transforms them by the inward work of the Spirit and is creating his new community into which Gentiles are admitted on the same terms as Jews, he breaks off into a rapturous doxology: 'Oh, the depth of the riches of the wisdom and knowledge of God! How unsearchable his judgments, and his paths beyond tracing out! . . . For from him and through him and to him are all things. To him be the glory for ever! Amen' (11:33–36). Earlier the apostle has seen the atoning death of Christ as a demonstration of God's justice and God's love; now he is overcome by a sense of God's wisdom – the wisdom to devise such a costly plan of salvation which both meets our needs and also satisfies his own character.

The cross as the wisdom and power of God is the main theme of 1 Corinthians 1:17 – 2:5, especially as contrasted with the wisdom and power of the world. It is Paul's mention of the 'gospel' which triggers his meditation, for he knows immediately that he is faced with a decision about its content. The choice is between 'words of human wisdom' and 'the cross of Christ'. If he were to choose human wisdom, the cross would be 'emptied', denuded, indeed destroyed (1:17). So he chooses 'the message of the cross', which he knows to be foolishness to those who are perishing, but at the same time is the power of God to those who are being saved (1:18). Powerless wisdom or foolish power: it was (and still is) a fateful choice. The one combination which is not an option is the

[32] T. J. Crawford, *Doctrine of Holy Scripture*, p. 335.

wisdom of the world plus the power of God.

The reason Paul opts for power against wisdom, God's power against the world's wisdom, is that God in Old Testament Scripture has already declared his intention to destroy the wisdom of the wise and frustrate the cleverness of the clever (1:19). So, if God has set himself against them, where are the wise, the scholars and the philosophers of this age to be found? Has not God already decided against them by making their wisdom foolish (1:20)? This is how he has done so. In his wisdom God first decreed that the world through its own wisdom should not know him, and then was pleased through the foolishness of the revealed and preached gospel to save believers (1:21). So it is again clear that power (saving power) is not in the world's wisdom but in God's foolishness, namely the gospel of Christ crucified.

This principle can be seen operating in the evangelization of Jews and Greeks, for both groups lay down conditions on which the gospel would be acceptable to them. 'Jews demand miraculous signs and Greeks look for wisdom' (1:22). In other words, they insist that the message must authenticate itself to them by power and wisdom respectively. In total contrast to their demands, however, 'we preach Christ crucified' (1:23), who does not even begin to conform to their criteria. On the contrary, the Jews find the cross 'a stumbling block' and the Gentiles 'foolishness', for it offends instead of impressing them, whereas to those who are called by God, whether Jews or Greeks, it is the exact opposite. Though crucified in weakness Christ is God's power, and though apparently foolish he is God's wisdom (1:24). For what men regard as God's foolishness is wiser than their wisdom, and what they regard as God's weakness is stronger than their strength (1:25). In brief, divine and human values are completely at variance with one another. And the cross, which as a way of salvation seems the height of impotence and folly, is actually the greatest manifestation of God's wisdom and power.

Paul caps his argument with two illustrations, the first taken from the Corinthians' experience of their call and conversion (1:26–31), and the second from his own experience of evangelism (2:1–5). As for them, by human standards not many of them were wise or powerful. In fact God deliberately chose what the world regards as foolish and feeble people, in order to shame the wise and the strong; he chose even the lowly, the despised and the non-existent to nullify what exists. His goal in this was to exclude human boasting. Boasting was entirely out of place, because it was God who had united them to Christ, and Christ who had become their wisdom (revealing God to them) and their power (bringing them justification, holiness and the promise of final redemption). Therefore, as Scripture says, if anybody boasts, he must boast neither in himself, nor in others, but in the Lord alone.

As for Paul the evangelist, when he came to Corinth, he had not come with a message of human wisdom. Nor had he come in his own strength. Instead, he had brought the foolish, revealed message of the cross, and he had come in personal weakness, fear and trembling, relying on the Holy Spirit's power to confirm the word. His whole purpose in coming to them in such folly and feebleness was that their faith would rest firmly on God's power, not men's wisdom.

What we have been hearing throughout this passage is variations on the theme of the wisdom and power of God, his wisdom through human folly and his power through human weakness. The gospel of the cross will never be a popular message, because it humbles the pride of our intellect and character. Yet Christ crucified is both God's wisdom (1:24) and ours (1:30). For the cross is God's way to satisfy his love and justice in the salvation of sinners. It therefore manifests his power too, 'the power of God for the salvation of everyone who believes' (Rom. 1:16).

So when we look at the cross we see the justice, love, wisdom and power of God. It is not easy to decide which is the most luminously revealed, whether the justice of God in judging sin, or the love of God in bearing the judgment in our place, or the wisdom of God in perfectly combining the two, or the power of God in saving those who believe. For the cross is equally an act, and therefore a demonstration, of God's justice, love, wisdom and power. The cross assures us that this God is the reality within, behind and beyond the universe.

In one of his great hymns Isaac Watts brought together God's self-revelation in the creation and the cross. After speaking of his handiwork in nature, he continues:

> But in the grace that rescued man
>   His brightest form of glory shines.
> Here, on the cross, 'tis fairest drawn
>   In precious blood and crimson lines.
>
> Here his whole name appears complete:
>   Nor wit can guess, nor reason prove,
> Which of the letters best is writ,
>   The power, the wisdom or the love.

9

The conquest of evil

It is impossible to read the New Testament without being impressed by the atmosphere of joyful confidence which pervades it, and which stands out in relief against the rather jejune religion that often passes for Christianity today. There was no defeatism about the early Christians; they spoke rather of victory. For example, 'thanks be to God! He gives us the victory . . .'. Again, 'in all these things (*sc.* adversities and dangers) we are more than conquerors . . .'. Once more, 'God . . . always leads us in triumphal procession . . .'. And each of Christ's letters to the seven churches of Asia ends with a special promise 'to him who overcomes'.[1] Victory, conquest, triumph, overcoming – this was the vocabulary of those first followers of the risen Lord. For if they spoke of victory, they knew they owed it to the victorious Jesus. They said so in the texts which I have so far quoted only in truncated form. What Paul actually wrote was: 'he gives us the victory *through our Lord Jesus Christ*', 'we are more than conquerors *through him who loved* us', and 'God . . . leads us in triumphal procession *in Christ*'. It is he who 'overcame', 'has triumphed', and moreover did it 'by the cross'.[2]

Of course any contemporary observer, who saw Christ die, would have listened with astonished incredulity to the claim that the Crucified was a Conqueror. Had he not been rejected by his own nation, betrayed, denied and deserted by his own disciples, and executed by authority from the Roman procurator? Look at him there, spread-eagled and skewered on his cross, robbed of all

---

[1] 1 Cor. 15:57; Rom. 8:37; 2 Cor. 2:14; Rev. 2 and 3.
[2] Rev. 3:21; 5:5; 12:11; Col. 2:15.

freedom of movement, strung up with nails or ropes or both, pinned there and powerless. It appears to be total defeat. If there is victory, it is the victory of pride, prejudice, jealousy, hatred, cowardice and brutality. Yet the Christian claim is that the reality is the opposite of the appearance. What looks like (and indeed was) the defeat of goodness by evil is also, and more certainly, the defeat of evil by goodness. Overcome there, he was himself overcoming. Crushed by the ruthless power of Rome, he was himself crushing the serpent's head (Gn. 3:15). The victim was the victor, and the cross is still the throne from which he rules the world.

> Fulfilled is now what David told
> In true prophetic song of old,
> How God the heathen's king should be,
> For God is reigning from the tree.

Here then is a further motif in the achievement of Christ's cross. In addition to the salvation of sinners (as indicated by the four images we considered in chapter 7) and the revelation of God (especially of his holy love, as considered in the last chapter), the cross secured the conquest of evil.

Gustav Aulen and *Christus Victor*

It is particularly Gustav Aulen, the Swedish theologian, who through his influential book *Christus Victor* (1930) reminded the church of this neglected truth. The book's original Swedish title means something like 'The Christian Concept of Atonement', but *Christus Victor* captures his emphasis better. His thesis, in a study which is more historical than apologetic, is that the traditional reconstruction of two main atonement theories is mistaken, namely the 'objective' or 'legal' view (Christ's death reconciling the Father), associated with Anselm, and the 'subjective' or 'moral' view (Christ's death inspiring and transforming us), associated with Abelard. For there is a third view which Aulen calls both 'dramatic' and 'classic'. It is 'dramatic' because it sees the atonement as a cosmic drama in which God in Christ does battle with the powers of evil and gains the victory over them. It is 'classic' because, he claims, it was 'the ruling idea of the Atonement for the first thousand years of Christian history' (pp. 22–23).

So Aulen was at pains to demonstrate that this concept of the atonement as a victory over sin, death and the devil was the dominant view of the New Testament; that it was held by all the

Greek Fathers from Irenaeus at the end of the second century to John of Damascus at the beginning of the eighth, and is therefore held by Eastern Orthodox churches today; that the leading Western Fathers believed it too (though often side by side with the 'objective' view), including Ambrose and Augustine, and Popes Leo the Great and Gregory the Great; that it was lost by medieval Catholic scholasticism; that Luther recovered it; but that subsequent Protestant scholasticism lost it again and reverted to the Anselmian notion of satisfaction.

Aulen is, therefore, very critical of Anselm's 'satisfaction' doctrine, which he calls 'Latin' and 'juridical'. He dismisses it a little contemptuously as 'really a sidetrack in the history of Christian dogma' (p. 31), in fact a deviation. His critique of Anselm is not altogether fair, however. He rightly underlines the truth that in the 'classic' view 'the work of atonement is regarded as carried through by God himself', that 'he himself is the effective agent in the redemptive work, from beginning to end' (p. 50), and that indeed 'the Atonement is, above all, a movement of God to man, not in the first place a movement of man to God' (p. 176). But he is unjust to represent Anselm's view of Christ's death as contradicting this, namely as 'an offering made to God by Christ as man' (p. 22), 'as it were from below' (p. 50), or 'a human work of satisfaction accomplished by Christ' (p. 104). For, as we saw in chapter 5, Anselm emphasized clearly that, although man *ought* to make satisfaction for sin, he *cannot*, for they are his sins for which satisfaction has to be made. Indeed, only God himself can, and therefore does, through Christ. In spite of what Aulen writes, Anselm's teaching is that, through the work of the unique God-man Christ Jesus, it is not only man who made satisfaction; it is God himself who was both the satisfier and the satisfied.

Nevertheless, Gustav Aulen was right to draw the church's attention to the cross as victory, and to show that by his death Jesus saved us not only from sin and guilt, but from death and the devil, in fact all evil powers, as well. His thesis was relevant too in a century torn apart by two World Wars and in a European culture aware of demonic forces. He was also correct in pointing out that 'the note of triumph', which 'sounds like a trumpet-call through the teaching of the early church' (p. 59), was largely absent from the cool logic of Anselm's *Cur Deus Homo?*. Luther, on the other hand, struck this note again. His hymns and catechisms reverberate with joy that God has rescued us from that 'monster' or 'tyrant' the devil, who previously held us in the captivity of sin, law, curse and death.

Another just criticism of Aulen's thesis is that he made too sharp a contrast between the 'satisfaction' and the 'victory' motifs, as if they are mutually incompatible alternatives. But the New Testament does not oblige us to choose between them, for it includes them both. Thus, God took the initiative and won the victory through Christ, but one of the tyrants from whom he liberated us was the very guilt which, according to Anselm, he died to atone for. An admirable attempt to combine the two concepts was made by the nineteenth-century Scottish commentator John Eadie:

> Our redemption is a work at once of price and of power – of expiation and of conquest. On the cross was the purchase made, and on the cross was the victory gained. The blood which wipes out the sentence against us was there shed, and the death which was the death-blow of Satan's kingdom was there endured.[3]

In fact all three of the major explanations of the death of Christ contain biblical truth and can to some extent be harmonized, especially if we observe that the chief difference between them is that in each God's work in Christ is directed towards a different person. In the 'objective' view God satisfies himself, in the 'subjective' he inspires us, and in the 'classic' he overcomes the devil. Thus Jesus Christ is successively the Saviour, the Teacher and the Victor, because we ourselves are guilty, apathetic and in bondage. P. T. Forsyth drew attention to this in the last chapter of his book *The Work of Christ* which he entitled 'The Threefold Cord'. He refers to the 'satisfactionary', 'regenerative' and 'triumphant' aspects of the work of Christ, and suggests that they are intertwined in 1 Corinthians 1:30, where Christ is made unto us 'justification, sanctification and redemption' (pp. 199–200). And although 'some souls . . . will gravitate to the great Deliverance, some to the great Atonement, and some to the great Regeneration' (p. 233), yet all are part of the Saviour's total accomplishment, 'the destruction of evil, the satisfaction of God, and the sanctification of men' (p. 202).

As we concentrate now on the theme of 'conquest', it may be helpful if we look first at the historic victory of Christ at the cross, and then at the victory of his people, which his victory has made possible.

[3] Quoted from John Eadie's Commentary on *Colossians* (p. 174) by T. J. Crawford in *Doctrine of Holy Scripture*, p. 127.

The victory of Christ

What the New Testament affirms, in its own uninhibited way, is that at the cross Jesus disarmed and triumphed over the devil, and all the 'principalities and powers' at his command. First-century hearers of the gospel will have had no difficulty in accepting this, for 'it is perhaps hard for modern man to realize how hag-ridden was the world into which Christ came'.[4] Still today in many countries people live in dread of malevolent spirits. And in the supposedly sophisticated West a new and alarming fascination with the occult has developed, which has been ably documented by Michael Green in his *I Believe in Satan's Downfall*. And yet at the same time many ridicule continuing belief in a personal devil, with evil spirits under him, as a superstitious anachronism. Rudolf Bultmann's dogmatic statement is well known: 'it is impossible to use electric light and the wireless, and to avail ourselves of modern medical and surgical discoveries, and at the same time believe in the New Testament world of demons and spirits.'[5] Michael Green sums up this anomaly of the coexistence of curiosity and incredulity by suggesting that two opposite attitudes would be equally pleasing to the devil: 'The first is that of excessive preoccupation with the Prince of evil. The second is that of excessive scepticism about his very existence' (p. 16). Michael Green goes on to give seven reasons why he believes in the existence of that immensely powerful, evil and cunning being who is called Satan or the devil. They relate to philosophy, theology, the environment, experience, the occult, Scripture and above all Jesus. It is a cogent case; I have nothing to add to it.

But how did God through Christ win the victory over him? The conquest is depicted in Scripture as unfolding in six stages, although the decisive defeat of Satan took place at the cross. Stage one is *the conquest predicted*. The first prediction was given by God himself in the Garden of Eden as part of his judgment on the serpent: 'And I will put enmity between you and the woman, and between your offspring and hers; he will crush your head, and you will strike his heel' (Gn. 3:15). We identify the woman's seed as the Messiah, through whom God's rule of righteousness will be established and the rule of evil eradicated. This being so, every Old Testament text which declares either God's present rule (*e.g.* 'Yours, O LORD, is the greatness and the power . . . . Yours, O LORD, is the kingdom . . .') or his future rule over the nations

[4] H. E. W. Turner, *Patristic Doctrine*, p. 47.
[5] Rudolf Bultmann, *Kerygma and Myth*, pp. 4–5.

through the Messiah (*e.g.* 'Wonderful Counsellor, Mighty God, Everlasting Father, Prince of Peace') may be understood as a further prophecy of the ultimate crushing of Satan.[6]

The second stage was *the conquest begun* in the ministry of Jesus. Recognizing him as his future conqueror, Satan made many different attempts to get rid of him, for example, through Herod's murder of the Bethlehem children, through the wilderness temptations to avoid the way of the cross, through the crowd's resolve to force him into a politico-military kingship, through Peter's contradiction of the necessity of the cross ('Get behind me, Satan'), and through the betrayal of Judas whom Satan actually 'entered'.[7] But Jesus was determined to fulfil what had been written of him. He announced that through him God's kingdom had come upon that very generation, and that his mighty works were visible evidence of it. We see his kingdom advancing and Satan's retreating before it, as demons are dismissed, sicknesses are healed and disordered nature itself acknowledges its Lord.[8] Moreover, Jesus sent out his disciples to preach and to heal as his representatives, and when they returned, excited that the demons had submitted to them in his name, he responded that he had seen 'Satan fall like lightning from heaven'. Here, however, is his most striking statement on this topic: 'When a strong man, fully armed, guards his own house, his possessions are safe. But when someone stronger attacks and overpowers him (*nikaō*, to gain the victory over), he takes away the armour in which the man trusted and divides up the spoils.' It is not difficult to recognize the strong man as a picture of the devil, the 'someone stronger' as Jesus Christ, and the dividing of the spoils (or, in Mark, the robbing of his house) as the liberation of his slaves.[9]

The 'overpowering' and 'binding' of the strong man did not take place, however, until the third and decisive stage, *the conquest achieved*, at the cross. Three times, according to John, Jesus referred to him as 'the prince of this world', adding that he was about to 'come' (*i.e.* launch his last offensive), but would be 'driven out' and 'condemned'.[10] He was evidently anticipating that at the time of his death the final contest would take place, in which the powers of darkness would be routed. It was by his death that he would 'destroy him who holds the power of death – that is, the devil –' and so set his captives free (Heb. 2:14–15).

Perhaps the most important New Testament passage in which

[6] 1 Ch. 29:11; Is. 9:6–7.
[7] Rev. 12:1ff.; Mt. 2:1–18; 4:1–11; Jn. 6:15; Mt. 16:23, RSV; Jn. 13:27.
[8] *E.g.* Mk. 1:24 (demons); Mt. 4:23 (sicknesses) and Mk. 4:39 (nature).
[9] Lk. 10:18; 11:21–22; Mk. 3:27.   [10] Jn. 12:31; 14:30; 16:11.

the victory of Christ is set forth is Colossians 2:13–15.

> He forgave us all our sins, having cancelled the written code, with its regulations, that was against us and that stood opposed to us; he took it away, nailing it to the cross. And having disarmed the powers and authorities, he made a public spectacle of them, triumphing over them by the cross.

Paul here brings together two different aspects of the saving work of Christ's cross, namely the forgiveness of our sins and the cosmic overthrow of the principalities and powers.[11] He illustrates the freeness and graciousness of God's forgiveness (*charizomai*) from the ancient custom of cancelling debts. 'The written code, with its regulations, that was against us' can hardly be a reference to the law in itself, since Paul regarded it as 'holy, righteous and good' (Rom. 7:12); it must rather refer to the broken law, which on that account was 'against us and stood opposed to us' with its judgment. The word Paul uses for this 'written code' is *cheirographon*, which was 'a hand-written document, specifically a certificate of indebtedness, a bond' (AG) or a 'signed confession of indebtedness, which stood as a perpetual witness against us'.[12] The apostle then employs three verbs to describe how God has dealt with our debts. He 'cancelled' the bond by 'wiping' it clean (as *exaleiphō* literally means) and then 'took it away, nailing it to the cross'. Jeremias thinks the allusion is to the *titulus*, the tablet fixed over a crucified person's head on which his crimes were written,

---

[11] Since about the Second World War, and in particular the publication of Hendrik Berkhof's *Christ and the Powers* and G. B. Caird's *Principalities and Powers*, there has been lively debate about the identity of Paul's 'principalities and powers'. Previously everybody seems to have agreed that he meant personal spiritual agencies, both angelic and demonic. But, not least because *archai* (rulers) and *exousiai* (authorities) are used by him in relation to political powers, it has been suggested that Paul himself had begun to 'demythologize' the concept of angels and demons, and that he sees them rather as structures of earthly existence and power, especially the state, but also tradition, convention, law, economics and even religion. Although this attempted reconstruction is popular in some evangelical (as well as liberal) groups, it remains unconvincing. The addition of 'in the heavenly realms' in the Ephesians passages, and the antithesis to 'flesh and blood' in Eph. 6:10, not to mention the world-wide extent of the powers' influence, seem to me to fit the concept of supernatural beings much more readily, although of course such beings can and do use structures as well as individuals as media of their ministry. For further study see my discussion in *Ephesians*, pp. 267–275; E. M. B. Green in *Satan's Downfall*, pp. 84 ff.; and especially the full discussion entitled 'Principalities and Powers', by P. T. O'Brien, pp. 110–150.

[12] F. F. Bruce, *Colossians*, p. 238.

and that on Jesus' *titulus* it was our sins, not his, which were inscribed.[13] In any case, God frees us from our bankruptcy only by paying our debts on Christ's cross. More than that. He has 'not only cancelled the debt, but also destroyed the document on which it was recorded'.[14]

Paul now moves from the forgiveness of our sins to the conquest of the evil powers, and uses three graphic verbs to portray their defeat. The first could mean that God in Christ 'stripped' them from himself like foul clothing, because they had closed in upon him and were clinging to him, and so 'discarded' them (NEB). Or better, it means that he 'stripped' them either of their weapons and so 'disarmed' them (NIV), or of 'their dignity and might'[15] and so degraded them. Secondly, 'he made a public spectacle of them', exhibiting them as the 'powerless powers'[16] they now are, and so, thirdly, 'triumphing over them by the cross', which is probably a reference to the procession of captives which celebrated a victory. Thus the cross, comments Handley Moule, was 'his scaffold from one viewpoint, his imperial chariot from another'.[17] Alexander Maclaren suggests a unified picture of Christ as 'the victor stripping his foes of arms and ornaments and dress, then parading them as his captives, and then dragging them at the wheels of his triumphal car'.[18]

All this is vivid imagery, but what does it actually mean? Are we to visualize a literal cosmic battle, in which the powers of darkness surrounded and attacked Christ on the cross, and in which he disarmed, discredited and defeated them? If it was unseen, as it would surely have to be, how did Christ make 'a public spectacle' of them? It seems that we are to think of his victory, though real and objective, in other terms.

First, it is surely significant that Paul brackets what Christ did to the *cheirographon* (cancelling and removing it) with what he did to the principalities and powers (disarming and conquering them). The bond he nailed to the cross; the powers he defeated by the cross. It does not seem necessary to insist on the latter being any more literal than the former. The important point is that both happened together. Is not his payment of our debts the way in which Christ has overthrown the powers? By liberating us from

[13] J. Jeremias, *Central Message*, p. 37.
[14] Peter O'Brien, *Colossians*, p. 133. *Cf.* p. 124.
[15] *Ibid.*, p. 127.   [16] *Ibid.*, p. 129.
[17] H. C. G. Moule, *Colossian Studies*, p. 159. It was 'as if the cross', wrote Calvin, 'which was full of shame, had been changed into a triumphal chariot!' (*Institutes*, II.xvi.6).
[18] Alexander Maclaren, *Colossians and Philemon*, p. 222.

these, he has liberated us from them.

Secondly, he overcame the devil by totally resisting his temptations. Tempted to avoid the cross, Jesus persevered in the path of obedience, and 'became obedient to death – even death on a cross' (Phil. 2:8). His obedience was indispensable to his saving work. 'For just as through the disobedience of the one man the many were made sinners, so also through the obedience of the one man the many will be made righteous' (Rom. 5:19). If he had disobeyed, by deviating an inch from the path of God's will, the devil would have gained a toehold and frustrated the plan of salvation. But Jesus obeyed; and the devil was routed. Provoked by the insults and tortures to which he was subjected, Jesus absolutely refused to retaliate. By his self-giving love for others, he 'overcame evil with good' (Rom. 12:21). Again, when the combined forces of Rome and Jerusalem were arrayed against him, he could have met power with power. For Pilate had no ultimate authority over him; more than twelve legions of angels would have sped to his rescue if he had summoned them; and he could have stepped down from the cross, as in jest they challenged him to do.[19] But he declined any resort to worldly power. He was 'crucified in weakness', though the weakness of God was stronger than human strength. Thus he refused either to disobey God, or to hate his enemies, or to imitate the world's use of power. By his obedience, his love and his meekness he won a great moral victory over the powers of evil. He remained free, uncontaminated, uncompromised. The devil could gain no hold on him, and had to concede defeat.[20] As F. F. Bruce has put it:

> As he was suspended there, bound hand and foot to the wood in apparent weakness, they imagined they had him at their mercy, and flung themselves upon him with hostile intent . . . . But he grappled with them and mastered them.[21]

So the victory of Christ, predicted immediately after the Fall and begun during his public ministry, was decisively won at the cross. Its remaining three stages were the outworkings of this.

Fourthly, the resurrection was *the conquest confirmed and announced*. We are not to regard the cross as defeat and the resurrection as victory. Rather, the cross was the victory won, and the resurrection the victory endorsed, proclaimed and demonstrated. 'It was impossible for death to keep its hold on him',

[19] Jn. 19:11; Mt. 26:53; Mk. 15:30.
[20] 2 Cor. 13:4; 1 Cor. 1:25; Jn. 14:30.
[21] F. F. Bruce, *Colossians*, p. 239.

because death had already been defeated. The evil principalities and powers, which had been deprived of their weapons and their dignity at the cross, were now in consequence put under his feet and made subject to him.[22]

Fifthly, *the conquest is extended* as the church goes out on its mission, in the power of the Spirit, to preach Christ crucified as Lord and to summon people to repent and believe in him. In every true conversion there is a turning not only from sin to Christ, but 'from darkness to light', 'from the power of Satan to God', and 'from idols to serve the living and true God'; there is also a rescue 'from the dominion of darkness . . . into the kingdom of the Son God loves'.[23] So every Christian conversion involves a power encounter in which the devil is obliged to relax his hold on some-body's life and the superior power of Christ is demonstrated. This being so, it may well be right to interpret the 'binding' of the dragon for a thousand years as coinciding with the 'binding' of the strong man which took place at the cross. For the result of the binding of Satan is that he is kept from 'deceiving the nations any more', which seems to refer to the evangelization of the nations which began after the great victory of the cross and its immediate sequel of Easter Day and Pentecost.[24]

Sixthly, we are looking forward to *the conquest consummated* at the Parousia. The interim between the two advents is to be filled with the church's mission. The Lord's Anointed is already reigning, but he is also waiting until his enemies become a footstool for his feet. On that day every knee will bow to him and every tongue confess him Lord. The devil will be thrown into the lake of fire, where death and Hades will join him. For the last enemy to be destroyed is death. Then, when all evil dominion, authority and power have been destroyed, the Son will hand over the kingdom to the Father, and he will be all in all.[25]

Is it correct, however, thus to attribute Christ's victory to his

[22] Acts 2:24; Eph. 1:20–23; 1 Pet. 3:22.

[23] Acts 26:18; 1 Thes. 1:9; Col. 1:13. Among animists, now usually called 'traditional religionists', who live in fear of the spirits, the concept of a 'power encounter' with Jesus Christ is particularly important. 'The turning of a people to serve the true and living God is normally a response to some evident and convincing demonstration of the power of Christ over the spirit powers (experiential), rather than a mental assent to truths about Jesus Christ (cognitive)' (*Christian Witness to Traditional Religionists of Asia and Oceania*, Lausanne Occasional Paper No. 16, p. 10). See also the Lausanne Occasional Papers which relate to Christian witness among similar peoples in Latin America and the Caribbean (No. 17) and in Africa (No. 18).

[24] Rev. 20:1–3; Mt. 28:18–20.

[25] Ps. 110:1; Phil. 2:9–11; Rev. 20:10, 14; 1 Cor. 15:24–28.

death? Was it not rather achieved by his resurrection? Was it not
by rising again from death that he conquered death? In fact, does
not this book's whole emphasis lie too heavily on the cross, and
insufficiently on the resurrection? Do the two events not belong
together, as Michael Green has argued powerfully in his recent
book, *The Empty Cross of Jesus*? It is essential that we address
ourselves to these questions.

To begin with, it is true beyond doubt that the death and resurrection of Jesus belong together in the New Testament, and that
the one is seldom mentioned without the other. Jesus himself, in
the three successive predictions of his passion which Mark records,
each time added that after three days he would rise again.[26]
According to John, he also said both that he would 'lay down' his
life and that he would 'take it up again'.[27] Moreover, it happened
as he said it would: 'I am the Living One; I was dead, and behold
I am alive for ever and ever' (Rev. 1:18). Next, it is equally clear
that the apostles spoke of the two together. The earliest apostolic
kerygma according to Peter was that he 'was handed over . . . by
God's set purpose and foreknowledge and . . . put to death . . . .
But God raised him from the dead', while Paul states as the original
and universal gospel that 'Christ died for our sins . . . was buried
. . . was raised . . . and . . . appeared'.[28] And Paul's letters are full
of phrases such as 'we believe that Jesus died and rose again' and
'those who live should . . . live . . . for him who died for them and
was raised again'.[29] Moreover, the two gospel sacraments were
acknowledged from the beginning to bear witness to both, since
in baptism the candidate symbolically dies and rises with Christ,
while at the Lord's Supper it is the risen Lord who makes himself
known to us through the very emblems which speak of his death.[30]
So this is not – or should not be – in dispute. It would be seriously
unbalanced to proclaim either the cross without the resurrection
(as I am afraid Anselm did) or the resurrection without the cross
(as do those who present Jesus as a living Lord rather than as an
atoning Saviour). It is therefore healthy to maintain an indissoluble
link between them.

Nevertheless, we need to be clear about the nature of the relation
between the death and resurrection of Jesus, and careful not to
ascribe saving efficacy to both equally. Michael Green avoids this
trap, for he strongly affirms that 'the cross of Jesus is the very core
of the gospel'.[31] It is indeed. When we examined the four images

[26] Mk. 8:31; 9:31; 10:34.　[27] Jn. 10:17–18; *cf.* 2:19.
[28] Acts 2:23–24; 1 Cor. 15:1–8.　[29] 1 Thes. 4:14; 2 Cor. 5:15.
[30] Rom. 6:1–4; Lk. 24:30–35.
[31] E. M. B. Green, *Empty Cross*, p. 11.

of salvation in chapter 7, it became apparent that it is 'by the blood of Jesus' that God's wrath against sin was propitiated, and by the same blood of Jesus that we have been redeemed, justified and reconciled. For it was by his death, and not by his resurrection, that our sins were dealt with. Even in the earliest apostolic *kerygma* already quoted Paul writes that 'Christ died for our sins'. Nowhere in the New Testament is it written that 'Christ rose for our sins'. But was it not by his resurrection that Christ conquered death? No, it was by his death that he destroyed him who holds the power of death (Heb. 2:14).

Of course the resurrection was essential to confirm the efficacy of his death, as his incarnation had been to prepare for its possibility. But we must insist that Christ's work of sin-bearing was finished on the cross, that the victory over the devil, sin and death was won there, and that what the resurrection did was to vindicate the Jesus whom men had rejected, to declare with power that he is the Son of God, and publicly to confirm that his sin-bearing death had been effective for the forgiveness of sins. If he had not been raised, our faith and our preaching would be futile, since his person and work would not have received the divine endorsement.[32] This is the implication of Romans 4:25, which at first sight seems to teach that Christ's resurrection is the means of our justification: 'He was delivered over to death for our sins and was raised to life for our justification.' Charles Cranfield explains: 'What was necessitated by our sins was, in the first place, Christ's atoning death, and yet, had his death not been followed by his resurrection, it would not have been God's mighty deed for our justification.'[33] In addition, because of the resurrection it is a living Christ who bestows on us the salvation he has won for us on the cross, who enables us by his Spirit not only to share in the merit of his death but also to live in the power of his resurrection, and who promises us that on the last day we too will have resurrection bodies.

James Denney expresses the relation between Jesus' death and resurrection in this way:

There can be no salvation from sin unless there is a living Saviour: this explains the emphasis laid by the apostle (*sc.* Paul) on the resurrection. But the living One can be a Saviour only because he has died: this explains the emphasis laid on the cross. The Christian believes in a living Lord, or he could not believe

[32] *E.g.* Acts 2:24; 5:31; Rom. 1:4; 1 Cor. 15:12ff.
[33] C. E. B. Cranfield, *Romans*, Vol. I, p. 252.

at all; but he believes in a living Lord who died an atoning death, for no other can hold the faith of a soul under the doom of sin.[34]

To sum up, the gospel includes both the death and resurrection of Jesus, since nothing would have been accomplished by his death if he had not been raised from it. Yet the gospel emphasizes the cross, since it was there that the victory was accomplished. The resurrection did not achieve our deliverance from sin and death, but has brought us an assurance of both. It is because of the resurrection that our 'faith and hope are in God' (1 Pet. 1:3, 21).

Entering into Christ's victory

For Christians as for Christ, life spells conflict. For Christians as for Christ it should also spell victory. We are to be victorious like the victorious Christ. Did not John write to the 'young men' of the churches he supervised because they had 'overcome the evil one'? Did not Jesus deliberately draw a parallel between himself and us in this respect, promising to him who overcomes the right to share his throne, just as he had overcome and shared his Father's throne?[35]

Yet the parallel is only partial. It would be utterly impossible for us by ourselves to fight and defeat the devil: we lack both the skill and the strength to do so. It would also be unnecessary to make the attempt, because Christ has already done it. The victory of Christians, therefore, consists of entering into the victory of Christ and of enjoying its benefits. We can thank God that 'he gives us the victory through our Lord Jesus Christ'. We know that Jesus, having been raised from the dead, is now seated at the Father's right hand in the heavenly realms. But God has 'made us alive with Christ . . ., and raised us up with Christ and seated us with him in the heavenly realms'. In other words, by God's gracious power we who have shared in Christ's resurrection share also in his throne. If God has placed all things under Christ's feet, they must be under ours too, if we are in him. To borrow Jesus' own metaphor, now that the strong man has been disarmed and bound, the time is ripe for us to raid his palace and plunder his goods.[36]

It is not quite so simple as that, however. For though the devil has been defeated, he has not yet conceded defeat. Although he has been overthrown, he has not yet been eliminated. In fact he

---

[34] James Denney, *Death of Christ*, p. 73.
[35] 1 Jn. 2:13; Rev. 3:21.
[36] 1 Cor. 15:57; Eph. 1:20–23; 2:4–6; Mk. 3:27.

continues to wield great power. This is the reason for the tension we feel in both our theology and our experience. On the one hand we are alive, seated and reigning with Christ, as we have just seen, with even the principalities and powers of evil placed by God under his (and therefore our) feet; on the other we are warned (also in Ephesians) that these same spiritual forces have set themselves in opposition to us, so that we have no hope of standing against them unless we are strong in the Lord's strength and clad in his armour.[37] Or here is the same paradox in different language. On the one hand, we are assured that, having been born of God, Christ keeps us safe 'and the evil one does not touch' us; on the other we are warned to watch out because the same evil one 'prowls around like a roaring lion looking for someone to devour'.[38]

Many Christians choose one or other of these positions, or oscillate unsteadily between them. Some are triumphalists, who see only the decisive victory of Jesus Christ and overlook the apostolic warnings against the powers of darkness. Others are defeatists, who see only the fearsome malice of the devil and overlook the victory over him which Christ has already won. The tension is part of the Christian dilemma between the 'already' and the 'not yet'. Already the kingdom of God has been inaugurated and is advancing; not yet has it been consummated. Already the new age (the age to come) has come, so that we have 'tasted . . . the powers of the coming age'; not yet has the old age completely passed away. Already we are God's sons and daughters, and no longer slaves; not yet have we entered 'the glorious freedom of the children of God'.[39] An overemphasis on the 'already' leads to triumphalism, the claim to perfection – either moral (sinlessness) or physical (complete health) – which belongs only to the consummated kingdom, the 'not yet'. An overemphasis on the 'not yet' leads to defeatism, an acquiescence in continuing evil which is incompatible with the 'already' of Christ's victory.

Another way of approaching this tension is to consider the implications of the verb *katargeō*, which, though often translated in our English versions as 'destroy', really falls short of that. It means rather to 'make ineffective or inactive', and is used of unproductive land and unfruitful trees. They are still there. They have not been destroyed. But they are barren. When this verb is applied to the devil, to our fallen nature and to death,[40] therefore, we know that they have not been completely 'destroyed'. For the devil is still very

[37] Eph. 1:20–23; 6:10–17.   [38] 1 Jn. 5:18; 1 Pet. 5:8.
[39] Heb. 6:5; 1 Jn. 2:8; Rom. 8:21.
[40] Heb. 2:14 (the devil); Rom. 6:6 (the 'flesh' or fallen nature); 2 Tim. 1:10 (death).

active, our fallen nature continues to assert itself, and death will go on claiming us until Christ comes. It is not, then, that they have ceased to exist, but that their power has been broken. They have not been abolished, but they have been overthrown.

John makes the important assertion that 'the reason why the Son of God appeared was that he might "undo" or "do away with" the works of the devil' (1 Jn. 3:8, literally). He came to confront and defeat the devil, and so undo the damage he had done. What are these 'works of the devil', the effects of his nefarious activity? Luther loved, for example, in his classic commentary on *Galatians*, to give a string of them. In one place he wrote of 'law, sin, death, the devil and hell' as constituting 'all the evils and miseries of mankind' (p. 162), and in another of 'sin, death and the curse' as 'those invincible and mighty tyrants' from which only Christ can set us free (p. 275). Anders Nygren in his famous commentary on *Romans* suggests that chapters 5 to 8 describe the life of the person who has been justified by faith: 'Chapter 5 says it means to be free from *wrath*. Chapter 6 says it is to be free from *sin*. Chapter 7 says free from *the law*. And Chapter 8 says we are free from *death*' (p. 188). My concern is that these lists omit any reference to 'the flesh' (our fallen human nature) and to 'the world' (godless society), which are familiar at least to church people in the trio 'the world, the flesh and the devil'. So the four 'works of the devil' from which Christ frees us, on which the New Testament writers seem to me to concentrate, are the law, the flesh, the world and death.

First, through Christ we are no longer under *the tyranny of the law*. It comes to many people as a surprise that the law, God's good gift to his people, in itself 'holy, righteous and good', could ever have become a tyrant which enslaves us. But that is exactly Paul's teaching. 'Before this faith came, we were held prisoners by the law, locked up until faith should be revealed.' The reason is that the law condemns our disobedience and so brings us under its 'curse' or judgment. But Christ has redeemed us from the law's curse by becoming a curse for us. It is in this sense that 'Christ is the end of the law' and we are no longer 'under' it.[41] It emphatically does not mean that there are now no moral absolutes except love, as the advocates of 'the new morality' taught in the 1960s, or that we now have no obligation to obey God's law, as other antinomians teach. No, since the tyranny of the law is its curse, it is from this that we are liberated by Christ, so that we are not 'under' it any more. The law no longer enslaves us by its condemnation.

[41] Gal. 3:23 and 13; Rom. 6:14; 10:4; Gal. 5:18.

The *cheirographon* we were thinking about earlier has been expunged. The first four verses of Romans 8 bring these strands together. They say that for those who are in Christ there is 'no condemnation' (v. 1), for God has already condemned our sins in Jesus Christ (v. 3), and he did it in order that 'the righteous requirements of the law might be fully met in us' (v. 4). So the same cross of Christ, which frees us from the law's condemnation, commits us to the law's obedience.

Secondly, through Christ we are no longer under *the tyranny of the flesh*. What Paul means by the 'flesh' (*sarx*) is our fallen nature or unredeemed humanity, everything that we are by birth, inheritance and upbringing before Christ renewed us. Because our 'flesh' is our 'self' in Adam, its characteristic is self-centredness. Paul supplies a catalogue of some of its worst and ugliest outworkings, including sexual immorality, idolatry and occult practices (misdirected worship), hatred, jealousy and anger, selfish ambition and dissensions, and drunkenness. Living this kind of life, we were 'enslaved by all kinds of passions and pleasures'. As Jesus himself said, 'everyone who sins is a slave to sin'. But he immediately added: 'if the Son sets you free, you will be free indeed.' And freedom from our fallen nature and its selfishness comes through the cross: 'For we know that our old self was crucified with him so that the body of sin might be rendered powerless, that we should no longer be slaves to sin.'[42] Christ by his cross has won the victory over the flesh as well as over the law.

Thirdly, through Christ we are no longer under *the tyranny of the world*. If the flesh is the foothold the devil has within us, the world is the means through which he exerts pressure upon us from without. For the 'world' in this context means godless human society, whose hostility to the church is expressed now by open ridicule and persecution, now by subtle subversion, the infiltration of its values and standards. John declares outspokenly that love for the world and love for the Father are mutually incompatible. For by worldliness he means 'the cravings of sinful man, the lust of his eyes and the boasting of what he has and does'. In the first expression 'sinful man' translates *sarx*. 'Flesh' and 'world' are inevitably linked, since 'world' is the community of unredeemed people, whose outlook is dictated by their unredeemed nature. Putting the three expressions together, it seems that the characteristics of the world which John emphasizes are its selfish desires, its superficial judgments (the eyes seeing only the surface appearance of things) and its arrogant materialism. Jesus made the claim,

[42] Gal. 5:19–21; Tit. 3:3; Jn. 8:34–36; Rom. 6:6.

however, 'I have overcome the world'. He totally rejected its distorted values and maintained his own godly perspective unsullied. John then adds that through Christ we can be overcomers too:

> for everyone born of God has overcome the world. This is the victory that has overcome the world, even our faith. Who is it that overcomes the world? Only he who believes that Jesus is the Son of God.[43]

It is when we believe in Jesus Christ that our values change. We no longer conform to the world's values, but find instead that we are being transformed by our renewed mind which grasps and approves the will of God. And nothing weans us from worldliness more than the cross of Christ. It is through the cross that the world has been crucified to us and we to the world,[44] so that we are freed from its tyranny.

Fourthly, through Christ we are no longer under *the tyranny of death*. It is sometimes said that, whereas our Victorian forebears had a morbid fascination with death, but never spoke of sex, the contemporary generation is obsessed with sex, while death is the great unmentionable. The fear of death is practically universal. The Duke of Wellington is reported as having said that 'that man must be a coward or a liar who could boast of never having felt a fear of death'. And Dr Samuel Johnson added that 'no rational man can die without uneasy apprehension'.[45] But Jesus Christ is able to set free even those who all their lives have been 'held in slavery by their fear of death'. This is because by his own death he has 'destroyed' (deprived of power) 'him who holds the power of death – that is, the devil' (Heb. 2:14).

Jesus Christ has not only dethroned the devil but dealt with sin. In fact, it is by dealing with sin that he has dealt with death. For sin is the 'sting' of death, the main reason why death is painful and poisonous. It is sin which causes death, and which after death will bring the judgment. Hence our fear of it. But Christ has died for our sins and taken them away. With great disdain, therefore, Paul likens death to a scorpion whose sting has been drawn, and to a military conqueror whose power has been broken. Now that we are forgiven, death can harm us no longer. So the apostle shouts defiantly: 'Where, O death, is your victory? Where, O death, is your sting?' There is of course no reply. So he shouts again, this

[43] 1 Jn. 2:15–16; Jn. 16:33; 1 Jn. 5:4–5.
[44] Rom. 12:1–2; Gal. 6:14.
[45] Boswell's *Life of Johnson*, Vol. II, p. 212.

time in triumph, not disdain: 'Thanks be to God! He gives us the victory through our Lord Jesus Christ' (1 Cor. 15:55–57).

What, then, should be the Christian's attitude to death? It is still an enemy, unnatural, unpleasant and undignified – in fact 'the last enemy to be destroyed'. Yet, it is a defeated enemy. Because Christ has taken away our sins, death has lost its power to harm and therefore to terrify. Jesus summed it up in one of his greatest affirmations: 'I am the resurrection and the life. He who believes in me will live, even though he dies; and whoever lives and believes in me will never die.'[46] That is, Jesus is the resurrection of believers who die, and the life of believers who live. His promise to the former is 'you will live', meaning not just that you will survive, but that you will be resurrected. His promise to the latter is 'you will never die', meaning not that you will escape death, but that death will prove to be a trivial episode, a transition to fullness of life.

The Christian conviction that Christ 'has destroyed death' (2 Tim. 1:10) has led some believers to deduce that he has also destroyed disease, and that from the cross we should claim healing as well as forgiveness. A popular exposition of this topic is *Bodily Healing and the Atonement* (1930) by the Canadian author T. J. McCrossan, which has recently been re-edited and re-published by Kenneth E. Hagin of the pentecostal Rhema Church. McCrossan states his case in these terms: 'All Christians should expect God to heal their bodies today, because Christ died to atone for our sicknesses as well as for our sins' (p. 10). He bases his argument on Isaiah 53:4, which he translates 'surely he hath borne our sicknesses and carried our pains'. He particularly emphasizes that the first Hebrew verb (*nasa'*) means to bear in the sense of 'suffering the punishment for something'. Since it is also used in Isaiah 53:12 ('he bore the sin of many'), 'the clear teaching . . . is that Christ bore our sicknesses in the very same way that he bore our sins' (p. 120).

There are three difficulties in the way of accepting this interpretation, however. First, *nasa'* is used in a variety of Old Testament contexts, including the carrying of the ark and other tabernacle furniture, the carrying of armour, weapons and children. It occurs in Isaiah 52:11 with reference to those who 'carry the vessels of the LORD'. So the verb in itself does not mean to 'bear the punishment of'. We are obliged to translate it thus only when sin is its object. That Christ 'bore' our sicknesses may (in fact, does) mean something quite different.

---

[46] 1 Cor. 15:26; Jn. 11:25–26.

Secondly, the concept McCrossan puts forward does not make sense. 'Bearing the penalty of sin' is readily intelligible, since sin's penalty is death and Christ died our death in our place. But what is the penalty of sickness? It has none. Sickness may itself *be* a penalty for sin, but it is not itself a misdemeanour which attracts a penalty. So to speak of Christ 'atoning for' our sicknesses is to mix categories; it is not an intelligible notion.

Thirdly, Matthew (who is the evangelist most preoccupied with the fulfilment of Old Testament Scripture) applies Isaiah 53:4 not to the atoning death but to the healing ministry of Jesus. It was in order to fulfil what was spoken through Isaiah, he writes, that Jesus 'healed all the sick'. So we have no liberty to reapply the text to the cross. It is true that Peter quotes the following verse 'by his wounds we are healed', but the contexts in both Isaiah and Peter make it clear that the 'healing' they have in mind is salvation from sin.[47]

We should not, therefore, affirm that Christ died for our sicknesses as well as for our sins, that 'there is healing in the atonement', or that health is just as readily available to everybody as forgiveness.

That does not mean, however, that our bodies are unaffected by the death and resurrection of Jesus. We should certainly take seriously these statements of Paul about the body:

We always carry around in our body the death of Jesus, so that the life of Jesus may also be revealed in our body. For we who are alive are always being given over to death for Jesus' sake, so that his life may be revealed in our mortal body (2 Cor. 4:10–11).

The apostle is referring to the infirmity and mortality of our human bodies, specially (in his case) in relation to physical persecution. It is, he says, like experiencing in our bodies the dying (or putting to death) of Jesus, and the purpose of this is that the life of Jesus may be revealed in our bodies. He does not seem to be referring to the resurrection of his body, for he comes to that later. Nor are his words exhausted in his survival of physical assaults, in which he was 'struck down, but not destroyed' (v. 9). No, he seems to be saying that now in our mortal bodies (which are doomed to die) there is being 'revealed' (twice repeated) the very 'life' of Jesus (also twice repeated). Even when we are feeling tired, sick and battered, we experience a vigour and vitality which are the life of

[47] Mt. 8:16–17; Is. 53:5; 1 Pet. 2:24.

the risen Jesus within us. Paul expresses the same thought in verse 16: 'Though outwardly we are wasting away, yet inwardly we are being renewed day by day.'

That the life of Jesus should be constantly revealed in our bodies; that God has put into the human body marvellous therapeutic processes which fight disease and restore health; that all healing is divine healing; that God can and sometimes does heal miraculously (without means, instantaneously and permanently) – these things we should joyfully and confidently affirm. But to expect the sick to be healed and the dead to be raised as regularly as we expect sinners to be forgiven, is to stress the 'already' at the expense of the 'not yet', for it is to anticipate the resurrection. Not till then will our bodies be entirely rid of disease and death.

We must now return to the four tyrants over which Christ has won the victory and from which in consequence he sets us free. The four tyrannies characterize the old 'aeon' (age) which was inaugurated by Adam. In it the law enslaves, the flesh dominates, the world beguiles and death reigns. The new 'aeon', however, which was inaugurated by Christ, is characterized by grace not law, the Spirit not the flesh, the will of God not the fashions of the world, and abundant life not death. This is the victory of Christ into which he allows us to enter.

The book of Revelation

No book of the New Testament bears a clearer or stronger testimony to Christ's victory than the Christian apocalypse which we know as 'the book of Revelation' or 'the Revelation to John'. More than half the occurrences of the 'victory' word group (*nikaō*, to overcome and *nikē*, victory) are to be found in this book. H. B. Swete wrote that from beginning to end it is a *Sursum corda*, because it summons its readers to lift up their drooping hearts, to take courage and to endure to the end. Michael Green has suggested that the liberation song 'We shall overcome' might have been written as 'the signature tune of the New Testament';[48] its triumphant strains are certainly heard throughout the book of Revelation.

In the ancient world it was assumed that every victory on the field of battle was won by gods rather than mere mortals: 'a god alone conquers, is unconquered and unconquerable'.[49] Hence the popularity of the goddess *Nikē*, who was often depicted on monu-

[48] E. M. B. Green, *Satan's Downfall*, p. 220.
[49] O. Bauernfeind's article on the *nikaō* word-group.

ments, and in whose honour the graceful little temple near the entrance to the Parthenon was built. I have sometimes wondered if it was in conscious contrast to *Nikē* that in the Revelation Jesus is called *ho Nikōn*, 'the Overcomer', and that his title is passed on to Christian overcomers too.[50]

Written almost certainly during the reign of the Emperor Domitian (AD 81–96), its background is the growth both of the persecution of the church (now systematic rather than spasmodic) and of the practice of emperor worship, the refusal of which by Christians often sparked off fresh outbreaks of persecution. What the book of Revelation does, in keeping with its apocalyptic genre, is to lift the curtain which hides the unseen world of spiritual reality and to show us what is going on behind the scenes. The conflict between the church and the world is seen to be but an expression on the public stage of the invisible contest between Christ and Satan, the Lamb and the dragon. This age-long battle is set forth in a series of dramatic visions which have been variously interpreted as depicting the historical development at that time (the 'praeterist' school), through the succeeding centuries (the 'historicist') or as a prelude to the End (the 'futurist'). None of these is altogether satisfactory, however. The visions cannot portray successive events in a continuous sequence, since the final judgment and victory are dramatized several times. It seems more probable, therefore, that the scenes overlap; that the whole history of the world between Christ's first coming (the victory won) and second (the victory conceded) is several times recapitulated in vision; and that the emphasis is on the conflict between the Lamb and the dragon which has already had a number of historical manifestations, and will have more before the End.

The book opens with references to Jesus Christ as 'the firstborn from the dead', 'the ruler of the kings of the earth' (1:5), 'the First and the Last' and 'the Living One' (1:17–18), and with a magnificent vision of him to justify these titles as the risen, ascended, glorified and reigning Lord. Next come the letters to the seven churches of the Roman province of Asia, each of which concludes with an appropriate promise to 'him who overcomes'. From Christ patrolling his churches on earth the focus then changes to Christ sharing God's throne in heaven. For four chapters (4 – 7) the throne is central, and everything is described in relation to it. Jesus Christ is portrayed as both Lion and Lamb (a combination of images which may indicate that his power is due to his self-sacrifice). He is seen 'standing in the centre of the throne'. The

---

[50] For *ho nikōn* see Rev. 2:7, 11, 17, 26; 3:5, 12, 21 (twice); 6:2; 21:7.

reason why he alone is worthy to open the sealed scroll (the book of history and destiny) is that he 'has triumphed' (5:5). And the nature of his triumph is that he was slain and by his blood has purchased for God people from every nation (5:9). We are intended to understand that the grim events which follow the breaking of the seals and the blowing of the trumpets (war, famine, plague, martyrdom, earthquake and ecological disasters) are nevertheless under the control of the Lamb, who is already reigning and whose perfect kingdom will soon be consummated (11:15–18).

My concern, however, is to reach the vision of chapter 12, which in some ways seems to be the centre of the book. John saw a pregnant woman, who had the sun as her garment, the moon as her foot-stool and twelve stars as her crown, and who was about to give birth to a Son whose destiny was to 'rule all the nations' (v. 5). He is evidently the Messiah, and she the Old Testament church out of whom the Messiah came. An enormous and grotesque red dragon, identified in verse 9 as 'that ancient serpent called the devil or Satan', stood in front of the woman, ready to 'devour her child the moment it was born'. But the child was 'snatched up to God and to his throne', and the woman fled to a desert place prepared for her by God (vv. 5–6).

War in heaven followed, in which 'the dragon and his angels' were defeated. As the Christ had been snatched from earth to heaven, the dragon was now hurled from heaven to earth. The victory must surely refer to the cross, since it was 'by the blood of the Lamb' (v. 11) that Christ's people overcame the dragon. No other weapon could be adequate, for the dragon is 'filled with fury, because he knows that his time is short' (v. 12).

This, then, is the situation. The devil has been defeated and dethroned. Far from this bringing his activities to an end, however, the rage he feels in the knowledge of his approaching doom leads him to redouble them. Victory over him has been won, but painful conflict with him continues. And in this conflict he relies on three allies who now appear (in John's vision) in the guise of two ugly monsters and a lewd and gaudy prostitute. It becomes evident that all three are symbols of the Roman empire, although in three different aspects, namely Rome the persecutor, Rome the deceiver and Rome the seducer.

The first monster, which John sees arising out of the sea, has seven heads and ten horns just like the dragon, and the dragon delegates to him his power, throne and sovereignty, so that he has a world-wide following. There is no need to go into the detail of interpretation (*e.g.* which heads and horns represent which emperors). What is of first importance is that the monster utters proud blasphemies against God (13:5), is given 'power to make war against the saints' and even (temporarily) 'to conquer them' (v. 7), and is worshipped by all but the Lamb's followers (v. 8). This is the absolute power of the Roman state. But the prophecy's fulfilment was not completed in the Roman empire. In every violent state, which opposes Christ, oppresses the church and demands the unquestioning homage of citizens, the horrible 'beast from the sea' raises again its ugly heads and aggressive horns.

The second monster arises 'out of the earth' (v. 11). He is evidently the first monster's henchman, since he exercises his authority and promotes his worship, and performs miraculous signs in order to do so. If it is the characteristic of the first beast to persecute, it is the characteristic of the second to deceive (v. 14). People are forced to worship the image of the first beast (an obvious reference to emperor worship) and to wear the mark of the beast, without which they will be unable to take part in business. This second beast is later called 'the false prophet' (19:20). Although in that generation he symbolized the promoters of emperor worship, in our day he stands for all false religion and ideology, which deflects worship to any object other than 'the living and true God'.

The dragon's third ally is not introduced for another few chapters, during which the Lamb's final victory is several times confidently forecast and celebrated.[51] This ally is called 'the great prostitute' (17:1). Once again without doubt she represents Rome, for she is referred to as 'Babylon the Great' (14:8 and 17:5), 'the great city that rules over the kings of the earth' (17:18), and a city which is situated on 'seven hills' (v. 9). But this time what is symbolized is the moral corruption of Rome. She sits on a scarlet beast (one of the kings on whom her authority rests), is adorned with purple and scarlet, gold, jewels and pearls, and holds in her hand a golden cup 'filled with abominable things and the filth of her adulteries' (v. 4). Such is her seductive power that the inhabitants of the earth are said to be 'intoxicated with the wine of her adulteries' (v. 2). Whether these adulteries are sexual immorality or spiritual idolatry, they were not her only offence. We read later of her 'excessive luxuries' (18:3) which resulted from her international commerce including a trade in slaves (vv. 11–13), unspecified 'sins' and 'crimes' (v. 5), and her boastful arrogance (v. 7). Her kings will make war against the Lamb, 'but the Lamb will overcome them', because he is 'Lord of lords and King of kings' (17:14). And in chapters 18 and 19 the fall of 'Babylon the Great' is not only

---

[51] E.g. Rev. 14:1–5; 15:1–4; 16:4–7.

described in graphic detail, but also vindicated as inevitable and just. Jesus the Victor is glimpsed on a white horse, as 'with justice he judges and makes war' (19:11–16). Then in the last three chapters are described the final destruction of Satan and death, the new heaven and new earth, and the New Jerusalem, in which there will be no tears, death, pain or night, as God establishes his perfect rule.

The devil has not changed his strategy. Although the Roman empire has long since passed away, other persecuting, deceiving and corrupting structures have arisen in its place. In some Hindu and Muslim countries today, in defiance of the United Nations' Declaration of Human Rights, to propagate the gospel and to profess conversion are offences punishable by imprisonment and even death. In the Soviet Union the psychiatric hospital is still in use as an alternative to prison. In most Marxist countries severe restrictions are placed on the teaching of the young and on all religious activities outside specially registered buildings. Wherever a non-Christian culture predominates, opportunities for higher education and prospects for promotion tend to be limited, and the full rights of citizenship denied. As for the 'beast from the earth' or 'false prophet', he is active through other religions, new cults and secular ideologies. Michael Green supplies in two chapters of his *I Believe in Satan's Downfall* well-documented information about both 'the fascination of the occult' and 'counterfeit religion'. I agree with him that these are still two of 'the strongest weapons in Satan's armoury' (p. 194). As for the 'great prostitute', the assault on traditional (*i.e.* biblical) Christian morality has now penetrated the defences of the church itself. On the sanctity of human life (*e.g.* in relation to abortion and experimentation on embryos) the church tends to be equivocal. There is no united witness against the immorality of indiscriminate weapons. Divorce is increasingly tolerated, even among Christian leaders. Sexual life-styles other than strict heterosexual monogamy are not always condemned. And we continue to enjoy in the West a level of affluence which is insensitive to the plight of the destitute millions.

The message of the book of Revelation is that Jesus Christ has defeated Satan and will one day destroy him altogether. It is in the light of these certainties that we are to confront his continuing malicious activity, whether physical (through persecution), intellectual (through deception) or moral (through corruption). How, then, can we enter into Christ's victory and prevail over the devil's power? How can we be numbered among the 'overcomers'? How can we hope to throw the enemy back, not only in our own lives but in the world he has usurped?

First, we are told to *resist the devil*. 'Resist him, standing firm in the faith.' Again, 'Resist the devil, and he will flee from you.'[52] We are not to be afraid of him. Much of his show of power is bluff, since he was overthrown at the cross, and we need the courage to call his bluff. Clad in the full armour of God, we can take our stand against him (Eph. 6:10–17). We are not to flee from him, but on the contrary to resist him so that he flees from us. Our own feeble voice, however, is not sufficiently authoritative to dismiss him. We cannot say in our own name, as Jesus could, 'Begone, Satan'. But we can do it in the name of Jesus. We have to claim the victory of the cross. 'In the name of Jesus Christ, of *Christus Victor*, who defeated you at the cross, begone, Satan.' It works. He knows his conqueror. He flees before him.

Secondly, we are told to *proclaim Jesus Christ*. The preaching of the cross is still the power of God. It is by proclaiming Christ crucified and risen that we shall turn people 'from darkness to light, and from the power of Satan to God' (Acts 26:18), and so the kingdom of Satan will retreat before the advancing kingdom of God. No other message has the same inherent force. No other name is defended and honoured by the Holy Spirit in the same way.

Both in our own lives, then, and in the church's mission it is only the cross of Christ, by which Satan has been defeated, which can prevail against him. It is still true today that 'they overcame him by the blood of the Lamb and by the word of their testimony; they did not love their lives so much as to shrink from death' (Rev. 12:11). Uncompromising witness to Christ is essential. So is the willingness, if necessary, to lay down our lives for his sake. But indispensable to both is the content of our faith and message, namely the objective, decisive victory of the Lamb over all the powers of darkness, which he won when he shed his blood on the cross.

[52] 1 Pet. 5:8–9; Jas. 4:7.

Part Four

Living under the cross

10

The community of celebration

Perhaps the reader has so far found this presentation of Christ's cross too individualistic. If so, the balance should be redressed in this section. For the same New Testament, which contains Paul's flash of individualism 'I have been crucified with Christ. . . . I live by faith in the Son of God, who loved me and gave himself for me', also insists that Jesus Christ 'gave himself for us to redeem us from all wickedness and to purify for himself a people that are his very own, eager to do what is good'.[1] Thus the very purpose of his self-giving on the cross was not just to save isolated individuals, and so perpetuate their loneliness, but to create a new community whose members would belong to him, love one another and eagerly serve the world. This community of Christ would be nothing less than a renewed and reunited humanity, of which he as the second Adam would be head. It would incorporate Jews and Gentiles on equal terms. In fact, it would include representatives from every nation. Christ died in abject aloneness, rejected by his own nation and deserted by his own disciples, but lifted up on the cross he would draw all men to himself. And from the Day of Pentecost onwards it has been clear that conversion to Christ means also conversion to the community of Christ, as people turn from themselves to him, and from 'this corrupt generation' to the alternative society which he is gathering round himself. These two transfers – of personal allegiance and social membership – cannot be separated.[2]

Much space is devoted in the New Testament to the portraiture

[1] Gal. 2:20; Tit. 2:14; Acts 2:40–41.
[2] Eph. 2:15; Rom. 5:12–19; Eph. 3:6; Rev. 7:9; Jn. 12:32 (*cf.* 11:52); Acts 2:40–47.

of this new, redeemed society – its beliefs and values, its standards, duties and destiny. The theme of this section is that the community of Christ is the community of the cross. Having been brought into being by the cross, it continues to live by and under the cross. Our perspective and our behaviour are now governed by the cross. All our relationships have been radically transformed by it. The cross is not just a badge to identify us, and the banner under which we march; it is also the compass which gives us our bearings in a disorientated world. In particular, the cross revolutionizes our attitudes to God, to ourselves, to other people both inside and outside the Christian fellowship, and to the grave problems of violence and suffering. We shall devote a chapter to each of these four relationships.

A new relationship to God

The four images of salvation, which we investigated in chapter 7, all bear witness to our new relationship to God. Now that he has acted in his love to turn aside his anger, we have been justified by him, redeemed for him and reconciled to him. And our reconciliation includes the concepts of 'access' and 'nearness', which are aspects of our dynamic knowledge of God or 'eternal life' (Jn. 17:3). This intimate relationship to God, which has replaced the old and painful estrangement, has several characteristics.

First, it is marked by *boldness*. The word the apostles loved to use for it is *parrēsia*, which means 'outspokenness, frankness, plainness of speech' (AG), both in our witness to the world and in our prayers to God. Through Christ we are now able to 'approach God with freedom (*parrēsia*) and confidence'. We have *parrēsia* because of Christ's high priesthood to come to God's 'throne of grace', and *parrēsia* by Christ's blood 'to enter the Most Holy Place' of God's very presence.[3] This freedom of access and this outspokenness of address to God in prayer are not incompatible with humility, for they are due entirely to Christ's merit, not ours. His blood has cleansed our consciences (in a way that was impossible in Old Testament days), and God has promised to remember our sins no more. So now we look to the future with assurance, not fear. We feel the power of Paul's logic that since, when we were God's enemies, we were both justified and reconciled through Christ's death, 'how much more', having been justified and reconciled, shall we be saved on the last day from God's wrath. Now that we are 'in Christ', we are confident that 'in all things'

[3] Eph. 3:12; Heb. 4:16; 10:19.

God is working for our good, and that nothing can separate us from his love.[4]

The second characteristic of our new relationship with God is *love*. Indeed, 'we love because he first loved us'. Previously we were afraid of him. But now love has driven out fear. Love begets love. God's love in Christ, which has in one sense liberated us, in another hems us in, because it leaves us no alternative but to live the rest of our lives for him, in adoring and grateful service.[5]

Joy is a third mark of those who have been redeemed by the cross. When the Babylonian exiles returned to Jerusalem, their 'mouths were filled with laughter' and their 'tongues with songs of joy'. The old alienation and humiliation were over; God had rescued and restored them. They likened their exhilaration to the revelries of harvest: 'Those who sow in tears will reap with songs of joy. He who goes out weeping, carrying seed to sow, will return with songs of joy, carrying sheaves with him.' How much more should we rejoice in the Lord, who have been redeemed from a much more oppressive slavery? The early Christians could hardly contain themselves: they shared their meals together 'with un-affected joy'.[6]

Boldness, love and joy are not to be thought of as purely private and interior experiences, however; they are to distinguish our public worship. The brief time we spend together on the Lord's Day, far from being divorced from the rest of our life, is intended to bring it into sharp focus. Humbly (as sinners), yet boldly (as forgiven sinners), we press into God's presence, responding to his loving initiative with an answering love of our own, and not only worshipping him with musical instruments but articulating our joy in songs of praise. W. M. Clow was right to draw our attention to singing as a unique feature of Christian worship, and to the reason for it:

There is no forgiveness in this world, or in that which is to come, except through the cross of Christ. 'Through this man is preached unto you the forgiveness of sins.' The religions of paganism scarcely knew the word. . . . The great faiths of the Buddhist and the Mohammedan give no place either to the need or the grace of reconciliation. The clearest proof of this is the simplest. It lies in the hymns of Christian worship. A Buddhist temple never resounds with a cry of praise. Mohammedan worshippers never sing. Their prayers are, at the highest, prayers

[4] Heb. 9:14; 8:12 and 10:17 (*cf.* Je. 31:34); Rom. 5:9–10; 8:28, 38–39.
[5] 1 Jn. 4:18–19; 2 Cor. 5:14–15.
[6] Ps. 126; Acts 2:46, NEB (*agalliasis* means 'exultation').

of submission and of request. They seldom reach the gladder note of thanksgiving. They are never jubilant with the songs of the forgiven.[7]

By contrast, whenever Christian people come together it is impossible to stop them singing. The Christian community is a community of celebration.

Paul expresses our common sense of joyful exhilaration by alluding to the best-known Jewish feast: 'Christ, our Passover lamb, has been sacrificed. Therefore let us keep the Festival . . .' (1 Cor. 5:7). Strictly speaking, 'Passover' referred to the communal meal which was eaten during the evening of the fifteenth Nisan, immediately after the killing of the paschal lambs that afternoon (Nisan 14), although it came to be applied also to the week-long Feast of Unleavened Bread which followed. The foundation of the people's rejoicing was their costly redemption from Egypt. Costlier still was the redeeming sacrifice of Jesus Christ on the cross. It is because he, our Paschal Lamb, has been slain, and because by the shedding of his precious life-blood we have been set free, that we are exhorted to keep the feast. In fact, the whole life of the Christian community should be conceived as a festival in which with love, joy and boldness we celebrate what God has done for us through Christ. In this celebration we find ourselves caught up in the worship of heaven, so that we join 'with angels and archangels, and with all the company of heaven' in giving God glory. And because the worship of God is in essence the acknowledgment of his worth, we unite with the heavenly chorus in singing of his worthiness as both Creator and Redeemer:

'You are worthy, our Lord and God,
    to receive glory and honour and power,
for you created all things,
    and by your will they were created
        and have their being' (Rev. 4:11).

'Worthy is the Lamb, who was slain,
    to receive power and wealth and wisdom and strength
    and honour and glory and praise!' (Rev. 5:12).

[7] W. M. Clow, *Cross in Christian Experience*, p. 278. If it be objected that in the Koran Allah is regularly styled 'the Compassionate, the Merciful' and sometimes 'the Forgiving One' (*e.g. Sura* 40), we would respond that, nevertheless, his forgiveness has to be earned and is never bestowed as a free gift on the undeserving. Hence the absence from Muslim worship of the note of jubilant celebration.

It is surprising that Paul's references to the Passover Lamb and the Paschal Feast come in the middle of an extremely solemn chapter, in which it has been necessary for him to upbraid the Corinthians for their moral laxity. One of their members is involved in an incestuous relationship. Yet they show no signs of humble grief or penitence. He instructs them to excommunicate the offender, and warns them of the danger that sin will spread in the community if decisive steps are not taken to eradicate it. 'Don't you know that a little yeast works through the whole batch of dough?' he asks (1 Cor. 5:6). It is this allusion to yeast (leaven) which reminds him of the Passover and its Feast of Unleavened Bread. As Christians 'keep the Festival', they must do it 'not with the old yeast, the yeast of malice and wickedness, but with bread without yeast, the bread of sincerity and truth' (v. 8). For the Christian festival is radically different from pagan festivals, which were usually accompanied by frenzy and often degenerated into an orgy of drunkenness and immorality. Holiness is to mark the Christian celebration, for Christ's ultimate purpose through the cross is 'to present you holy in his sight, without blemish and free from accusation' (Col. 1:22).

Christ's sacrifice and ours

Although the Christian life is a continuous festival, the Lord's Supper is the particular Christian equivalent to the Passover. It is therefore central to the church's life of celebration. It was instituted by Jesus at Passover-time, indeed during the Passover meal itself, and he deliberately replaced the ceremonial recitation 'This is the bread of affliction which our fathers ate' with 'This is my body given for you. . . . This is my blood shed for you. . .'. The bread and wine of the Christian festival oblige us to look back to the cross of Christ, and to recall with gratitude what he suffered and accomplished there.

Protestant churches have traditionally referred to Baptism and the Lord's Supper as either 'sacraments of the gospel' (because they dramatize the central truths of the good news) or 'sacraments of grace' (because they set forth visibly God's gracious saving initiative). Both expressions are correct. The primary movement which the gospel sacraments embody is from God to man, not man to God. The application of water in baptism represents either cleansing from sin and the outpouring of the Spirit (if it is administered by affusion) or sharing Christ's death and resurrection (if by immersion) or both. We do not baptize ourselves. We submit to baptism, and the action done to us symbolizes the saving work of

Christ. In the Lord's Supper, similarly, the essential drama consists of the taking, blessing, breaking and giving of bread, and the taking, blessing, pouring and giving of wine. We do not (or should not) administer the elements to ourselves. They are given to us; we receive them. And as we eat the bread and drink the wine physically, so spiritually by faith we feed on Christ crucified in our hearts. Thus, in both sacraments we are more or less passive, recipients not donors, beneficiaries not benefactors.

At the same time, baptism is recognized as an appropriate occasion for the confession of faith, and the Lord's Supper for the offering of thanksgiving. Hence the increasingly popular use of 'Eucharist' (*eucharistia*, 'thanksgiving') as a name for the Lord's Supper. And since 'sacrifice' is another word for 'offer', it is not surprising that the term 'eucharistic sacrifice' came to be invented. But is it legitimate? What does it imply?

To begin with, we should all be able to agree on five ways in which what we do at the Lord's Supper is related to the self-sacrifice of Christ on the cross. First, we *remember* his sacrifice: 'do this in remembrance of me', he said (1 Cor. 11:24–25). Indeed, the prescribed actions with the bread and wine make the remembrance vivid and dramatic. Secondly, we *partake* of its benefits. The purpose of the service goes beyond 'commemoration' to 'communion' (*koinōnia*): 'Is not the cup of thanksgiving for which we give thanks a participation in the blood of Christ? And is not the bread that we break a participation in the body of Christ?' (1 Cor. 10:16). For this reason the Eucharist is rightly called the 'Holy Communion' (since through it we may share in Christ) and the 'Lord's Supper' (since through it we may feed, even feast, on Christ). Thirdly, we *proclaim* his sacrifice: 'For whenever you eat this bread and drink this cup, you proclaim the Lord's death until he comes' (1 Cor. 11:26). Although his death took place centuries ago, the proclamation of it continues today. Yet the Supper is a temporary provision. It looks forward to the Lord's coming as well as back to the Lord's death. It is not only a feast upon Christ crucified but a foretaste of his heavenly banquet. It thus spans the whole period between his two comings. Fourthly, we *attribute our unity* to his sacrifice. For we never partake of the Lord's Supper alone, in the privacy of our own room. No, we 'come together' (1 Cor. 11:20) in order to celebrate. And we recognize that it is our common share in the benefits of Christ's sacrifice which has united us: 'Because there is one loaf, we, who are many, are one body, for we all partake of the one loaf' (1 Cor. 10:17). Fifthly, we *give thanks* for his sacrifice, and in token of our thanksgiving offer ourselves, our souls and bodies as 'living sacrifices' to his service (Rom. 12:1).

So then, whenever we share in the Lord's Supper, his sacrifice on the cross is remembered, partaken of, proclaimed, acknowledged as the ground of our unity, and responded to in grateful worship. The question which remains, however, is whether there is any closer relationship still between the sacrifice Christ offered on the cross and the sacrifice of thanksgiving we offer in the Eucharist, between his 'dying' sacrifice and our 'living' sacrifices. It is this which has divided Christendom since the sixteenth century, and is a topic of anxious ecumenical debate today. We cannot talk about the church as a 'community of celebration', without delving more deeply into the nature of the eucharistic celebration.

Already in the immediate post-apostolic period the early church Fathers began to use sacrificial language in relation to the Lord's Supper. They saw in it a fulfilment of Malachi 1:11. ' "In every place incense and pure offerings will be brought to my name, because my name will be great among the nations," says the LORD Almighty.'[8] But the unconsecrated bread and wine as 'pure offerings' were symbols of the creation, for which the people gave thanks. The ancient authors also regarded the people's prayers and praises, and alms for the poor, as an offering to God. It was not until Cyprian, Bishop of Carthage in the middle of the third century, that the Lord's Supper itself was called a true sacrifice, in which the passion of the Lord was offered to God by priests, whose sacrificial role was said to parallel that of the Old Testament priests. From this beginning the eucharistic doctrine of medieval Catholicism eventually developed, namely that the Christian priest offered Christ, really present under the forms of bread and wine, as a propitiatory sacrifice to God for the sins of the living and the dead. And it was against this that the Reformers vigorously protested.

Although Luther and Calvin diverged from one another in their eucharistic teaching, all the Reformers were united in rejecting the sacrifice of the mass, and were concerned to make a clear distinction between the cross and the sacrament, between Christ's sacrifice offered for us and our sacrifices offered through him. Cranmer expressed the differences with lucidity:

One kind of sacrifice there is, which is called a propitiatory or

---

[8] Mal. 1:11 is quoted in the *Didache* xiv.1; it was also used by Irenaeus, Tertullian, Jerome and Eusebius. See the survey of patristic references to 'sacrifice' in Daniel Waterland's *Review of the Doctrine of the Eucharist*, pp. 347–388. See also Michael Green's essay 'Eucharistic Sacrifice', especially pp. 71–78.

merciful sacrifice, that is to say, such a sacrifice as pacifieth God's wrath and indignation, and obtaineth mercy and forgiveness for all our sins. . . . And although in the Old Testament there were certain sacrifices called by that name, yet in very deed there is but one such sacrifice whereby our sins be pardoned, and God's mercy and favour obtained, which is the death of the Son of God, our Lord Jesu Christ; nor never was any other sacrifice propitiatory at any time, nor never shall be. This is the honour and glory of this our High Priest, wherein he admitteth neither partner nor successor . . .

Another kind of sacrifice there is, which doth not reconcile us to God, but is made of (*sc.* by) them that be reconciled by Christ, to testify our duties unto God, and to show ourselves thankful unto him. And therefore they be called sacrifices of laud, praise and thanksgiving.

The first kind of sacrifice Christ offered to God for us; the second kind we ourselves offer to God by (*sc.* through) Christ.[9]

Once this vital distinction had been made, Cranmer was determined to be consistent in its application. The ordained minister could still be called a 'priest', because this English word is simply a contraction of the word 'presbyter' (elder), but every reference to an 'altar' was eliminated from the Book of Common Prayer and replaced by 'table', 'holy table', 'Lord's table' or 'Communion table'. For Cranmer saw clearly that the Communion service is a supper served by a minister from a table, not a sacrifice offered by a priest on an altar. The shape of his final Communion Service exhibits the same determination, for the thankful self-offering of the people was taken out of the Prayer of Consecration (where it was in his first Communion Service, replacing the offering of Christ himself in the medieval mass) and judiciously placed after the reception of the bread and wine as a 'Prayer of Oblation'. In this way, beyond any possibility of misunderstanding, the people's sacrifice was seen to be their offering of praise in responsive gratitude for Christ's sacrifice, whose benefits they had again received by faith.

Scripture undergirds Cranmer's doctrine, both in safeguarding the uniqueness of Christ's sacrifice and in defining our sacrifices as expressing our thanksgiving, not securing God's favour. The unique finality of Christ's sacrifice on the cross is indicated by the adverb *hapax* or *ephapax* (meaning 'once for all'), which is applied to it five times in the letter to the Hebrews. For example, 'Unlike

[9] *Cranmer On the Lord's Supper*, p. 235.

the other high priests, he does not need to offer sacrifices day after day, first for his own sins, and then for the sins of the people. He sacrificed for their sins *once for all* when he offered himself.' Again, 'now he has appeared *once for all* at the end of the ages to do away with sin by the sacrifice of himself'.[10] That is why, unlike the Old Testament priests who stood to perform their temple duties, repeatedly offering the same sacrifices, Jesus Christ, having made 'one sacrifice for sins for ever', sat down at God's right hand, resting from his finished work (Heb. 10:11–12).

Although his work of atonement has been accomplished, he still has a continuing heavenly ministry, however. This is not to 'offer' his sacrifice to God, since the offering was made once for all on the cross; nor to 'present' it to the Father, pleading that it may be accepted, since its acceptance was publicly demonstrated by the resurrection; but rather to 'intercede' for sinners on the basis of it, as our advocate. It is in this that his 'permanent priesthood' consists, for intercession was as much a priestly ministry as sacrifice: 'he always lives to intercede' for us.[11]

The uniqueness of Christ's sacrifice does not mean, then, that we have no sacrifices to offer, but only that their nature and purpose are different. They are not material but spiritual, and their object is not propitiatory but eucharistic, the expression of a responsive gratitude. This is the second biblical undergirding of Cranmer's position. The New Testament describes the church as a priestly community, both a 'holy priesthood' and a 'royal priest-hood', in which all God's people share equally as 'priests'.[12] This is the famous 'priesthood of all believers', on which the Reformers laid great stress. In consequence of this universal priesthood, the word 'priest' (*hiereus*) is never in the New Testament applied to the ordained minister, since he shares in offering what the people offer, but has no distinctive offering to make which differs from theirs.

What spiritual sacrifices, then, do the people of God as a 'holy priesthood' offer to him? Eight are mentioned in Scripture. First, we are to present our bodies to him for his service, as 'living sacrifices'. This sounds like a material offering, but it is termed our 'spiritual worship' (Rom. 12:1), presumably because it pleases God only if it expresses the worship of the heart. Secondly, we offer God our praise, worship and thanksgiving, 'the fruit of lips that confess his name'.[13] Our third sacrifice is prayer, which is said to

---

[10] Heb. 7:27; 9:26. *Cf.* Heb. 9:12, 28; 10:10; and also Rom. 6:10 and 1 Pet. 3:18.
[11] Heb. 7:23–25; 1 Jn. 2:1–2.   [12] 1 Pet. 2:5, 9; Rev. 1:6.
[13] Heb. 13:15. *Cf.* Pss. 50:14, 23; 69:30–31; 116:17.

ascend to God like fragrant incense, and our fourth 'a broken and contrite heart', which God accepts and never despises.[14] Fifthly, faith is called a 'sacrifice and service'. So too, sixthly, are our gifts and good deeds, for 'with such sacrifices God is pleased'.[15] The seventh sacrifice is our life poured out like a drink offering in God's service, even unto death, while the eighth is the special offering of the evangelist, whose preaching of the gospel is called a 'priestly duty' because he is able to present his converts as 'an offering acceptable to God'.[16]

These eight are all, in Daniel Waterland's words, 'true and evangelical sacrifices', because they belong to the gospel not the law, and are thankful responses to God's grace in Christ.[17] They are spiritual and 'intrinsic' too, being 'either good thoughts, good words or good ways, all of them issues of the heart'.[18] And, he continued, the Eucharist may be termed a 'sacrifice' only because it is an occasion both for remembering Christ's sacrifice and for making a responsive, comprehensive offering of ours.

The Catholic Counter-Reformation

The Protestant Reformation, including its careful distinctions between Christ's sacrifice and ours, was condemned by the Roman Catholic Church at the Council of Trent (1545–64). Its Session XXII (1562) focused on the sacrifice of the mass.

> Inasmuch as in this divine sacrifice which is celebrated in the mass is contained and immolated in an unbloody manner the same Christ who once offered himself in a bloody manner on the altar of the cross, the holy council teaches that this is truly propitiatory . . . . For, appeased by this sacrifice, the Lord grants the grace and gift of penitence, and pardons even the gravest crimes and sins. For the victim is one and the same, the same now offering by the ministry of priests who then offered himself on the cross, the manner alone of the offering being different.[19]

> If anyone says that in the mass a true and real sacrifice is not offered to God, . . . let him be anathema. (Canon 1)

[14] Rev. 5:8; 8:3–4; *cf.* Mal. 1:11; Ps. 51:17; *cf.* Ho. 14:1–2.
[15] Phil. 2:17; 4:18; Heb. 13:16; *cf.* Acts 10:4.
[16] Phil. 2:17; 2 Tim. 4:6; Rom. 15:16.
[17] Daniel Waterland, *Review of the Doctrine of the Eucharist*, pp. 344–345.
[18] *Ibid.*, p. 601.
[19] H. J. Schroeder (ed.), *Canons and Decrees*, Session xxii, chapter 2.

If anyone says that by those words *Do this for a commemoration of me* Christ did not institute the Apostles priests, or did not ordain that they and other priests should offer his own body and blood, let him be anathema. (Canon 2)

If anyone says that the sacrifice of the mass is one only of praise and thanksgiving; or that it is a mere commemoration of the sacrifice consummated on the cross but not a propitiatory one, let him be anathema. (Canon 3)

The Canons of the Council of Trent remain in force as part of the Roman Catholic Church's official teaching. Their substance has been confirmed within the last half-century, for example, in two papal encyclicals. Pius XI in *Ad Catholici Sacerdotii* (1935) described the mass as being in itself 'a real sacrifice ... which has a real efficacy'. Moreover, 'the ineffable greatness of the human priest stands forth in all its splendour', because he 'has power over the very body of Jesus Christ'. He first 'makes it present upon our altars' and next 'in the name of Christ himself he offers it a victim infinitely pleasing to the Divine Majesty' (pp. 8–9). In *Mediator Dei* (1947) Pius XII affirmed that the eucharistic sacrifice 'represents', 're-enacts', 'renews' and 'shows forth' the sacrifice of the cross. At the same time he described it as being itself 'truly and properly the offering of a sacrifice' (para. 72), and said that 'on our altars he (Christ) offers himself daily for our redemption' (para. 77). He added that the mass 'in no way derogates from the dignity of the sacrifice of the cross', since it is 'a reminder to us that there is no salvation but in the cross of our Lord Jesus Christ' (para. 83). But in spite of this claim, to call the Eucharist in the same paragraph 'the daily immolation' of Christ inevitably detracts from the historical finality and eternal sufficiency of the cross.

There are three particularly obnoxious elements in these statements of the Council of Trent and subsequent papal encyclicals, which need to be clarified. The implications are that the sacrifice of the mass, being a daily though unbloody immolation of Christ, (1) is distinct from his 'bloody' sacrifice on the cross, and supplementary to it, (2) is made by human priests and (3) is 'truly propitiatory'. By contrast the Reformers insisted, as we must, that the sacrifice of Christ (1) took place once for all on the cross (so that it cannot be re-enacted or supplemented in any way), (2) was made by himself (so that human beings cannot make it or share in making it), and (3) was a perfect satisfaction for sin (so that any mention of additional propitiatory sacrifices is gravely derogatory to it).

Theologians of the Catholic tradition in more recent times, however, together with some scholars of other traditions, have proposed a variety of more moderate positions. While wishing to retain a concept of eucharistic sacrifice which links our sacrifice to Christ's, they have at the same time denied that his unique sacrifice could in any way be repeated or supplemented, or that we can offer Christ, or that the Eucharist is propitiatory. Some make all three denials together.

Although slightly out of chronological sequence, it seems appropriate to begin with the Second Vatican Council (1962–65). On the one hand, the bishops quoted and endorsed the findings of the Council of Trent 400 years previously, for instance that Christ 'is present in the sacrifice of the mass, . . . "the same one now offering, through the ministry of priests, who formerly offered himself on the cross" '.[20] Crude statements also appear, as when priests are told to instruct the faithful 'to offer to God the Father the divine victim in the sacrifice of the mass'.[21] On the other hand, there are two new emphases, first that the Eucharist is not a repetition but a perpetuation of the cross, and secondly that the eucharistic offering is made not by priests but by Christ and his whole people together. For example, Christ is said to have 'instituted the Eucharistic Sacrifice . . . in order to perpetuate the sacrifice of the Cross throughout the centuries until he should come again'.[22] Then the role of priests is stated thus that, 'acting in the person of Christ (they) join the offering of the faithful to the sacrifice of their Head. Until the coming of the Lord . . . they re-present and apply in the sacrifice of the mass the one sacrifice of the New Testament, namely the sacrifice of Christ offering himself once and for all to his Father as a spotless victim'.[23]

One senses in these statements, both in what they say and in what they leave unsaid, the struggle to get away from the crudities of Trent. Yet the two new emphases are still unacceptable, for the offering of the cross cannot be 'perpetuated', nor can our offering be 'joined' to Christ's. The 'Agreed Statement on the Eucharist' produced by ARCIC (the Anglican Roman Catholic International Commission) seems to back away even further from Trent. The commissioners not only decline to call the Eucharist 'propitiatory', but insist strongly on the absolute finality of the cross: 'Christ's death on the cross . . . was the one, perfect and sufficient sacrifice for the sins of the world. There can be no repetition of or addition

[20] *Constitution on the Sacred Liturgy*, I.1.7.
[21] *Decree on the Ministry and Life of Priests*, II.5.
[22] *Constitution on the Sacred Liturgy*, II.47.
[23] *Dogmatic Constitution on the Church*, III.28.

to what was then accomplished once for all by Christ. Any attempt to express a nexus between the sacrifice of Christ and the Eucharist must not obscure this fundamental fact of the Christian faith.'[24]

The cross and the Eucharist

What nexus is there, then, between the cross and the Eucharist? Recent suggestions have emphasized two main ideas, namely the eternal, heavenly ministry of Jesus and the church's union with him as his body.

According to the former, Christ's sacrifice is thought of as 'prolonged' (or 'perpetuated', as at Vatican II), so that he is conceived as continuously offering himself to the Father. Dom Gregory Dix, for example, developed this concept in *The Shape of the Liturgy*. He rejected the view that the death of Jesus was 'the moment of his sacrifice'. On the contrary, he argued, 'his sacrifice was something which began with his humanity and which has its eternal continuance in heaven' (pp. 242–243). R. J. Coates has explained the importance which this idea has for its advocates, namely that the church somehow shares in Christ's continuous self-offering, whereas of course 'the church cannot offer Christ at the earthly altar, if he is not offering himself at a heavenly altar'.[25] But the New Testament does not represent Christ as eternally offering himself to the Father. To be sure, Father, Son and Holy Spirit give themselves to each other in love eternally, but that is reciprocal, and in any case is quite different from Christ's specific historical sacrifice for sin. It is also true that the incarnation involved sacrifice, since by becoming flesh the Son both 'emptied himself' and 'humbled himself' (Phil. 2:7–8), and throughout his public ministry he demonstrated that he had come 'not to be served but to serve'. But, according to his teaching and that of his apostles, the climax of his incarnation and ministry was his self-giving on the cross as a ransom for many (Mk. 10:45). It is this historical act, involving his death for our sins, which Scripture calls his sin-bearing sacrifice and which was finished once for all. Not only can it not be repeated, but it cannot be extended or prolonged. 'It is finished,' he cried. That is why Christ does not have his altar in heaven, but only his throne. On it he sits, reigning, his atoning work done, and intercedes for us on the basis of what has been

[24] *Final Report* of the Anglican Roman Catholic International Commission, p. 13. See also the evangelical assessment and critique entitled *Evangelical Anglicans and the ARCIC Final Report*, issued on behalf of the Church of England Evangelical Council.

[25] R. J. Coates, 'Doctrine of Eucharistic Sacrifice', p. 135.

done and finished. Richard Coates was right to urge us to maintain 'the lonely eminence of the sacrifice of Calvary'.[26]

This is the theme of Alan Stibbs' neglected monograph *The Finished Work of Christ* (1954). He quotes Michael Ramsey's argument that since Christ is for ever priest and 'priesthood means offering', therefore in Christ 'there is for ever that spirit of self-offering which the sacrifice of Calvary uniquely disclosed in our world of sin and death' (p. 5). Similarly, Donald Baillie maintained that the divine sin-bearing was not confined to one moment of time, but that there is 'an eternal atonement in the very being and life of God', of which the cross was the incarnate part (p. 6). Over against such views Alan Stibbs shows that Christ's self-offering for our salvation 'is unmistakably represented in Scripture as exclusively earthly and historical, the purpose of the incarnation, wrought out in flesh and blood, in time and space, under Pontius Pilate', and that 'by this once-for-all finished happening the necessary and intended atoning work was completely accomplished' (p. 8). Could Christ not be continuously offering in heaven, however, the sacrifice which he made once-for-all on earth? Indeed is it not necessary to affirm this, since he is called in Hebrews 'a priest for ever'? No. Eternal priesthood does not necessitate eternal sacrifice. Stibbs goes on to draw a helpful analogy between priesthood and motherhood:

> Admittedly the act of offering was necessary to constitute Christ a priest . . ., just as the act of child-bearing is necessary to constitute a woman a mother. But that truth does not mean in the case of motherhood that henceforth, to those who resort to her as 'mother', such a woman is always giving them birth. Her act of child-bearing is for them not only an indispensable but also a finished work. What they now enjoy are other complementary ministries of motherhood, which lie beyond the child-bearing. Similarly with Christ's priesthood his propitiatory offering is not only an indispensable but also a finished work . . . . (Now, however) as with motherhood, beyond such successful discharge of the fundamental function of priesthood there lie other complementary throne ministries of grace, which the priest fulfils for the benefit of his already reconciled people (in particular, his heavenly intercession) (pp. 30–31).

The second emphasis of what I have called more 'moderate' positions is related to the thoroughly scriptural teaching that the

[26] *Ibid.*, p. 143.

church is the body of Christ, living in union with its head. But this biblical doctrine has come to be developed in an unbiblical way, namely that the body of Christ offers itself to God in and with its head. This notion has been widely held. A popular exposition of it was given by Gabriel Hebert in 1951; it influenced the Anglican bishops who assembled at the 1958 Lambeth Conference:

> The eucharistic sacrifice, that storm-centre of controversy, is finding in our day a truly evangelical expression from the 'catholic' side, when it is insisted that the sacrificial action is not any sort of re-immolation of Christ, nor a sacrifice additional to his one sacrifice, but a participation in it. The true celebrant is Christ the High Priest, and the Christian people are assembled as members of his body to present before God his sacrifice, and to be themselves offered up in sacrifice through their union with him.[27]

In endorsing this, the Lambeth bishops added their own statement, that 'we ourselves, incorporate in the mystical body of Christ, are the sacrifice we offer. Christ with us offers us in himself to God'.[28] William Temple had earlier written something almost identical: 'Christ in us presents us with himself to the Father; we in him yield ourselves to be so presented.'[29]

What is important about these last statements is that there is no question either of Christ's sacrifice being repeated or of our offering him. Instead, it is Christ the head who offers his body with himself to the Father. The ARCIC Agreed Statement says something similar, namely that in the Eucharist 'we enter into the movement of Christ's self-offering' (pp. 14, 20), or are caught up into it by Christ himself. Professor Rowan Williams, a widely respected contemporary Anglo-Catholic theologian, has expressed his view that this, namely 'our being "offered" in and by Christ', is 'the basic fact of the Eucharist'.[30]

Other suggested reconstructions attempt to mingle not our sacrifice, but either our obedience or our intercession, with Christ's. Professor C. F. D. Moule, for example, stressing the *koinōnia* by which we are 'in Christ', united to him, has written that 'the two

---

[27] G. Hebert, in *Ways of Worship*, ed. P. Edwall, E. Hayman and W. D. Maxwell. Quoted in the 1958 *Lambeth Conference Papers*, Part 2, pp. 84, 85.
[28] Lambeth 1958, Part 2, p. 84.
[29] William Temple, *Christus Veritas*, p. 242.
[30] Rowan Williams, in *Essays on Eucharistic Sacrifice*, ed. Colin Buchanan, p. 34.

obediences – Christ's and ours, Christ's in ours and ours in Christ's – are offered to God together'.[31] *Baptism, Eucharist and Ministry*, on the other hand, the so-called 'Lima Text' (1982), which is the fruit of fifty years' ecumenical discussion and claims 'significant theological convergence', focuses on intercession rather than obedience. Declaring that the Christ events (*e.g.* his birth, death and resurrection) 'are unique and can neither be repeated nor prolonged', it nevertheless affirms that 'in thanksgiving and intercession the church is united with the Son, its great high priest and intercessor',[32] and that 'Christ unites the faithful with himself and includes their prayers within his own intercession, so that the faithful are transfigured and their prayers accepted' (II.4).

What can be objected to, it may be asked, in such statements as these? They deliberately avoid the three 'obnoxious elements' in traditional Roman Catholic documents which I mentioned earlier. Once it has been firmly established that Christ's self-sacrifice is unrepeatable, that the Eucharist is not propitiatory, and that our offerings are not meritorious, must Calvary and Eucharist still be kept apart? After all, the New Testament calls us priests and summons us to offer our eight 'spiritual sacrifices' to God. It also sets Christ's self-giving love and obedience before us as the model to which we should aspire. So what could be better or healthier than to allow our self-offering to be caught up in his? Would not the perfection of his compensate for the imperfection of ours? More than that, as Vatican II put it, would not 'the spiritual sacrifice of the faithful' then be 'made perfect in union with the sacrifice of Christ'?[33] Is this not appropriate and reasonable? Would it not be perversely obstinate to object?

I am afraid there are real and grave objections, however. The first is that, as a matter of fact, the New Testament authors never express the concept of our offering being united to Christ's. What they do is exhort us to give ourselves (as a sacrifice) in loving obedience to God in three ways. First, 'like' Christ: 'live a life of love, just as Christ loved us and gave himself up for us as a fragrant offering and sacrifice to God' (Eph. 5:2). His self-offering is to be the model of ours. Secondly, the spiritual sacrifices we offer to God are to be offered 'through' Christ (1 Pet. 2:5), our Saviour and Mediator. Since they are all tainted with self-centredness, it is only through him that they become acceptable. Thirdly, we are to give

[31] C. F. D. Moule, *Sacrifice of Christ*, p. 52.

[32] *Baptism, Eucharist and Ministry*, II.8. See also *Evangelical Anglicans and the Lima Text*, an assessment and critique, drafted by Tony Price for the Church of England Evangelical Council.

[33] *Decree on the Ministry and Life of Priests*, I.2.

ourselves in sacrifice 'unto' or 'for' Christ, constrained by his love to live for him alone the new life-from-death which he has given us (2 Cor. 5:14–15). Thus, we are to offer ourselves 'like', 'through' and 'for' Christ. These are the prepositions which the New Testament uses; it never suggests that our offerings may be made 'in' or 'with' Christ. And if it were important to see our self-offering as identified with Christ's, it is strange that the New Testament never says so. To be sure, it is 'in Christ' that we are justified, forgiven, adopted and made a new creation, but it is never said that we worship God 'in' Christ, in union with him, joining our praises with his. Even when we shall join the heavenly host in worship, and our self-offering is at last purged of all imperfection, – even then our praise is not said to be united with Christ's. No, he will remain the object of our worship; he will not become our fellow-worshipper, nor shall we become his (see Rev. 4 – 7).

That brings me to the second objection, which is surely the reason why the New Testament refrains from describing our worship as offered 'in and with' Christ. It is that the self-offerings of the Redeemer and of the redeemed are so qualitatively different from one another that it would be a glaring anomaly to attempt to mingle them. We need to go back to Cranmer's distinction between the two sorts of sacrifice, 'propitiatory' (atoning for sin) and – though he did not use this word – 'eucharistic' (expressing praise and homage). It is vital to remember that Christ's sacrifice was both, whereas ours are only 'eucharistic'. The death of Jesus was not only a perfect example of self-giving love, as Abelard stressed, in which he gave himself to the Father in obedience to his will; he also gave himself as a ransom for us, dying our death in our place. He therefore died both as our substitute, thus sparing us what otherwise we should have had to experience, and as our representative or example, thus showing us what we ourselves should also do. If the cross were only the latter, it might have been possible to associate our self-offering more closely with his, in spite of the difference, much as he called God 'Father' and permitted us to do the same. But the cross was first and foremost a propitiatory sacrifice, and in that sense absolutely unique. We need greater clarity in disentangling the two meanings of the cross, so that we see the uniqueness of what Daniel Waterland often called 'the grand sacrifice of the cross'[34] and 'the high tremendous sacrifice of Christ God-Man' (p. 37). Then we will conclude that it is not only anomalous, but actually impossible, to associate our sacrifices with his, or even to think of asking him to draw ours up into his. The

---

[34] Daniel Waterland, *Review of the Doctrine of the Eucharist*, p. 343.

only appropriate relationship between the two will be for ours to express our humble and adoring gratitude for his.

There is now an important criticism of this evangelical emphasis to consider. When we are thinking of our conversion, it is said, our sacrifices do indeed appear only as penitent and unworthy responses to the cross. But does not the situation change once we have come to Christ and been welcomed home? Do we not then have something to offer, which can be caught up into Christ's offering? This is a point Professor Rowan Williams has made. He wants to retrieve 'the idea that the effect of Christ's sacrifice is precisely to make us "liturgical" beings, capable of offering ourselves, our praises and our symbolic gifts to a God who we know will receive us in Christ'.[35] Again, 'the effect of Christ's offering is to make us capable of offering, to count us worthy to stand and serve as priests' (p. 30). Is it then necessary for the liturgy so to be constructed as to cast us in the role of unconverted unbelievers, and to recapitulate our salvation? Could it not rather regard us as being already in Christ, already God's children, and then unite our thanksgiving to our Father with Christ's self-offering on the cross (pp. 26–27)? These questions are not without appeal. They make a substantive point. Nevertheless, I think they must be answered in the negative. For our offerings are still tainted with sin and need to be offered 'through' Christ, rather than 'in and with' him. Besides, his sacrifice not only towers above ours in quality; it also differs from ours in character. It is not appropriate, therefore, to mix the two. Nor is it safe. The pride of our hearts is so deeply ingrained and so subtly insidious that it would be easy for us to nurse the idea that we have something of our own to offer God. Not that Rowan Williams thinks so. He is quite explicit that we have nothing to offer before we have received. This being so, and granted our hungry human vanity, should not this truth be explicitly set forth in the Lord's Supper? I agree with Roger Beckwith and Colin Buchanan, whom Rowan Williams quotes, that 'all progress in the Christian life depends upon a recapitulation of the original terms of one's acceptance with God' (p. 26). The liturgy must remind us of these, and not allow us to forget them.

Michael Green got this right in preparation for the 1967 National Evangelical Anglican Congress at Keele:

We never outgrow the fact that we are sinners still, totally dependent each day on the grace of God to the underserving. We do not come to offer; in the first place we come to receive. The very

[35] Rowan Williams, *Eucharistic Sacrifice*, p. 27.

nature of a supper declares this. We are the hungry, coming to be fed. We are the undeserving, welcomed freely at the Lord's Table.[36]

What can be said, in conclusion of this discussion of 'eucharistic sacrifice', about the relationship between Christ's sacrifice and ours? I think we have to insist that they differ from one another too widely for it ever to be seemly to associate them. Christ died for us while we were still sinners and enemies. His self-giving love evokes and inspires ours. So ours is always secondary and responsive to his. To try to unite them is to blur the primary and the secondary, the source and the stream, initiative and response, grace and faith. A proper jealousy for the uniqueness of Christ's sacrifice for sin will lead us to avoid any formulation which could conceivably detract from it.

I come back to where this chapter began. The Christian community is a community of the cross, for it has been brought into being by the cross, and the focus of its worship is the Lamb once slain, now glorified. So the community of the cross is a community of celebration, a eucharistic community, ceaselessly offering to God through Christ the sacrifice of our praise and thanksgiving. The Christian life is an unending festival. And the festival we keep, now that our Passover Lamb has been sacrificed for us, is a joyful celebration of his sacrifice, together with a spiritual feasting upon it. In this celebratory feast we are all participants. But what is it that we share in? Not in the offering of Christ's sacrifice, nor even in the movement of it, but only in the benefits he achieved by it. For this costly sacrifice, and for the precious blessings it has won for us, we shall never cease, even in eternity, to honour and adore the Lamb.

[36] E. M. B. Green, from his chapter 'Christ's Sacrifice and Ours', relating Holy Communion to the cross, in *Guidelines*, p. 116.

11

Self-understanding and self-giving

The cross revolutionizes our attitude to ourselves as well as to God. So the community of the cross, in addition to being a community of celebration, is also a community of self-understanding. This may sound like a reversion to individualism. But it should not be so, since self-understanding is with a view to self-giving. How can one give what one does not know one has? That is why the quest for one's own identity is essential.

Who are we, then? How should we think of ourselves? What attitude should we adopt towards ourselves? These are questions to which a satisfactory answer cannot be given without reference to the cross.

A low self-image is comparatively common today. Many people have crippling inferiority feelings. Sometimes their origin is in a deprived childhood, sometimes in a more recent tragedy of being unwanted and unloved. The pressures of a competitive society make matters worse. And other modern influences make them worse still. Wherever people are politically or economically oppressed, they feel demeaned. Racial and sexual prejudice, and the trauma of being declared 'redundant', can undermine anybody's self-confidence. Technology demotes persons, as Arnold Toynbee once put it, 'into serial numbers punched on a card, designed to travel through the entrails of a computer'. Meanwhile, ethologists such as Desmond Morris tell us that we are nothing but animals, and behaviourists such as B. F. Skinner that we are nothing but machines, programmed to make automatic responses to external stimuli. No wonder many people today feel worthless nonentities.

In over-reaction to this set of influences is the popular 'human potential' movement in the opposite direction. 'Be yourself, express yourself, fulfil yourself!' it cries. It emphasizes 'the power of positive thinking', together with the need for 'possibility thinking' and 'positive mental attitudes'. With the laudable desire to build self-esteem, it gives the impression that our potentiality for development is virtually limitless. A whole literature has grown up round this concept, which has been well described and documented by Dr Paul Vitz in his book *Psychology as Religion: The Cult of Self-worship*. 'Psychology has become a religion', he writes, 'in particular a form of secular humanism based on worship of the self' (p. 9). He begins by analysing 'the four most important self-theorists', namely Erich Fromm, Carl Rogers, Abraham Maslow and Rollo May, all of whom, with different twists and turns, teach the intrinsic goodness of human nature, and the consequent need for unconditional self-regard, self-awareness and self-actualization. These self-theories have been popularized by 'transactional analysis' ('*I'm OK; you're OK*') and EST (Erhard Seminar Training) which Dr Vitz rightly calls 'an amazingly literal self-deification' (pp. 31 ff.). He also cites an advertisement in *Psychology Today* as an illustration of 'selfist jargon': 'I love me. I am not conceited. I'm just a good friend to myself. And I like to do whatever makes me feel good . . .' (p. 62). This self-absorption has been well captured in a limerick:

> There once was a nymph named Narcissus,
> Who thought himself very delicious;
>   So he stared like a fool
>   At his face in a pool,
> And his folly today is still with us.[1]

Unfortunately, many Christians seem to have allowed themselves to be sucked into this movement, under the false impression that the Mosaic command, endorsed by Jesus, that we love our neighbour as ourselves is a command to love ourselves as well as our neighbour. But it really is not. Three arguments may be adduced.

First, and grammatically, Jesus did not say 'the first commandment is to love the Lord your God, the second to love your neighbour, and the third to love yourself'. He spoke only of the first great commandment and of the second which was like it. The addition of 'as yourself' supplies a rough and ready, practical guide to neighbour-love, because 'no-one ever hated his own body' (Eph.

[1] Quoted by John Piper of Bethel College, Minneapolis, in a 1977 article in *Christianity Today*, entitled 'Is Self-love biblical?'.

5:29). In this respect it is like the Golden Rule to 'do to others what you would have them do to you' (Mt. 7:12). Most of us do love ourselves. So we know how we would like to be treated, and this will tell us how to treat others. Self-love is a fact to be recognized and a rule to be used, not a virtue to be commended.

Secondly, and linguistically, the verb is *agapaō*, and *agapē* love means self-sacrifice in the service of others. It cannot therefore be self-directed. The concept of sacrificing ourselves in order to serve ourselves is a nonsense.

Thirdly, and theologically, self-love is the biblical understanding of sin. Sin is being curved in on oneself (as Luther put it). One of the marks of 'the last days' is that people will be 'lovers of self' instead of 'lovers of God' (2 Tim. 3:1–5). Their love will be misdirected from God and neighbour to self.

How then should we regard ourselves? How can we renounce the two extremes of self-hatred and self-love, and neither despise nor flatter ourselves? How can we avoid a self-evaluation which is either too low or too high, and instead obey Paul's admonition, 'think of yourself with sober judgment' (Rom. 12:3)? The cross of Christ supplies the answer, for it calls us both to self-denial and to self-affirmation. But before we are in a position to consider these complementary exhortations, it tells us that we are already new people because we have died and risen with Christ.

It is in this respect that the death of Jesus must rightly be called 'representative' as well as 'substitutionary'.

A 'substitute' is one who acts in place of another in such a way as to render the other's action unnecessary.

A 'representative' is one who acts on behalf of another, in such a way as to involve the other in his action.

Thus, a person who in former days served in the army (for pay) instead of a conscript was a 'substitute'. So is the footballer who plays instead of another who has sustained an injury. The conscript and the injured player are now inactive; they have been replaced.

An agent, however, who serves as the 'representative' of his firm, is deputed to act on its behalf. He does not speak instead of the firm, but for it. The firm is committed to what he says and does.

Just so, as our substitute Christ did for us what we could never do for ourselves: he bore our sin and judgment. But as our representative he did what we by being united to him have also done: we have died and risen with him.

Paul's most extensive exposition of this extraordinary yet wonderful theme comes at the beginning of Romans 6.[2] It was

---

[2] Rom. 6:1–14; *cf*. Gal. 2:20; Col. 2:20 and 3:1–14; 2 Cor. 5:14–15.

occasioned by the evil suggestion that since, when sin increased, grace increased all the more, we might just as well go on sinning, so that grace may increase still further (5:20 – 6:1). Paul indignantly repudiates the idea, for the simple reason that 'we died to sin' and therefore can live in it no longer (6:2). When did that death take place? At our baptism: 'don't you know that all of us who were baptized into Christ Jesus were baptized into his death? We were therefore buried with him through baptism into death in order that, just as Christ was raised from the dead through the glory of the Father, we too may live a new life' (6:3–4). So then baptism visibly dramatizes our participation in the death and resurrection of Jesus. That is why we may be said to have 'died to sin', so that we should live in it no longer.

The missing piece in the jigsaw puzzle is that Christ's death (in which we have shared by faith inwardly and by baptism outwardly) was a death to sin: 'the death he died, he died to sin once for all; but the life he lives, he lives to God' (v. 10). There is only one sense in which it may be said that Jesus 'died to sin', and that is that he bore its penalty, since 'the wages of sin is death' (v. 23). Having paid sin's wage (or borne its penalty) by dying, he has risen to a new life. So have we, by union with him. We too have died to sin, not in the sense that we have personally paid its penalty (Christ has done that in our place, instead of us), but in the sense that we have shared in the benefit of his death. Since the penalty of sin has been borne, and its debt paid, we are free from the awful burden of guilt and condemnation. And we have risen with Christ to a new life, with the sin question finished behind us. How then can we possibly go on living in the sin to which we have died? It is not impossible, for it is still necessary for us to take precautions against letting sin reign within us (vv. 12–14). But it is inconceivable, because it is incompatible with the fact of our death and resurrection with Jesus. It is death and resurrection which have cut us off from our old life; how can we ever think of returning to it? That is why we have to 'reckon' or 'count' ourselves 'dead to sin but alive to God in Christ Jesus' (v. 11). This does not mean that we are to pretend we have died to sin and risen to God, when we know very well that we have not. On the contrary, we know that, by union with Christ, we have shared in his death and resurrection, and so have ourselves died to sin and risen to God; we must therefore constantly remember this fact and live a life consistent with it. William Tyndale expressed it in characteristically vivid terms at the end of his prologue to his work on *Romans*:

Now go to, reader, and according to the order of Paul's writing, even so do thou .... Remember that Christ made not this atonement that thou shouldest anger God again; neither died he for thy sins, that thou shouldest live still in them; neither cleansed he thee, that thou shouldest return, as a swine, unto thine old puddle again; but that thou shouldest be a new creature, and live a new life after the will of God, and not of the flesh.[3]

Barth grasped the radical nature of this teaching and alluded to it in his section on Justification. 'The sentence which was executed as the divine judgment in the death of Jesus is that ... I am the man of sin, and that this man of sin and therefore I myself am nailed to the cross and crucified (in the power of the sacrifice and obedience of Jesus Christ in my place), that I am therefore destroyed and replaced ....' This is the negative side of justification. But 'in the same judgment in which God accuses and condemns us as sinners, and gives us up to death, he pardons us and places us in a new life before him and with him'. These two belong together, 'our real death and our real life beyond death', the destruction by death and the replacement by resurrection, the No and the Yes of God to the same person.[4]

Granted this fundamental fact about all who are in Christ, namely that we have died and risen with him, so that our old life of sin, guilt and shame has been terminated and an entirely new life of holiness, forgiveness and freedom has begun, what is to be our attitude to our new self? Because our new self, though redeemed, is still fallen, a double attitude will be necessary, namely self-denial and self-affirmation, both illumined by the cross.

Self-denial

First, the call to self-denial. The invitation of Jesus is plain: 'If anyone would come after me, he must deny himself and take up his cross and follow me' (Mk. 8:34). Jesus has just for the first time clearly predicted his sufferings and death. It 'must' happen to him, he says (v. 31). But now he expresses implicitly a 'must' for his followers as well. He must go to the cross; they must take up their cross and follow him. Indeed, they must do it 'daily'. And, as the negative counterpart, if anybody does not take his cross and follow him, he is not worthy of him and cannot be his disciple.[5] In this way, one might say, every Christian is both a Simon of Cyrene and a Barabbas. Like Barabbas we escape the cross, for

[3] William Tyndale, *Doctrinal Treatises*, p. 510.
[4] K. Barth, *Church Dogmatics*, IV.1, pp. 515–516, 543.
[5] Lk. 9:23; Mt. 10:38; Lk. 14:27.

Christ died in our place. Like Simon of Cyrene we carry the cross, for he calls us to take it up and follow him (Mk. 15:21).

The Romans had made crucifixion a common sight in all their colonized provinces, and Palestine was no exception. Every rebel condemned to crucifixion was compelled to carry his cross, or at least the *patibulum* (the cross beam), to the scene of his execution. Plutarch wrote that 'every criminal condemned to death bears his cross on his back'.[6] So John wrote of Jesus that 'carrying his own cross, he went out to The Place of the Skull' (19:17). To take up our cross, therefore, and follow Jesus, is 'to put oneself into the position of a condemned man on his way to execution'.[7] For if we are following Jesus with a cross on our shoulder, there is only one place to which we are going: the place of crucifixion. As Bonhoeffer put it, 'When Christ calls a man, he bids him come and die'.[8] Our 'cross', then, is not an irritable husband or a cantankerous wife. It is instead the symbol of death to the self.

Although Jesus may have had the possibility of martyrdom in his mind, the universal nature of his call ('if anyone . . .') suggests a broader application. It is surely self-denial which, by this vivid imagery, Jesus is describing. To deny ourselves is to behave towards ourselves as Peter did towards Jesus when he denied him three times. The verb is the same (*aparneomai*). He disowned him, repudiated him, turned his back on him. Self-denial is not denying to ourselves luxuries such as chocolates, cakes, cigarettes and cocktails (though it may include this); it is actually denying or disowning ourselves, renouncing our supposed right to go our own way. 'To deny oneself is . . . to turn away from the idolatry of self-centredness.'[9] Paul must have been referring to the same thing when he wrote that those who belong to Christ 'have crucified the sinful nature with its passions and desires' (Gal. 5:24). No picture could be more graphic than that: an actual taking of hammer and nails to fasten our slippery fallen nature to the cross and thus do it to death. The traditional word for this is 'mortification'; it is the sustained determination by the power of the Holy Spirit to 'put to death the misdeeds of the body', so that through this death we may live in fellowship with God.[10]

In fact, Paul writes in his letters of three different deaths and resurrections, which are part and parcel of our Christian experience. Much confusion arises when we fail to distinguish between

[6] Quoted by Martin Hengel in *Crucifixion*, p. 77.
[7] H. B. Swete, *St Mark*, p. 172.
[8] Dietrich Bonhoeffer, *Cost of Discipleship*, p. 79.
[9] C. E. B. Cranfield in his *Mark*, p. 281.
[10] Rom. 8:13. *Cf.* Col. 3:5; 1 Pet. 2:24.

them. The first (which we have already considered) is the death to sin and subsequent life to God, which happens to all Christians by virtue of our union with Christ in his death and resurrection. By it we share in the benefits both of Christ's death (its forgiveness) and of his resurrection (its power). This is inherent in our conversion/baptism.

The second is the death to self, called variously taking up the cross, or denying, crucifying or mortifying ourselves. As a result, we live a life of fellowship with God. This death is not something which has happened to us, and which we are now told to 'reckon' or remember, but something which we must deliberately do ourselves, though by the power of the Spirit, putting our old nature to death. Indeed all Christians have done it, in the sense that it is an essential aspect of our original and continuing repentance, and we cannot be Christ's disciples without it. But we have to maintain this attitude, that is, take up the cross daily.

The third kind of death and resurrection I mentioned in chapter 9. It is the carrying about in our bodies of the dying of Jesus, so that the life of Jesus may be revealed in our bodies (2 Cor. 4:9–10). Plainly the arena for this is our bodies. It refers to their infirmity, persecution and mortality. It is in this connection that Paul could say both 'I die daily' (1 Cor. 15:30–31) and 'we face death all day long' (Rom. 8:36). For it is a continuous physical frailty. But then the 'resurrection', the inward vitality or renewal from the life of Jesus within us, is continuous too (2 Cor. 4:16).

To sum up, the first death is *legal*; it is a death to sin by union with Christ in his death to sin (bearing its penalty), and the resultant resurrection with him leads to the new life of freedom which justified sinners enjoy. The second death is *moral*; it is a death to self as we put to death the old nature and its evil desires, and the resurrection which follows leads to a new life of righteousness in fellowship with God. The third death is *physical*; it is a death to safety, a 'being given over to death for Jesus' sake', and the corresponding resurrection is Jesus' strength which he makes perfect in our weakness. The legal death was a 'death unto sin once and for all', but the moral and physical deaths are daily – even continuous – experiences for the Christian disciple.

I wonder how my readers have reacted thus far, especially to the emphasis on dying to self, or rather putting it to death by crucifying or mortifying it? I expect (and hope) that you have felt uneasy about it. I have expressed an attitude to the self so negative that I must almost seem to have aligned myself with the bureaucrats and technocrats, the ethologists and behaviourists, in demeaning human beings. It is not that what I have written is untrue (for it was Jesus who told us to take up our cross and follow him to death), but that it is only one side of the truth. It implies that our self is wholly bad, and that it must on that account be totally repudiated, indeed 'crucified'.

Self-affirmation

But we must not overlook another strand in Scripture. Alongside Jesus' explicit call to self-denial is his implicit call to self-affirmation (which is not at all the same thing as self-love). Nobody who reads the Gospels as a whole could possibly gain the impression that Jesus had a negative attitude to human beings himself, or encouraged one in others. The opposite is the case.

Consider, first, his *teaching* about people. It is true that he drew attention to the evil and ugly things which issue from the human heart (Mk. 7:21–23). He also spoke, however, of the 'value' of human beings in God's sight. They are 'much more valuable' than birds or beasts, he said.[11] What was the ground of this value judgment? It must have been the doctrine of creation, which Jesus took over from the Old Testament, namely that human beings are the crown of God's creative activity, and that he made man male and female in his own image. It is the divine image we bear which gives us our distinctive value. In his excellent little book *The Christian Looks at Himself* Dr Anthony Hoekema quotes a young American black who, rebelling against the inferiority feelings inculcated in him by whites, put up this banner in his room: 'I'm me and I'm good, 'cause God don't make junk' (p. 15). It may have been bad grammar, but it was good theology.

Secondly, there was Jesus' *attitude* to people. He despised nobody and disowned nobody. On the contrary, he went out of his way to honour those whom the world dishonoured, and to accept those whom the world rejected. He spoke courteously to women in public. He invited little children to come to him. He spoke words of hope to Samaritans and Gentiles. He allowed leprosy sufferers to approach him, and a prostitute to anoint and kiss his feet. He made friends with the outcasts of society, and ministered to the poor and hungry. In all this diversified ministry his compassionate respect for human beings shone forth. He acknowledged their value and loved them, and by loving them he further increased their value.

Thirdly, and in particular, we must remember Jesus' *mission and death* for human beings. He had come to serve, not to be served,

[11] Mt. 6:26; 12:12.

he said, and to give his life as a ransom instead of the many. Nothing indicates more clearly the great value Jesus placed on people than his determination to suffer and die for them. He was the Good Shepherd who came into the desert, braving the hardship and risking the peril, in order to seek and to save only one lost sheep. Indeed, he laid down his life for the sheep. It is only when we look at the cross that we see the true worth of human beings. As William Temple expressed it, 'My worth is what I am worth to God; and that is a marvellous great deal, for Christ died for me.'[12]

We have seen so far that the cross of Christ is both a proof of the value of the human self and a picture of how to deny or crucify it. How can we resolve this biblical paradox? How is it possible to value ourselves and to deny ourselves simultaneously?

This question arises because we discuss and develop alternative attitudes to ourselves before we have defined the 'self' we are talking about. Our 'self' is not a simple entity that is either wholly good or wholly evil, and therefore to be either totally valued or totally denied. Instead, our 'self' is a complex entity of good and evil, glory and shame, which on that account requires that we develop more subtle attitudes to ourselves.

What we are (our self or personal identity) is partly the result of the creation (the image of God) and partly the result of the Fall (the image defaced). The self we are to deny, disown and crucify is our fallen self, everything within us that is incompatible with Jesus Christ (hence his commands 'let him deny *himself*' and then 'let him follow *me*'). The self we are to affirm and value is our created self, everything within us that is compatible with Jesus Christ (hence his statement that if we lose ourselves by self-denial we shall find ourselves). True self-denial (the denial of our false, fallen self) is not the road to self-destruction but the road to self-discovery.

So then, whatever we are by creation we must affirm: our rationality, our sense of moral obligation, our sexuality (whether masculinity or femininity), our family life, our gifts of aesthetic appreciation and artistic creativity, our stewardship of the fruitful earth, our hunger for love and experience of community, our awareness of the transcendent majesty of God, and our inbuilt urge to fall down and worship him. All this (and more) is part of our created humanness. True, it has been tainted and twisted by sin. Yet Christ came to redeem it, not to destroy it. So we must gratefully and positively affirm it.

Whatever we are by the Fall, however, we must deny or

---

[12] William Temple, *Citizen and Churchman*, p. 74.

repudiate: our irrationality, our moral perversity, our blurring of sexual distinctives and lack of sexual self-control, the selfishness which spoils our family life, our fascination with the ugly, our lazy refusal to develop God's gifts, our pollution and spoliation of the environment, the anti-social tendencies which inhibit true community, our proud autonomy, and our idolatrous refusal to worship the living and true God. All this (and more) is part of our fallen humanness. Christ came not to redeem this but to destroy it. So we must strenuously deny or repudiate it.

So far I have deliberately oversimplified the contrast between our createdness and our fallenness. The picture needs now to be modified, indeed enriched, in two ways. Both enrichments are due to the introduction into the human scene of the redemption of Christ. Christians can no longer think of themselves only as 'created and fallen', but rather as 'created, fallen and redeemed'. And the injection of this new element gives us both more to affirm and more to deny.

First, we have more to affirm. For we have not only been created in God's image, but re-created in it. God's gracious work in us, which is variously portrayed in the New Testament as 'regeneration', 'resurrection', 'redemption', *etc.*, is essentially a re-creation. Our new self has been 'created to be like God in true righteousness and holiness', and it 'is being renewed in knowledge in the image of its Creator'. Indeed, every person who is in Christ 'is a new creation'.[13] This means that our mind, our character and our relationships are all being renewed. We are God's children, Christ's disciples and the Holy Spirit's temple. We belong to the new community which is the family of God. The Holy Spirit enriches us with his fruit and gifts. And we are God's heirs, looking forward with confidence to the glory which will one day be revealed. Becoming a Christian is a transforming experience. By changing us, it also changes our self-image. We now have much more to affirm, not boastfully but gratefully. Dr Hoekema is right to make this his main emphasis in *The Christian Looks at Himself*. He mentions the hymn 'Beneath the Cross of Jesus', which in many ways is magnificent and moving. But not the end of one verse, which goes like this:

> And from my smitten heart, with tears,
> Two wonders I confess, –
> The wonder of his glorious love,
> And my own worthlessness.

[13] Eph. 4:24; Col. 3:10; 2 Cor. 5:17.

No, no, Dr Hoekema objects. We cannot sing that. 'And my unworthiness' would express the truth, but not 'my own worthless-ness' (p. 16). How can we declare 'worthless' what Jesus Christ has declared of 'value'? Is it 'worthless' to be a child of God, a member of Christ and an heir of the kingdom of heaven? So then, a vital part of our self-affirmation, which in reality is an affirmation of the grace of God our Creator and Redeemer, is what we have become in Christ. 'The ultimate basis for our positive self-image must be God's acceptance of us in Christ' (p. 102).

Secondly, Christians have more to deny as well as more to affirm. So far I have included only our fallenness in what needs to be denied. Sometimes, however, God calls us to deny to ourselves things which, though not wrong in themselves or attributable to the Fall, yet stand in the way of our doing his particular will for us. This is why Jesus, whose humanity was perfect and not fallen, still had to deny himself. We are told that he 'did not consider equality with God something to be grasped', that is, to be selfishly enjoyed (Phil. 2:6). It was his already. He did not 'make himself equal with God' as his critics complained (Jn. 5:18); he was eter-nally equal with him, so that he and his Father were 'one' (Jn. 10:30). Yet he did not cling to the privileges of this status. Instead, he 'emptied himself' of his glory. Yet the reason he laid it aside is not that it was not his by right, but that he could not retain it and at the same time fulfil his destiny to be God's Messiah and Mediator. He went to the cross in self-denial, not of course because he had done anything to deserve death, but because this was his Father's will for him according to Scripture, and to that will he voluntarily surrendered himself. Throughout his life he resisted the temptation to avoid the cross. In Max Warren's succinct words, 'all Christ's living was a dying'.[14] He denied himself in order to give himself for us.

The very same principle is applicable to Christ's followers. 'Let this mind be in you', Paul wrote. For he knew the call to self-denial in his own apostolic experience. He had legitimate rights, for example to marriage and to financial support, which he deliberately denied himself because he believed this was God's will for him. He also wrote that mature Christians should be willing to renounce their rights and limit their liberties so as not to cause immature brothers and sisters to sin. Still today some Christian people are called to forgo married life, or a secure job, or professional promotion, or a comfortable home in a salubrious suburb, not because any of these things is wrong in itself, but because they are

[14] M. A. C. Warren, *Interpreting the Cross*, p. 81.

incompatible with a particular call of God to go overseas or live in the inner city or identify more closely with the world's poor and hungry people.

There is, therefore, a great need for discernment in our self-understanding. Who am I? What is my 'self'? The answer is that I am a Jekyll and Hyde, a mixed-up kid, having both dignity, because I was created and have been re-created in the image of God, and depravity, because I still have a fallen and rebellious nature. I am both noble and ignoble, beautiful and ugly, good and bad, upright and twisted, image and child of God, and yet sometimes yielding obsequious homage to the devil from whose clutches Christ has rescued me. My true self is what I am by creation, which Christ came to redeem, and by calling. My false self is what I am by the Fall, which Christ came to destroy.

Only when we have discerned which is which within us, shall we know what attitude to adopt towards each. We must be true to our true self and false to our false self. We must be fearless in affirming all that we are by creation, redemption and calling, and ruthless in disowning all that we are by the Fall.

Moreover, the cross of Christ teaches us both attitudes. On the one hand, the cross is the God-given measure of the value of our true self, since Christ loved us and died for us. On the other hand, it is the God-given model for the denial of our false self, since we are to nail it to the cross and so put it to death. Or, more simply, standing before the cross we see simultaneously our worth and our unworthiness, since we perceive both the greatness of his love in dying, and the greatness of our sin in causing him to die.

Self-sacrificial love

Neither self-denial (a repudiation of our sins) nor self-affirmation (an appreciation of God's gifts) is a dead end of self-absorption. On the contrary, both are means to self-sacrifice. Self-understanding should lead to self-giving. The community of the cross is essentially a community of self-giving love, expressed in the worship of God (which was our theme in the previous chapter) and in the service of others (which is our theme at the end of this chapter). It is to this that the cross consistently and insistently calls us.

The contrast between the standards of the cross and of the world is nowhere more dramatically set forth than in the request of James and John and in the response of Jesus to them.

Then James and John, the sons of Zebedee, came to him.

'Teacher,' they said, 'We want you to do for us whatever we ask.'

'What do you want me to do for you?' he asked.

They replied, 'Let one of us sit at your right and the other at your left in your glory.'

'You don't know what you are asking,' Jesus said. 'Can you drink the cup I drink or be baptized with the baptism I am baptized with?'

'We can,' they answered.

Jesus said to them, 'You will drink the cup I drink and be baptized with the baptism I am baptized with, but to sit at my right or left is not for me to grant. These places belong to those for whom they have been prepared.'

When the ten heard about this, they became indignant with James and John. Jesus called them together and said, 'You know that those who are regarded as rulers of the Gentiles lord it over them, and their high officials exercise authority over them. Not so with you. Instead, whoever wants to become great among you must be your servant, and whoever wants to be first must be slave of all. For even the Son of Man did not come to be served, but to serve, and to give his life as a ransom for many' (Mk. 10:35–45).

Verse 35 ('We want you to do for us whatever we ask') and verse 45 ('the Son of Man came to serve . . . and to give'), the one introducing and the other concluding this story, portray the sons of Zebedee and the Son of Man in irreconcilable disagreement. They speak a different language, breathe a different spirit and express a different ambition. James and John want to sit on thrones in power and glory; Jesus knows that he must hang on a cross in weakness and shame. The antithesis is total.

There was, first, the choice *between selfish ambition and sacrifice*. The brothers' statement 'We want you to do for us whatever we ask' surely qualifies as the worst, most blatantly self-centred prayer ever prayed. They seem to have anticipated that there would be an unholy scramble for the most honourable seats in the kingdom; so they judged it prudent to make an advance reservation. Their request to 'sit in state' (NEB) with Jesus was nothing but 'a bright mirror of human vanity'.[15] It was the exact opposite of true prayer, whose purpose is never to bend God's will to ours, but always to bend our will to his. Yet the world (and even the church) is full of Jameses and Johns, go-getters and status-seekers, hungry for honour and prestige, measuring life by achieve-

[15] Calvin, *Commentary on a Harmony of the Evangelists*, Vol. II, p. 417.

ment, and everlastingly dreaming of success. They are aggressively ambitious for themselves.

This whole mentality is incompatible with the way of the cross. 'The Son of Man did not come to be served, but to serve, and to give . . . .' He renounced the power and glory of heaven and humbled himself to be a slave. He gave himself without reserve and without fear, to the despised and neglected sections of the community. His obsession was the glory of God and the good of human beings who bear his image. To promote these, he was willing to endure even the shame of the cross. Now he calls us to follow him, not to seek great things for ourselves, but rather to seek first God's rule and God's righteousness.[16]

The second choice was *between power and service*. It seems clear that James and John wanted power as well as honour. Asking to 'sit' each side of Jesus in his glory, we may be quite sure they were not dreaming of seats on the floor, or on cushions, stools or chairs, but on thrones. They rather fancied themselves with a throne each. We know they came from a well-to-do family, because their father Zebedee had employees in his fishing business on the lake. Perhaps they missed having servants to wait on them, but were willing to forgo that luxury for a while, provided that they were compensated with thrones in the end. The world loves power. 'You know that those who are regarded as rulers of the Gentiles lord it over them,' said Jesus, 'and their high officials exercise authority over them' (v. 42). Was he thinking of Rome, whose emperors had coins struck featuring their head with the inscription 'he who deserves adoration'? Or was he thinking of the Herods, who, though only puppet kings, ruled like tyrants? The lust for power is endemic to our fallenness.

It is also totally incompatible with the way of the cross, which spells service. Jesus' affirmation that 'the Son of Man did not come to be served, but to serve' was startlingly original. For the Son of Man in Daniel's vision was given power so that all nations would serve him (7:13–14). Jesus claimed the title, but changed the role. He had not come to be served, but rather to be the 'servant of the Lord' of the Servant Songs. He fused the two portraits. He was both the glorious Son of Man and the suffering servant; he would enter glory only by suffering. Again, he calls us to follow. In the secular world rulers continue to throw their weight about, manipulate, exploit and tyrannize others. 'Not so with you' (v. 43), said Jesus emphatically. His new community is to be organized on a different principle and according to a different model – humble

---

[16] Je. 45:5; Mt. 6:33.

287

service, not oppressive power. Leadership and lordship are two distinct concepts. The symbol of an authentically Christian leadership is not the purple robe of an emperor, but the coarse apron of a slave; not a throne of ivory and gold, but a basin of water for the washing of feet.

The third choice was, and still is, *between comfort and suffering*. By asking for thrones in glory, James and John were wanting comfortable security in addition to honour and power. Following Jesus, they had become vagrants, even vagabonds. Did they miss their pleasant home? When Jesus replied to their question with a counter-question as to whether they could share his cup and his baptism as well as his throne, their riposte was a glib 'we can' (vv. 38–39). But surely they did not understand. They were daydreaming about the goblets of wine at the Messianic banquet, preceded by the luxurious pre-banquet baths which Herod was known to love. Jesus, however, was referring to his sufferings. They would indeed share his cup and baptism, he said, without enlightening them. For James was to lose his head at the hand of Herod Antipas, and John was to suffer a lonely exile.

The spirit of James and John lingers on, especially in us who have been cushioned by affluence. It is true that inflation and unemployment have brought to many a new experience of insecurity. Yet we still regard security as our birthright and 'safety first' as a prudent motto. Where is the spirit of adventure, the sense of uncalculating solidarity with the underprivileged? Where are the Christians who are prepared to put service before security, compassion before comfort, hardship before ease? Thousands of pioneer Christian tasks are waiting to be done, which challenge our complacency, and which call for risk.

Insistence on security is incompatible with the way of the cross. What daring adventures the incarnation and the atonement were! What a breach of convention and decorum that Almighty God should renounce his privileges in order to take human flesh and bear human sin! Jesus had no security except in his Father. So to follow Jesus is always to accept at least a measure of uncertainty, danger and rejection for his sake.

Thus James and John coveted honour, power and comfortable security, while the whole career of Jesus was marked by sacrifice, service and suffering. Mark, who is increasingly acknowledged as a theologian-evangelist as well as a historian, sandwiches the request of James and John between two explicit references to the cross. It is the glory of Christ's cross which shows up their selfish ambition for the shabby, tatty, threadbare thing it was. It also highlights the choice, which faces the Christian community in every generation, between the way of the crowd and the way of the cross.

Spheres of service

Granted that the community of Christ is a community of the cross, and will therefore be marked by sacrifice, service and suffering, how will this work itself out in the three spheres of home, church and world?

Life in a Christian home, which should in any case be characterized by natural human love, should be further enriched by supernatural divine love, that is, the love of the cross. It should mark all Christian family relationships, between husband and wife, parents and children, brothers and sisters. For we are to 'submit to one another out of reverence for Christ' (Eph. 5:21), the Christ whose humble and submissive love led him even to the cross. Yet it is specially husbands who are singled out. 'Husbands, love your wives, just as Christ loved the church and gave himself up for her to make her holy, . . . and to present her to himself as a radiant church . . .' (vv. 25–27). This Ephesians passage is commonly regarded as being very hard on wives, because they are to recognize the 'headship' God has given to their husbands and submit to them. But it is arguable that the quality of self-giving love required of husbands is even more demanding. For they are to love their wives with the love which Christ has for his bride the church. This is Calvary love. It is both self-sacrificial (he 'gave himself up for her', v. 25) and constructive ('to make her holy' and resplendent, growing into her full potential, vv. 26–27). It is also caring and protective: 'husbands ought to love their wives as their own bodies', for 'no-one ever hated his own body, but he feeds it and cares for it, just as Christ does the church' (vv. 28–29). Christian homes in general, and Christian marriages in particular, would be more stable and more satisfying if they were marked by the cross.

We turn now from the home to the church, and begin with pastors. We saw in an earlier chapter that there is a place for authority and discipline in the community of Jesus. Nevertheless, his emphasis was not on these things but on the new style of leadership which he introduced, distinguished by humility and service. Paul himself felt the tension. As an apostle he had received from Christ a special degree of authority. He could have come to the recalcitrant Corinthian church 'with a whip', and was 'ready to punish every act of disobedience', if he had to. But he did not want to be 'harsh' in the use of his authority, which the Lord Jesus had given him for building them up, not for tearing them down.

He would much prefer to come as a father visiting his dear children. It was the tension between the death and resurrection of Jesus, between weakness and power. He could exercise power, since Christ 'lives by God's power'. But since 'he was crucified in weakness', it is 'the meekness and gentleness of Christ' which Paul wants most to exhibit.[17] If Christian pastors adhered more closely to the Christ who was crucified in weakness, and were prepared to accept the humiliations which weakness brings, rather than insisting on wielding power, there would be much less discord and much more harmony in the church.

The cross is to characterize all our relationships in Christ's community, however, and not just the relationship between pastors and people. We are to 'love one another', John insists in his first letter, both because God is love in his being and because he has showed his love by sending his Son to die for us. And this love always expresses itself in unselfishness. We are to 'do nothing out of selfish ambition or vain conceit, but in humility consider others better than' ourselves. Positively, we are each of us to look not only to our own interests, 'but also to the interests of others'. Why? Why this renunciation of selfish ambition and this cultivation of an unselfish interest in others? Because this was the attitude of Christ, who both renounced his own rights and humbled himself to serve others. In fact, the cross sweetens all our relationships in the church. We have only to remember that our fellow Christian is a 'brother (or sister) for whom Christ died', and we will never disregard, but always seek to serve, their truest and highest welfare. To sin against them would be to 'sin against Christ'.[18]

If the cross is to mark our Christian life in the home and the church, this should be even more so in the world. The church tends to become very preoccupied with its own affairs, obsessed with petty, parochial trivia, while the needy world outside is waiting. So the Son sends us out into the world, as the Father had sent him into the world. Mission arises from the birth, death and resurrection of Jesus. His birth, by which he identified himself with our humanity, calls us to a similar costly identification with people. His death reminds us that suffering is the key to church growth, since it is the seed which dies which multiplies. And his resurrection gave him the universal lordship which enabled him both to claim that 'all authority' was now his and to send his church to disciple the nations.[19]

[17] 1 Cor. 4:21; 2 Cor. 10:6–18; 13:10; 1 Cor. 4:13–14; 2 Cor. 13:10 and 10:1.
[18] 1 Jn. 4:7–12; Phil. 2:3–4; 1 Cor. 8:11–13.
[19] Jn. 17:18; 20:21; 12:24; Mt. 28:18–20.

In theory we know very well the paradoxical principle that suffering is the path to glory, death the way to life, and weakness the secret of power. It was for Jesus, and it still is for his followers today. But we are reluctant to apply the principle to mission, as the Bible does. In the shadowy image of Isaiah's suffering servant, suffering was to be the condition of his success in bringing light and justice to the nations. As Douglas Webster has written, 'mission sooner or later leads into passion. In biblical categories . . . the servant must suffer. . . . Every form of mission leads to some form of cross. The very shape of mission is cruciform. We can understand mission only in terms of the cross . . .'.[20]

This biblical vision of suffering service has been largely eclipsed in our day by the unbiblical 'prosperity gospel' (which guarantees personal success) and by triumphalist notions of mission (which employ military metaphors that do not comfortably fit the humble image of the suffering servant). By contrast, Paul dared to write to the Corinthians: 'so then, death is at work in us, but life is at work in you' (2 Cor. 4:12). The cross lies at the very heart of mission. For the cross-cultural missionary it may mean costly individual and family sacrifices, the renunciation of economic security and professional promotion, solidarity with the poor and needy, repenting of the pride and prejudice of supposed cultural superiority, and the modesty (and sometimes frustration) of serving under national leadership. Each of these can be a kind of death, but it is a death which brings life to others.

In all evangelism there is also a cultural gulf to bridge. This is obvious when Christian people move as messengers of the gospel from one country or continent to another. But even if we remain in our own country, Christians and non-Christians are often widely separated from one another by social sub-cultures and lifestyles as well as by different values, beliefs and moral standards. Only an incarnation can span these divides, for an incarnation means entering other people's worlds, their thought-world, and the worlds of their alienation, loneliness and pain. Moreover, the incarnation led to the cross. Jesus first took our flesh, then bore our sin. This was a depth of penetration into our world in order to reach us, in comparison with which our little attempts to reach people seem amateur and shallow. The cross calls us to a much more radical and costly kind of evangelism than most churches have begun to consider, let alone experience.

The cross calls us to social action too, because it summons us to the imitation of Christ:

[20] Douglas Webster, *Yes to Mission*, pp. 101–102.

291

This is how we know what love is: Jesus Christ laid down his life for us. And we ought to lay down our lives for our brothers. If anyone has material possessions and sees his brother in need but has no pity on him, how can the love of God be in him? Dear children, let us not love with words or tongue but with actions and in truth (1 Jn. 3:16–18).

According to John's teaching here, love is essentially self-giving. And since our most valuable possession is our life, the greatest love is seen in laying it down for others. Just as the essence of hate is murder (as with Cain), so the essence of love is self-sacrifice (as with Christ). Murder is taking another person's life; self-sacrifice is laying down one's own. God does more, however, than give us a paramount exhibition of love in the cross; he puts his love within us. With the love of God both revealed to us and indwelling us, we have a double, inescapable incentive to give ourselves in love to others. Moreover, John makes it clear that to lay down our life for others, though the supreme form of self-giving, is not its only expression. If one of us 'has' a possession, 'sees' someone else who needs it, and then fails to relate what he 'has' to what he 'sees' in terms of practical action, he cannot claim to have God's love in him. So love gives food to the hungry, shelter to the homeless, help to the destitute, friendship to the lonely, comfort to the sad, provided always that these gifts are tokens of the giving of the self. For it is possible to give food, money, time and energy, and yet somehow withhold oneself. But Christ gave himself. Though rich, he became poor, in order to make us rich. We know this grace of his, Paul writes, and we must emulate it. Generosity is indispensable to the followers of Christ. There was an almost reckless extravagance about Christ's love on the cross; it challenges the calculating coldness of our love.

Yet, as we have repeatedly noted throughout this book, the cross is a revelation of God's justice as well as of his love. That is why the community of the cross should concern itself with social justice as well as with loving philanthropy. It is never enough to have pity on the victims of injustice, if we do nothing to change the unjust situation itself. Good Samaritans will always be needed to succour those who are assaulted and robbed; yet it would be even better to rid the Jerusalem-Jericho road of brigands. Just so Christian philanthropy in terms of relief and aid is necessary, but long-term development is better, and we cannot evade our political responsibility to share in changing the structures which inhibit development. Christians cannot regard with equanimity the injustices which spoil God's world and demean his creatures. Injustice must bring pain to the God whose justice flared brightly at the cross; it should bring pain to God's people too. Contemporary injustices take many forms. They are international (the invasion and annexation of foreign territory), political (the subjugation of minorities), legal (the punishment of untried and unsentenced citizens), racial (the humiliating discrimination against people on the ground of race or colour), economic (the toleration of gross North-South inequality and of the traumas of poverty and unemployment), sexual (the oppression of women), educational (the denial of equal opportunity for all) or religious (the failure to take the gospel to the nations). Love and justice combine to oppose all these situations. If we love people, we shall be concerned to secure their basic rights as human beings, which is also the concern of justice. The community of the cross, which has truly absorbed the message of the cross, will always be motivated to action by the demands of justice and love.

As an illustration of how a Christian community can be comprehensively stimulated by the cross, I would like to mention the Moravian Brethren, founded by Count Nikolaus von Zinzendorf (1700–60). In 1722 he welcomed some pietistic Christian refugees from Moravia and Bohemia to his estate in Saxony, where he helped them to form a Christian community under the name 'Herrnhut'. The Moravians' stress was on Christianity as a religion of the cross and of the heart. They defined a Christian as one who has 'an inseparable friendship with the Lamb, the slaughtered Lamb'.[21] Their seal bears the inscription in Latin 'Our Lamb has conquered; let us follow him', and the ensign on their boats was of a lamb passant with a flag in a blood-coloured field (p. 97). They were deeply concerned for Christian unity and believed that the Lamb would be the ground of it, since all who 'adhere to Jesus as the Lamb of God' are one (p. 106). Indeed, Zinzendorf himself declared that 'the Lamb Slain' was from the beginning the foundation on which their church was built (p. 70).

First, they were certainly a community of celebration. They were great singers, and the focus of their worship at Herrnhut was Christ crucified.

> In Jesus' blood their element
> They swim and bathe with full content (p. 70).

No doubt they were too preoccupied with the wounds and the blood of Jesus. At the same time they never forgot the resurrection.

[21] A. J. Lewis, *Zinzendorf*, p. 107.

They were sometimes called 'the Easter people' because it was the risen Lamb whom they adored (p. 74).

As for self-understanding, their particular brand of pietism seems to have enabled them to come to terms with themselves. Their emphasis on the cross brought them to genuine humility and penitence. But it also gave them a strong assurance of salvation and quiet confidence in God. 'We are the Saviour's happy people', Zinzendorf said (p. 73). It was in fact their joy and fearlessness, when face to face with death as their ship was sinking in an Atlantic storm, which brought John Wesley under conviction of sin and was an important link in the chain which led to his conversion.

But the Moravians are best known as a missionary movement. While still a schoolboy Zinzendorf founded 'the Order of the Grain of Mustard Seed', and he never lost his missionary zeal. Again, it was the cross which stimulated him and his followers to this expression of self-giving love. Between 1732 and 1736 Moravian missions were founded in the Caribbean, Greenland, Lapland, North and South America, and South Africa, while later they began missionary work in Labrador, among Australian aboriginals and on the Tibetan border. The heathen know there is a God, taught Zinzendorf, but they need to know of the Saviour who died for them. 'Tell them about the Lamb of God', he urged, 'till you can tell them no more' (p. 91).

This healthy emphasis on the cross arose largely from his own conversion experience. Sent as a young man of 19 to visit the capital cities of Europe, in order to complete his education, he found himself one day in the art gallery of Düsseldorf. He stood before Domenico Feti's *Ecce Homo*, in which Christ is portrayed wearing the crown of thorns, and under which the inscription reads: 'All this I did for thee; what doest thou for me?' Zinzendorf was deeply convicted and challenged. 'There and then', A. J. Lewis writes, 'the young Count asked the crucified Christ to draw him into "the fellowship of his sufferings" and to open up a life of service to him' (p. 28). He never went back on this commitment. He and his community were passionately concerned for 'the enthronement of the Lamb of God'.

12

Loving our enemies

'To live under the cross' means that every aspect of the Christian community's life is shaped and coloured by it. The cross not only elicits our worship (so that we enjoy a continuous, eucharistic celebration) and enables us to develop a balanced self-image (so that we learn both to understand ourselves and to give ourselves), but it also directs our conduct in relation to others, including our enemies. We are to 'be imitators of God ... as dearly loved children' and to 'live a life of love, just as Christ loved us and gave himself up for us ...' (Eph. 5:1–2). More than that, we are to exhibit in our relationships that combination of love and justice which characterized the wisdom of God in the cross.

Conciliation and discipline

But how in practice we are to combine love and justice, mercy and severity, and so walk the way of the cross, is often hard to decide and harder still to do. Take 'conciliation' or 'peace-making' as an example. Christian people are called to be 'peacemakers' (Mt. 5:9) and to 'seek peace and pursue it' (1 Pet. 3:11). At the same time, it is recognized that peace-making can never be a purely unilateral activity. The instruction to 'live at peace with everyone' is qualified by the two conditions 'if it is possible' and 'as far as it depends on you' (Rom. 12:18). What are we to do, then, when it proves impossible to live at peace with somebody because he or she is unwilling to live at peace with us? The place to begin our answer is with the beatitude already quoted. For there, in pronouncing peacemakers 'blessed', Jesus added that 'they will be called sons (or daughters) of God'.[1] He must have meant that peace-making is such a characteristically divine activity, that those who engage in it thereby disclose their identity and demonstrate their authenticity as God's children.

If our peace-making is to be modelled on our heavenly Father's, however, we shall conclude at once that it is quite different from appeasement. For the peace which God secures is never cheap peace, but always costly. He is indeed the world's pre-eminent peacemaker, but when he determined on reconciliation with us, his 'enemies', who had rebelled against him, he 'made peace' through the blood of Christ's cross (Col. 1:20). To reconcile himself to us, and us to himself, and Jews, Gentiles and other hostile groups to each other, cost him nothing less than the painful shame of the cross. We have no right to expect, therefore, that we shall be able to engage in conciliation work at no cost to ourselves, whether our involvement in the dispute is as the offending or offended party, or as a third party anxious to help enemies to become friends again.

What form might the cost take? Often it will begin with sustained, painstaking listening to both sides, the distress of witnessing the mutual bitterness and recriminations, the struggle to sympathize with each position, and the effort to understand the misunderstandings which have caused the communication breakdown. Honest listening may uncover unsuspected faults, which will in their turn necessitate their acknowledgment, without resorting to face-saving subterfuges. If we are ourselves to blame, there will be the humiliation of apologizing, the deeper humiliation of making restitution where this is possible, and the deepest humiliation of all, which is to confess that the wounds we have caused will take time to heal and cannot light-heartedly be forgotten. If, on the other hand, the wrong has not been done by us, then we may have to bear the embarrassment of reproving or rebuking the other person, and thereby risk forfeiting his or her friendship. Although the followers of Jesus never have the right to refuse forgiveness, let alone to take revenge, we are not permitted to cheapen forgiveness by offering it prematurely when there has been no repentance. 'If your brother sins,' Jesus said, 'rebuke him', and only then 'if he repents, forgive him' (Lk. 17:3).

The incentive to peace-making is love, but it degenerates into appeasement whenever justice is ignored. To forgive and to ask for forgiveness are both costly exercises. All authentic Christian peace-making exhibits the love and justice – and so the pain –

---

[1] Mt. 5:9; *cf.* 5:48 and Lk. 6:36.

of the cross.

Turning from social relationships in general to family life in particular, Christian parents will want their attitude to their children to be marked by the cross. Love is the indispensable atmosphere within which children grow into emotional maturity. Yet this is not the soft, unprincipled love which spoils the children, but the 'holy love' which seeks their highest welfare, whatever the cost. Indeed, since the very concept of human fatherhood is derived from the eternal fatherhood of God (Eph. 3:14–15), Christian parents will naturally model their love on his. Consequently, true parental love does not eliminate discipline, since 'the Lord disciplines those whom he loves'. Indeed, it is when God disciplines us that he is treating us as his sons and daughters. If he did not discipline us, it might show us to be his illegitimate, not his authentic, children (Heb. 12:5–8). Genuine love gets angry too, being hostile to everything in the children which is inimical to their highest good. Justice without mercy is too strict, and mercy without justice too lenient. Besides, children know this instinctively. They have an inborn sense of both. If they have done something which they know is wrong, they also know that they deserve punishment, and they both expect and want to receive it. They also know at once if the punishment is being administered either without love or contrary to justice. The two most poignant cries of a child are 'Nobody loves me' and 'It isn't fair'. Their sense of love and justice comes from God, who made them in his image, and who revealed himself as holy love at the cross.

The same principle applies to the church family as to the human family. Both kinds of family need discipline, and for the same reason. Yet nowadays church discipline is rare, and where it does take place, it is often administered clumsily. Churches tend to oscillate between the extreme severity which excommunicates members for the most trivial offences and the extreme laxity which never even remonstrates with offenders. Yet the New Testament gives clear instructions about discipline, on the one hand its necessity for the sake of the church's holiness, and on the other its constructive purpose, namely, if possible, to 'win over' and 'restore' the offending member. Jesus himself made it abundantly plain that the object of discipline was not to humiliate, let alone to alienate, the person concerned, but rather to reclaim him. He laid down a procedure which would develop by stages. Stage one is a private, one-to-one confrontation with the offender, 'just between the two of you', during which, if he listens, he will be won over. If he refuses, stage two is to take several others along in order to establish the rebuke. If he still refuses to listen, the church is to be told, so that he may have a third chance to repent. If he still obstinately refuses to listen, only then is he to be excommunicated (Mt. 18:15–17). Paul's teaching was similar. A church member 'caught in a sin' is to be 'restored' in a spirit of gentleness and humility; this would be an example of bearing each other's burdens and so fulfilling Christ's law of love (Gal. 6:1–2). Even a 'handing over to Satan', by which presumably Paul was referring to the excommunication of a flagrant offender, had a positive purpose, either that he might be 'taught not to blaspheme' (1 Tim. 1:20), or at least that 'his spirit (might be) saved on the day of the Lord' (1 Cor. 5:5). Thus all disciplinary action was to exhibit the love and justice of the cross.

More perplexing than these examples from the life of individuals, family and church is the administration of justice by the state. Can God's revelation in the cross be applied to this area too? More particularly, may the state use force, or would this be incompatible with the cross? Of course the cross was itself a conspicuous act of violence by the authorities, involving a gross violation of justice and a brutal execution. Yet it was an equally conspicuous act of non-violence by Jesus, who allowed himself to be unjustly condemned, tortured and executed without resistance, let alone retaliation. Moreover, his behaviour is set forth in the New Testament as the model of ours: 'if you suffer for doing good and you endure it, this is commendable before God. To this you were called, because Christ suffered for you, leaving you an example, that you should follow in his steps' (1 Pet. 2:20–21). Yet this text provokes many questions. Does the cross commit us to a non-violent acceptance of all violence? Does it invalidate the process of criminal justice and the so-called 'just war'? Does it prohibit the use of every kind of force, so that it would be incompatible for a Christian to be a soldier, policeman, magistrate or prison officer?

Christian attitudes to evil

The best way to seek answers to these questions is to look carefully at the twelfth and thirteenth chapters of Paul's letter to the Romans. They are part of the apostle's plea to his Christian readers to respond adequately to 'the mercies of God'. For eleven chapters he has been unfolding God's mercy both in giving his Son to die for us and in bestowing on us the full salvation he thus obtained for us. How should we respond to the divine mercy? We are (1) to present our bodies to *God* as a living sacrifice, and with renewed minds to discern and to do his will (12:1–2); (2) to think of *ourselves* with sober judgment, neither flattering nor despising ourselves (v. 3); (3) to love *each other*, using our gifts to serve each other, and living together in harmony and humility (vv. 4–13, 15–16); and (4) we are to bless our persecutors and do good to our *enemies* (vv. 14, 17–21). In other words, when the mercies of God lay hold of us, all our relationships are radically transformed: we obey God, understand ourselves, love one another and serve our enemies.

It is the fourth of these relationships which particularly concerns us now. The opposition of unbelievers is assumed. The stumbling-block of the cross (which offers salvation as a free and unmerited gift), the love and purity of Jesus (which shame human selfishness), the priority commands to love God and neighbour (which leave no room for self-love) and the call to take up our cross (which is too threatening) – these things arouse opposition to us because they arouse opposition to our Lord and his gospel. This, then, is the background to our study of Romans 12. There are people who 'persecute' us (v. 14), who do 'evil' to us (v. 17), who may even be described as our 'enemies' (v. 20). How should we react to our persecutors and enemies? What do the mercies of God require of us? How should the cross, in which God's mercy shines at its brightest, affect our conduct? Specially instructive, in the following section of Romans 12 and 13, are Paul's four references to good and evil:

Love must be sincere. Hate what is evil; cling to what is good. . . .

Bless those who persecute you; bless and do not curse. Rejoice with those who rejoice; mourn with those who mourn. Live in harmony with one another. Do not be proud, but be willing to associate with people of low position. Do not be conceited.

Do not repay anyone evil for evil. Be careful to do what is right in the eyes of everybody. If it is possible, as far as it depends on you, live at peace with everyone. Do not take revenge, my friends, but leave room for God's wrath, for it is written: 'It is mine to avenge; I will repay,' says the Lord. On the contrary:

'If your enemy is hungry, feed him;
if he is thirsty, give him something to drink.
In doing this, you will heap burning coals on his head.'
Do not be overcome by evil; but overcome evil with good.

Everyone must submit himself to the governing authorities, for there is no authority except that which God has established. The authorities that exist have been established by God. Consequently, he who rebels against the authority is rebelling against what God has instituted, and those who do so will bring judgment on themselves. For rulers hold no terror for those who do right, but for those who do wrong. Do you want to be free from fear of the one in authority? Then do what is right and he will commend you. For he is God's servant to do you good. But if you do wrong, be afraid, for he does not bear the sword for nothing. He is God's servant, an agent of wrath to bring punishment on the wrongdoer. Therefore, it is necessary to submit to the authorities, not only because of possible punishment but also because of conscience.

This is also why you pay taxes, for the authorities are God's servants, who give their full time to governing. Give everyone what you owe him: If you owe taxes, pay taxes; if revenue, then revenue; if respect, then respect; if honour, then honour (Rom. 12:9, 14 – 13:7).

This passage seems to be a self-conscious meditation on the theme of good and evil. Here are the apostle's four allusions to them:

Hate what is evil; cling to what is good (12:9).

Do not repay anyone evil for evil. Be careful to do what is right in the eyes of everybody (12:17).

Do not be overcome by evil; but overcome evil with good (12:21).

He is God's servant to do you good . . . He is God's servant, an agent of wrath to bring punishment on the evildoer (13:4).

In particular, these verses define what our Christian attitude to evil should be.

First, *evil is to be hated*. 'Love must be sincere. Hate what is evil; cling to what is good' (12:9). This juxtaposition of love and hate sounds incongruous. Normally we regard them as mutually exclusive. Love expels hate, and hate love. But the truth is not so simple. Whenever love is 'sincere' (literally, 'without hypocrisy'), it is morally discerning. It never pretends that evil is anything else, or condones it. Compromise with evil is incompatible with love. Love seeks the highest good of others and therefore hates the evil which spoils it. God hates evil because his love is holy love; we must hate it too.

Secondly, *evil is not to be repaid*. 'Do not repay anyone evil for evil . . . . Do not take revenge, my friends' (12:17, 19). Revenge and retaliation are absolutely forbidden to the people of God. For to repay evil for evil is to add one evil to another. And if we hate evil, how can we add to it? The Sermon on the Mount is clearly being echoed here. 'Do not resist an evil person', Jesus had said. That is, as the context clarifies, 'do not retaliate'. And at the cross Jesus perfectly exemplified his own teaching, for 'when they hurled their insults at him, he did not retaliate; when he suffered, he made no threats' (1 Pet. 2:23). Instead, we are to 'do what is right' (12:17) and to 'live at peace with everyone' (12:18). That is, good not evil, and peace not violence, are to characterize our lives.

Thirdly, *evil is to be overcome*. It is one thing to hate evil and another to refuse to repay it; better still is to conquer or overcome it. 'Do not be overcome by evil; but overcome evil with good' (12:21). How to do this Paul has indicated in the previous verses, echoing more words from the Sermon on the Mount. Jesus had said: 'Love your enemies, do good to those who hate you, bless those who curse you, pray for those who ill-treat you.'[2] Now Paul writes: 'Bless those who persecute you' (12:14), and 'if your enemy is hungry, feed him' (12:20). We are to wish good to people by blessing them, and to do good to people by serving them. In the new community of Jesus curses are to be replaced by blessings, malice by prayer, and revenge by service. In fact, prayer purges the heart of malice; the lips which bless cannot simultaneously curse; and the hand occupied with service is restrained from taking revenge. To 'heap burning coals' on an enemy's head sounds an unfriendly act, incompatible with loving him. But it is a figure of speech for causing an acute sense of shame – not in order to hurt or humiliate him, but in order to bring him to repentance, and so to 'overcome evil with good'. The tragedy of repaying evil for evil is that we thereby add evil to evil and so *increase* the world's tally of evil. It causes what Martin Luther King called 'the chain reaction of evil', as hate multiplies hate and violence multiplies violence in 'a descending spiral of destruction'.[3] The glory of loving and serving our enemies, however, is that we thereby *decrease* the amount of evil in the world. The supreme example is the cross. Christ's willingness to bear the scorn of men and the wrath of God has brought salvation to millions. The cross is the only alchemy which turns evil into good.

Fourthly, *evil is to be punished*. If we were to stop with the first three attitudes to evil, we would be guilty of grave biblical selectivity and therefore imbalance. For Paul goes on to write of the punishment of evil by the state. All careful readers of these chapters

[2] Lk. 6:27–28; *cf.* Mt. 5:44.
[3] Martin Luther King, *Strength to Love*, p. 51.

notice the contrast – even apparent contradiction – which they contain. We are told both that we are not to avenge ourselves and that God will avenge (12:19). Again, we are told both that we are not to repay anyone evil for evil and that God will repay (12:17, 19). Thus vengeance and retaliation are first forbidden us, and then attributed to God. Is that not intolerable? No. The reason these things are forbidden us is not because evil does not deserve to be punished (it does, and should be), but because it is *God's* prerogative to punish it, not ours.

So how does God punish evil? How is his wrath expressed against evil-doers? The answer which immediately springs to mind is 'at the last judgment', and that is true. The unrepentant are 'storing up wrath' against themselves 'for the day of God's wrath, when his righteous judgment will be revealed' (Rom. 2:5). But must we wait till then? Is there no way in which God's wrath against evil is revealed now? There is, according to Paul. The first is in the progressive deterioration of a godless society, by which God 'gives over' to their uncontrolled depravity of mind and conduct those who deliberately smother their knowledge of God and of goodness (Rom. 1:18–32). That is an outworking of God's wrath. The second is through the judicial processes of the state, since the law enforcement officer is 'God's servant, an agent of wrath to bring punishment on the wrongdoer' (13:4). In this sense, Dr Cranfield writes, the state is 'a partial, anticipatory, provisional manifestation of God's wrath against sin'.[4]

It is important to note that Paul uses the same vocabulary at the end of Romans 12 and at the beginning of Romans 13. The words 'wrath' (*orgē*) and 'revenge/punishment' (*ekdikēsis* and *ekdikos*) occur in both passages. Forbidden to God's people in general, they are assigned to God's 'servants' in particular, namely officials of the state. Many Christians find great difficulty in what they perceive here to be an ethical 'dualism'.[5] I should like to try to clarify this issue.

First, Paul is not distinguishing between *two entities*, church and state, as in Luther's well-known doctrine of the two kingdoms, the kingdom of God's right hand (the church) having a spiritual responsibility exercised through the power of the gospel, and the

[4] C. E. B. Cranfield, Commentary on *Romans*, vol. II, p. 666.

[5] Discussion of this 'dualism' may be found, for example, in Jean Lasserre's *War and the Gospel*, pp. 23 ff., 128 ff. and 180 ff.; in David Atkinson's *Peace in Our Time?*, pp. 102–107 and 154–157; in the debate between Ronald Sider and Oliver O'Donovan, published as *Peace and War*, pp. 7–11 and 15; and to some extent in my own *Message of the Sermon on the Mount*, pp. 103–124.

kingdom of his left hand (the state) having a political or temporal responsibility exercised through the power of the sword. Jean Lasserre calls this 'the traditional doctrine' (for Calvin held it too, though he expressed it in different terms) and sums it up thus:

> God has charged the church with the duty of preaching the gospel, and the state with the duty of ensuring the political order; the Christian is both member of the church and citizen of the nation; as the former he must obey God by conforming to the gospel ethic . . .; as the latter he must obey God by conforming to the political ethic of which the state is the judge . . . .[6]

It is true that God gives church and state different responsibilities, even if it needs to be stressed that they overlap, are not directed by different ethics and are both under Christ's lordship. But this is not really the issue in Romans 12 and 13.

Secondly, Paul is not distinguishing between *two spheres* of Christian activity, private and public, so that (to put it crudely) we must love our enemies in private but may hate them in public. The concept of a double standard of morality, private and public, is to be firmly rejected; there is only one Christian morality.

Thirdly, what Paul is doing is to distinguish between *two roles*, personal and official. Christians are always Christians (in church and state, in public and private), under the same moral authority of Christ, but are given different roles (at home, at work and in the community) which make different actions appropriate. For example, a Christian in the role of a policeman may use force to arrest a criminal, which in the role of a private citizen he may not; he may as a judge condemn a prisoner who has been found guilty, whereas Jesus told his disciples 'do not judge, or you too will be judged'; and he may as an executioner (assuming that capital punishment may in some circumstances be justified) kill a condemned man, although he is forbidden to commit murder. (Capital punishment and the prohibition of murder go together in the Mosaic law.) This is not to say that arresting, judging and executing are in themselves wrong (which would establish different moralities for public and private life), but that they are right responses to criminal behaviour, which however God has entrusted to particular officials of the state.

This, then, is the distinction which Paul is making in Romans 12 and 13 between the non-repayment of evil and the punishment of evil. The prohibitions at the end of chapter 12 do not mean that

[6] Jean Lasserre, *War and the Gospel*, p. 132.

evil should be left unrequited pending the day of judgment, but that the punishment should be administered by the state (as the agent of God's wrath) and that it is inappropriate for ordinary citizens to take the law into their own hands. It is this distinction which Christian pacifists find it hard to come to terms with. They tend to rest their case on Jesus' teaching and example of non-retaliation, assuming that retaliation is intrinsically wrong. But retaliation is not wrong, since evil deserves to be punished, should be punished, and in fact will be punished. Jesus himself said that 'the Son of Man ... will reward each person according to what he has done' (Mt. 16:27, where the verb is similar to that in Rom. 12:19). This truth appears even in Peter's account of Jesus' own non-retaliation. When he was insulted, he did not answer back. When he suffered, he did not threaten. But we must not deduce from this that he was condoning evil. For what did he do in place of retaliation? 'He entrusted himself to him who judges justly' (1 Pet. 2:23). In Paul's language, he left it to the wrath of God. So even when Jesus was praying for the forgiveness of his executioners, and even when he was giving himself in holy love for our salvation, the necessity of divine judgment on evil was not absent from his mind. Indeed, he himself was overcoming evil at that very moment only by enduring its just punishment himself.

The authority of the state

This brings us to another perplexing question in seeking to relate the cross to the problem of evil, namely how Christians should regard the state and its authority. A careful study of Romans 13 should help us to avoid the extremes of divinizing it (pronouncing it always right) or demonizing it (pronouncing it always wrong). The Christian attitude to the state should rather be one of critical respect. Let me try to sum up Paul's teaching here about the state's authority under four heads relating to its *origin*, the *purpose* for which it has been given, the *means* by which it should be exercised and the *recognition* which it should be accorded. In each case a limitation is placed on the authority of the state.

First, the *origin* of its authority is God. 'Everyone must submit himself to the governing authorities, for there is no authority except that which God has established' (v. 1a). 'The authorities that exist have been established by God' (v. 1b). 'Consequently, he who rebels against the authority is rebelling against what God has instituted' (v. 2). This perspective was already clear in the Old Testament.[7]

---

[7] *E.g.* Je. 27:5–6; Dn. 2:21; 4:17, 25, 32; 5:21; 7:27.

We are not to think of the functions of the state in terms of 'authority' only, however, but of 'ministry' too. For 'the one in authority' (which seems to be a generic reference which could include any state official from policeman to judge) 'is God's servant to do you good' (v. 4a). Again, 'he is God's servant, an agent of wrath to bring punishment on the wrongdoer' (v. 4b). Yet again, the reason why we are to pay taxes is that the authorities are 'God's servants, who give their full time to governing' (v. 6).

I confess that I find it extremely impressive that Paul writes of both the 'authority' and the 'ministry' of the state; that three times he affirms the state's authority to be God's authority; and that three times he describes the state and its ministers as God's ministers, using two words (*diakonos* and *leitourgos*) which elsewhere he applied to his own ministry as apostle and evangelist, and even to the ministry of Christ.[8] I do not think there is any way of wriggling out of this, for example by interpreting the paragraph as a grudging acquiescence in the realities of political power. No. In spite of the defects of Roman government, with which he was personally familiar, Paul emphatically declared its authority and ministry to be God's. It is the divine origin of the state's authority which makes Christian submission to it a matter of 'conscience' (v. 5).

Nevertheless, the fact that the state's authority has been delegated to it by God, and is therefore not intrinsic but derived, means that it must never be absolutized. Worship is due to God alone, and to his Christ, who is the lord of all rule and authority (Eph. 1:21–22) and 'the ruler of the kings of the earth' (Rev. 1:5; *cf.* 19:16). The state must be respected as a divine institution; but to give it our blind, unqualified allegiance would be idolatry. The early Christians refused to call Caesar 'lord'; that title belonged to Jesus alone.

Secondly, the *purpose* for which God has given authority to the state is in order both to reward (and so promote) good and to punish (and so restrain) evil. On the one hand, then, the state 'commends' (expresses its approbation of) those who do good (v. 3) – by the honours it bestows on its outstanding citizens – and exists to 'do you good' (v. 4). This phrase is not explained, but it surely covers all the social benefits of good government, preserving the peace, maintaining law and order, protecting human rights, promoting justice and caring for the needy. On the other hand, the state, as the minister of God and agent of his wrath, punishes

---

[8] For *diakonos* applied to Christ see Rom. 15:8, and to Paul 2 Cor. 6:4. For *leitourgos* applied to Christ see Heb. 8:2, and to Paul Rom. 15:16.

wrongdoers (v. 4), bringing them to justice. Modern states tend to be better at the latter than the former. Their structures for law enforcement are more sophisticated than those for the positive encouragement of good citizenship by rewarding public service and philanthropy. Yet punishments and rewards go together. The apostle Peter also brackets them when, perhaps echoing Romans 13, and certainly writing after Christians had begun to suffer persecution in Rome, he affirms the same divine origin and constructive purpose of the state as 'sent by God to punish those who do wrong and to commend those who do right' (1 Pet. 2:14).

Nevertheless, the state's double function requires a high degree of discernment. Only the good is to be rewarded, only the evil punished. There is no warrant here for the arbitrary distribution of favours or penalties. This is specially so in relation to law enforcement. In peacetime the innocent must be protected, and in wartime non-combatants must be guaranteed immunity. Police action is discriminate action, and the Bible consistently expresses its horror at the shedding of innocent blood. The same principle of discrimination is an essential aspect of the 'just war' theory. It is why all use of indiscriminate weapons (atomic, biological and chemical) and all indiscriminate use of conventional weapons (*e.g.* the saturation bombing of civilian cities) are outlawed by this text and deeply offensive to the Christian conscience.

Thirdly, the *means* by which the state's authority is exercised must be as controlled as its purposes are discriminate. In order to protect the innocent and punish the guilty it is clearly necessary for coercion sometimes to be used. Authority implies power, although we have to distinguish between violence (the uncontrolled and unprincipled use of power) and force (its controlled and principled use to arrest evil-doers, hold them in custody, bring them to trial, and if convicted and sentenced oblige them to bear their punishment). The state's authority may even extend to the judicial taking of life. For most commentators interpret the 'sword' which the state bears (v. 4) as the symbol not just of its general authority to punish, but of its specific authority either to inflict capital punishment or to wage war or both.[9] Luther and Calvin argued that it was legitimate to extrapolate in this paragraph to include the 'just war', since the 'evil-doers' the state has authority to punish may be aggressors who threaten it from without, as well as criminals who threaten it from within.

[9] *Machaira*, the word Paul uses of the state's 'sword' here, may sometimes be translated 'dagger' or 'knife', but is used several times in the New Testament to symbolize death by execution or in war (*e.g.* Mt. 10:34; Lk. 21:24; Acts 12:2; Rom. 8:35; Heb. 11:37).

Of course there are obvious differences between sentencing and punishing a criminal on the one hand, and declaring and waging war against an aggressor on the other. In particular, in warfare there is neither a judge nor a court. In declaring war a state is acting as judge in its own cause, since as yet no independent body exists to arbitrate in international disputes. And the set procedures and cool, dispassionate atmosphere of the lawcourt have no parallel on the battlefield. Nevertheless, as Professor Oliver O'Donovan has shown, the development of the just war theory 'represented a systematic attempt to interpret acts of war by analogy with acts of civil government',[10] and so to see them as belonging to 'the context of the administration of justice' and as subject to 'the restraining standards of executive justice'.[11] In fact, the more a conflict can be represented in terms of the quest for justice, the stronger will be the case for its legitimacy.

The state's use of force, being strictly limited to the particular purpose for which it is given, must with equal strictness be limited to particular people, *i.e.* bringing criminals to justice. No possible excuse can be found in Romans 13 for the repressive measures of a police state. In all civilized nations both police and army have instructions to use 'minimum necessary force' – sufficient only to accomplish its task. In war force has to be controlled as well as discriminate. The Christian conscience protests against the appalling overkill capacity of current nuclear arsenals.

Fourthly, the due *recognition* of the state's authority is laid down. Citizens are to 'submit' to the governing authorities because God has established them (v. 1). In consequence, those who 'rebel' against them are rebelling against God, and bring his judgment upon them (v. 2). It is necessary to 'submit', however, not only to avoid punishment but also to maintain a good conscience (v. 5). What, then, is included in our 'submission'? Certainly we shall obey laws (1 Pet. 2:13) and pay taxes (v. 6). We shall also pray for rulers (1 Tim. 2:1–2). Example, taxes and prayer are three ways of encouraging the state to fulfil its God-given responsibilities. Whether we go further and suggest that due 'submission' will include co-operation, and even participation in the work of the state, is likely to depend on whether our ecclesiology is Lutheran, Reformed or Anabaptist. Speaking for myself, since the authority and ministry of the state are God's, I can see no reason for avoiding, and every reason for sharing in, its God-appointed service.

Nevertheless, there must be limits to our submission. Although

[10] Oliver O'Donovan, *Pursuit of a Christian View of War*, p. 13.
[11] *Ibid.*, p. 14.

(in theory, according to God's purpose) 'rulers hold no terror for those who do right, but for those who do wrong' (v. 3), Paul knew that a Roman procurator had condemned Jesus to death, and he had himself on occasion been the victim of Roman injustice. So what should Christians do if the state misuses its God-given authority, perverts its God-given ministry and begins to promote evil and punish good? What if it ceases to be God's minister and becomes the devil's, persecutes the church instead of protecting it, and exercises a malevolent authority derived not from God but from the dragon (Rev. 13)? What then? We reply that Christians should still respect an evil state, much as children should respect bad parents, but meek submission is not required of them. The apostle gives no encouragement to totalitarian rule. We have a duty to criticize and protest, agitate and demonstrate, and even (in extreme situations) resist to the point of law-breaking disobedience. Civil disobedience is, in fact, a biblical concept honoured particularly by Daniel and his friends in the Old Testament and by the apostles Peter and John in the New.[12] The principle is clear. Since the state's authority has been given it by God, we must submit right up to the point where to obey the state would be to disobey God. At that point, if the state commands what God forbids, or forbids what God commands, we disobey the state in order to obey God. As the apostles said to the Sanhedrin, 'We must obey God rather than men!'[13]

If in extreme circumstances disobedience is permissible, is rebellion permissible too? Certainly the Christian tradition of the 'just war' has sometimes been extended to include the 'just revolution'. But the same stringent conditions have been laid down for armed revolt as for war. These relate to justice (the need to overthrow a manifestly evil tyranny), restraint (last resort only, all other options having been exhausted), discrimination and control (in the use of force), proportion (the suffering caused must be less than that being endured), and confidence (a reasonable expectation of success). A conscientious application of these principles will make the drastic step of rebellion very rare.

Let me sum up the aspects and corresponding limitations of the state's authority. Because its authority has been delegated to it by God, we must respect but not worship it. Because the purpose of its authority is to punish evil and promote goodness, it has no excuse for arbitrary government. To fulfil this purpose it may use coercion, but only minimum necessary force, not indiscriminate

[12] As examples of civil disobedience see Ex. 1:15–21; Dn. 3:1–18 and 6:1–14; Acts 4:13–20.
[13] Acts 5:29; *cf.* 4:19.

violence. We are to respect the state and its officials, giving them a discerning submission, not an uncritical subservience.

Overcoming evil with good

Having moved, in our study of Romans 12 and 13, from the hatred of evil, through the non-repayment and the conquest of evil, to its punishment, we are left with a problem of harmonization. We have seen that evil is to be both not repaid and repaid, depending on who is the agent. But how can evil be at one and the same time 'overcome' (12:21) and 'punished' (13:4)? This is a more difficult question and goes to the heart of the debate between Christian pacifists and just war theorists. The Christian mind goes at once to the cross of Christ, because there they were reconciled. God overcame our evil by justifying us only because he first condemned it in Christ, and by redeeming us only because he first paid the ransom-price. He did not overcome evil by refusing to punish it, but by accepting the punishment himself. At the cross human evil was both punished and overcome, and God's mercy and justice were both satisfied.

How, then, can these two be reconciled in our attitudes to evil today? In the light of the cross, Christians cannot come to terms with any attitude to evil which either bypasses its punishment in an attempt to overcome it, or punishes it without seeking to overcome it. Certainly the state as the agent of God's wrath must witness to his justice, in punishing evil-doers. But Christian people also want to witness to his mercy. It is over-simple to say that individuals are directed by love, states by justice. For individual love should not be indifferent to justice, nor should the state's administration of justice overlook that love for neighbour which is the fulfilment of the law. Moreover, the state is not under obligation in its pursuit of justice to demand the highest penalty the law permits. The God who laid down the 'life for life' principle himself protected the life of the first murderer (Gn. 4:15). Extenuating circumstances will help to temper justice with mercy. The retributive (punishing the evil-doer) and the reformative (reclaiming and rehabilitating him) go hand in hand, for then evil is simultaneously punished and overcome.

It is considerably more difficult to imagine such a reconciliation in war, when nations rather than individuals are involved. But at least Christians must struggle with the dilemma and try not to polarize over it. 'Just war' theorists tend to concentrate on the need to resist and punish evil, and to overlook the other biblical injunction to overcome it. Pacifists, on the other hand, tend to concentrate on the need to overcome evil with good, and to forget that according to Scripture evil deserves to be punished. Can these two biblical emphases be reconciled? Christians will at least stress the need to look beyond the defeat and surrender of the national enemy to its repentance and rehabilitation. The so-called 'politics of forgiveness', recently developed by Haddon Willmer,[14] is relevant here. David Atkinson sums up this emphasis well:

> Forgiveness is a dynamic concept of change. It refuses to be trapped into a fatalistic determinism. It acknowledges the reality of evil, wrong and injustice, but it seeks to respond to wrong in a way that is creative of new possibilities. Forgiveness signals an approach to wrong in terms, not of peace at any price, nor of a destructive intention to destroy the wrongdoer, but of a willingness to seek to reshape the future in the light of the wrong, in the most creative way possible.[15]

On the cross, by both demanding and bearing the penalty of sin, and so simultaneously punishing and overcoming evil, God displayed and demonstrated his holy love; the holy love of the cross should characterize our response to evil-doers today.

[14] Haddon Willmer, in *Third Way* (May, 1979).
[15] David Atkinson, *Peace in our Time?*, p. 167.

13

Suffering and glory

The fact of suffering undoubtedly constitutes the single greatest challenge to the Christian faith, and has been in every generation. Its distribution and degree appear to be entirely random and therefore unfair. Sensitive spirits ask if it can possibly be reconciled with God's justice and love.

On 1 November 1755 Lisbon was devastated by an earthquake. Being All Saints Day, the churches were full at the time, and thirty of them were destroyed. Within six minutes 15,000 people had died and 15,000 more were dying. One of many stunned by the news was the French philosopher and writer, Voltaire. For months he alluded to it in his letters in terms of passionate horror. How could anybody now believe in the benevolence and omnipotence of God? He ridiculed Alexander Pope's lines in his *Essay on Man*, which had been written in a secure and comfortable villa in Twickenham:

> And, spite of pride, in erring reason's spite,
> One truth is clear, Whatever is, is right.

Voltaire had always revolted against this philosophy of Optimism. Would Pope have repeated his glib lines if he had been in Lisbon? They seemed to Voltaire illogical (interpreting evil as good), irreverent (attributing evil to Providence) and injurious (inculcating resignation instead of constructive action). He first expressed his protest in his *Poem on the Disaster of Lisbon*, which asks why, if God is free, just and beneficent, we suffer under his rule. It is the old conundrum that God is either not good or not almighty. Either he wants to stop suffering but cannot, or he could but will not.

311

Whichever it is, how can we worship him as God? Voltaire's second protest was to write his satirical novel *Candide*, the story of an ingenuous young man, whose teacher Dr Pangloss, a professor of Optimism, keeps blandly assuring him that 'all is for the best in the best of all possible worlds', in defiance of their successive misfortunes. When they are shipwrecked near Lisbon, Candide is nearly killed in the earthquake, and Pangloss is hanged by the Inquisition. Voltaire writes: 'Candide, terrified, speechless, bleeding, palpitating, said to himself: "If this is the best of all possible worlds, what can the rest be?" '[1]

The problem of suffering is far from being of concern only to philosophers, however. It impinges upon nearly all of us personally; few people go through life entirely unscathed. It may be a child-hood deprivation resulting in lifelong emotional turmoil, or a congenital disability of mind or body. Or suddenly and without warning we are overtaken by a painful illness, redundancy at work, poverty or bereavement. Or again, perhaps we are afflicted by involuntary singleness, a broken love affair, an unhappy marriage, divorce, depression or loneliness. Suffering comes in many unwel-come forms, and sometimes we not only ask God our agonized questions 'Why?' and 'Why me?' but even like Job rage against him, accusing him of injustice and indifference. I know of no Christian leader who has been more forthright in confessing his anger than Joseph Parker, who was minister of the City Temple from 1874 until his death in 1902. He says in his autobiography that up to the age of 68 he never had a religious doubt. Then his wife died, and his faith collapsed. 'In that dark hour', he wrote, 'I became almost an atheist. For God had set his foot upon my prayers and treated my petitions with contempt. If I had seen a dog in such agony as mine, I would have pitied and helped the dumb beast; yet God spat upon me and cast me out as an offence – out into the waste wilderness and the night black and starless.'[2]

It needs to be said at once that the Bible supplies no thorough solution to the problem of evil, whether 'natural' evil or 'moral', that is, whether in the form of suffering or of sin. Its purpose is more practical than philosophical. Consequently, although there are references to sin and suffering on virtually every page, its concern is not to explain their origin but to help us to overcome them.

My object in this chapter is to explore what relation there might

[1] See S. G. Tallentyre, *Life of Voltaire*, Vol. II, pp. 25–27 and *Voltaire* by Colonel Hamley, pp. 168–177.
[2] Quoted by Leslie J. Tizard in *Preaching*, p. 28.

be between the cross of Christ and our sufferings. So I shall not elaborate other standard arguments about suffering which the textbooks include, but only mention them as an introduction.

First, according to the Bible suffering is an alien intrusion into God's good world, and will have no part in his new universe. It is a Satanic and destructive onslaught against the Creator. The book of Job makes that clear. So do Jesus' description of an infirm woman as 'bound by Satan', his 'rebuking' of disease as he rebuked demons, Paul's reference to his 'thorn in the flesh' as 'a messenger of Satan' and Peter's portrayal of Jesus' ministry as 'healing all who were under the power of the devil'.[3] So whatever may be said later about the 'good' which God can bring out of suffering, we must not forget that it is good out of evil.

Secondly, suffering is often due to sin. Of course originally disease and death entered the world through sin. But I am now thinking of contemporary sin. Sometimes suffering is due to the sin of others, as when children suffer from unloving or irresponsible parents, the poor and hungry from economic injustice, refugees from the cruelties of war, and road casualties caused by drunken drivers. At other times suffering can be the consequence of our own sin (the reckless use of our freedom) and even its penalty. We must not overlook those biblical passages where sickness is attributed to the punishment of God.[4] At the same time we must firmly repudiate the dreadful Hindu doctrine of *karma* which attributes all suffering to wrong-doing in this or a previous existence, and the almost equally dreadful doctrine of Job's so-called comforters. They trotted out their conventional orthodoxy that all personal suffering is due to personal sin, and one of the major purposes of the book of Job is to contradict that popular but wrong-headed notion. Jesus categorically rejected it too.[5]

Thirdly, suffering is due to our human sensitivity to pain. Misfortune is made worse by the hurt (physical or emotional) which we feel. But the pain sensors of the central nervous system give valuable warning-signals, necessary for personal and social survival. Perhaps the best illustration of this is the discovery by Dr Paul Brand at Vellore Christian Hospital in South India that Hansen's disease ('leprosy') numbs the extremities of the body, so that the ulcers and infections which develop are secondary problems, due to loss of feeling. Nerve reactions have to *hurt* if we are to protect ourselves. 'Thank God for inventing pain!' wrote Philip Yancey; 'I

---

[3] Lk. 13:16 and 4:35, 39; 2 Cor. 12:7; Acts 10:38.
[4] *E.g.* Dt. 28:15 ff.; 2 Ki. 5:27; Pss. 32:3–5; 38:1–8; Lk. 1:20; Jn. 5:14; 1 Cor. 11:30.
[5] *E.g.* Lk. 13:1–5; Jn. 9:1–3.

don't think he could have done a better job. It's beautiful.'[6]

Fourthly, suffering is due to the kind of environment in which God has placed us. Although most human suffering is caused by human sin (C. S. Lewis reckoned four-fifths of it, and Hugh Silvester nineteen-twentieths, *i.e.* 95%[7]), natural disasters such as flood, hurricane, earthquake and drought are not. True, it can be argued that God did not intend the earth's 'inhospitable areas' to be inhabited, let alone increased by ecological irresponsibility.[8] Yet most people go on living where they were born and have no opportunity to move. What can one say, then, about the so-called 'laws' of nature which in storm and tempest relentlessly overwhelm innocent people? C. S. Lewis went so far as to say that 'not even Omnipotence could create a society of free souls without at the same time creating a relatively independent and "inexorable" Nature'.[9] 'What we need for human society', Lewis continued, 'is exactly what we have – a neutral something', stable and having 'a fixed nature of its own', as the arena in which we may act freely towards each other and him.[10] If we lived in a world in which God prevented every evil from happening, like Superman in Alexander Salkind's films, free and responsible activity would be impossible.

There have always been some who insist that suffering is meaningless, and that no purpose whatever can be detected in it. In the ancient world these included both the Stoics (who taught the need to submit with fortitude to nature's inexorable laws) and the Epicureans (who taught that the best escape from a random world was indulgence in pleasure). And in the modern world secular existentialists believe that everything, including life, suffering and death, is meaningless and therefore absurd. But Christians cannot follow them down that blind alley. For Jesus spoke of suffering as being both 'for God's glory', that God's Son might be glorified through it, and 'so that the work of God might be displayed'.[11] This seems to mean that in some way (still to be explored) God is at work revealing his glory in and through suffering, as he did (though differently) through Christ's. What then is the relationship between Christ's sufferings and ours? How does the cross speak to us in our pain? I want to suggest from Scripture six possible answers to these questions, which seem to rise gradually from the simplest to the most sublime.

[6] Philip Yancey, *Where is God when it hurts?*, p. 23.
[7] C. S. Lewis, *Problem of Pain*, p. 77; Hugh Silvester, *Arguing with God*, p. 32.
[8] Hugh Silvester, *Arguing with God*, p. 80.
[9] C. S. Lewis, *Problem of Pain*, p. 17.   [10] *Ibid.*, p. 19.
[11] Jn. 11:4 and 9:3.

Patient endurance

First, the cross of Christ is *a stimulus to patient endurance*. Even though suffering has to be recognized as evil and therefore resisted, there nevertheless comes a time when it has to be realistically accepted. It is then that the example of Jesus, which is set before us in the New Testament for our imitation, becomes an inspiration. Peter directed his readers' attention to it, especially if they were Christian slaves with harsh masters during the Neronian persecution. It would be no particular credit to them if they were beaten for some wrong-doing and took it patiently. But if they suffered for doing good and endured it, this would be pleasing to God. Why? Because undeserved suffering is part of their Christian calling, since Christ himself had suffered for them, leaving them an example, that they should follow in his steps. Though sinless, he was insulted, but he never retaliated (1 Pet. 2:18–23). Jesus set an example of perseverance as well as of non-retaliation, which should encourage us to persevere in the Christian race. We need to 'fix our eyes on Jesus', for he 'endured the cross, scorning its shame'. So then: 'Consider him who endured such opposition from sinful men, so that you will not grow weary and lose heart' (Heb. 12:1–3).

Although both these examples relate specifically to opposition or persecution, it seems legitimate to give them a wider application. Christians in every generation have gained from the sufferings of Jesus, which culminated in the cross, the inspiration to bear undeserved pain patiently, without either complaining or hitting back. True, there are many kinds of suffering he did not have to endure. Yet his sufferings were remarkably representative. Take Joni Eareckson as an example. In 1967, when she was a beautiful, athletic teenager, she had a terrible diving accident in Chesapeake Bay, which left her a quadriplegic. She has told her story with affecting honesty, including her times of bitterness, anger, rebellion and despair, and how gradually, through the love of her family and friends, she came to trust the sovereignty of God and to build a new life of mouth-painting and public speaking under the signal blessing of God. One night, about three years after her accident, Cindy one of her closest friends, sitting by her bedside, spoke to her of Jesus, saying, 'Why, he was paralysed too.' It had not occurred to her before that on the cross Jesus was in similar pain to hers, unable to move, virtually paralysed. She found this thought deeply comforting.[12]

---

[12] Joni Eareckson with Joe Musser, *Joni*, p. 96. See also her second book *A Step Further*, in which she writes more about God's sovereignty and his eternal purpose.

Mature holiness

Secondly, the cross of Christ is *the path to mature holiness*. Extraordinary as it may sound, we can add 'it was for him, and it is for us'. We need to consider the implications of two rather neglected verses in the letter to the Hebrews:

> In bringing many sons to glory, it was fitting that God . . . should make the Author of their salvation perfect through suffering (2:10).

> Although he was a son, he learned obedience from what he suffered and, once made perfect, he became the source of eternal salvation for all who obey him (5:8–9; *cf.* 7:28).

Both verses speak of a process in which Jesus was 'made perfect', and both ascribe the perfecting process to his 'suffering'. Not of course that he was ever imperfect in the sense that he had done wrong, for Hebrews underlines his sinlessness.[13] It was rather that he needed further experiences and opportunities in order to become *teleios*, 'mature'. In particular, 'he learned obedience from what he suffered'. He was never disobedient. But his sufferings were the testing-ground in which his obedience became full-grown.

If suffering was the means by which the sinless Christ became mature, so much the more do we need it in our sinfulness. Significantly, James uses the same language of 'perfection' or 'maturity' in relation to Christians. Just as suffering led to maturity through obedience for Christ, so it leads to maturity through perseverance for us.

> Consider it pure joy, my brothers, whenever you face trials of many kinds, because you know that the testing of your faith develops perseverance. Perseverance must finish its work so that you may be mature (*teleioi*) and complete, not lacking anything (Jas. 1:2–4; *cf.* Rom. 5:3–5).

Three graphic images are developed in Scripture to illustrate how God uses suffering in pursuance of his purpose to make us holy, in other words, Christlike. They are the father disciplining his children, the metalworker refining silver and gold, and the gardener pruning his vine. The father-children picture is already seen in Deuteronomy, where Moses says: 'Know then in your heart that

[13] *E.g.* Heb. 4:15; 7:26.

as a man disciplines his son, so the LORD your God disciplines you.' The metaphor is taken up again in the book of Proverbs, where it is stressed that a father's discipline is an expression of his love for his children, and the Proverbs verses are quoted in the letter to the Hebrews and echoed in Jesus' message to the Laodicean church.[14] The Hebrews passage is the longest. It teaches that fatherly discipline marks out the true sons from the illegitimate; that God disciplines us only 'for our good', namely 'that we may share in his holiness'; that at the time discipline is painful not pleasant, but that later 'it produces a harvest of righteousness and peace', not indeed for everybody (for some rebel against the discipline), but for those who submit to it and so are 'trained by it'.

The second picture of God as the refiner of silver and gold occurs three times in the Old Testament, where it is made clear that the place of refinement for Israel was 'the furnace of affliction', and Peter applies it to the testing of our Christian faith in 'all kinds of trials'. The process will be distressing, but through it our faith ('of greater worth than gold') will both be proved genuine and result in glory to Jesus Christ.[15]

The third picture Jesus himself developed in his allegory of the vine, in which the fruitfulness of the branches (almost certainly a symbol of Christian character) will depend not only on their abiding in the vine, but also on their being pruned by the vine-dresser. Pruning is a drastic process, which often looks cruel, as the bush is cut right back and left jagged and almost naked. But when the spring and summer come round again, there is much fruit.[16]

All three metaphors describe a negative process, disciplining the child, refining the metal and pruning the vine. But all three also underline the positive result – the child's good, the metal's purity, the vine's fruitfulness. We should not hesitate to say, then, that God intends suffering to be a 'means of grace'. Many of his children can repeat the psalmist's statement: 'Before I was afflicted I went astray, but now I obey your word' (Ps. 119:67). For if God's love is holy love, as it is, then it is concerned not only to act in holiness (as in the cross of Christ), but also to promote holiness (in the people of God). As we have already seen, suffering fosters perseverance and purifies faith. It also develops humility, as when Paul's thorn in the flesh was to keep him 'from becoming conceited'. And it deepens insight, as through the pain of Hosea's unrequited love

[14] Dt. 8:5; Pr. 3:11–12; Heb. 12:5–11; Rev. 3:19.
[15] Ps. 66:10; Is. 48:10; Zc. 13:9; 1 Pet. 1:6–7.
[16] Jn. 15:1–8. *Cf.* Is. 5:1–7, especially v. 7, and Gal. 5:22–23, as evidence that the 'fruit' means righteous and Christlike character.

for Gomer there was revealed to him the faithfulness and patience of Yahweh's love for Israel.[17] Nor should we overlook the benefits which can come into other people's lives, such as the heroic unselfishness of those who care for the sick, the senile and the handicapped, and the spontaneous upsurge of generosity towards the hungry peoples of sub-Saharan Africa.

The Roman Catholic church has traditionally spoken of 'redemptive suffering'. Its official teaching is that, even after the guilt of our misdeeds has been forgiven, their due of punishment still has to be completed either in this life or in purgatory (which is 'the church suffering'). Thus pardon does not remit penance, for punishment has to be added to forgiveness. The best penances, moreover, are not those appointed by the church but those sent from God himself – namely 'crosses, sicknesses, pains' – which atone for our sins. There are, in fact, 'two reasons for suffering for sin: first, atonement to God, and second the re-making of our souls'. For suffering subdues our bodily appetites, cleanses and restores us.[18]

This kind of teaching, which appears both to underplay the completeness with which God through Christ has redeemed and forgiven us, and to ascribe atoning efficacy to our sufferings, is very offensive to the Protestant mind and conscience. Some Roman Catholics use the term 'redemptive suffering', however, simply to indicate that affliction, although it embitters some, transforms others. Mary Craig writes of 'the redemptive power of suffering' in this sense. She describes how two of her four sons were born with severe abnormalities, her second son Paul with the disfiguring and incapacitating Höhler's syndrome, and her fourth Nicholas with Down's syndrome. She tells the story of her spiritual struggle without self-pity or melodrama. In the final chapter of her book, significantly entitled *Blessings*, she meditates on the meaning of suffering, and it is now that she introduces the word 'redemptive'. 'In the teeth of the evidence', she writes, 'I do not believe that any suffering is ultimately absurd or pointless', although 'it is often difficult to go on convincing oneself' of this. At first, we react with incredulity, anger and despair. Yet 'the value of suffering does not lie in the pain of it, . . . but in what the sufferer makes of it. . . . It is in sorrow that we discover the things which really matter; in sorrow that we discover ourselves' (pp. 133–144).

Since Jesus Christ is the one and only Redeemer, and the New Testament never uses redemption language of anything we do, we

[17] 2 Cor. 12:7–10 and Ho. 1 – 3.
[18] George D. Smith (ed.), *Teaching of the Catholic Church*, pp. 1141–1146.

will be wise not to talk of 'redemptive suffering'. 'Creative suffering', a term popularized by Dr Paul Tournier's last book, would be better, so long as it is not imagined that suffering actually creates anything. But it does stimulate 'creativity', which is his point. He begins by referring to an article written by Dr Pierre Rentchnick of Geneva in 1975 entitled 'Orphans Lead the World'. From the life-stories of history's most influential politicians he had made the astonishing discovery that nearly 300 of them were orphans, from Alexander the Great and Julius Caesar through Charles V and Louis XIV to George Washington, Napoleon and (less happily) Lenin, Hitler, Stalin and Castro. This naturally struck Dr Tournier, since he had long lectured on the importance for the child's development of a father and mother performing their roles harmoniously – which is exactly what the most influential politicians never had! Dr Rentchnick developed a theory that 'the insecurity consequent upon emotional deprivation must have aroused in these children an exceptional will to power'. The same was evidently true of religious leaders, since, for example, Moses, the Buddha, Confucius and Mohammed were also all orphans.[19] Professor André Haynal, a psychoanalyst, has worked further on the theory, and suggests that 'deprivation' of any kind (not just being orphaned) lies behind 'creativity' (which he prefers to 'will to power'). Finally, Dr Tournier confirms the theory from his own clinical experience. For fifty years his patients have confided in him their pains and conflicts. 'I have seen them change through suffering', he says (p. 15). Not that suffering (which is an evil) is the *cause* of growth; but it is its *occasion* (p. 29). Why, then, do some grow through handicap, while others do not? Their reaction depends, he thinks, 'more on the help they receive from others than on their hereditary disposition' (p. 32), and in particular it depends on love. 'Deprivations without the aid of love spell catastrophe', while 'the decisive factor in making deprivation bear fruit is love' (p. 34). So it is not so much suffering which matures people, as the way they react to suffering (p. 37). 'While suffering may not be creative in itself, we are scarcely ever creative without suffering .... One could also say that it is not suffering which makes a person grow, but that one does not grow without suffering' (p. 110).

Biblical teaching and personal experience thus combine to teach that suffering is the path to holiness or maturity. There is always an indefinable something about people who have suffered. They have a fragrance which others lack. They exhibit the meekness and

[19] Paul Tournier, *Creative Suffering*, pp. 1–5.

gentleness of Christ. One of the most remarkable statements Peter makes in his first letter is that 'he who has suffered in his body is done with sin' (4:1). Physical affliction, he seems to be saying, actually has the effect of making us stop sinning. This being so, I sometimes wonder if the real test of our hunger for holiness is our willingness to experience any degree of suffering if only thereby God will make us holy.

Suffering service

Thirdly, the cross of Christ is *the symbol of suffering service*. We are familiar with the four or five 'Servant Songs' of Isaiah which together make up the portrait of the 'suffering servant of the Lord',[20] and we began in the last chapter to consider the link between suffering and service. Meek in character and conduct (never shouting or raising his voice), and gentle in his dealings with others (never breaking bruised reeds or snuffing out smouldering wicks), he has nevertheless been called by Yahweh since before his birth, filled with his Spirit and receptive to his Word, with a view to bringing Israel back to him and being a light to the nations. In this task he perseveres, setting his face like a flint, although his back is beaten, his beard pulled out, his face spat upon, and he himself is led like a lamb to the slaughter and dies, bearing the sins of many. Nevertheless, as a result of his death, many will be justified and the nations sprinkled with blessing. What is particularly striking in this composite picture is that suffering and service, passion and mission belong together. We see this clearly in Jesus, who is the suffering servant *par excellence*, but we need to remember that the servant's mission to bring light to the nations is also to be fulfilled by the church (Acts 13:47). For the church, therefore, as for the Saviour, suffering and service go together.

More than this. It is not just that suffering belongs to service, but that suffering is indispensable to fruitful or effective service. This is the inescapable implication of the words of Jesus:

'The hour has come for the Son of Man to be glorified. I tell you the truth, unless an ear of wheat falls to the ground and dies, it remains only a single seed. But if it dies, it produces many seeds. The man who loves his life will lose it, while the man who hates his life in this world will keep it for eternal life. Whoever serves me must follow me; and where I am, my servant also will be. My Father will honour the one who serves me . . . .'

[20] Is. 42:1–4; perhaps 44:1–5; 49:1–6; 50:4–9; 52:13 – 53:12.

'But I, when I am lifted up from the earth, will draw all men to myself.' He said this to show the kind of death he was going to die (Jn. 12:23–26, 32–33).

It is hard to accept this lesson from the agricultural harvest. Death is more than the way to life; it is the secret of fruitfulness. Unless it falls into the ground and dies, the kernel of wheat remains a single seed. If it stays alive, it stays alone; but if it dies it multiplies. First and foremost Jesus was referring to himself. Did certain Greeks wish to see him? He was about to be 'glorified' in death. Soon he would be lifted up on his cross to draw people of all nations to himself. During his earthly ministry he restricted himself largely to 'the lost sheep of the house of Israel', but after his death and resurrection, he would have universal authority and a universal appeal.

But Jesus was not speaking only of himself. He was uttering a general principle, and went on to apply it to his disciples who must follow him and like him lose their lives (vv. 25–26) – not necessarily in martyrdom but at least in self-giving, suffering service. For us as for him, the seed must die to multiply.

Paul is the most notable example of this principle. Consider these texts taken from three different letters:

> For this reason I, Paul, the prisoner of Christ Jesus for the sake of you Gentiles – I ask you . . . not to be discouraged because of my sufferings for you, which are your glory (Eph. 3:1, 13).

> Now I rejoice in what was suffered for you, and I fill up in my flesh what is still lacking in regard to Christ's afflictions, for the sake of his body, which is the church (Col. 1:24).

> This is my gospel, for which I am suffering . . . . Therefore I endure everything for the sake of the elect, that they too may obtain the salvation that is in Christ Jesus, with eternal glory (2 Tim. 2:8–10).

Paul states in all three texts that his sufferings are being endured 'for the sake of you Gentiles', 'for the sake of Christ's body' or 'for the sake of the elect'. Since he is doing it for them, he believes they will derive some benefit from his sufferings. What is this? In the Colossians verse he refers to his sufferings as filling up what was still lacking in Christ's afflictions. We can be certain that Paul is not attaching any atoning efficacy to his sufferings, partly because he knew Christ's atoning work was finished on the cross, and partly because he uses the special word 'afflictions' (*thlipseis*) which denotes his persecutions. It is these which were unfinished, for he continued to be persecuted in his church. What benefit, then, did Paul think would come to people through his sufferings? Two of the three texts link the words 'sufferings' and 'glory'. 'My sufferings . . . are your glory', he tells the Ephesians. Again, 'salvation . . . with eternal glory' will be obtained by the elect because of the sufferings Paul is enduring (2 Tim. 2:8–10). It sounds outrageous. Does Paul really imagine that his sufferings will obtain their salvation and glory? Yes, he does. Not directly, however, as if his sufferings had saving efficacy like Christ's, but indirectly because he was suffering for the gospel which they must hear and embrace in order to be saved. Once again, suffering and service were bracketed, and the apostle's sufferings were an indispensable link in the chain of their salvation.

The place of suffering in service and of passion in mission is hardly ever taught today. But the greatest single secret of evangelistic or missionary effectiveness is the willingness to suffer and die. It may be a death to popularity (by faithfully preaching the unpopular biblical gospel), or to pride (by the use of modest methods in reliance on the Holy Spirit), or to racial and national prejudice (by identification with another culture), or to material comfort (by adopting a simple lifestyle). But the servant must suffer if he is to bring light to the nations, and the seed must die if it is to multiply.

The hope of glory

Fourthly, the cross of Christ is *the hope of final glory*. Jesus clearly looked beyond his death to his resurrection, beyond his sufferings to his glory, and indeed was sustained in his trials by 'the joy set before him' (Heb. 12:2). It is equally clear that he expected his followers to share this perspective. The inevitability of suffering is a regular theme in his teaching and that of the apostles. If the world had hated and persecuted him, it would hate and persecute his disciples also. Suffering was, in fact, a 'gift' of God to all his people, and part of their calling. They should not therefore be surprised by it, as if something strange were happening to them. It was only to be expected. Nothing could be more forthright than Paul's assertion that 'everyone who wants to live a godly life in Christ Jesus will be persecuted'.[21] Further, in suffering *like* Christ

[21] *E.g.* Mt. 5:10–12; Jn. 15:18–21; Phil. 1:30; 1 Thes. 3:3; 1 Pet. 2:21; 4:12; 2 Tim. 3:12.

they were suffering *with* Christ. They were more than spectators of his sufferings now, more than witnesses, more even than imitators; they were actually participants in his sufferings, sharing his 'cup' and his 'baptism'.[22] So, as they share in his sufferings, they would also share in his glory. The indispensability of suffering was to be seen not only as due to the antagonism of the world but as a necessary preparation. 'Through many tribulations we must enter the kingdom of God', the apostles warned the new converts in Galatia. It is understandable, therefore, that the countless multitude of the redeemed whom John saw before God's throne were described both as having 'come out of the great tribulation' (in the context surely a synonym for the Christian life) and as having 'washed their robes and made them white in the blood of the Lamb'.[23]

It is, then, the hope of glory which makes suffering bearable. The essential perspective to develop is that of the eternal purpose of God, which is to make us holy or Christlike. We ought frequently to meditate on the great New Testament texts which bring together the past and future eternities within a single horizon. For 'God chose us in Christ before the creation of the world to be holy and blameless in his sight'. His purpose is to present us 'before his glorious presence without fault and with great joy'. It is when these horizons are in our view that we 'consider . . . our present sufferings are not worth comparing with the glory that will be revealed in us', because 'our light and momentary troubles are achieving for us an eternal glory that far outweighs them all'. And what is this 'glory', this ultimate destiny, towards which God is working everything together for good, including our sufferings? It is that we may 'be conformed to the likeness of his Son'. The future prospect which makes suffering endurable, then, is not a reward in the form of a 'prize', which might lead us to say 'no pain, no palm' or 'no cross, no crown', but the only reward of priceless value, namely the glory of Christ, his own image perfectly re-created within us. 'We shall be like him, for we shall see him as he is.'[24]

This is the dominant theme of the book *Destined For Glory* by Margaret Clarkson, the Canadian hymn-writer and authoress. Born into a 'loveless and unhappy' home, and afflicted from childhood with painful headaches and crippling arthritis, suffering has

[22] *E.g.* Mk. 10:38; 2 Cor. 1:5; Phil. 3:10; 1 Pet. 4:13; 5:1.
[23] *E.g.* Acts 14:22 (RSV); Rom. 8:17; 2 Tim. 2:11–12; 1 Pet. 4:13; 5:1, 9–10; Rev. 7:9, 14.
[24] Eph. 1:4; Jude 24; Rom. 8:18; 2 Cor. 4:17; Rom. 8:28–29; 1 Jn. 3:2.

been her lifelong companion. In earlier days she experienced the full range of human responses to pain, including 'rage, frustration, despair' and even temptation to suicide (pp. vii ff.). But gradually she came to believe in the sovereignty of God, namely that God 'displays his sovereignty over evil by using the very suffering that is inherent in evil to assist in the working out of his eternal purpose' (p. 37). In this process he has developed an alchemy greater than that sought by the early chemists who tried to turn base metals into gold. For 'the only true alchemist is God'. He succeeds even in the 'transmutation of evil into good' (p. 103). We are 'destined for glory', the 'glory for which he created us – to make us like his Son' (p. 125). It is summed up in a verse of one of Margaret Clarkson's hymns (p. xii):

> O Father, you are sovereign,
>   The Lord of human pain,
> Transmuting earthly sorrows
>   To gold of heavenly gain.
> All evil overruling,
>   As none but Conqueror could,
> Your love pursues its purpose –
>   Our souls' eternal good.

We may well respond, of course, that we do not want God to change us, especially if the necessary means he uses is pain. 'We may wish, indeed,' wrote C. S. Lewis, 'that we were of so little account to God that he left us alone to follow our natural impulses – that he would give over trying to train us into something so unlike our natural selves: but once again, we are asking not for more love, but for less . . . . To ask that God's love should be content with us as we are is to ask that God should cease to be God . . . .'[25]

This vision of suffering as the path to glory for the people of God is undoubtedly biblical. One cannot say the same, however, for attempts to universalize the principle and apply it to all suffering without exception. Consider, for example, one of the official books published in preparation for the sixth assembly of the World Council of Churches in Vancouver (1983), whose advertised title was 'Jesus Christ, the Life of the World'. This book, although written by John Poulton, arose out of a meeting of twenty-five representative theologians, whose views he therefore incorporates. One of its main themes is that there is a parallel

---

[25] C. S. Lewis, *Problem of Pain*, pp. 32, 36.

between the death and resurrection of Jesus on the one hand and the suffering and triumphs of the contemporary world on the other. In this way the whole of human life is represented as a eucharistic celebration. 'Might we not say', John Poulton asks, 'that wherever there is the conjunction of suffering and joy, of death and life, *there is eucharist?*' [26] The basis for this interpretation is the fact that 'the pattern of self-sacrifice and new beginnings is not one that only members of the Christian church experience and live by. Outside their circle, others too seem to reflect it, sometimes quite remarkably' (p. 66). Indeed, John Poulton continues, the criss-crossing of pain and joy, suffering and security, betrayal and love is discernible in everyday life everywhere. It reflects winter and spring, and Good Friday and Easter. Old-style evangelism is no longer needed, therefore. The new evangelism will be the Holy Spirit's work in 'bringing into focus in Jesus Christ a shape already glimpsed in human experience' (p. 66).

This is not the gospel of the New Testament, however. Scripture gives us no liberty to assert that all human suffering leads to glory. True, Jesus referred to wars, earthquakes and famines as 'the beginning of birth pains' heralding the emergence of the new world, and Paul similarly likened nature's frustration, bondage to decay and groans to 'the pains of childbirth'.[27] But these are references to the promise of cosmic renewal for both society and nature; they are not applied in the Bible to the salvation of individuals or peoples.

Another example is the moving attempt made by Dr Ulrich Simon, a German Jewish Christian who fled to England in 1933, and whose father, brother and other relatives perished in Nazi concentration camps, to apply the death-resurrection, sufferings-glory principle to the holocaust. In his *A Theology of Auschwitz* (1967) he tried to 'show the pattern of Christ's sacrifice, which summarizes all agonies, as the reality behind Auschwitz' (pp. 13–14). For the holocaust (which of course means 'burnt offering') 'is no less a sacrifice than that prefigured in the Scriptures', that is to say, in the suffering servant of the Lord (pp. 83–84). In this way, 'the mechanics of murder were turned into a Godward oblation', and those who gave their lives in the gas chambers became identified with 'the supreme sacrifice by way of a sharing analogy' (p. 84); they were even scapegoats, bearing the sins of the German people (p. 86). But now 'the dead of Auschwitz have risen from the dust' (p. 91), and their resurrection is seen in Israel's return to the land, in the conquest of antisemitism which

[26] John Poulton, *Feast of Life*, p. 52.   [27] Mk. 13:8; Rom. 8:22.

'both led to Auschwitz and was redeemed there' (p. 93), and in the contemporary Jewish witness to the world concerning the sacredness of human life and the loving brotherhood of all men (p. 95). The corn of wheat, having fallen into the ground, has borne this fruit. Thus the sufferings of Auschwitz, Ulrich Simon claims, are 'within the pattern of creation and redemption' (p. 102). In particular, by interpreting the holocaust 'in the light of the suffering Christ' and by seeing its aftermath as 'reflected in the triumph of the Crucified One', it has been possible to give 'spiritual meaning to the meaningless' (p. 104). 'We venture to attribute the glory of the ascended Christ to the gassed millions' (p. 105).

One cannot fail to be touched by this attempted reconstruction, and one fully appreciates Dr Simon's reasons for wanting to develop a 'timeless, universal and cosmic conception of Christ's work' (p. 110). But I fear this kind of 'theology of Auschwitz' is speculative rather than scriptural. I believe there is a better and more biblical way to relate the cross to Auschwitz, and I will come to it shortly. Meanwhile, within the community of those whom God in mercy has redeemed, it should be possible for us to echo Paul's affirmations that 'we also rejoice in our sufferings' because 'we rejoice in the hope of the glory of God' (Rom. 5:2–3).

So far, in seeking to discern the relationships between Christ's sufferings and ours, apart from the inspiration of his example, we have seen that suffering (for us as for Jesus) is God's appointed path to sanctification (mature holiness), multiplication (fruitful service) and glorification (our final destiny). I hope it does not sound glib. It is easy to theorize, I know. But things look different when the horizon closes in upon us, a horror of great darkness engulfs us, and no glimmer of light shines to assure us that suffering can yet be productive. At such times we can only cling to the cross, where Christ himself demonstrated that blessing comes through suffering.

Faith and the book of Job

Fifthly, the cross of Christ is *the ground of a reasonable faith*. All suffering, physical and emotional, sorely tries our faith. How can it be reasonable, when calamity overwhelms us, to continue to trust in God? The best answer to this question is provided by the book of Job. It will be worth our while to clarify its thesis.

Job is introduced as a 'blameless and upright' man, who 'feared God and shunned evil'. But then (after we as readers have been permitted a glimpse into the deliberations of the heavenly council chamber), Job is overtaken by a series of personal tragedies: he is deprived successively of his livestock, his servants, his sons and daughters, and his health. It would be hard to exaggerate the magnitude of the disasters which have overwhelmed him. In the rest of the book the full spectrum of possible responses to suffering is rehearsed in the dialogue which develops between Job, his three so-called 'comforters', the young man Elihu and finally God himself. Each of the four proposes a different attitude, and specially noteworthy in each is the place accorded to the self.

Job's own attitude is a mixture of *self-pity* and *self-assertion*. Refusing to follow his wife's advice that he should 'curse God and die', he nevertheless begins by cursing the day of his birth and then longs with anguish for the day of his death. He utterly rejects the accusations of his three friends. Instead, he frames his own accusations against God. God is being brutally cruel to him, even ruthless. Worse still, God has altogether denied him justice (27:2). The contest between them is grossly unfair, since the contestants are so unequal. If only there were a mediator to arbitrate between them! If only he himself could find God, in order personally to press charges against him! Meanwhile, he vehemently maintains his innocence and is confident that one day he will be vindicated.

By contrast, the attitude recommended by Job's friends may best be described as *self-accusation*. Job is suffering because he is sinful. His afflictions are the divine penalty for his misdeeds. That is the conventional orthodoxy about the wicked, which they repeat *ad nauseam*. 'All his days the wicked man suffers torment', says Eliphaz (15:20). 'The lamp of the wicked is snuffed out', adds Bildad (18:5), while Zophar's contribution is that 'the mirth of the wicked is brief' (20:5). From this basic premise they draw the inevitable deduction that Job is suffering for his wickedness: 'Is not your wickedness great? Are not your sins endless?' (22:5). But Job will have none of it. His friends are 'worthless physicians' (13:4) and 'miserable comforters' (16:2), who talk nothing but 'nonsense' and even 'falsehood' (21:34). And God later confirms Job's verdict. He refers to their 'folly', and says that they 'have not spoken' of him 'what is right', as his servant Job has (42:7–8).

Elihu enters next. Although he is angry because Job has been 'justifying himself rather than God' (32:2), he is diffident on account of his youth to speak. When he does, it is not altogether easy to distinguish his position from that of Job's three comforters. For sometimes he too repeats the old orthodoxy. He also anticipates Yahweh's speech about creation. Yet it seems right to call the attitude he recommends *self-discipline*, for his distinctive emphasis is that God speaks in many ways (including suffering) in order 'to turn man from wrongdoing and keep him from pride'

(33:14, 17). So God makes people 'listen to correction' and 'speaks to them in their affliction' (36:10, 15). Indeed, 'who is a teacher like him?' (v. 22). His teaching is even a kind of 'wooing' (v.16), in which he pleads with people to repent and so seeks to deliver them from their distress.

At last, when Job, the comforters and Elihu have exhausted their arguments, Yahweh reveals himself and speaks. Judging from Job's response, the recommended attitude now may be called *self-surrender*. God is far from joining Job's three friends in their accusations, and he does not blame Job for maintaining his innocence (42:8). He takes his complaints seriously, and therefore replies to him. Yet Job has uttered 'words without knowledge', since it is never right to blame, accuse, let alone 'correct' God (40:2). 'Would you discredit my justice?' God asks (40:8). And Job replies: 'My ears had heard of you but now my eyes have seen you. Therefore I despise myself and repent in dust and ashes' (42:5–6). Previously he has defended, pitied and asserted himself, and accused God. Now he despises himself, and worships God. What has he 'seen' which has converted him from self-assertion to self-surrender?

Job has been invited to look afresh at the creation, and has glimpsed the glory of the Creator. God bombards him with questions. Where was he when the earth and the sea were made? Can he control the snow, the storm and the stars? Does he possess the expertise to supervise and sustain the animal world – lions and mountain goats, the wild donkey and the wild ox, the ostrich and the horse, hawks and eagles? Above all, can Job comprehend the mysteries and subdue the strength of *behemoth* the hippopotamus and *leviathan* the crocodile? What God gave Job was a comprehensive introduction to the wonders of nature, and thereby a revelation of his creative genius, which silenced Job's accusations and led him – even in the midst of his continued bereavement, suffering and pain – to humble himself, repent of his rebellion, and trust God again.

If it was reasonable for Job to trust the God whose wisdom and power have been revealed in creation, how much more reasonable is it for us to trust the God whose love and justice have been revealed in the cross? The reasonableness of trust lies in the known trustworthiness of its object. And no-one is more trustworthy than the God of the cross. The cross assures us that there is no possibility of a miscarriage of justice or of the defeat of love either now or on the last day. 'He who did not spare his own Son, but gave him up for us all – how will he not also, along with him, graciously give us all things?' (Rom. 8:32). It is the self-giving of God in the gift of his Son which convinces us that he will withhold nothing from us that we need, and allow nothing to separate us from his love (vv. 35–39). So between the cross, where God's love and justice began to be clearly revealed, and the day of judgment when they will be completely revealed, it is reasonable to trust in him.

We have to learn to climb the hill called Calvary, and from that vantage-ground survey all life's tragedies. The cross does not solve the problem of suffering, but it supplies the essential perspective from which to look at it. Since God has demonstrated his holy love and loving justice in a historical event (the cross), no other historical event (whether personal or global) can override or disprove it. This must surely be why the scroll (the book of history and destiny) is now in the hands of the slain Lamb, and why only he is worthy to break its seals, reveal its contents and control the flow of the future.

The pain of God

There is a sixth way in which Christ's sufferings are related to ours. It is the most important of the series. It is that the cross of Christ is *the proof of God's solidary love*, that is, of his personal, loving solidarity with us in our pain. For the real sting of suffering is not misfortune itself, nor even the pain of it or the injustice of it, but the apparent God-forsakenness of it. Pain is endurable, but the seeming indifference of God is not. Sometimes we picture him lounging, perhaps dozing, in some celestial deck-chair, while the hungry millions starve to death. We think of him as an armchair spectator, almost gloating over the world's suffering, and enjoying his own insulation from it. Philip Yancey has gone further and uttered the unutterable which we may have thought but to which we have never dared to give voice: 'If God is truly in charge, somehow connected to all the world's suffering, why is he so capricious, unfair? Is he the cosmic sadist who delights in watching us squirm?'[28] Job had said something similar: God 'mocks the despair of the innocent' (9:23).

It is this terrible caricature of God which the cross smashes to smithereens. We are not to envisage him on a deck-chair, but on a cross. The God who allows us to suffer, once suffered himself in Christ, and continues to suffer with us and for us today. Since the cross was a once-for-all historical event, in which God in Christ bore our sins and died our death because of his love and justice,

[28] P. Yancey, *Where is God when it hurts?*, p. 63.

we must not think of it as expressing an eternal sin-bearing in the heart of God. What Scripture does give us warrant to say, however, is that God's eternal holy love, which was uniquely exhibited in the sacrifice of the cross, continues to suffer with us in every situation in which it is called forth. But is it legitimate to speak of a suffering God? Are we not impeded from doing so by the traditional doctrine of the divine impassibility? The Latin adjective *impassibilis* means 'incapable of suffering' and therefore 'devoid of emotion'. Its Greek equivalent *apathēs* was applied by the philosophers to God, whom they declared to be above pleasure and pain, since these would interrupt his tranquillity.

The early Greek Fathers of the church took over this notion somewhat uncritically. In consequence, their teaching about God sometimes sounds more Greek than Hebrew. It was also ambivalent. True, they knew that Jesus Christ the Incarnate Son suffered, but not God himself. Ignatius wrote to Polycarp, for example, of the God 'who cannot suffer, who for our sakes accepted suffering', that is, in Christ.[29] Similarly, Irenaeus affirmed that by reason of the incarnation 'the invisible was made visible, the incomprehensible comprehensible, and the impassible passible'.[30] True again, they knew that the Old Testament authors wrote freely of the love, pity, anger, sorrow and jealousy of God. But they added that these were anthropomorphisms which are not to be taken literally, since the divine nature is unmoved by all emotions.[31] Gregory Thaumaturgus in the third century even wrote that 'in his suffering God shows his impassibility'.

These and other ancient church Fathers deserve our understanding. They were wanting above all to safeguard the truths that God is perfect (so that nothing can add to or subtract from him) and that God is changeless (so that nothing can disturb him).[32] We today should still wish to maintain these truths. God cannot be influenced against his will from either outside or inside. He is never the unwilling victim either of actions which affect him from without or of emotions which upset him from within. As William Temple put it, 'there is a highly technical sense in which God, as Christ revealed him, is "without passions"; for he is Creator and supreme,

[29] Ignatius, *Ad Polycarp* 3. *Cf.* his *Ad Eph.* vii. 2.

[30] Irenaeus, *Adversus Haereses* iii.16.6.

[31] See *e.g.* Clement of Alexandria's *Stromateis* v.11 and Origen's *Ezek. Hom.* vi.6. A useful survey of patristic quotations and references is given by J. K. Mozley in his *Impassibility of God*. See also *Suffering of the Impassible God* by B. R. Brasnett.

[32] Statements that God does not change his mind, his justice or his compassion may be found in Nu. 23:19; 1 Sa. 15:29; Ezk. 18:25; and Mal. 3:6.

and is never "passive" in the sense of having things happen to him except with his consent; also he is constant, and free from gusts of feeling carrying him this way and that'. Nevertheless, Temple rightly went on to say that the term 'impassible' as used by most theologians really meant 'incapable of suffering', and that 'in this sense its predication of God is almost wholly false'.[33]

It is true that Old Testament language is an accommodation to our human understanding, and that God is represented as experiencing human emotions. Yet, to acknowledge that his feelings are not *human* is not to deny that they are *real*. If they are only metaphorical, 'then the only God left to us will be the infinite iceberg of metaphysics'.[34] In contrast to this, we may be thankful to the Jewish scholar Abraham Heschel, who in his book *The Prophets* refers to their 'pathetic theology', because they portray a God of feeling. The frequent Old Testament 'anthropopathisms' (which ascribe human suffering to God) are not to be rejected as crude or primitive, he writes, but rather to be welcomed as crucial to our understanding of him: 'the most exalted idea applied to God is not infinite wisdom, infinite power, but infinite concern' (p. 241). Thus, before the flood Yahweh was 'grieved' that he had made human beings, 'and his heart was filled with pain', and when his people were oppressed by foreigners during the time of the Judges, Yahweh 'could bear Israel's misery no longer'.[35] Most striking of all are the occasions when through the prophets God expresses his 'yearning' and 'compassion' for his people and addresses Israel direct: 'I have loved you with an everlasting love . . . . Can a mother forget the baby at her breast . . .? Though she may forget, I will not forget you! . . . How can I give you up, Ephraim? How can I hand you over, Israel? . . . My heart is changed within me; all my compassion is aroused.'[36]

If God's full and final self-revelation was given in Jesus, moreover, then his feelings and sufferings are an authentic reflection of the feelings and sufferings of God himself. The Gospel writers attribute to him the whole range of human emotions, from love and compassion through anger and indignation to sorrow and joy. The stubbornness of human hearts caused him distress and anger. Outside Lazarus' tomb, in the face of death, he both 'wept' with grief and 'snorted' with indignation. He wept again over Jerusalem, and uttered a lament over her blindness and obstinacy. And still

[33] William Temple, *Christus Veritas*, p. 269.
[34] Vincent Tymms, quoted by J. K. Mozley, *Impassibility of God*, p. 146.
[35] Gn. 6:6–7; Jdg. 10:16.
[36] Je. 31:20; 31:3; Is. 49:15; Ho. 11:8.

today he is able 'to sympathize with our weaknesses', feeling with us in them.[37]

The best way to confront the traditional view of the impassibility of God, however, is to ask 'what meaning there can be in a love which is not costly to the lover'.[38] If love is self-giving, then it is inevitably vulnerable to pain, since it exposes itself to the possibility of rejection and insult. It is 'the fundamental Christian assertion that God is love', writes Jürgen Moltmann, 'which in principle broke the spell of the Aristotelian doctrine of God' (*i.e.* as 'impassible'). 'Were God incapable of suffering . . ., then he would also be incapable of love', whereas 'the one who is capable of love is also capable of suffering, for he also opens himself to the suffering which is involved in love'.[39] That is surely why Bonhoeffer wrote from prison to his friend Eberhard Bethge, nine months before his execution: 'only the Suffering God can help.'[40]

Worthy of special mention, as a doughty opponent of false views of the divine impassibility, is the Japanese Lutheran scholar Kazoh Kitamori. He wrote his remarkable book *Theology of the Pain of God* in 1945, not long after the first atomic bombs had destroyed Hiroshima and Nagasaki. It was inspired, he tells us, by Jeremiah 31:20, where God describes his heart as 'yearning' or 'pained' for Ephraim, even as 'broken'. 'The heart of the gospel was revealed to me as the "pain of God",' he writes (p. 19). To begin with, God's anger against sin gives him pain. 'This wrath of God is absolute and firm. We may say that the recognition of God's wrath is the beginning of wisdom.' But God loves the very people with whom he is angry. So 'the "pain" of God reflects his will to love the object of his wrath'. It is his love and his wrath which together produce his pain. For here, in Luther's arresting phrase, is 'God striving with God'. 'The fact that this fighting God is not two different gods but the same God causes his pain' (p. 21). The pain of God is 'a synthesis of his wrath and love' (p. 26) and is 'his essence' (p. 47). It was supremely revealed in the cross. For 'the "pain of God" results from the love of the One who intercepts and blocks his wrath towards us, the One who himself is smitten by his wrath' (p. 123). This is strikingly bold phraseology. It helps us to understand how God's pain continues whenever his wrath and

---

[37] Mk. 3:5; Jn. 11:35, 38; Lk. 13:34–35; 19:41–44; Heb. 4:15. See also B. B. Warfield's essay 'The Emotional Life of our Lord', reprinted from *Biblical and Theological Studies* (Scribners, 1912) in *The Person and Work of Christ*, ed. Samuel G. Craig, pp. 93–145.

[38] H. Wheeler Robinson, *Suffering Human and Divine*, p. 176.

[39] Jürgen Moltmann, *Crucified God*. See the whole section pp. 222–230.

[40] Dietrich Bonhoeffer, *Letters and Papers*, p. 361.

love, his justice and mercy, are in tension today.

Looking at the world during the second half of this century, there have probably been two outstandingly conspicuous examples of human suffering, the first being hunger and poverty on a global scale, and the second the Nazi holocaust of six million Jews. How does the cross speak to such evils as these?

It is reckoned that one thousand million people today, because they lack the basic necessities of life, may rightly be described as 'destitute'. Many of them eke out a pitiful existence in the slums and shanty towns of Africa and Asia, the *barriadas* of Spanish Latin America and the *favelas* of Brazil. The penury of the people, the overcrowding in their ramshackle shelters, the lack of elementary sanitation, the virtual nakedness of the children, the hunger, disease, unemployment and absence of education – all this adds up to a horrific tally of human need. It is not surprising that such slums are hotbeds of bitterness and resentment; the wonder is that the sheer inhumanity and injustice of it all does not breed an even more virulent anger. Rolf Italiaander imagines a poor man from one of the *favelas* of Rio de Janeiro, who climbs laboriously up to the colossal statue of Christ, 2,310 feet high, which towers above Rio, 'the Christ of Corcovado'. The poor man speaks to the statue:

> I have climbed up to you, Christ, from the filthy, confined quarters down there . . . to put before you, most respectfully, these considerations: there are 900,000 of us down there in the slums of that splendid city . . . . And you, Christ, . . . do you remain here at Corcovado surrounded by divine glory? Go down there into the *favelas*. Come with me into the *favelas* and live with us down there. Don't stay away from us; live among us and give us new faith in you and in the Father. Amen.[41]

What would Christ say in response to such an entreaty? Would he not say 'I did come down to live among you, and I live among you still'?

This is, in fact, how some Latin American theologians are presenting the cross today. In his *Christology at the Crossroads*, for example, Professor Jon Sobrino of El Salvador develops a protest both against a purely academic theology which fails to take appropriate action and against the traditional, mournful 'mystique' of the cross which is too passive and individualistic. Instead, he seeks to relate the cross to the modern world and its social injustice.

[41] Quoted from Walbert Bühlmann, *Coming of the Third Church*, p. 125.

Was God himself, he asks, 'untouched by the historical cross because he is essentially untouchable?' (p. 190). No, no. 'God himself, the Father, was on the cross of Jesus.' In addition, 'God is to be found on the crosses of the oppressed' (p. 201). Provided that Professor Sobrino is not denying the fundamental, atoning purpose of the cross, I do not think we should resist what he is affirming. Here is his summary: 'On the cross of Jesus God himself is crucified. The Father suffers the death of the Son and takes upon himself the pain and suffering of history.' And in this ultimate solidarity with human beings God 'reveals himself as the God of love' (pp. 224, 371).

What, then, about the holocaust? 'After Auschwitz', said Richard Rubinstein, 'it is impossible to believe in God.' One Sunday afternoon, in a sub-camp of Buchenwald, a group of learned Jews decided to put God on trial for neglecting his chosen people. Witnesses were produced for both prosecution and defence, but the case for the prosecution was overwhelming. The judges were Rabbis. They found the accused guilty and solemnly condemned him.[42] It is understandable. The sheer bestiality of the camps and the gas chambers, and the failure of God to intervene on behalf of his ancient people, in spite of their frequent and fervent prayers, have shaken many people's faith. I have already said that I do not think the way to interpret Auschwitz and its aftermath is in terms of death and resurrection. Is there, then, another way? I think Elie (Eliezer) Wiesel can help us. Born a Hungarian Jew, and now an internationally acclaimed author, he has given us in his book *Night* a deeply moving account of his boyhood experiences in the death camps of Auschwitz, Buna and Buchenwald. He was not quite fifteen when the Gestapo arrived to deport all Jews from Sighet in the spring of 1944. They travelled by train for three days, eighty in each cattle wagon. On arrival at Auschwitz, the men and women were segregated, and Elie never saw his mother or sister again. 'Never shall I forget that night, the first night in camp, which has turned my life into one long night, seven times cursed and seven times sealed. Never shall I forget that smoke (*sc.* of the crematorium) . . . . Never shall I forget those flames which consumed my faith for ever . . . . Never shall I forget those moments which murdered my God and my soul, and turned my dreams to dust . . . .' (p. 45). A bit later he wrote: 'Some talked of God, of his mysterious ways, of the sins of the Jewish people, and of their future deliverance. But I had ceased to pray. How I sympathised

---

[42] Rabbi Hugo Gryn first heard this story from an uncle of his who survived Buchenwald. It has been told by several Jewish authors, and also by Gerald Priestland in *Case Against God*, p. 13.

with Job! I did not deny God's existence, but I doubted his absolute justice' (p. 57).

Perhaps the most horrifying experience of all was when the guards first tortured and then hanged a young boy, 'a child with a refined and beautiful face', a 'sad-eyed angel'. Just before the hanging Elie heard someone behind him whisper, 'Where is God? Where is he?' Thousands of prisoners were forced to watch the hanging (it took the boy half an hour to die) and then to march past, looking him full in the face. Behind him Elie heard the same voice ask, 'Where is God now?' 'And I heard a voice within me answer him: "Where is he? Here he is – he is hanging here on this gallows . . . ." ' (pp. 75–77). His words were truer than he knew, for he was not a Christian. Indeed, in every fibre of his being he rebelled against God for allowing people to be tortured, butchered, gassed and burned. 'I was alone – terribly alone in a world without God and without man. Without love or mercy' (p. 79). Could he have said that if in Jesus he had seen God on the gallows?

There is good biblical evidence that God not only suffered in Christ, but that God in Christ suffers with his people still. Is it not written of God, during the early days of Israel's bitter bondage in Egypt, not just that he saw their plight and 'heard their groaning', but that 'in all their distress he too was distressed'? Did Jesus not ask Saul of Tarsus why he was persecuting him, thus disclosing his solidarity with his church? It is wonderful that we may share in Christ's sufferings; it is more wonderful still that he shares in ours. Truly his name is 'Emmanuel', 'God with us'. But his 'sympathy' is not limited to his suffering with his covenant people. Did Jesus not say that in ministering to the hungry and thirsty, the stranger, the naked, the sick and the prisoner, we would be ministering to him, indicating that he identified himself with all needy and suffering people?[43]

I could never myself believe in God, if it were not for the cross. The only God I believe in is the One Nietzsche ridiculed as 'God on the cross'. In the real world of pain, how could one worship a God who was immune to it? I have entered many Buddhist temples in different Asian countries and stood respectfully before the statue of the Buddha, his legs crossed, arms folded, eyes closed, the ghost of a smile playing round his mouth, a remote look on his face, detached from the agonies of the world. But each time after a while I have had to turn away. And in imagination I have turned instead to that lonely, twisted, tortured figure on the cross, nails through hands and feet, back lacerated, limbs wrenched, brow bleeding

[43] Ex. 2:24; Is. 63:9; Acts 9:4; Mt. 1:23; 25:34–40.

from thorn-pricks, mouth dry and intolerably thirsty, plunged in God-forsaken darkness. That is the God for me! He laid aside his immunity to pain. He entered our world of flesh and blood, tears and death. He suffered for us. Our sufferings become more manageable in the light of his. There is still a question mark against human suffering, but over it we boldly stamp another mark, the cross which symbolizes divine suffering. 'The cross of Christ . . . is God's only self-justification in such a world' as ours.[44]

The playlet entitled 'The Long Silence' says it all:

At the end of time, billions of people were scattered on a great plain before God's throne.

Most shrank back from the brilliant light before them. But some groups near the front talked heatedly – not with cringing shame, but with belligerence.

'Can God judge us? How can he know about suffering?' snapped a pert young brunette. She ripped open a sleeve to reveal a tattooed number from a Nazi concentration camp. 'We endured terror . . . beatings . . . torture . . . death!'

In another group a Negro boy lowered his collar. 'What about this?' he demanded, showing an ugly rope burn. 'Lynched . . . for no crime but being black!'

In another crowd, a pregnant schoolgirl with sullen eyes. 'Why should I suffer' she murmured, 'It wasn't my fault.'

Far out across the plain there were hundreds of such groups. Each had a complaint against God for the evil and suffering he permitted in his world. How lucky God was to live in heaven where all was sweetness and light, where there was no weeping or fear, no hunger or hatred. What did God know of all that man had been forced to endure in this world? For God leads a pretty sheltered life, they said.

So each of these groups sent forth their leader, chosen because he had suffered the most. A Jew, a Negro, a person from Hiroshima, a horribly deformed arthritic, a thalidomide child. In the centre of the plain they consulted with each other. At last they were ready to present their case. It was rather clever.

Before God could be qualified to be their judge, he must endure what they had endured. Their decision was that God should be sentenced to live on earth – as a man!

'Let him be born a Jew. Let the legitimacy of his birth be doubted. Give him a work so difficult that even his family will think him out of his mind when he tries to do it. Let him be

[44] P. T. Forsyth, *Justification of God*, p. 32.

betrayed by his closest friends. Let him face false charges, be tried by a prejudiced jury and convicted by a cowardly judge. Let him be tortured.

'At the last, let him see what it means to be terribly alone. Then let him die. Let him die so that there can be no doubt that he died. Let there be a great host of witnesses to verify it.'

As each leader announced his portion of the sentence, loud murmurs of approval went up from the throng of people assembled.

And when the last had finished pronouncing sentence, there was a long silence. No-one uttered another word. No-one moved. For suddenly all knew that God had already served his sentence.

Edward Shillito, shattered by the carnage of the First World War, found comfort in the fact that Jesus was able to show his disciples the scars of his crucifixion. It inspired him to write his poem 'Jesus of the Scars':

> If we have never sought, we seek thee now;
>   Thine eyes burn through the dark, our only stars;
> We must have sight of thorn-marks on thy brow,
>   We must have thee, O Jesus of the scars.
>
> The heavens frighten us; they are too calm;
>   In all the universe we have no place.
> Our wounds are hurting us; where is the balm?
>   Lord Jesus, by thy scars we know thy grace.
>
> If, when the doors are shut, thou drawest near,
>   Only reveal those hands, that side of thine;
> We know today what wounds are, have no fear;
>   Show us thy scars, we know the countersign.
>
> The other gods were strong; but thou wast weak;
>   They rode, but thou didst stumble to a throne;
> But to our wounds only God's wounds can speak,
>   And not a god has wounds, but thou alone.[45]

---

[45] Edward Shillito, *Jesus of the Scars*, published after World War I, and quoted by William Temple in his *Readings in St John's Gospel*, pp. 384–385.

Conclusion

The pervasive influence
of the cross

In the first chapter I sought to establish the centrality of the cross in the mind of Christ, in Scripture and in history; in the last we shall consider how from that centre the influence of the cross spreads outwards until it pervades the whole of Christian faith and life.

But before developing this theme, it may be helpful to survey the territory we have crossed.

In answer to the question 'Why did Christ die?' we reflected that, although Judas delivered him to the priests, the priests to Pilate, and Pilate to the soldiers, the New Testament indicates both that the Father 'gave him up' and that Jesus 'gave himself up' for us. That led us to look below the surface of what was happening, and to investigate the implications of Jesus' words in the upper room, the Garden of Gethsemane and the cry of dereliction.

It had already become evident that his death was related to our sins, and so in Part Two we came to the very heart of the cross. We began by broaching the problem of forgiveness as constituted by the conflict between the majesty of God and the gravity of sin. And although we rejected other 'satisfaction' theories, we concluded in chapter 5 that God must 'satisfy himself'. That is, he cannot contradict himself, but must act in a way that expresses his perfect character of holy love. But how could he do this? Our answer (chapter 6) was that in order to satisfy himself he substituted himself in Christ for us. We dared to affirm 'self-satisfaction by self-substitution' as the essence of the cross.

In Part Three we looked beyond the cross itself to its consequences, indeed its achievement in three spheres: the salvation of sinners, the revelation of God and the conquest of evil. As for salvation, we studied the four words 'propitiation', 'redemption', 'justification' and 'reconciliation'. These are New Testament 'images', metaphors of what God has done in and through Christ's death. 'Substitution', however, is not another image; it is the reality which lies behind them all. We then saw (chapter 8) that God has fully and finally revealed his love and justice by exercising them in the cross. When substitution is denied, God's self-disclosure is obscured, but when it is affirmed, his glory shines forth brightly. Having thus far concentrated on the cross as both objective achievement (salvation from sin) and subjective influence (through the revelation of holy love), we agreed that *Christus Victor* is a third biblical theme, which depicts Christ's victory over the devil, the law, the flesh, the world and death, and our victory through him (chapter 9).

Part Four I have entitled 'Living under the cross', because the Christian community is essentially a community of the cross. Indeed, the cross has radically altered all our relationships. We now worship God in continuous celebration (chapter 10), understand ourselves and give ourselves in the service of others (chapter 11), love our enemies, seeking to overcome evil with good (chapter 12), and face the perplexing problem of suffering in the light of the cross (chapter 13).

Seven affirmations in the letter to the Galatians

In order, in conclusion, to emphasize the pervasive influence of the cross, namely that we cannot eliminate it from any area of our thinking or living, we shall look through Paul's letter to the Galatians. There are two main reasons for this choice. First, it is arguably his first letter. This is not the place to assess the pros and cons of the 'South Galatian' and 'North Galatian' theories. The similarity of the contents with the letter to the Romans may suggest the later date, but the situation presupposed in Galatians fits the Acts chronology much better and strongly favours the earlier date. In this case the letter was written about AD 48, within fifteen years of the death and resurrection of Jesus. Secondly, the gospel according to Paul in Galatians (which he defends, along with his apostolic authority, as coming from God, not man) focuses on the cross. Indeed the letter contains seven striking affirmations about the death of Jesus, each of which illumines a different facet of it. When we put them together, we have an amazingly comprehensive grasp of the pervasive influence of the cross.

1. The cross and salvation (1:3–5)

> Grace and peace to you from God our Father and the Lord Jesus
> Christ, who gave himself for our sins to rescue us from the
> present evil age, according to the will of our God and Father,
> to whom be glory for ever and ever. Amen.

These words form part of Paul's introductory salutation. Usually
such an epistolary greeting would be casual or conventional. But
Paul uses it to make a carefully balanced theological statement
about the cross, which indicates what his concern in the letter is
going to be.

First, *the death of Jesus was both voluntary and determined*. On
the one hand, he 'gave himself for our sins', freely and voluntarily.
On the other, his self-giving was 'according to the will of our God
and Father'. God the Father purposed and willed the death of his
Son and foretold it in the Old Testament Scriptures. Yet Jesus
embraced this purpose of his own accord. He set his will to do his
Father's will.

Secondly, *the death of Jesus was for our sins*. Sin and death are
integrally related throughout Scripture as cause and effect, as we
have seen. Usually the one who sins and the one who dies are the
same person. Here, however, although the sins are ours, the death
is Christ's: *he* died for *our* sins, bearing their penalty in our place.

Thirdly, *the purpose of Jesus' death was to rescue us*. Salvation
is a rescue operation, undertaken for people whose plight is so
desperate that they cannot save themselves. In particular, he died
to rescue us 'out of the present evil age'. Since Christ inaugurated
the new age, the two ages at present overlap. But he died to rescue
us from the old age and secure our transfer into the new, so that
already we might live the life of the age to come.

Fourthly, *the present result of Jesus' death is grace and peace*.
'Grace' is his free and unmerited favour, and 'peace' is the reconciliation with him and with each other which grace has achieved. The
life of the age to come is a life of grace and peace. Paul continues
to allude to it in the following verses, in which he expresses his
astonishment that the Galatians have so quickly deserted the one
who had called them 'by the grace of Christ' (v. 6). For the call of
God is a call of grace, and the gospel of God is the gospel of grace.

Fifthly, *the eternal result of Jesus' death is that God will be
glorified for ever*. The references in verses 3–5 to grace and glory,
as part of the same sentence, are striking. Grace comes from God;
glory is due to God. The whole of Christian theology is encapsu-
lated in that epigram.

Here, then, in one pregnant sentence, is Paul's first statement in Galatians about the cross. Although it was determined eternally by the Father's will, Jesus gave himself voluntarily for us. The nature of his death was the penalty for our sins, and its purpose was to rescue us from the old age and transfer us to the new, in which we receive grace and peace now, and God receives glory for ever.

2. The cross and experience (2:19–21)

For through the law I died to the law so that I might live for God. I have been crucified with Christ and I no longer live, but Christ lives in me. The life I live in the body, I live by faith in the Son of God, who loved me and gave himself for me. I do not set aside the grace of God, for if righteousness could be gained through the law, Christ died for nothing!

If we were not already familiar with verse 20, it would strike us as quite extraordinary. That Jesus Christ was crucified under Pontius Pilate is an established historical fact; but what could Paul possibly mean by writing that *he* had been crucified with Christ? As a physical fact it was manifestly not true, and as a spiritual fact it was hard to understand.

We need to examine the context. Verses 15–21 are in general about justification, how a righteous God can declare the unrighteous righteous. But in particular they assert that sinners are justified not by the law (referred to 7 times) but by God's grace through faith. Three times in verse 16 the apostle insists that nobody can be justified by the law. It would hardly have been possible to state more forcibly than this the impossibility of self-justification, that is, of winning God's acceptance by obeying the law. Why is this? Because the law condemns sin and prescribes death as its penalty. Thus the function of the law is to condemn, not to justify.

Since the law clamours for my death as a law-breaker, how can I possibly be justified? Only by meeting the law's requirement and dying the death it demands. If I were to do this myself, however, that would be the finish of me. So God has provided another way. Christ has borne the penalty of my law-breaking, and the blessing of what he has done has become mine because I am united with him. Being one with Christ, I am able to say 'I died to the law' (v. 19), meeting its demands, because 'I have been crucified with Christ' and now he lives in me (v. 20).

As in Romans 6, so in Galatians 2, the assertion of our death and resurrection with Christ is Paul's answer to the charge of antinomianism. Granted, nobody can be justified by law-observance. But that does not mean that I am free to break the law. On the contrary, it is inconceivable that I should continue in sin. Why so? Because I have died; I have been crucified with Christ; my old sinful life has received the condemnation it deserved. In consequence I (the old, sinful, guilty I) live no longer. But Christ lives in me. Or, since plainly I am still alive, I can say that the life I now live is an entirely different life. It is the old 'I' (sinful, rebellious, guilty) which lives no longer. It is the new 'I' (justified and free from condemnation) who lives by faith in the Son of God who loved me and gave himself for me.

It is important to grasp that Paul is referring to the death and resurrection of Christ, and to our death and resurrection through union with him. He puts the same truth in two ways. Regarding the *death* of our old life, he can say both 'he loved me and gave himself for me' and 'I died . . . I have been crucified with Christ'. Regarding the *resurrection* to new life, he can say both 'Christ lives in me' and 'I live for God' (v. 19) or 'I live by faith in the Son of God' (v. 20).

To sum up, Christ died for me, and I died with him, meeting the law's demands and paying sin's just penalty. Then Christ rose again and lives, and I live through him, sharing in his resurrection life. Justification by faith, then, does not set aside God's grace (v. 21). Nor (as in Rom. 6) does it presume on it, saying 'where sin abounds, grace abounds much more'. No, justification by faith magnifies the grace of God, declaring that it is by his grace alone. It is the notion of justification by law which sets aside the grace of God, for if a righteous status before God were attainable by law-obedience, then Christ's death was superfluous.

3. The cross and preaching (3:1–3)

You foolish Galatians! Who has bewitched you? Before your very eyes Jesus Christ was clearly portrayed as crucified. I would like to learn just one thing from you: Did you receive the Spirit by observing the law, or by believing what you heard? Are you so foolish? After beginning with the Spirit, are you now trying to attain your goal by human effort?

Paul has just described (in 2:11–14) his public showdown with Peter in Antioch, because Peter had withdrawn from table fellowship with Gentile Christians and so in effect had contradicted God's free acceptance of them by his grace. He has gone on to rehearse

342

the arguments he had used with Peter to prove the doctrine of justification by faith. Now he breaks out into an expression of astonished indignation. He accuses the Galatians of folly. Twice he uses the word 'senseless' (*anoētos*), which is to be lacking in *nous*, intelligence. Their folly is so uncharacteristic and so unacceptable that he asks who has 'bewitched' them. He implies that a spell must have been cast over them, perhaps by the Archdeceiver, though doubtless through human false teachers. For their present distortion of the gospel is totally incompatible with what they have heard from Paul and Barnabas. He therefore reminds them of his preaching when he was with them. He 'publicly portrayed' (RSV) Jesus Christ before their eyes as having been crucified for them. How then could they imagine that, having begun their Christian life by faith in Christ crucified, they needed to continue it by their own achievement?

There is much to learn from this text about the preaching of the gospel.

First, *gospel-preaching is proclaiming the cross*. True, the resurrection must be added (1:1; 2:19–20). So must Jesus' birth of a woman, and under the law (4:4). But the gospel is in essence the good news of Christ crucified.

Secondly, *gospel-preaching is proclaiming the cross visually*. Paul uses a remarkable verb, *prographō*. Usually it means to 'write previously', for example, 'as I have already written' (Eph. 3:3). But *graphō* can sometimes mean to draw or paint, rather than to write, and *pro* can mean 'before' in space (before our eyes) rather than in time (previously). So Paul here likens his gospel-preaching either to a huge canvas painting or to a placard publicly exhibiting a notice or advertisement. The subject of his painting or placard was Jesus Christ on the cross. Of course it was not literally a painting; the picture was created by words. Yet it was so visual, so vivid, in its appeal to their imagination, that the placard was presented 'before your very eyes'. One of the greatest arts or gifts in gospel-preaching is to turn people's ears into eyes, and to make them *see* what we are talking about.

Thirdly, *gospel-preaching proclaims the cross visually as a present reality*. Jesus Christ had been crucified at least fifteen years before Paul was writing, and in our case nearly two millennia ago. What Paul did by his preaching (and we must do by ours) was to bring that event out of the past into the present. The ministry of both word and sacrament can do this. It can overcome the time-barrier and make past events present realities in such a way that people have to respond to them. Almost certainly none of Paul's readers had been present at the crucifixion of Jesus; yet Paul's preaching brought it before their eyes so that they could see it, and into their existential experience so that they must either accept or reject it.

Fourthly, *gospel-preaching proclaims the cross as a visual, present and permanent reality.* For what we (like Paul) are to placard before people's eyes is not just *Christos staurōtheis* (aorist) but *Christos estaurōmenos* (perfect). The tense of the verb emphasizes not so much that the cross was a historical event of the past as that its validity, power and benefits are permanent. The cross will never cease to be God's power for salvation to believers.

Fifthly, *gospel-preaching proclaims the cross also as the object of personal faith.* Paul did not placard Christ crucified before their eyes so that they might simply gape and stare. His purpose was to persuade them to come and put their trust in him as their crucified Saviour. And this is what they had done. The reason for Paul's astonishment was that, having received justification and the Spirit by faith, they should imagine that they could continue in the Christian life by their own achievements. It was a contradiction of what Paul had presented before their eyes.

4. *The cross and substitution (3:10–14)*

All who rely on observing the law are under a curse, for it is written: 'Cursed is everyone who does not continue to do everything written in the Book of the Law.' Clearly no-one is justified before God by the law, because, 'The righteous will live by faith.' The law is not based on faith; on the contrary, 'The man who does these things will live by them.' Christ redeemed us from the curse of the law by becoming a curse for us, for it is written: 'Cursed is everyone who is hanged on a tree.' He redeemed us in order that the blessing given to Abraham might come to the Gentiles through Christ Jesus, so that by faith we might receive the promise of the Spirit.

These verses constitute one of the clearest expositions of the necessity, meaning and consequence of the cross. Paul expresses himself in such stark terms that some commentators have not been able to accept what he writes about the 'curse' which Christ 'became' for us. A. W. F. Blunt, for example, wrote in his commentary: 'The language here is startling, almost shocking. We should not have dared to use it.'[1] Jeremias also called it a 'shocking phrase'

---

[1] A. W. F. Blunt, *Galatians*, p. 96.

and spoke of its 'original offensiveness'.[2] Nevertheless, the apostle Paul did use this language, and Blunt was surely correct in adding that 'Paul means every word of it'. So we have to come to terms with it.

Several attempts have been made to soften it. First, it has been suggested that Paul deliberately de-personalized the 'curse' by calling it 'the curse of the law'. But the expression in Deuteronomy 21:23 is 'God's curse'; it cannot seriously be entertained that Paul is contradicting Scripture. Secondly, it has been proposed that his 'becoming' a curse expresses the sympathy of Christ for law-breakers, not an objective acceptance of their judgment. Here is Blunt's interpretation: 'It was not by a forensic fiction that Christ bore our sins, but by an act of genuine fellow feeling', like a mother who has a son who goes wrong and who 'feels his guilt to be hers as well'.[3] But this is an evasion; it does not do justice to Paul's words. As Jeremias put it, 'became' is 'a circumlocution for the action of God'.

Thirdly, it is said, Paul's statement that Christ became 'a curse' for us falls short of saying that he was actually 'cursed'. But according to Jeremias, 'curse' is 'a metonym for "the cursed one" ', and we should translate the phrase 'God made Christ a cursed one for our sake'. It is then parallel to 'God made him who had no sin to be sin for us' (2 Cor. 5:21). And we shall be able to accept the two phrases, and indeed worship God for their truth, because 'God was in Christ reconciling' (2 Cor. 5:19) even while he made Christ both sin and a curse.

Luther grasped very clearly what Paul meant, and expressed its implications with characteristic directness:

> Our most merciful Father, seeing us to be oppressed and over-whelmed with the curse of the law, and so to be holden under the same that we could never be delivered from it by our own power, sent his only Son into the world and laid upon him all the sins of all men, saying: Be thou Peter that denier; Paul that persecutor, blasphemer and cruel oppressor; David that adulterer; that sinner which did eat the apple in Paradise; that thief which hanged upon the cross; and briefly, be thou the person which hath committed the sins of all men; see therefore that thou pay and satisfy for them.[4]

We need to feel the logic of Paul's teaching. First, *all who rely*

[2] Joachim Jeremias, *Central Message*, p. 35.
[3] A. W. F. Blunt, *Galatians*, p. 97.
[4] Martin Luther, *Epistle to the Galatians*, p. 272.

on the law are under a curse. At the beginning of verse 10 Paul again uses the expression he used three times in 2:16, namely 'those who are of works of law' (literally), which NIV elaborates as 'all who rely on observing the law'. The reason Paul can declare such to be 'under a curse' is that Scripture says they are: 'Cursed is everyone who does not continue to do everything written in the Book of the Law' (*cf.* Dt. 27:26). No human being has ever 'continued' to do 'everything' the law requires. Such a continuous and comprehensive obedience has been given by no-one except Jesus. So 'clearly' (v. 11) nobody 'is justified before God by the law', because nobody has kept it. Besides, Scripture also says that 'the righteous will live by his faith' (Hab. 2:4), and living 'by faith' and living 'by law' are two completely different states (v. 12). The conclusion is unavoidable. Although theoretically those who obey the law will live, in practice none of us will, because none of us has obeyed. Therefore we cannot obtain salvation that way. On the contrary, far from being saved by the law, we are cursed by it. The curse or judgment of God, which his law pronounces on law-breakers, rests upon us. This is the appalling predicament of lost humankind.

Secondly, *Christ redeemed us from the curse of the law by becoming a curse for us.* This is probably the plainest statement in the New Testament of substitution. The curse of the broken law rested on us; Christ redeemed us from it by becoming a curse in our place. The curse that lay on us was transferred to him. He assumed it, that we might escape it. And the evidence that he bore our curse is that he hung on a tree, since Deuteronomy 21:23 declares such a person cursed (v. 13).

Thirdly, Christ did this *in order that in him the blessing of Abraham might come to the Gentiles ... by faith* (v. 14). The apostle moves deliberately from the language of cursing to that of blessing. Christ died for us not only to redeem us from the curse of God, but also to secure for us the blessing of God. He had promised centuries previously to bless Abraham and through his posterity the Gentile nations. And this promised blessing Paul here interprets as 'justification' (v. 8) and 'the Spirit' (v. 14); all who are in Christ are thus richly blessed.

To sum up, because of our disobedience we were under the curse of the law. Christ redeemed us from it by bearing it in our place. As a result, we receive by faith in Christ the promised blessing of salvation. The sequence is irresistible. It prompts our humble worship that God in Christ, in his holy love for us, was willing to go to such lengths, and that the blessings we enjoy today are due to the curse he bore for us on the cross.

5. *The cross and persecution (5:11; 6:12)*

> Brothers, if I am still preaching circumcision, why am I still being persecuted? In that case the offence of the cross has been abolished.

> Those who want to make a good impression outwardly are trying to compel you to be circumcised. The only reason they do this is to avoid being persecuted for the cross of Christ.

The cross of Christ is mentioned in both these verses, and in 5:11 it is called an 'offence' or 'stumbling-block' (*skandalon*). In both verses too there is a reference to persecution. According to 5:11 Paul is being persecuted because he preaches the cross; according to 6:12 the false teachers are avoiding persecution by preaching circumcision instead of the cross. So the alternative for Christian evangelists, pastors and teachers is to preach either circumcision or the cross.

To 'preach circumcision' is to preach salvation by the law, that is, by human achievement. Such a message removes the offence of the cross, which is that we cannot earn our salvation; it therefore exempts us from persecution.

To 'preach the cross' (as in 3:1) is to preach salvation by God's grace alone. Such a message is a stumbling-block (1 Cor. 1:23) because it is grievously offensive to human pride; it therefore exposes us to persecution.

There are, of course, no Judaizers in the world today, preaching the necessity of circumcision. But there are plenty of false teachers, inside as well as outside the church, who preach the false gospel (which is not a gospel, 1:7) of salvation by good works. To preach salvation by good works is to flatter people and so avoid opposition. To preach salvation by grace is to offend people and so invite opposition. This may seem to some to pose the alternative too starkly. But I do not think so. All Christian preachers have to face this issue. Either we preach that human beings are rebels against God, under his just judgment and (if left to themselves) lost, and that Christ crucified who bore their sin and curse is the only available Saviour. Or we emphasize human potential and human ability, with Christ brought in only to boost them, and with no necessity for the cross except to exhibit God's love and so inspire us to greater endeavour.

The former is the way to be faithful, the latter the way to be popular. It is not possible to be faithful and popular simultaneously. We need to hear again the warning of Jesus: 'Woe to you when all men speak well of you' (Lk. 6:26). By contrast, if we preach the cross, we may find that we are ourselves hounded to the cross. As Erasmus wrote in his treatise *On Preaching*: 'Let him (*sc.* the preacher) remember that the cross will never be lacking to those who sincerely preach the gospel. There are always Herods, Ananiases, Caiaphases, Scribes and Pharisees.'[5]

6. *The cross and holiness (5:24)*

Those who belong to Christ Jesus have crucified the sinful nature with its passions and desires.

It is essential to see this text (as indeed every text) in its context. Paul in Galatians 5 is concerned with the meaning of moral freedom. He declares that it is not self-indulgence but self-control, not serving ourselves but serving each other in love (v. 13). Behind this alternative is the inner conflict of which all Christian people are conscious. The apostle calls the protagonists 'the flesh' (our fallen nature with which we are born) and 'the Spirit' (the Holy Spirit himself who indwells us when we are born again). In verses 16–18 he describes the contest between the two, because the desires of the flesh and of the Spirit are contrary to each other.

The acts of the flesh (vv. 19–21) include sexual immorality, religious apostasy (idolatry and witchcraft), social breakdown (hatred, discord, jealousy, temper, selfish ambition and factions) and uncontrolled physical appetites (drunkenness and orgies). The fruit of the Spirit (vv. 22–23), however, the graces which he causes to ripen in the people he fills, include love, joy and peace (specially in relation to God), patience, kindness and goodness (in relation to each other), and faithfulness, gentleness and self-control (in relation to ourselves).

How then can we ensure that the desires of the Spirit predominate over the desires of the flesh? Paul replies that it depends on the attitude which we adopt to each. According to verse 24 we are to 'crucify' the flesh, with its evil passions and desires. According to verse 25 we are to 'live by' and 'keep in step with' the Spirit.

My concern in this chapter is with verse 24, because of its assertion that those who belong to Christ have 'crucified' their flesh or sinful nature. It is an astonishing metaphor. For crucifixion was a horrible, brutal form of execution. Yet it illustrates graphically what our attitude to our fallen nature is to be. We are not to coddle or cuddle it, not to pamper or spoil it, not to give it any

[5] Quoted by Roland H. Bainton, in *Erasmus of Christendom*, p. 323.

encouragement or even toleration. Instead, we are to be ruthlessly fierce in rejecting it, together with its desires. Paul is elaborating the teaching of Jesus about 'taking up the cross' and following him. He is telling us what happens when we reach the place of execution: the actual crucifixion takes place. Luther writes that Christ's people nail their flesh to the cross, 'so that although the flesh be yet alive, yet can it not perform that which it would do, forasmuch as it is bound both hand and foot, and fast nailed to the cross'.[6] And if we are not ready to crucify ourselves in this decisive manner, we shall soon find that instead we are 'crucifying the Son of God all over again'. The essence of apostasy is 'changing sides from that of the Crucified to that of the crucifiers'.[7]

The crucifixions of Galatians 2:20 and 5:24 refer to two quite different things, as mentioned in an earlier chapter. The first says that we have been crucified with Christ (it has happened to us as a result of our union with Christ), and the second that the people of Christ have themselves taken action to crucify their old nature. The first speaks of our freedom from the condemnation of the law by sharing in *Christ's* crucifixion, the second of our freedom from the power of the flesh by ensuring *its* crucifixion. These two, namely to have been crucified with Christ (passive) and to have crucified the flesh (active), must not be confused.

7. The cross and boasting (6:14)

May I never boast except in the cross of our Lord Jesus Christ, through which the world has been crucified to me, and I to the world.

There is no exact equivalent in the English language to *kauchaomai*. It means to boast in, glory in, trust in, rejoice in, revel in, live for. The object of our boast or 'glory' fills our horizons, engrosses our attention, and absorbs our time and energy. In a word, our 'glory' is our obsession.

Some people are obsessed with themselves and their money, fame or power; the false teachers in Galatia were triumphalists, obsessed with the number of their converts (v. 13); but Paul's obsession was with Christ and his cross. That which the average Roman citizen regarded as an object of shame, disgrace and even disgust was for Paul his pride, boasting and glory. Moreover, we cannot dismiss this as Pauline idiosyncrasy. For, as we have seen, the cross was

[6] Martin Luther, *Epistle to the Galatians*, p. 527.
[7] Heb. 6:4–6; 10:26–27. *Cf.* C. F. D. Moule, *Sacrifice of Christ*, p. 30.

central to the mind of Christ, and has always been central to the faith of the church.

First, to glory or boast in the cross is to see it as *the way of acceptance with God*. The most important of all questions is how we, as lost and guilty sinners, may stand before a just and holy God. It was to answer this question loud and clear that Paul, in the passionate heat of his controversy with the Judaizers, dashed off his letter to the Galatians. Like them some people today still trust in their own merits. But God forbid that we should boast except in the cross. The cross excludes all other kinds of boasting (Rom. 3:27).

Secondly, to glory or boast in the cross is to see it as *the pattern of our self-denial*. Although Paul writes of only one cross ('the cross of our Lord Jesus Christ'), he refers to two crucifixions, even three. On the same cross on which our Lord Jesus Christ was himself crucified, 'the world has been crucified to me, and I to the world'. The 'world' thus crucified (repudiated) does not of course mean the people of the world (for we are called to love and serve them), but the values of the world, its godless materialism, vanity and hypocrisy (for we are told not to love these, but to reject them). 'The flesh' has already been crucified (5:24); now 'the world' joins it on the cross. We ought to keep the two main crucifixions of 6:14 in close relation to each other – Christ's and ours. For they are not two, but one. It is only the sight of Christ's cross which will make us willing, and even anxious, to take up ours. It is only then that we shall be able with integrity to repeat Paul's words after him that we glory in nothing but the cross.

We have now considered Paul's seven great affirmations about the cross in the letter to the Galatians, and have looked at them in the order in which they occur. It may be helpful, in conclusion, to re-arrange and group them in theological rather than chronological order, in order to grasp yet more firmly the centrality and pervasiveness of the cross in every sphere of Christian living.

First, the cross is *the ground of our justification*. Christ has rescued us from the present evil age (1:4) and redeemed us from the curse of the law (3:13). And the reason why he has delivered us from this double bondage is that we may stand boldly before God as his sons and daughters, declared righteous and indwelt by his Spirit.

Secondly, the cross is *the means of our sanctification*. This is where the three other crucifixions come in. We have been crucified with Christ (2:20). We have crucified our fallen nature (5:24). And the world has been crucified to us, as we have been to the world

(6:14). So the cross means more than the crucifixion of Jesus; it includes our crucifixion, the crucifixion of our flesh and of the world.

Thirdly, the cross is *the subject of our witness*. We are to placard Christ crucified publicly before people's eyes, so that they may see and believe (3:1). In doing so, we must not bowdlerize the gospel, extracting from it its offence to human pride. No, whatever the price may be, we preach the cross (the merit of Christ), not circumcision (the merit of man); it is the only way of salvation (5:11; 6:12).

Fourthly, the cross is *the object of our boasting*. God forbid that we should boast in anything else (6:14). Paul's whole world was in orbit round the cross. It filled his vision, illumined his life, warmed his spirit. He 'gloried' in it. It meant more to him than anything else. Our perspective should be the same.

If the cross is not central in these four spheres for us, then we deserve to have applied to us that most terrible of all descriptions, 'enemies of the cross of Christ' (Phil. 3:18). To be an enemy of the cross is to set ourselves against its purposes. Self-righteousness (instead of looking to the cross for justification), self-indulgence (instead of taking up the cross to follow Christ), self-advertisement (instead of preaching Christ crucified) and self-glorification (instead of glorying in the cross) – these are the distortions which make us 'enemies' of Christ's cross.

Paul, on the other hand, was a devoted friend of the cross. So closely had he identified himself with it, that he suffered physical persecution for it. 'I bear on my body the marks of Jesus' (Gal. 6:17), he wrote, the wounds and scars he had received in proclaiming Christ crucified, the *stigmata* which branded him as Christ's authentic slave.

The *stigmata* of Jesus, in the spirit if not in the body, remain a mark of authentication for every Christian disciple, and especially every Christian witness. Campbell Morgan expressed it well:

> It is the crucified man that can preach the cross. Said Thomas 'except I shall see in his hands the print of the nails . . . I will not believe'. Dr. Parker of London said that what Thomas said of Christ, the world is saying about the church. And the world is also saying to every preacher: Unless I see in your hands the print of the nails, I will not believe. It is true. It is the man . . . who has died with Christ, . . . that can preach the cross of Christ.[8]

[8] G. Campbell Morgan, *Evangelism*, pp. 59–60.

Bibliography

Only works mentioned in the text are included in the Bibliography. With a few exceptions non-English works are given in an accessible English translation where a suitable one is widely available.

Abelard, P. *See* Fairweather, E. (ed.), *A Scholastic Miscellany*.

Anderson, J. N. D., *Morality, Law and Grace* (Tyndale Press, 1972).

Anglican Roman Catholic International Commission (ARCIC), *Final Report* (Catholic Truth Society and SPCK, 1982).

Anselm, *Cur Deus Homo?* (1098), tr. Edward S. Prout (Religious Tract Society, 1880).

Atkinson, David, *Peace in Our Time?* (IVP, 1985).

Atkinson, James, *Rome and Reformation Today*. Latimer Studies no. 12 (Latimer House, 1982).

Aulen, Gustav, *Christus Victor* (1930; SPCK, 1931).

Bailey, Kenneth, *The Cross and the Prodigal* (Concordia, 1973).

Bainton, Roland H., *Erasmus of Christendom* (1969; Collins, 1970).

Baptism, Eucharist and Ministry. Faith and Order Paper no. 111 (World Council of Churches, 1982).

Barclay, O. R., *Whatever Happened to the Jesus Lane Lot?* (IVP, 1977).

Barclay, William, *Crucified and Crowned* (SCM, 1961).

Barraclough, Geoffrey (ed.), *The Christian World*: A social and cultural history of Christianity (Thames & Hudson, 1981).

Barth, Karl, *Church Dogmatics*, ed. G. W. Bromiley and T. F. Torrance, tr. G. W. Bromiley (T. & T. Clark, 1956–57).

Bauernfeind, O., '*nikaō*', in *Theological Dictionary of the New Testament*, vol. IV (Eerdmans, 1967), pp. 942–945.

Baxter, Richard, *The Saints' Everlasting Rest* (1650), in *Practical Works*, vol. xxiii, ed. William Orme (James Duncan, 1830).

Beckwith, R. T., Duffield, G. E. and Packer, J. I., *Across the Divide* (Marcham Manor Press, 1977).

Beeson, Trevor, *Discretion and Valour*: Religious Conditions in Russia and Eastern Europe (Collins, 1974).

Behm, Johannes, '*haima*', in *Theological Dictionary of the New Testament*, vol. I (Eerdmans, 1964), pp. 172–177.

Berkhof, Hendrik, *Christ and the Powers*, tr. John Howard Yoder (Herald Press, 1962).

Berkouwer, G. C., *The Work of Christ* (Eerdmans, 1965).

Blunt, A. W. F., *The Epistle of Paul to the Galatians. The Clarendon Bible* (OUP, 1925).

Bonhoeffer, Dietrich, *The Cost of Discipleship*, tr. R. H. Fuller (1937; SCM, 1964).

— *Letters and Papers from Prison* (1953; SCM, 1971).

Boswell, James, *Life of Johnson*. 2 vols. (Dutton, 1927).

Brasnett, B. R., *The Suffering of the Impassible God* (SPCK, 1928).

Bruce, F. F., *Colossians. See under* Simpson, E. K. and Bruce, F. F.

Brunner, Emil, *Man in Revolt*: A Christian anthropology, tr. Olive Wyon (1937; Lutterworth, 1939).

— *The Mediator*, tr. Olive Wyon (1927; Westminster Press, 1947).

Buchanan, Colin (ed.), *Essays on Eucharistic Sacrifice in the Early Church*. Grove Liturgical Study no. 40 (Grove Books, 1984).

Büchsel, F., '*allassō* and *katallassō*', in *Theological Dictionary of the New Testament*, vol. I (Eerdmans, 1964), pp. 251–259.

— and Hermann, J., '*hilaskomai*', in *Theological Dictionary of the New Testament*, vol. III (Eerdmans, 1965), pp. 300–323.

Bühlmann, Walbert, *The Coming of the Third Church* (1974; Orbis, 1978).

Bultmann, Rudolf, *Kerygma and Myth*, ed. Hans Werner Bartsch, tr. R. H. Fuller, 2 vols. (1948; SPCK, 1953).

Bushnell, Horace, *Forgiveness and Law*, grounded in principles interpreted by human analogies (Scribner, Armstrong & Co, 1874).

— *The Vicarious Sacrifice*, grounded in principles of universal obligation (Alexander Strahan, 1866).

Buttrick, George A., *Jesus Came Preaching*. The 1931 Yale Lectures (Scribner, 1931).

Caird, G. B., *Principalities and Powers*; A Study in Pauline Theology (Clarendon Press, 1956).

Calvin, John, *Commentary on a Harmony of the Evangelists Matthew, Mark and Luke*, tr. W. Pringle. 3 vols. (Eerdmans, 1965).

— *Commentary on the Gospel According to St John*, tr. T. H. L. Parker. 2 vols. (Oliver & Boyd, 1961).

— *Institutes of the Christian Religion* (1559), in the *Library of Christian Classics*, vols. XX and XXI, ed. John T. McNeill, tr. Ford Lewis Battles (Westminster Press, 1960).

Campbell, John McLeod, *The Nature of the Atonement*, and its relation to remission of sins and eternal life (1856; Macmillan, 4th ed. 1873).

Carey, George L., 'Justification by Faith in Recent Roman Catholic Theology', in *The Great Acquittal*, ed. Gavin Reid (Collins, 1980).

— 'The Lamb of God and Atonement Theories', *Tyndale Bulletin* 32 (1983), pp. 97–122.

Christian Witness to Traditional Religionists of Asia and Oceania. Lausanne Occasional Paper no. 16 (Lausanne Committee for World Evangelization, 1980).

Church of England Evangelical Council, *Evangelical Anglicans and the ARCIC Final Report* (Grove Books, 1982).

Cicero, *Against Verres*, tr. L. H. G. Greenwood, *The Verrine Orations*. 2 vols. (Heinemann, 1928–35).

— *In Defense of Rabirius*, tr. H. G. Hodge, *The Speeches of Cicero* (Heinemann, 1927), pp. 452–491.

Clarkson, Margaret, *Destined for Glory*: the meaning of suffering (Eerdmans and Marshalls, 1983).

Clement of Alexandria, *Stromateis* (Miscellanies), in *The Ante-Nicene Fathers*, vol. II, ed. A. Roberts and J. Donaldson (1885; Eerdmans, 1975), pp. 299–567.

Clow, W. M., *The Cross in Christian Experience* (Hodder & Stoughton, 1910).

Coates, R. J., 'The Doctrine of Eucharistic Sacrifice in Modern Times', in *Eucharistic Sacrifice*, ed. J. I. Packer (Church Book Room Press, 1962), pp. 127–153.

Coggan, F. Donald (ed.), *Christ and the Colleges*: a history of the Inter-Varsity Fellowship of Evangelical Unions (IVFEU, 1934).

— *The Glory of God*: Four studies in a ruling biblical concept (CMS, 1950).

Council of Trent. *See* Schroeder, H. J., *Canons and Decrees*.

Cox, Harvey G., *On Not Leaving it to the Snake* (1964; SCM, 1968).

Craig, Mary, *Blessings*: an autobiographical fragment (Hodder & Stoughton, 1979).

Bibliography

Cranfield, C. E. B., *The Epistle to the Romans. International Critical Commentary*. 2 vols. (T. & T. Clark, 1975–79).
— *The Gospel According to St Mark. Cambridge Greek New Testament Commentary* series (CUP, 1959).
Cranmer, Thomas, *On the Lord's Supper* (1550); reprinted from *The Remains of Thomas Cranmer*, ed. H. Jenkyns (1833; Thynne, 1907).
— *First Book of Homilies* (1547; SPCK, 1914).
Crawford, Thomas J., *The Doctrine of Holy Scripture Respecting the Atonement* (Wm Blackwood, 1871; 5th ed. 1888).
Cullmann, Oscar, *Baptism in the New Testament*, tr. J. K. L. Reid (1950; SCM, 1951).
— *The Christology of the New Testament*, tr. S. C. Guthrie and C. A. M. Hall (1957; SCM, 1959).
Cyprian, *Ad Thibaritanos* and *De Lapsis*, in *The Ante-Nicene Fathers*, vol. V, trans. Ernest Wallis (Eerdmans, 1981).

Dale, R. W., *The Atonement* (Congregational Union, 1894).
Denney, James, 'Anger', in *A Dictionary of Christ and the Gospels*, ed. James Hastings, vol. I (T. & T. Clark, 1906), pp. 60–62.
— *The Atonement and the Modern Mind* (Hodder & Stoughton, 1903).
— *The Death of Christ*, ed. R. V. G. Tasker (1902; Tyndale Press, 1951).
Didache, in *Early Christian Fathers*, vol. I, tr. and ed. Cyril C. Richardson (SCM, 1953), pp. 161–179.
Dimock, Nathaniel, *The Doctrine of the Death of Christ*: in relation to the sin of man, the condemnation of the law, and the dominion of Satan (Elliot Stock, 1890).
Dix, Gregory (ed.), *The Apostolic Tradition of St Hippolytus of Rome* (SPCK, 1937).
— *The Shape of the Liturgy* (Dacre Press, 1945).
Dodd, C. H., *The Bible and the Greeks* (Hodder & Stoughton, 1935).
— *The Epistle of Paul to the Romans. The Moffatt New Testament Commentary* (Hodder & Stoughton, 1932).
— '*hilaskesthai*, Its Cognates, Derivatives and Synonyms, in the Septuagint', *Journal of Theological Studies* 32 (1931), pp. 352–360.
— *The Johannine Epistles. The Moffatt New Testament Commentary* (Hodder & Stoughton, 1946).
Dunstone, A. S., *The Atonement in Gregory of Nyssa* (Tyndale Press, 1964).

Eareckson, Joni, *Joni* (Zondervan, 1976).
— *A Step Further* (Zondervan, 1978).
Edwall, P., Hayman, E. and Maxwell, W. D. (eds.), *Ways of Worship* (SCM, 1951).
England, R. G., *Justification Today: The Roman Catholic and Anglican Debate*. Latimer Studies no. 4 (Latimer House, 1979).
Epistle to Diognetus, in *The Ante-Nicene Fathers*, vol. I, ed. A. Roberts and J. Donaldson (1885; Eerdmans, 1981), pp. 23–30.

Fairweather, Eugene (ed.), *A Scholastic Miscellany: Anselm to Ockham. Library of Christian Classics*, vol. X (Macmillan, 1970).
Fichtner, Johannes, 'orgē', in *Theological Dictionary of the New Testament*, vol. V (Eerdmans, 1967), pp. 394–408.
Forsyth, P. T., *The Cruciality of the Cross* (Hodder & Stoughton, 1909).
— *The Justification of God* (Duckworth, 1916).
— *The Work of Christ* (Hodder & Stoughton, 1910).
Foxe, John, *Book of Martyrs* (1554; Religious Tract Society, 1926).
Franks, Robert S., *A History of the Doctrine of the Work of Christ*, in its ecclesiastical development (Hodder & Stoughton, 1918).
— *The Work of Christ*: A historical study of Christian doctrine (1918; Thomas Nelson, 1962).

Gandhi, Mahatma, *An Autobiography* (1948; Jonathan Cape, 1966).
Glasser, William, *Reality Therapy*: a new approach to psychiatry (Harper & Row, 1965).
Glover, T. R., *The Jesus of History* (SCM, 1917; 2nd ed. 1920).
Gough, Michael, *The Origins of Christian Art* (Thames & Hudson, 1973).
Green, E. M. B., 'Christ's Sacrifice and Ours', in *Guidelines*: Anglican Evangelicals Face the Future, ed. J. I. Packer (Falcon, 1967), pp. 89–117.
— *The Empty Cross of Jesus* (Hodder & Stoughton, 1984).
— 'Eucharistic Sacrifice in the New Testament and the Early Fathers', in *Eucharistic Sacrifice*, ed. J. I. Packer (Church Book Room Press, 1962), pp. 58–83.
— *I Believe in Satan's Downfall* (1981; Hodder & Stoughton, 1984).
Green, Peter, *Watchers by the Cross*: thoughts on the seven last words (Longmans Green, 1934).
Gregory of Nazianzus, *Orations*, in *Nicene and Post-Nicene*

Fathers, vol. III, ed. Philip Schaff and Henry Wace, tr. C. G. Browne and J. E. Swallow (1893; Eerdmans, 1981), pp. 203–434.

Gregory of Nyssa, *The Catechetical Oration*, in *Nicene and Post-Nicene Fathers*, vol. V, ed. Philip Schaff and Henry Wace, tr. W. Moore and H. A. Wilson (1892; Eerdmans, 1979), pp. 473–509.

Grotius, Hugo, *A Defence of the Catholic Faith concerning the Satisfaction of Christ against Faustus Socinus* (1617), tr. F. H. Foster (W. F. Draper, 1889).

Grubb, Norman P., *Once Caught, No Escape: My Life Story* (Lutterworth, 1969)

Guillebaud, H. E., *Why the Cross?* (IVF, 1937).

Hamley, Colonel (Edward Bruce), *Voltaire* (W. Blackwood & Sons, 1877).

Hanson, A. T., *The Wrath of the Lamb* (SPCK, 1959).

Hardy, Alister, *The Divine Flame* (Collins, 1966).

Hart, H. L. A., *Punishment and Responsibility* (OUP, 1968).

Hebert, G. *See under* Edwall, P. *et al.*, *Ways of Worship*.

Heiler, Friedrich, *The Gospel of Sadhu Sundar Singh* (1924; George Allen & Unwin, 1927).

Hengel, Martin, *The Atonement*: the origin of the doctrine in the New Testament, tr. John Bowden (1980; SCM, 1981).

— *Crucifixion*, tr. John Bowden (1976; SCM and Fortress Press, 1977); originally *Mors turpissima crucis*.

Heschel, Abraham, *The Prophets* (Harper & Row, 1962).

Hoekema, Anthony A., *The Christian Looks at Himself* (Eerdmans, 1975).

Hooker, Richard, *Of the Laws of Ecclesiastical Polity* (1593–97), in *The Works of Richard Hooker*, ed. John Keble. 3 vols. (OUP, 3rd ed. 1845).

— 'Sermon on Habakkuk i. 4' (1585), in *The Works of Richard Hooker*, ed. John Keble, vol. III (OUP, 3rd ed. 1845), pp. 483–547.

Ignatius, *Ad Ephesios*, in *The Ante-Nicene Fathers*, vol. I, ed. A. Roberts and J. Donaldson (1885; Eerdmans, 1981), pp. 49–58.

— *Ad Polycarp*, in *The Ante-Nicene Fathers*, vol. I, ed. A. Roberts and J. Donaldson (1885; Eerdmans, 1981), 99–100.

Imbert, Jean, *Le Procès de Jésus* (Presses Universitaires de France, 1980).

Irenaeus, *Adversus Haereses*, in *The Ante-Nicene Fathers*, vol. I, ed. A. Roberts and J. Donaldson (1885; Eerdmans, 1981), pp. 315–567.

Jeeves, Malcolm A., Berry, R. J. and Atkinson, David, *Free to Be Different* (Marshalls, 1984).

Jeremias, Joachim, *The Central Message of the New Testament* (1955; SCM, 1966).

— *The Eucharistic Words of Jesus*, tr. N. Perrin (OUP, 1955).

— and Zimmerli, W., *'pais Theou'*, in *Theological Dictionary of the New Testament*, vol. V (Eerdmans, 1967), pp. 654–717.

— *'polloi'*, in *Theological Dictionary of the New Testament*, vol. VI (Eerdmans, 1968).

— and Zimmerli, W., *The Servant of God* (1952; SCM, 1957).

Josephus, *Jewish Antiquities*, tr. H. St J. Thackeray, Ralph Marcus *et al.* 6 vols. (Heinemann, 1930–65).

— *Jewish War*, tr. H. St J. Thackeray. 2 vols. (Heinemann, 1927–28).

Justin Martyr, *Dialogue with Trypho a Jew*, in *The Ante-Nicene Fathers*, vol. I, ed. A. Roberts and J. Donaldson (1885; Eerdmans, 1981), pp. 194–270.

— *First Apology*, in *The Ante-Nicene Fathers*, vol. I, ed. A. Roberts and J. Donaldson (1885; Eerdmans, 1981), pp. 163–187.

Kidner, F. D., *Sacrifice in the Old Testament* (Tyndale Press, 1952).

King, Martin Luther, *Strength to Love* (1963; Hodder & Stoughton, 1964).

Kitamori, Kazoh, *Theology of the Pain of God* (1946; SCM, 1966).

Koran, The, tr. N. J. Dawood (Penguin, 3rd revised ed. 1958).

Küng, Hans, *Justification: The Doctrine of Karl Barth and a Catholic Reflection* (1957; Burns & Oates, 1964).

Lambeth Conference, *1958 Lambeth Conference Papers* (SPCK, 1958).

Lasserre, Jean, *War and the Gospel* (James Clarke, 1962).

Lewis, A. J., *Zinzendorf: The Ecumenical Pioneer*. A study in the Moravian contribution to Christian mission and unity (SCM, 1962).

Lewis, C. S., *The Four Loves* (Geoffrey Bles, 1960).

— 'The Humanitarian Theory of Punishment', in *Churchmen Speak*, ed. Philip E. Hughes (Marcham Manor Press, 1966), pp. 39–44.

— *The Problem of Pain* (1940; Collins Fontana, 1957).

— *Surprised by Joy* (Geoffrey Bles, 1955).

Lewis, W. H. (ed.), *Letters of C. S. Lewis* (Geoffrey Bles, 1966).

Loane, Marcus L., *Archbishop Mowll* (Hodder & Stoughton, 1960).

Lombard, Peter, *Book of Sentences* (*Sententiarum Libri Quatuor*), in *Opera Omnia*, ed. J.-P. Migne, vol. 192 (Paris, 1880), pp. 521–1112.

Lucian, *The Passing of Peregrinus*, tr. A. M. Harman, in *The Works of Lucian*, vol. 5 (Heinemann, 1936), pp. 2–51.

Luther, Martin, *Commentary on the Epistle to the Galatians* (1535; James Clarke, 1953).

— *Letters of Spiritual Counsel*, in the *Library of Christian Classics*, vol. XVIII, ed. Theodore G. Tappert (SCM, 1955).

Mackintosh, Robert, *Historic Theories of the Atonement* (Hodder, 1920).

Maclaren, Alexander, *The Epistles of Paul to the Colossians and Philemon. The Expositor's Bible* (Hodder & Stoughton, 1896).

Marshall, I. H., *The Work of Christ* (Paternoster Press, 1969).

McCrossan, T. J., *Bodily Healing and the Atonement*, ed. Roy Hicks and Kenneth E. Hagin (1930; Faith Library Publications, 1982).

McGrath, Alister, 'The Moral Theory of the Atonement: An Historical and Theological Critique', *Scottish Journal of Theology* 38 (1985), pp. 205–220.

Menninger, Karl, *Whatever Became of Sin?* (Hawthorn Books, 1973).

Miller, J. H., 'Cross' and 'Crucifix', in *The New Catholic Encyclopedia*, vol. 4 (McGraw Hill, 1980), pp. 473–479 and 485.

Moberly, R. C., *Atonement and Personality* (1901).

Moltmann, Jürgen, *The Crucified God*: The cross of Christ as the foundation and criticism of Christian theology (1973; SCM, 1974).

Morgan, G. Campbell, *Evangelism* (Henry E. Walter, 1964).

Morris, Leon, *The Apostolic Preaching of the Cross* (Tyndale Press, 1955).

— *The Atonement*: Its meaning and significance (IVP, 1983).

— *The Cross in the New Testament* (Paternoster Press, 1965).

— 'The use of *hilaskesthai* etc. in Biblical Greek', *The Expository Times* lxii.8 (1951), pp. 227–233.

Moule, C. F. D., *The Sacrifice of Christ* (Hodder & Stoughton, 1956).

Moule, Handley C. G., *Colossian Studies* (Hodder & Stoughton, 1898).

Mowrer, O. Hobart, *The Crisis in Psychiatry and Religion* (Van Nostrand, 1961).

Mozley, J. K., *The Doctrine of the Atonement* (Duckworth, 1915).

— *The Impassibility of God*: a survey of Christian thought (CUP, 1926).

Muggeridge, Malcolm, *Jesus Rediscovered* (Collins, 1969).

Murray, Iain H., *David Martyn Lloyd-Jones* (Banner of Truth, 1982).

Murray, John, *The Epistle to the Romans*. 2 vols. in 1 (Marshall, Morgan & Scott, 1960–65).

— *Redemption Accomplished and Applied* (Eerdmans, 1955; Banner of Truth, 1961).

Neil, William, *Apostle Extraordinary* (Religious Education Press, 1965).

Neill, S. C., *Christian Faith Today* (Penguin, 1955).

— *Crises of Belief* (Hodder & Stoughton, 1984).

— 'Jesus and History', in *Truth of God Incarnate*, ed. E. M. B. Green (Hodder & Stoughton, 1977).

Nicole, Roger R., 'C. H. Dodd and the Doctrine of Propitiation', *Westminster Theological Journal* xvii.2 (1955), pp. 117–157.

Nietzsche, Friedrich, *The Anti-Christ* (1895; Penguin, 1968).

Nygren, Anders, *Agape and Eros*: a study of the Christian idea of love, tr. A. G. Hebert. 2 vols. (SPCK, 1932–39).

— *A Commentary on Romans* (1944; Fortress Press, 1949).

O'Brien, Peter, *Commentary on Colossians. Word Biblical Commentary*, vol. 44 (Word Books, 1982).

— 'Principalities and Powers, Opponents of the Church', in *Biblical Interpretation and the Church*: Text and Context, ed. D. A. Carson (Paternoster Press, 1984), pp. 110–150.

O'Donovan, Oliver, *In Pursuit of a Christian View of War*. Grove Booklets on Ethics no. 15 (Grove Books, 1977).

Origen, *Ezek. Hom.*, in *Opera Omnia*, ed. J.-P. Migne, vol. 13 (Paris, 1862), pp. 663–767.

Orr, James, *The Progress of Dogma* (Hodder & Stoughton, 1901).

Packer, J. I., 'Justification', in *New Bible Dictionary* (IVP, 2nd ed. 1982), pp. 646–649.

— 'What Did the Cross Achieve? The Logic of Penal Substitution', *Tyndale Bulletin* 25 (1974), pp. 3–45.

Paterson, W. P., 'Sacrifice', in *A Dictionary of the Bible*, ed. James Hastings (T. & T. Clark, 1902), pp. 329–349.

Philo, *Ad Gaium*, tr. C. D. Yonge, in *Works*, vol. 4 (Henry G. Bohn, 1855).

Piper, John, 'Is Self-love biblical?', *Christianity Today*, 12 August 1977, p. 6.

Pius XI, *Ad Catholici Sacerdotii* (Catholic Truth Society, 1935).

Pius XII, *Mediator Dei* (Catholic Truth Society, 1947).

Plato, *Phaedo*, tr. H. N. Fowler (Heinemann, 1914), pp. 200–403.

Pocknee, Cyril E., *The Cross and Crucifix in Christian Worship and Devotion*. Alcuin Club Tracts xxxii (Mowbray, 1962).

Poulton, John, *The Feast of Life*: a theological reflection on the theme Jesus Christ – the life of the world (World Council of Churches, 1982).

Price, Tony, *Evangelical Anglicans and the Lima Text*. Grove Worship series no. 92 (Grove Books, 1985).

Priestland, Gerald, *The Case Against God* (Collins, 1984).

— *Priestland's Progress*: one man's search for Christianity now (BBC, 1981).

Ramsey, A. Michael, *The Glory of God and the Transfiguration of Christ* (Longmans Green, 1949).

Rashdall, Hastings, *The Idea of Atonement in Christian Theology* (Macmillan, 1919).

Robinson, H. Wheeler, *Suffering Human and Divine* (SCM, 1940).

Sanday, W. and Headlam, A. C., *The Epistle to the Romans. International Critical Commentary* (T. & T. Clark, 5th ed. 1902).

Schroeder, H. J., *The Canons and Decrees of the Council of Trent* (1941; Tan Books, 1978).

Shaw, George Bernard, *Major Barbara* (1905).

Sider, Ronald and O'Donovan, Oliver, *Peace and War: a debate about pacifism* (Grove Books, 1985).

Silvester, Hugh, *Arguing with God* (IVP, 1971).

Simon, Ulrich E., *A Theology of Auschwitz* (Gollancz, 1967).

Simpson, E. K. and Bruce, F. F., *Commentary on the Epistles to the Ephesians and the Colossians. New London Commentary* (Marshalls, 1957); *New International Commentary on the New Testament* (Eerdmans, 1957).

Simpson, P. Carnegie, *The Fact of Christ* (Hodder & Stoughton, 1900).

Skinner, B. F., *Beyond Freedom and Dignity* (1971; Pelican, 1973).

Smith, George D. (ed.), *The Teaching of the Catholic Church* (Burns Oates, 2nd ed. 1952).

Sobrino, Jon, *Christology at the Crossroads* (1976; Orbis, SCM, 1978).

Socinus, Faustus, *De Jesu Christo Servatore* (1578), tr. Thomas Rees (London, 1818).

Stählin, Gustav, 'orgē', in *Theological Dictionary of the New Testament*, vol. V (Eerdmans, 1967), pp. 419–447.

Stibbs, Alan M., *The Finished Work of Christ*. The 1952 Tyndale Biblical Theology Lecture (Tyndale Press, 1954).

— *The Meaning of the Word 'Blood' in Scripture* (Tyndale Press, 1948).

Stott, John R. W., *The Message of Ephesians: God's New Society. The Bible speaks today* series (IVP, 1979).

— *The Message of the Sermon on the Mount: Christian Counter-Culture. The Bible speaks today* series (IVP, 1978).

Swete, H. B., *The Gospel According to St Mark* (Macmillan, 1898).

Tallentyre, S. G., *The Life of Voltaire*. 2 vols. (London, 1903).

Tasker, R. V. G., *The Biblical Doctrine of the Wrath of God* (Tyndale Press, 1951).

Tatlow, Tissington, *The Story of the Student Christian Movement of Great Britain and Ireland* (SCM, 1933).

Taylor, Vincent, *The Atonement in New Testament Teaching* (Epworth Press, 1940).

— *Forgiveness and Reconciliation*: a study in New Testament theology (Macmillan, 2nd. ed. 1946).

— *Jesus and His Sacrifice*: a study of the passion-sayings in the Gospels (Macmillan, 1937).

Temple, William, *Christus Veritas* (Macmillan, 1924).

— *Citizen and Churchman* (Eyre & Spottiswoode, 1941).

— *Readings in St John's Gospel*. 2 vols. (Macmillan, 1939–40).

Tertullian, *Adversus Praxean*, in *The Ante-Nicene Fathers*, tr. Holmes, vol. III, ed. A. Roberts and J. Donaldson (Eerdmans, 1973), pp. 597–627.

— *De Carne Christi*, in *The Ante-Nicene Fathers*, tr. Holmes, vol. III, ed. A. Roberts and J. Donaldson (Eerdmans, 1973), pp. 521–542.

— *De Corona*, in *The Ante-Nicene Fathers*, tr. S. Thelwall, vol. III, ed. A. Roberts and J. Donaldson (Eerdmans, 1973), pp. 93–103.

Thompson, R. J. and Beckwith, R. T., 'Sacrifice and Offering', in *New Bible Dictionary* (IVP, 2nd ed. 1982), pp. 1045–1054.

Tizard, L. J., *Preaching*: the art of communication (OUP, 1959).

Tournier, Paul, *Creative Suffering* (1981; SCM, 1982).

Treuherz, J., *Pre-Raphaelite Paintings* (Lund Humphries, 1980).

Turner, H. E. W., *The Patristic Doctrine of Redemption* (Mowbray, 1952).

Tyndale, William, *Doctrinal Treatises*. Parker Society (CUP, 1848).

Vanstone, W. H., *Love's Endeavour, Love's Expense*: the response of being to the Love of God (Darton, Longman & Todd, 1977).

Vidler, Alec R., *Essays in Liberality* (SCM, 1957).

Vitz, Paul, *Psychology as Religion: The Cult of Self-Worship* (Eerdmans, 1977).

Vivekananda, Swami, *Speeches and Writings* (G. A. Natesan, Madras, 3rd ed.).

Wace, Henry, *The Sacrifice of Christ*: its vital reality and efficacy (1898; Church Book Room Press, 1945).

Wallace, Ronald S., *The Atoning Death of Christ* (Marshalls, 1981).

Warfield, B. B., *Biblical Doctrines* (OUP, 1929).

— *The Person and Work of Christ*, ed. Samuel G. Craig (Presbyterian & Reformed Publishing Company, 1950).

Warren, M. A. C., *Interpreting the Cross* (SCM, 1966).

Waterland, Daniel, *A Review of the Doctrine of the Eucharist* (1737; Clarendon Press, 1896).

Webster, Douglas, *In Debt to Christ* (Highway Press, 1957).

— *Yes to Mission* (SCM, 1966).

Wells, David F., *Revolution in Rome* (IVP, 1972).

— *The Search for Salvation* (IVP, 1978).

Wenham, G. J., *Numbers. Tyndale Old Testament Commentaries* (IVP, 1981).

Westcott, B. F., *Commentary on the Epistles of John* (Macmillan, 1883).

— *The Epistle to the Hebrews* (1889; Macmillan, 3rd ed. 1903).

— *The Historic Faith* (Macmillan, 6th ed. 1904).

Westminster Confession of Faith: The Proposed Book of Confessions of the Presbyterian Church in the United States (1976), pp. 77–101.

Whale, J. S., *Victor and Victim*: the Christian doctrine of redemption (CUP, 1960).

White, Douglas, 'The Nature of Punishment and Forgiveness', in *Papers in Modern Churchmanship*, no. II, ed. C. F. Russell (Longmans Green, 1924), pp. 6–9.

Wiesel, Elie, *Night* (1958; Penguin, 1981).

Williams, Rowan, *Eucharistic Sacrifice – The Roots of a Metaphor*. Grove Liturgical Study no. 31 (Grove Books, 1982).

Willmer, Haddon, in *Third Way*, May 1979.

Wright, Tom, 'Justification: The Biblical Basis and its Relevance for Contemporary Evangelicalism', in *The Great Acquittal*, ed. Gavin Reid (Collins, 1980).

Yancey, Philip, *Where is God when it hurts?* (Zondervan, 1977).

Zwemer, Samuel M., *The Glory of the Cross* (Marshall, Morgan & Scott, 1928).

Index of biblical references

Index of biblical references

366

Index of biblical references

368

373

Author index

Subject index

Subject index

THE CROSS OF CHRIST
STUDY GUIDE

It's all too easy just to read through a book like this without letting its message take root in our lives. That's where this study guide is designed to help. It sets out questions which will help you get to the heart of what the author has written and challenge you to apply what you learn to your own life. Though suitable for individual use, the guide is intended primarily for small groups of Christians meeting, perhaps for an hour or two each week, to study, discuss and pray together.

The guide provides material for each of the fourteen sections of the book. When used by a group with limited time, the leader should decide beforehand which questions are most appropriate for the group to discuss during the meeting and which should perhaps be left for group members to work through by themselves or in smaller groups during the week. In order to be able to contribute fully and learn from the group meetings, each member of the group should read through the relevant chapter of the book before each session.

It is important not to let these studies become merely academic exercises. Guard against this by making time to discuss how what you learn works out in practice for you. Make sure you begin and end each study with a period of worship and prayer. Ask the Holy Spirit to reveal the truths of the cross to you and inspire you to renewed love and obedience. Bear in mind these words from the author's preface: 'We can stand before [the cross] only with a bowed head and a broken spirit. And there we remain until the Lord Jesus speaks to our hearts his word of pardon and acceptance, and we, gripped by his love and brimful of thanksgiving, go out into the world to live our lives in his service' (p. 12).

PART ONE:
Approaching the cross

SESSION ONE

Chapter 1: *The centrality of the cross* (pp. 17–46)

The author's intention in this first chapter is to show that, according to the views of Jesus and the early church presented in the New Testament, the cross of Christ is *the* central feature of Christianity. Despite the opposition which it arouses, there are good reasons for our continuing to share this perspective today.

1   These days we have become used to the cross as the symbol of our faith. But it was a rather surprising choice in the context of the first century. Why was this (pp. 23f.)?

2   The first Christians seem to have caught the idea from Jesus himself. Read Mark 8:31–32; 9:30–32; 10:32–34. What is the striking thing about these predictions (p. 27)?

3   John shares the same perspective as the other gospel writers. How does he draw attention to it (pp. 28f.)?

4   How did Jesus know that his death was inevitable (pp. 29ff.)?

5 This focus on the centrality of Jesus' death also comes across in the preaching of Peter and Paul recorded by Luke in Acts. Divide into twos or threes and let each sub-group look up one or two of the passages mentioned (Acts 2:14–39; 3:12–26; 4:8–12; 5:29–32; 10:34–43; 13:16–41; 14:15–17; 17:2–3 and 22–31; 28:23–31). What did they understand about the *meaning* of the cross (pp. 33ff.)? Why is the use of the term 'tree' especially significant?

6 '. . . the three major letter-writers of the New Testament – Paul, Peter and John – are unanimous in witnessing to [the centrality of the cross], as are also the letter to the Hebrews and the Revelation' (p. 35). How can this statement be supported (pp. 35ff.)?

7 'There is no greater cleavage between faith and unbelief than in their respective attitudes to the cross' (p. 40). What recent experience have you had of this divide?

8 Islam is an example of a religion which cannot accept the centrality of the cross (p. 40ff.). Why is this?

9 Given the opposition that it arouses, what reasons would you give for continuing to hold to the centrality of the cross?

SESSION TWO

Chapter 2: Why did Christ die? (pp. 47–62)

This chapter examines the human factors which brought about the crucifixion of Jesus. Behind all these, however, lies Jesus' understanding of his Father's will. It was this that led him to go to his death quite deliberately.

1 These gospel writers make it clear that though legal procedures were followed at Jesus' trial, the death sentence was a gross miscarriage of justice. See Matthew 26:57–58; Mark 14:57–59; Luke 23:1–2, 13–16; John 18:38; 19:6. Why was this (p. 48)?

2 Read Luke 23:1–25. What does this passage reveal about Pilate (pp. 50f.)?

3 'It is easy to condemn Pilate and overlook our own equally devious behaviour' (p. 51). Why did Pilate do what he did? In what ways are you like him?

4 Why was the Jewish establishment so opposed to Jesus (pp. 52ff.)? In what ways are you like them?

5 Why is it misleading to say that Judas Iscariot was merely the victim of forces outside his control (pp. 55f.)?

6 What motives lay behind Judas' betrayal of Jesus (pp. 56f.)?

7 'Jesus had said that it is impossible to serve God and money' (p. 58). In what respects have you found this to be true in your experience?

8 'Before we can begin to see the cross as something done *for* us (leading us to faith and worship), we have to see it as something done *by* us (leading us to repentence)' (pp. 59–60). *Is* this how you see the cross? Spend some time reflecting on the extent to which you share the characteristics exhibited by Pilate, Caiaphas and Judas.

9 Why is it inaccurate to call Jesus a 'martyr' (pp. 60ff.)?

SESSION THREE

Chapter 3: Looking below the surface (pp. 63–84)

We have seen that, although human agents were involved, the crucifixion of Jesus was primarily a result of his giving himself up to do his Father's will. We move on to consider why it was that God intended his Son to die in this way.

1   What are the four stages which the author suggests in answer to the question 'Why did Christ die?' (pp. 63ff.)? Make sure you can back up your answers from Scripture.

But does this account fit the facts? The rest of this chapter looks at the gospel writers' accounts of the events surrounding Jesus' death to see whether or not they support the message outlined later in the New Testament.

2   Read Mark 14:22–24. What does the institution of the Lord's Supper teach us about how Jesus himself understood the significance of his coming death (pp. 67ff.)?

3   What does the fact that the meal took place in the context of the Passover festival add to our understanding (pp. 71f.)?

4   Read Matthew 26:36–46. Why is it 'ludicrous to suppose that [Jesus] was now afraid of pain, insult and death' (p. 74)? What then did Jesus mean by the 'cup' from which he prayed to be delivered?

5   Read Mark 15:33–34. Just before Jesus died he cried out,

quoting Psalm 22:1. What explanations have been suggested for why he did this (pp. 80f.)? Which do you find the most persuasive?

6   'The agony in the garden opens a window on the greater agony of the cross. If to bear man's sin and God's wrath was so terrible in anticipation, what must the reality have been like?' (p. 77). How does this affect your attitude to sin?

7   Look back over your study so far. In what way has your understanding of sin, of God and of salvation been enlarged?

PART TWO:
The heart of the cross

SESSION FOUR

Chapter 4: The problem of forgiveness
(pp. 87–110)

But why can't God just forgive us? Why should our pardon depend on the death of Christ? This is the problem which the author tackles in this chapter. The answer lies in our having a better understanding of the seriousness of sin and the majesty of God.

1   What do you understand by the word 'sin'? According to the Bible (*e.g.* Romans 8:7; 1 John 3:4), what is the *essence* of sin (pp. 90f.)?

2   'But how can we be held responsible for our sin? After all, we can't help it!' How would you answer this (pp. 91ff.)?

3   'If human beings have sinned (which they have), and if they are responsible for their sins (which they are), then they are guilty before God' (p. 96). How would you answer someone who complained that talking about guilt in this way was unduly morbid (pp. 96ff.)?

4   'A full acknowledgment of human responsibility, and therefore guilt, far from diminishing the dignity of

393

human beings, actually enhances it' (p. 101). How is this the case?

5 Many people find it difficult to think of God being angry and punishing sin. How would you answer the following ways of getting round the problem:

   a 'The God of wrath belongs to the Old Testament, while the God of the New Testament is love' (p. 103).

   b 'God's wrath is an inevitable process of cause and effect in a moral universe, not the personal attitude of God to man' (pp. 103ff.).

6 What differences are there between God's wrath and human anger?

7 The author quotes five metaphors used in the Bible to illustrate the fact that God's holiness cannot co-exist with human sin (pp. 106ff.). What does the perspective given by these pictures say to your life and that of your church?

8 'It must even be said that our evangelical emphasis on the atonement is dangerous if we come to it too quickly' (p. 109). Why is this?

SESSION FIVE

Chapter 5: Satisfaction for sin (pp. 111–132)

The last chapter concluded that the gravity of sin and the character of God make it impossible for God simply to forgive us. We turn now to the concept of 'satisfaction' and the question 'Who needs to be satisfied?'

1 In the early church, many held that Jesus' death was the compensation which God was obliged to pay to *the devil* in order to secure mankind's freedom from his power. How did this view come about (pp. 112ff.)? What is wrong with it?

2 Another view is that God is in a similar dilemma to that faced by Darius in Daniel 6 (see especially verses 13–17) and that the death of Jesus was necessary in order to secure our freedom from the penalty demanded by *the law*. Why is this view inadequate (pp. 114ff.)?

3 Three other suggestions have been made since: Anselm held that it was *God's honour* that, having been offended by sin, needed to be satisfied (pp. 117ff.). The Reformers, with their emphasis on justification, stressed the need for the way of salvation to satisfy *God's justice* (pp. 120f.). Grotius developed the view that God cannot simply forgive sins because he must satisfy *the moral order* of the world he governs (pp. 121ff.). Discuss the advantages and drawbacks of each view. What limitation do they all share (p. 123)?

4 God judges sinners 'because he must, if he is to remain true to himself' (p. 124). The author mentions four ways

395

in which the Bible describes this (pp. 124ff.). Read the following passages and discuss how they help our understanding of divine anger and the need for satisfaction: Judges 2:12–13; 2 Kings 22:13, 17; Hosea 8:5; Ezekiel 5:13; Ezekiel 20:44.

5 The author quotes Emil Brunner: 'The cross is the only place where the loving, forgiving, merciful God is revealed in such a way that we perceive that his holiness and his love are equally infinite' (p. 131). What distortions occur when either one of these attributes is ignored? In what ways is *your* thinking distorted?

SESSION SIX

Chapter 6: The self-substitution of God
(pp. 133–163)

We have seen that the solution to the problem of human sin must take full account of God's holiness. 'How then could God express simultaneously his holiness in judgment and his love in pardon?' (p. 134). The answer lies in God's substitution of himself in our place.

1 Old Testament sacrifices 'were the God-intended preparation for the sacrifice of Christ' (p. 134). What two basic ideas lay behind the Old Testament sacrifices (p. 135)? How was the idea of substitution expressed?

2 Read Leviticus 17:11. What does this verse teach about blood and atonement (p. 138)?

3 We saw in an earlier study that the death of Christ (the 'Lamb of God') is seen by New Testament writers as the fulfilment of the Passover. What does the Passover story in Exodus 11 – 13 reveal about God and his way of dealing with human sin (pp. 139ff.)?

Another illustration of the principle of substitution is seen in the New Testament's use of 'sin-bearing'. Here we face two important questions. First, does 'bearing sin' always mean receiving the *penalty* of sin? Secondly, does 'bearing sin' necessarily imply *substitution*, with the innocent party taking the place of the guilty and enduring his penalty?

4 What objections have been raised to the notion of 'penal substitution' as the description of what Jesus achieved

through his death on the cross (pp. 141ff.)? How does
the Bible help to answer them (pp. 143ff.)?

5 Read through Isaiah 53. The author quotes Jeremias:
'No other passage from the Old Testament was as
important to the Church as Isaiah 53' (p. 145). Why is
this (pp. 145ff.)? Look at Mark 10:45 and 14:24. What
light do these verses shed on Jesus' own understanding
of the significance of his death?

6 Read 2 Corinthians 5:21 and Galatians 3:13–14. What do
these verses add to what we have already seen
(pp. 148f.)?

A further question concerns how we are to think of the One
who 'took our place, bore our sin, became our curse,
endured our penalty, died our death' (p. 149). There are three
possibilities: a) Jesus was just a man; b) Jesus was simply God
and only appeared to be a man; c) Jesus was (and is) the
unique God-man.

7 What problems arise when we think of the Jesus who
died on the cross as merely a man (pp. 150f.)?

8 'We must not . . . speak of God punishing Jesus or of
Jesus persuading God . . .' (p. 151). Why not? How then
should we speak of the relationship between God and
Jesus on the cross?

9 What are the apparent advantages in thinking of the
Jesus who died on the cross as God alone (pp. 152ff.)?

10 But despite this, 'it is misleading to say that "God died"'
(p. 155). Why is this the case?

11 We are left with the third alternative: our substitute was 'neither Christ alone (since that would make him a third party thrust in between us and God), nor God alone (since that would undermine the historical incarnation), but *God in Christ*, who was truly and fully both God and man, and who on that account was uniquely qualified to represent both God and man and to mediate between them' (p. 156). List some of the biblical evidence for this statement (pp. 157f.).

12 'At the root of every caricature of the cross there lies a distorted Christology' (*i.e.*, a distorted view of who Jesus is) (p. 160). Why is this the case?

13 On the basis of this chapter, what might you say to someone who said that they were doing their best to get to heaven and that they hoped God would overlook their minor failings?

PART THREE:
The achievement of the cross

SESSION SEVEN

Chapter 7: The salvation of sinners
(pp. 167–203)

The *heart* of the cross is God's substitution of himself in our place. We move on in Part Three to think about what this self-sacrifice *achieved* under the headings of salvation, revelation and conquest. In this chapter, the author discusses four complementary word-pictures used by the Bible to describe the meaning of salvation.

1 The first image is that of *propitiation*. What does it mean? Why have some people been unhappy with it as a way of describing the effect of Jesus' death (pp. 168ff.)? How would you answer their objections?

2 Secondly, there is the image of *redemption*. Why is 'ransom' a more appropriate term than 'deliverance' (pp. 175ff.)?

3 By what are we held captive (p. 178)? Why is it important to affirm that 'even our release from these

captivities does not complete our redemption' (p. 178)?

4   What was the price paid for our redemption (pp. 179f.)? What does this mean?

5   What are the practical implications of the fact that 'the person of the redeemer . . . has proprietary rights over his purchase' (pp. 181f.)? How far do you acknowledge this in your life?

6   *Justification* is the third image, recalling the picture of the lawcourt. What is the difference between justification and forgiveness (p. 182)? Why is it 'the heart and hub . . . of the whole economy of God's saving grace' (p. 183)?

7   What objections are there to this notion (pp. 183f.)?

8   Why was the Reformers' teaching on justification by faith rejected by the Roman Catholic Church (pp. 183f., 187)?

9   What do 'justification', 'regeneration' and 'sanctification' mean (pp. 185f.)? Why is it important to distinguish clearly between them?

10 How would you answer someone who said that 'justification by faith is merely a "legal fiction", with God pronouncing us righteous when we are not really righteous at all' (pp. 187ff.)?

11 The author summarizes Paul's teaching on justification (pp. 189ff.). Why is it important to maintain that our justification a) has its source in God's grace, b) is grounded in the shedding of Christ's blood, c) has its means through faith, d) brings about a personal relationship with Christ?

401

12 The fourth image is of *reconciliation*. What are the results of our being reconciled to God (pp. 193ff.)?

13 Read 2 Corinthians 5:18–21. What does this passage teach about reconciliation (pp. 196ff.)?

14 Why is it misleading to talk of substitution as a 'theory of the atonement' (pp. 202f.)?

SESSION EIGHT

Chapter 8: The revelation of God
(pp. 204–226)

The cross was God's decisive means of acting on our behalf and securing our salvation. It was also an event through which he made himself known to us, an aspect which we consider in this chapter.

1 What do you understand by the word 'glory'? In what ways is the cross a demonstration of the glory of God (pp. 204ff.)?

2 What does 'theodicy' mean (p. 207)? Can you think of any times when you have experienced the 'apparently unjust ways of God'?

3 Read Acts 17:30–31. What perspective does this give to your answer to question 2 (p. 208)?

4 Although God's justice will be fully made known at the end of history, it has in fact already been revealed. Read Romans 3:21–26. What three main explanations have been given for what Paul means by 'a righteousness from God' in verse 21 (pp. 209ff.)? With which do you agree?

5 According to this passage, why did God present Jesus as the 'sacrifice of atonement'? What does this mean and how does it help in the search for a theodicy (pp. 210ff.)?

6 Read 1 John 3:16 and 4:10. 'If we are looking for a definition of love, we should look not in a dictionary,

but at Calvary' (p. 212). In what ways does the cross reveal the nature of true love?

7 How do you know that God loves *you*? Read Romans 5:5, 8. What do these verses tell us about God's authentic love (pp. 213ff.)?

8 The author quotes Moltmann: 'The Son suffers dying, the Father suffers the death of the Son. The grief of the Father here is just as important as the death of the Son. The Fatherlessness of the Son is matched by the Sonlessness of the Father' (p. 216). In the light of this statement, how might you answer the claim that, in view of the world's suffering, God's love is an illusion?

9 Summarize Abelard's view of the atonement (pp. 217ff.). How would you answer him?

10 Some people assert that 'forgiveness without atonement' was taught by Jesus himself, for example in the Parable of the Prodigal Son (pp. 221ff.). Is this view justifiable?

11 Read 1 Corinthians 1:17 – 2:5. In what ways is the message of the cross 'foolishness to those who are perishing' (pp. 224ff.)? How did the Christians at Corinth know that the cross is 'actually the greatest manifestation of God's wisdom and power' (p. 225)?

12 Are you ever embarrassed by the message of the cross? Why do you think this is? Discuss possible solutions to this problem.

SESSION NINE

Chapter 9: The conquest of evil (pp. 227–251)

The Christian claim is that, despite the appearance of total
defeat, the cross of Christ was 'the throne from which he
rules the world' (p. 228). This chapter examines the basis for
this claim.

1 What is Aulen's view of the atonement. Why does he
   call it a) 'dramatic' and b) 'classic' (pp. 228ff.)? Is he
   right?

2 What are the six stages by which God, through Christ,
   has won the victory over the devil (pp. 231ff.)?

3 Read Colossians 2:13–15. How does Paul describe the
   conquest achieved by Christ on the cross (pp. 233ff.)?

4 Why is it wrong to 'regard the cross as defeat and the
   resurrection as victory' (pp. 235ff.)? What is the correct
   relation between Jesus' death and his resurrection?

5 Why is it important to say that the parallel between our
   victory and Christ's victory is only partial (pp. 239ff.)?

6 'The victory of Christians . . . consists of entering into
   the victory of Christ and of enjoying its benefits'
   (p. 239). What does this mean?

7 In connection with Christian victory, what is wrong
   with a) triumphalism and b) defeatism (pp. 240f.)? How
   can we avoid each of these positions?

405

STUDY GUIDE

8 The author identifies the law, the flesh, the world and death as the four tyrants from which we are set free through Christ. What difference does being a Christian make to your attitudes to these things (pp. 241ff.)?

9 What is misleading about the statement that 'Christ bore our sicknesses in the very same way that he bore our sins' (pp. 244ff.)? What then is the effect of Christ's death and resurrection on our physical bodies (pp. 245f.)?

10 'What the book of Revelation does . . . is to lift the curtain which hides the unseen world of spiritual reality and to show us what is going on behind the scenes' (p. 247). Read Revelation 11:15 – 12:12 to get a taste of the perspective which sees the church's continuing conflict with the devil in the context of the victory of the Lamb. What does the author identify as the devil's allies in this conflict (pp. 248ff.)?

11 In what ways do you wage war against these things? How can they and their master be overcome (pp. 250f.)?

PART FOUR:
Living under the cross

SESSION TEN

Chapter 10: *The community of celebration* (pp. 255–273)

Jesus' self-sacrifice on the cross 'was not just to save isolated individuals, and so perpetuate their loneliness, but to create a new community whose members would belong to him, love one another and eagerly serve the world' (p. 255). We move on then to consider the relationship of the cross to the Christian community.

1 What characteristics mark the Christian's intimate relationship to God (pp. 256f.)?

2 '. . . whenever Christian people come together it is impossible to stop them singing' (p. 258). Why is this?

3 Why is the Lord's Supper 'central to the church's life of celebration' (p 259)?

Different ways of understanding the sense in which the Lord's Supper may be called a 'sacrifice' have 'divided Christendom since the sixteenth century, and [are] a topic of anxious ecumenical debate today' (p. 261).

4   Why did the sixteenth-century Reformers reject the
    'sacrifice of the mass' (pp. 261f.)?

5   What 'spiritual sacrifices' do Christians offer (pp. 263f.)?

6   How did the Catholic Counter-Reformation react to the
    emphases made by the Reformers (pp. 264ff.)? Why was
    this?

7   In recent times, more moderate positions have been
    proposed. One is that 'the Eucharist is not a repetition but
    a perpetuation of the cross' (p. 266). What does this mean?
    How far does this accord with New Testament teaching
    (pp. 266ff.)?

8   Another suggestion is that the Eucharist is a sacrifice
    because, in offering ourselves to God as living sacrifices,
    we participate in what Christ did on the cross (pp. 268ff.).
    How far does this accord with New Testament teaching
    (pp. 269ff.)?

9   Rowan Williams has written that 'the effect of Christ's
    offering is to make us capable of offering, to count us
    worthy to stand and serve as priests' (p. 272). Why is it
    nevertheless important to maintain a clear distinction
    between Christ's sacrifice on the cross and what takes
    place in a service of Holy Communion?

SESSION ELEVEN

Chapter 11: Self-understanding and self-giving (pp. 274–294)

A true understanding of the cross of Christ revolutionizes our attitude to God. But it also radically alters the way we see ourselves, a subject which this chapter explores in greater detail.

1 What sort of things lead people to have a low self-image? How has the modern world reacted to this (pp. 274f.)?

2 Jesus told us to love our neighbours as ourselves. Why is it wrong to interpret this as meaning 'love yourself' (pp. 275f.)?

3 The cross gives a new attitude to ourselves because it tells us that as those who are in Christ, we have become new people. This is because Christ died and rose again as our representative. What does this mean (p. 276)?

4 Read Romans 6:1–14. Paul draws out the practical consequences of Jesus' death being representative as well as substitutionary. What are they and how do they apply to you (pp. 277f.)?

5 We move on to ask what our attitude should be to the new self we have through the death and resurrection of Jesus. What does the author suggest (p. 278)? Why is this?

6 'Self-denial is not denying to ourselves luxuries such as chocolates, cakes, cigarettes and cocktails . . .' (p. 279). What is it then?

7   Three different sorts of death and resurrection can be found in Paul's writing. What are they and why is it important to distinguish between them (pp. 280ff.)?

8   What is the difference between self-affirmation and self-love (p. 281)? On what basis can we have a positive attitude to ourselves (pp. 281ff.)?

9   How can we resolve the biblical tension between valuing ourselves and denying ourselves at the same time (pp. 282f.)?

10 Our redemption by Christ gives us 'both more to affirm and more to deny' about ourselves (p. 283). What does the author mean (pp. 283ff.)? What practical application does this have for you?

11 'Self-understanding should lead to self-giving . . . It is to this that the cross consistently and insistently calls us' (p. 285). Read Mark 10:35–45. What was there about James and John which was opposed to the way of the cross (pp. 286ff.)? What aspects do you have in common with them?

12 In practical terms, how should the way of the cross be seen in a) a Christian home and b) the church (pp. 289f.)? How does this work out in *your* home and *your* church?

13 'If the cross is to mark our Christian life in the home and the church, this should be even more so in the world' (p. 290). In what ways (pp. 290ff.)?

14 'There was an almost reckless extravagance about Christ's love on the cross; it challenges the calculating coldness of our love' (p. 292). Does it? In what ways?

SESSION TWELVE

Chapter 12: Loving our enemies (pp. 295–310)

' "To live under the cross" means that every aspect of the Christian community's life is shaped and coloured by it' (p. 295). That includes our conduct to our enemies, the subject of this chapter.

1 What is the difference between peace-making and appeasement (pp. 295f.)? What is unsatisfactory about the latter?

2 'Justice without mercy is too strict, and mercy without justice is too lenient' (p. 297). How should this apply in a) a Christian home and b) the church? How does it work out in *your* home and *your* church?

3 We turn now to the administration of justice by the state and the question of whether or not the use of force by the state is compatible with the cross. Look at Romans 12:9 and then 12:14 – 13:7 and note the four references Paul makes to good and evil.

4 Paul makes it clear that although God will punish evil at the last judgment, his wrath against evil is also being revealed now. In what ways is this true (pp. 302ff.)?

5 'Retaliation is not wrong . . .' (p. 304). Why not?

6 The author sums up Paul's teaching under four headings (pp. 304ff.). What are these? What limitations are imposed on the state's authority?

411

7   Under what circumstances might it be right to disobey
    the law (p. 307f.)? Is armed revolt against the state ever
    justified?

8   God 'did not overcome evil by refusing to punish it, but
    by accepting the punishment himself' (p. 309). How
    should this affect the way we treat our enemies?

SESSION THIRTEEN

Chapter 13: Suffering and glory (pp. 311–337)

'The fact of suffering undoubtedly constitutes the single greatest challenge to the Christian faith' (p. 311). Although the Bible hints at answers to the intellectual problem of suffering (see pp. 313f.), its chief concern is practical, enabling us to *overcome* suffering. The purpose of this chapter is to consider how the cross helps us in this.

1   Read 1 Peter 2:18–23. What does this passage teach about the relationship between our suffering and that of Christ (p. 315)?

2   Read Hebrews 2:10 and 5:8–9. In what sense did Jesus need to be made 'perfect' (p. 316)? Read James 1:2–4. What positive benefit can suffering have? How have you found this to be the case in your own experience?

3   Three images are used in the Bible to illustrate how God uses suffering in our lives. What are they and what do they teach us (pp. 316ff.)?

4   'It is not just that suffering belongs to service, but that suffering is indispensable to fruitful or effective service' (p. 320). Why is this? In what ways have you found this principle working out in practice?

5   Read Hebrews 12:2. What does this verse indicate about how Jesus was sustained in his suffering (pp. 322f.)?

6   'The essential perspective to develop is that of the eternal purpose of God, which is to make us holy or Christlike' (p. 323). Is this the way you see suffering?

7 Does *all* human suffering lead to glory? What is the New Testament's perspective on this question (pp. 324ff.)?

8 We turn to the story of Job, a man who was overwhelmed by calamity for no apparent reason. What attitude did he take to his suffering (p. 327). How did his friends try to help him?

9 When they have finished, God speaks. Read Job 40:1–9. On what basis should Job have trusted God (p. 328)? Read Romans 8:32. What additional reason do we have to continue to trust God in the midst of suffering?

10 'The real sting of suffering is . . . the apparent God-forsakenness of it' (p. 329). How does the cross help us here?

11 Why did some early Christians find it difficult to believe that God himself can suffer (pp. 330f.)? What does the Bible say?

12 How then does the cross speak to evils such as global hunger and the Nazi holocaust (pp. 333ff.)?

Conclusion

SESSION FOURTEEN

The pervasive influence of the cross (pp. 338–351)

The author's concluding assertion is that 'we cannot eliminate the cross from any area of our thinking or living' (p. 339). To emphasize this, he considers seven affirmations about the cross made by Paul in his letter to the Galatians.

1   The cross and salvation. Read Galatians 1:3–5. What do these verses teach about the cross of Christ (pp. 340f.)?

2   The cross and experience. Read Galatians 2:19–21. What exactly does Paul mean by claiming that he has been 'crucified with Christ' (pp. 341f.)? Can you say what Paul says here?

3   The cross and preaching. Read Galatians 3:1–3. What does this passage teach about the place of the cross in the preaching of the gospel (pp. 342ff.)?

4   The cross and substitution. Read Galatians 3:10–14. What is 'startling, almost shocking' about this passage? What does it mean (pp. 345f.)?

5 The cross and persecution. Read Galatians 5:11 and 6:12. 'It is not possible to be faithful and popular simultaneously' (p. 347). Why not? To what extent are you tempted to blunt the message of the cross in the way you communicate the gospel to others?

6 The cross and holiness. Read Galatians 5:19–26. How can we 'ensure that the desires of the Spirit predominate over the desires of the flesh' (p. 348)? How does this work out in practice?

7 The cross and boasting. Read Galatians 6:14. '. . . Paul's obsession was with Christ and his cross' (p. 349). Why was this? To what extent do you share Paul's attitude?

8 '. . . the world is saying to every preacher: Unless I see in your hands the print of the nails, I will not believe' (p. 351). What does this mean? How does it apply to you?